DISARMAMENT SKETCHES

DISARMAMENT SKETCHES

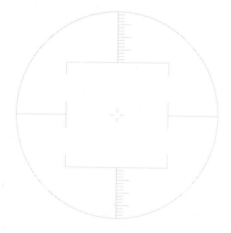

Three Decades of Arms Control and International Law

Thomas Graham Jr.

INSTITUTE FOR GLOBAL AND REGIONAL SECURITY STUDIES · SEATTLE

UNIVERSITY OF WASHINGTON PRESS · SEATTLE AND LONDON

This publication was supported in part by the
Donald R. Ellegood International Publications Endowment

Library of Congress Cataloging-in-Publication Data

Graham, Thomas, 1933–
    Disarmament sketches : three decades of arms control and international law /
Thomas Graham Jr.
        p.   cm.
    Includes index.
    ISBN 0-295-98212-8 (hbk. : alk. paper)
    1. Arms control—United States—History.   2. Arms control—History.   I. Title.
KZ5624.G73   2002
327.1'74'0973—dc21   2002002792

To my mother and father

AND

to my wife, Christine

CONTENTS

FOREWORD

President Kennedy once said, "Mankind must put an end to war or war will put an end to mankind." I believe this to be as true today as it was some forty years ago. Like no other time in history, the nuclear age has witnessed the birth of technologies so dangerous as to bring about the potential annihilation of hundreds of thousands, even millions, of people, none of whom would have been responsible for the decision involved in bringing about such unspeakable disaster, not to mention the incalculable damage to our natural environment. From Hiroshima to the walk in the woods to the Comprehensive Test Ban Treaty, my own relationship with nuclear weapons and my own efforts to mitigate the danger of their potential employment have spanned seven decades and the administrations of eleven presidents. Across the years, I have been humbled and honored by the opportunity to work toward this most important of objectives with so many colleagues who, while divided by their means, were united in their dedication to this common cause.

Few have been as consistently enthusiastic and effective as Tom Graham. For thirty years, he has been an indefatigable warrior for the true and just in the long battle to reduce the risk of nuclear war through equitable and verifiable arms control measures. The issues surrounding that battle have been serious and complex. Some have been among and within the executive agencies; others among the executive, legislative, and judicial branches of the government; and others have involved continuous coordination with and among our allies. Tom has been at the center of those controversies longer than anyone else. He has known the history, the semantics, the ambiguities, and the politics of these issues.

Be it limitations on and reductions in strategic nuclear arsenals, conventional armed forces, antiballistic missile systems, chemical and biological weapons, nuclear testing, space weapons, or small arms, Tom's career has traversed the complicated fields of nearly every major arms control battle. Indeed, he was involved in all of the major arms control and nonproliferation negotiations in which the United States participated over the past thirty years. As legal advisor, senior arms control representative, or chief negotiator, Tom was a central figure in *inter alia* the ABM, SALT II, START I, START II, INF, CFE, CTBT, and NPT treaties, just to set forth some of the acronyms that have written the story of his illustrious career. Through it all he has kept his objectivity and common sense, his commitment and integrity, his drive and focus, qualities that help to explain the high regard in which he is held by his supporters and critics alike. Few are as qualified to write an account of the evolution of attempts to control, limit, and reduce armaments during the second half of the Cold War and in its aftermath as Tom, a task which he has assiduously undertaken with the same thoroughness, evenhandedness, and attention to detail that I long ago came to expect from him.

Having served in the administration of every president from Nixon to Clinton and participated in every major arms control treaty negotiation from 1970 to 1997, Tom has continued to build upon his exemplary record of public service since his retirement from government, bringing the same effectiveness and vigor to the nongovernmental community that he brought to the government. He has also spent much time teaching students over the years, for which I commend him. He understands, as do I, the importance of finding and inspiring the next generation of men and women who will toil in this garden. This book is the most recent example of Tom's record.

Ambassador Paul H. Nitze
Washington, D.C.
February 2001

ACKNOWLEDGMENTS

In putting this book together, I benefited from the assistance and support of a number of energetic and helpful people. I must first recognize my colleague Damien LaVera for his outstanding editorial work and his sage advice as this manuscript took its final form. He combined a firm grasp of the subject matter and a very real literary ability with a keen editor's eye. Damien has a great future ahead of him both in the national security field and with the written word.

Next I would like to thank Janet Rupp for her help in the early stages of this narrative. This book was written primarily during long plane rides, and Janet effectively converted my verbose scribbling into a readable manuscript.

Everyone at the University of Washington Press and the Henry M. Jackson School of International Studies at the University of Washington was of great assistance. Chris Jones at the Jackson School and Michael Duckworth of the University of Washington Press were positive and helpful partners. And Toby Dalton of the Jackson School, who edited the manuscript for the University of Washington Press, did an excellent job and was a pleasure to work with.

Rosemarie Forsythe, David Koplow, and Janne Nolan were generous with their time in reading the text at an early date and offered superb advice and real encouragement. Rob Nicholas twice reviewed the entire text toward the end of the process from a technical and editorial perspective, giving me much helpful assistance, and John Rhinelander carefully and thoughtfully reviewed the material on the ABM Treaty. Jim Woolsey my lawyer, during some trying times in the 1980s and during the State Department review, provided wise guidance. I also benefited considerably from suggestions and advice by former collegues during that same review. Stephanie Powell, a current colleague, gave me excellent research assistance as the text neared completion.

So many outstanding people have counseled, advised, and inspired me over the years that I could not begin to name them all. Indeed, one of the great benefits that flows from a career in arms control and disarmament is the opportunity to get to know so many remarkable and talented people. It has been one of my life's greatest pleasures. That said, however, I would be remiss if I failed to thank Paul Nitze for the special inspiration that he has been to me for the last twenty-five years.

I have dedicated this book to my parents and to my wife, Christine, thereby recognizing their importance to me; their love and support have been central to my life. But, finally, I would like to say something to Eliza, Tommy,

Thomas, Clover, and Missy. In writing this book, I have attempted to explain to you as well as to others where I came from, how I spent my professional life for many years, and what I tried to do. My hopes for the future are very much with all of you.

PROLOGUE

This volume, in addition to being a personal history, is intended as a chronicle of the U.S. arms control and disarmament policymaking process during the late twentieth century. It is also an accounting of the role played in that process by the agency for which I worked for twenty-seven years, the United States Arms Control and Disarmament Agency (ACDA).

This book sets forth my personal recollections of the events described and is not a precise, exact accounting of the subject. In this, I am motivated by the style of General Douglas MacArthur's autobiography entitled *Reminiscences*, which I read many years ago. It has no footnotes and does not pretend to be objective. My purpose is to tell a story in an interesting way, while attempting to record the facts of those times and the issues as honestly as I can remember them. I do have some notes and tapes, but they are secondary. This book is written largely from recollection rather than research. Thus, I beg the reader's indulgence as I present my reminiscences and opinions. I should also note that quotation marks are often used throughout, not usually to present a precise quote, but rather to set forth the gist of what I remember from the conversation and to present the story in a conversational format. Only occasionally will I present precise excerpts or quotes, which will be indicated.

"Arms control, non-proliferation, and disarmament" is the phrase used to describe the subject of this volume. It used to be called "arms control and disarmament," with non-proliferation considered a subset of arms control. In distinguishing between arms control and disarmament, arms control could be said to refer to limitations, either numerical or otherwise, placed on a particular class of arms, while disarmament could be used to refer to the elimination of a certain type of armament. Disarmament can mean reductions as well as elimination, however. But the two terms were and are often used interchangeably. With the end of the Cold War and the increased threat of the proliferation of weapons of mass destruction as the principal threat to the security of the civilized world, non-proliferation has been receiving separate billing. Thus, I shall use in these pages the two terms "arms control" and "disarmament" interchangeably to mean all forms of arms limitation and regulation, including both reduction and elimination, and shall not repeat the phrase "arms control, non-proliferation, and disarmament," or "arms control and disarmament," except when necessary for clarity. Often, I shall simply use the word "disarmament," which is the word in longest usage of the three and is the most eloquent.

U.S. policy in these areas is developed and established by the president and his national security bureaucracy. The general practice of past presidential administrations has been to establish committees for various disarmament subjects such as the test ban, chemical weapons, the Nuclear Non-Proliferation Treaty (NPT), conventional armed forces in Europe, strategic nuclear arms negotiations, intermediate-range nuclear arms, etc., at the assistant secretary level. In the national security policy process, they report to a deputies committee, which reports to a committee of agency principals (or agency heads). For the most part, the principals committee meetings are chaired by the assistant to the president for national security affairs—the national security advisor. The other members of the disarmament principals committee during my government career were the secretary of state, the secretary of defense, the director of central intelligence (DCI), the director of ACDA, the chairman of the Joint Chiefs of Staff (JCS), and, depending on the issue, the secretary of energy, who has authority over the nation's nuclear stockpile. This committee operates on the basis of consensus; if any member dissents from a proposed course of action, the issue is sent for decision to the president, who is advised of the views of the committee by the national security advisor. The National Security Council (NSC), a statutory committee actually chaired by the president with many of the same cabinet officials as members or advisors, also exists, but is rarely used for developing disarmament policy.

The deputies committee is composed of the same agencies but is represented at the deputy level, for example, the deputy national security advisor as chairman, the deputy secretary of state, and the vice chairman of the Joint Chiefs of Staff. It too operates on the basis of consensus. If an issue can be settled at the deputies level it does not proceed to the principals level, and if the principals can all agree on an issue it never goes to the president for decision. Below the deputies are the various working-level committees and their subcommittees established to address specific disarmament issues. These are where the disarmament issue under consideration will be introduced first. Here the various agencies are represented by experts on the particular subject that the committee has been set up to address (e.g., strategic nuclear arms negotiations, chemical weapons negotiations) at the level of assistant secretary or an agency's equivalent. These committees also operate on the basis of consensus and often have frequent and long meetings— unlike the deputies and principals committees, which hold strictly time limited and scripted meetings. Much of the work is actually accomplished and agreed upon at the working-group level.

In order to oversee the conduct of a particular negotiation, a backstopping committee is formed, which will have a membership similar to the working-level committee. The backstopping committee receives and responds to requests for guidance from U.S. disarmament negotiating delegations overseas. If the issue is difficult, it will be referred to the working-group committee and on up the line if agreement cannot be reached. At the working-group level, both the interagency committee and the backstopping committee are usually not chaired by an NSC staff representative but by an official from the State Department or (formerly) ACDA.

U.S. disarmament negotiating delegations mirror the interagency community. The chairman of the delegation, typically an ambassador, represents the president and in the past usually—but not always—came from ACDA, and now usually from the State Department. There were also representatives from ACDA, State, the Office of the Secretary of Defense (OSD), the Office of the Chairman of the Joint Chiefs of Staff (OJCS), the Central Intelligence Agency (CIA), and, if appropriate, the Department of Energy (DOE). Interagency consensus on a move to be made with a negotiating partner—for example, Russia or several states at a conference—is considered desirable, but sometimes the chairman will decide an intra-delegation dispute himself since he represents the president.

In addition to the front-channel exchanges with the backstopping committee, which sends the instructions within which the delegation is to operate, the chairman has a private cable channel to the national security advisor, called a back-channel, and occasionally will get direct orders from the national security advisor speaking for the president without regard for consensus. All the other agency representatives maintain back-channels to their home agencies, often to make sure certain issues are raised in the interagency process, but there was an unwritten rule that before an agency representative sends a back-channel cable—which no one else sees, unlike the front-channel cables which everyone sees—he or she shows it privately to the delegation chairman.

Overall delegation policy and objectives are often set by presidential decision memoranda signed by the president and reflecting discussions up through the pyramid of committees to the principals committee. This policy is adjusted day to day by backstopping cables, responses to requests for guidance from the delegation, and issues put forth in the working-group committees. Some of these are designed to chip away at various parts of the presidential decision memorandum as agencies seek to re-fight old battles that they lost during the development of the memorandum. In all of this, personal relationships are important in causing policy decisions to go one way or the other. If the delegation chairman has a close personal relationship with the national security advisor, or (formerly) the director of ACDA with the secretary of state, it can make a difference.

For thirty-eight years, until 1999, the focal point of arms control policy development in the U.S. government was the director of ACDA, with four assistant directors for Strategic Affairs (e.g., strategic nuclear weapons negotiations), Multilateral Affairs (e.g., the comprehensive test ban), Nonproliferation, and Verification, working with the director of Political Military Affairs (PM) at the State Department. Now, following the absorption of ACDA by the State Department, this role is filled by the undersecretary of state for arms control and international security, with four subordinate assistant secretaries—PM, Nonproliferation (NP), Arms Control (AC), and Verification and Compliance (VC). Also, the assistant secretary of defense for international security policy (ISP) has always and will continue to play an important role in the evolution of arms control policy.

As the Cold War wore on, American political leaders increasingly came to realize the paramount importance of disarmament in avoiding an overwhelmingly disastrous nuclear war and, also important, in maintaining a channel of communication with the Soviet Union that would not be disrupted during times of tension. This recognition took shape in the form of a proposal to Congress by President Kennedy in 1961. In testimony from Secretary of State Dean Rusk, Secretary of Defense Robert McNamara, and Ambassador John J. McCloy—one of the early Cold War "wise men" serving as a consultant to President Kennedy—it was argued that disarmament is too important and technical a subject to leave in the hands of a larger agency with many other responsibilities or at the White House where the staff support for dealing with this subject in a comprehensive way does not exist. But where to locate it? To place it in the Department of Defense would create an obvious conflict of interest. Placing the locus for disarmament policy within the State Department would also create an inherent contradiction, it was said, as the primary mission of the department is to improve relations with other countries, whereas disarmament policy often goes in the opposite direction, for example, castigating China for selling nuclear technology to Pakistan. Sometimes, quite understandably, this important fundamental mission of the State Department can develop into a protectiveness in various department offices and bureaus toward certain countries for which a particular office or bureau is responsible, a tendency sometimes uncharitably referred to as "clientitis." While such a designation is unfair, the tendency in this direction in the department is real and it often runs counter to disarmament objectives.

For example, under the so-called Pressler Amendment passed in the early 1980s, the United States was required to cut off all foreign aid, including military aid, to Pakistan unless the president each year could certify that Pakistan was not in possession of a nuclear explosive device. Every year from 1985 until 1991—when President Bush found he could no longer do so—Presidents Reagan and Bush duly made the certification, even though by the late 1980s it was clear that the conditions for certification could not be met. The war in Afghanistan was going on during most of that period and every year the Department of State (as well as the Department of Defense) recommended that the president sign the certification because State wanted to maintain good relations with Pakistan so as to better influence the course of the war. Every year beginning in 1986, ACDA recommended against certification because Pakistan did have the capability to construct a nuclear device. Thus the mission of good relations with an important regional ally can run directly counter to disarmament considerations. This was understood even in 1961, as one can see from a review of the testimony during consideration of the ACDA Act establishing the agency, where it was provided that ACDA would be an independent agency. (The Senate version of the bill had provided for a semi-autonomous agency within the Department of State, but the House of Representatives preferred an independent agency. In the conference report, the proposal for an independent agency won out.)

An independent agency to advocate disarmament solutions to national security problems was established in 1961. The director reported to the president, attended all principals committee meetings in any way related to disarmament, and was a statutory advisor to the National Security Council. The lower-level committees all had an ACDA representative. This meant that at all levels of government up to the cabinet level an independent official was present to place the disarmament alternative in competition with military, economic, and other proposed solutions to national security questions.

Disarmament is not an end in itself, but merely one part of a national security policy. Sometimes United States security can best be maintained by military action and sometimes through economic measures, bilateral diplomacy, or disarmament negotiations. But it is important that the president and the NSC have all the options before them when developing national security policy. If the central responsibility for disarmament policy is located within the Department of State, as it has been since April 1, 1999, there is always a risk that disarmament considerations will be buried whenever they conflict with the department's primary mission, and thus the president and the NSC will not have the disarmament option available for consideration.

This is not to say that the disarmament option should always prevail; it clearly should not. But it should be one of the competing considerations before the president to achieve the best policy results. The Pakistan matter is a case in point. It was important that the president have before him the option of invoking the Pressler Amendment, and to be aware of the arguments for and against invoking it. Arguably, during the war in Afghanistan it should not have been invoked even though the conditions of the law had been met. But the president, in making his decision, needed to know about these legal requirements. If there had not been an independent ACDA, these considerations would never have reached the president. They would have remained somewhere in the Department of State. And presidents did pay attention to these arguments. President Reagan said in early 1989 just before he left office that he was certifying Pakistan again, but this was the last year he would be able to do so in good conscience. And President Bush, after certifying once, refused thereafter to do so. But, of course, the war in Afghanistan had ended by that time.

There are many other such examples in the history of ACDA. In the 1960s, the State Department opposed the negotiation of a nuclear non-proliferation treaty; it was only ACDA that championed it. When the NPT was signed in

1968, it had clearly become a centerpiece of United States and world security, and is even more so today. During the Bush administration it was only ACDA that was interested in completing the negotiation of the Chemical Weapons Convention (CWC), which was signed in January 1993. Now the CWC is an important part of the international system of constraints inhibiting the proliferation of weapons of mass destruction. It was ACDA alone that argued for the negotiation of a zero-yield Comprehensive Nuclear Test Ban Treaty (CTBT) in 1995 and in 1993 for the continuation of the U.S. nuclear testing moratorium begun in 1992, which led directly to the signing of the CTBT in 1996 and the establishment of the long overdue world consensus against nuclear explosions. In addition, the indefinite extension of the NPT in 1995 would not have happened had it not been for an independent ACDA. No other U.S. government agency thought it was possible, but the United States led the world to this result. And there are other examples of important developments for U.S. security that only took place because of an independent ACDA, for example, 1) the United States' insistence on (and the consequent eventual acceptance of) intrusive verification for disarmament treaties, including on-site inspection; 2) pressing the case against the former Soviet Union for its violation of the 1972 Antiballistic Missile (ABM) Treaty caused by the construction of a ballistic missile early warning radar near Krasnoyarsk in Siberia; and 3) charging violations of the Biological Weapons Convention (BWC) against the former Soviet Union in 1980 as a result of a suspicious outbreak of anthrax in Sverdlovsk (now Ekaterinburg).

In 1997, despite this record of success, ACDA was traded to the Senate Foreign Relations Committee chairman in exchange for ratification of the CWC. It became clear in December 1996 that the administration had decided—based on a December 1996 communication from incoming National Security Advisor Sandy Berger to ACDA Director John Holum—that the ACDA "independent box" had to disappear. ACDA, represented by John Holum, Deputy Director Ralph Earle, Executive Assistant to the Director Barbara Starr, and myself, tried to negotiate the best arrangement that was possible for the disarmament function to reside in the State Department. What was negotiated on paper from January to April 1997 and developed in the detailed agency-to-agency discussions in 1997 and 1998 is quite good. If fully and honestly implemented, it could even strengthen the disarmament function in the government. The ability of the responsible official to raise disarmament issues with the president is preserved. Whether an independent disarmament function will in fact be preserved, and whether this arrangement will be properly implemented in the future, depends entirely on the commitment of the people involved. Without question an independent agency is preferable because the independence of the disarmament function is secure, even when the agency is not in political favor, a common condition in the period from 1961 to 1997.

With the elimination of ACDA in 1999, this precious national security benefit may have been lost, since the disarmament official (the undersecretary of state for arms control and international security) in the future will attend the relevant decision meetings as a direct employee of the secretary of state. The negotiated arrangement with the Department of State was probably the best that could be achieved at the time, but it is all important that the authorities preserved for the undersecretary to protect the independence of the arms control process be exercised and observed.

Thus, despite its many accomplishments, a decision to eliminate the agency was taken in 1997 and implemented in 1999. General Edward Rowny, a long-time opponent of many of the disarmament efforts and an important figure in most, had nonetheless testified in favor of CWC ratification. At the ACDA farewell meeting (ironically scheduled on April 1, 1999), he stated that if he had known that ACDA would be sold to achieve CWC ratification, he would have testified against the treaty.

ACDA over the years was attacked often and was downgraded several times, but it survived. Its mission was central to U.S. national security interests during the Cold War. This mission was just as important thereafter with the emergence of the proliferation of weapons of mass destruction, principally nuclear weapons, as the major threat to U.S. and world security. Despite its many successes, ACDA always had many enemies who wished to do away with it or at least render it impotent—disarmament is an emotional subject, after all. But after every reverse, ACDA came back stronger than ever and went on to further success in advancing the nation's interests. The turbulent history of this agency, an agency that contributed so much to the security of this country, and its ultimate demise are central to the story in this volume.

DISARMAMENT SKETCHES

CHAPTER ONE POLITICS, LOUISVILLE AND WASHINGTON, D.C.

I come from a political family. My great-uncle, Robert Connor, was lieutenant governor of Wisconsin under Governor Robert LaFollette and chairman of the Republican Party in Wisconsin for many years. I remember once asking my grandmother, "Granny, are you a Democrat or a Republican?" Elizabeth Malcolm Connor Graham looked at me with scorn and replied, "I was forty before I saw a Democrat!"

My grandmother's sister was the grandmother of Melvin Laird, President Nixon's secretary of defense. I always especially admired Mel and his political career. He was a great secretary of defense and an outstanding politician in the best sense of that word. Early in his congressional career, while serving as ranking Republican on the House Appropriations Committee, he was referred to as "the Richelieu of the cheese belt," his congressional district being in central Wisconsin. This important part of my heritage is deeply Republican, but progressive Republican. My guiding light with respect to political views since 1968 has been Mel Laird. I used the term "progressive Republican" to indicate that part of the political spectrum which used to be called "eastern establishment Republicans." Many of the present-day heirs to this tradition are sometimes referred to as "moderate" Republicans. This is the tradition to which I adhere. It means being an internationalist and being conservative with respect to some social issues and liberal with respect to others. Personally, I am pro-choice on abortion, but I support the death penalty; I became opposed to the Vietnam War, but I strongly objected to the campus protests.

My grandfather, Thomas Jackson Graham (named after Stonewall by my great-grandfather, a major in the Union Army, First Indiana Volunteers), was a Presbyterian minister who moved to Louisville, Kentucky, in 1920 to take over the Warren Memorial Presbyterian Church, the largest Presbyterian church in the city at that time. My father was at Princeton then and, inspired by Woodrow Wilson, decided to break with his Republican upbringing and become a Democrat. He remained an active Democrat all his life and was a mover and shaker in Louisville, serving as the party treasurer of the Jefferson County (Louisville) Democratic Party organization for thirty years and as chairman of the Sinking Fund (a part-time assignment with the civic organization that managed the city's long-term investments) for fifteen years. He finally was kicked out as treasurer in 1966 because he joined the reelection campaign of Republican Senator John Sherman Cooper, one of his longtime friends, whose first statewide campaign he had helped finance in 1946.

My father stood for mayor of Louisville in 1948—much against my mother's wishes. The incumbent, Marion E. Taylor, had died after just a year in office. The twelve-man Board of Aldermen was charged with electing a successor to serve out the remainder of the four-year term. A vigorous contest ensued between my father and Charles Farnesly, an interesting and eccentric man. (After his political career, Farnesly ran an organization named the Lost Cause Press and he drove, as I recall, a 1919 Rolls-Royce automobile.) On the day of the vote, one of my father's supporters was sick and did not attend, and the result was a 5–5 tie (the chairman only voted in case of a tie). The chairman, Daniel Byck, a neighbor of ours, voted for Mr. Farnesly, much to the relief of my mother, who never liked politics. Charles Farnesly went on to serve seven years as mayor and a term or two in Congress, while my father returned to his investment business and part-time political career.

My father and mother gave me a golden childhood. It was sufficiently joyous that an old family retainer once said to me when I was a teenager, "Mister Tom, your childhood has been so happy that you are sure to have some bad when you grow up." I have always remembered that—it has both good and bad connotations. Louisville when I was growing up in the 1940s and 1950s, while not perfect, was itself a rather golden place. It was reasonably prosperous, a tight-knit neighborly community, crime was nonexistent, and divorce was virtually unknown. Although alcoholism was a huge problem (particularly among business leaders—alcohol was the tranquilizer, the sedative of that place in those times), drugs were not present at all. And politics was fun.

I went with my father to the 1952 Democratic Convention in Chicago, accompanied by Wilson Wyatt, who among many other things was our family lawyer. Wyatt became Adlai Stevenson's campaign manager and Governor Stevenson was a classmate of my father's at Princeton, so at the age of eighteen I felt myself very much in the middle of things. Alban Barkely, longtime Kentucky senator and vice president under President Harry S. Truman, was the candidate of the Kentucky delegation, but it was clear early on that he had no chance for the nomination, in part because of his age. Senator Richard Russell was a favorite of my father's, but I remember traveling by cab from the train station to our hotel in Chicago and seeing a placard being held by a man near the hotel which said, "Russell unfair to labor," and my father saying, "probably a lot of people have that view." Apparently many of the delegates did.

My father arranged for me to attend three other Democratic national conventions in various capacities in 1960, 1964, and 1968. In the summer of 1960, my classmate from Harvard Law School George Daly and I finished our second year with a driving tour around the West that included four days at the convention in Los Angeles. We had gallery seats, which were briefly challenged by Wendell Ford, then head of the Kentucky Young Democrats, later governor and longtime senator. My best memory of that convention was Minnesota Senator Eugene McCarthy's nominating speech for Adlai Stevenson, to the effect of, as I recall: "Let the prophet not be without honor in his own country." Because of its eloquence, it made as strong an impression upon me as any political speech that I have since heard.

In 1964 my father joined the so-called President's Club, which gave members certain privileges in exchange for a contribution of, I believe, $5,000 to the Democratic Party. Among the privileges were two free-floating passes to sit on the floor with the delegates at the national convention anywhere one could find a seat, which he gave to me. That convention was, of course, simply a ratification of President Lyndon Johnson and his vice presidential selection, Hubert Humphrey. The only real excitement was the ouster of the official, segregationist delegation from Mississippi and its replacement on the floor by an alternate delegation called the Mississippi Freedom Democrats. As I remember, this result was effected by a media campaign and pressure put on the convention leadership by African-American Democratic leaders from the North. I was seated on the floor with the Kentucky delegation when this happened. I turned around to watch the Mississippi Freedom Democrats file in to their seats—in the lead was someone who looked like none other than Stuart Lampe, a student at Harvard from Ghana whom I had met at law school. He went on to join the staff of the Ghanaian Embassy in Washington, where I understood he was living in 1964. This suggested to me that the Freedom Democrats were perhaps not all grassroots Mississippians, but rather their delegation may have contained an outsider or two.

The other special memory that I have from that convention is of a huge billboard along the boardwalk—the convention was in Atlantic City that year—dominated by a picture of Senator Barry Goldwater with the caption, "In your heart you know he's right." With the perspective of thirty-six years, having in mind what the Johnson administration did in Vietnam (campaigning on the basis of "Asian boys to fight Asian wars" while at that same time secretly conducting a huge American build-up in Vietnam), the left-wing extremism on college campuses in the 1960s and early 1970s, and the later rise of the radical right, perhaps he was right and in our hearts we should have known it. My father came to know Barry Goldwater through the League of Cities/Conference of Mayors organization—Senator Goldwater at the time was on the Phoenix City Council and my father was chairman of the Sinking Fund in Louisville. In his later years, my father referred to himself as a Goldwater Democrat. When I was young, I thought of myself as a liberal, but I remember the shock in 1962 when I picked up a copy of Goldwater's *Conscience of a Conservative* and found that I agreed with almost all of it.

Having grown up in Louisville, the Kentucky Derby has always been important to me. In 2001, I attended my forty-first Derby and that made thirty-five out of the last thirty-seven. One of my standard frivolities is to remark that some people have Christmas, some people have Yom Kippur, some people have Ramadan, I have Derby Day. My father was on the Board of Directors of Churchill Downs for thirty years and, among other things, designed the official silver Derby Julep Cup. He and my mother—almost always a winner on the Derby—took me for the first time when I was thirteen; Citation was the horse that year. To me, the Derby is a time to relate to tradition, be with one's family, and have a wonderful time. I was always a shy person, with some but limited ambition. Going to the Derby as an early teenager brought me out a bit.

In high school, I by chance found myself asked to join the very old and prestigious Louisville high school fraternity called the Athenaeum Literary Association (ALA), which dated back to 1862. (Many of Louisville's business and civic leaders had gone to my high school and had been members of the ALA over the decades.) By an even greater chance I was elected president of the ALA in my senior year of high school. Several of my closest lifelong friendships came from my membership in the organization. Becoming a member and then president gave me some self-confidence and ambition.

My high school, Louisville Male High School, while being perhaps one of Louisville's oldest and most venerable institutions, was everything the name implied. It was an all-male, all-white public high school, but one of very high academic standards. Being all-male and public, it was somewhat unusual, and families that had moved to Louisville recently, as opposed to old-line types, began a campaign to make Male co-educational in the 1940s. This touched off perhaps the greatest political battle of that era in Louisville's history; bitter campaigns for School Board membership ensued, friendships broke up. By one camp it was seen as a direct assault on one of Louisville's sacred institutions, by the other as essential reform to move away from prehistoric practices. Eventually, the co-education side won and my class (1951) was the last to graduate without girls. By contrast, the racial integration of Louisville public schools after the 1954 Supreme Court decision was accomplished promptly and without incident in 1956. The foolishness of segregation reminds me of one of the many wise sayings of Harry Golden, the editor in the 1950s of a newspaper in North Carolina called the *Carolina Israelite*— a voice of reason in those times. He wrote, as I recall: "No white Southerner objects to standing next to a Negro, only sitting next to one, so the solution to the integration problem is simply to move the chairs out of the schools." Thankfully, Louisville was spared much of the tumult of this issue.

However, even after public school integration, Louisville remained to a degree a segregated city. There was considerable resistance to Martin Luther King Jr.'s campaign to integrate Louisville's restaurants and lunchrooms more than a decade later. After the co-education battle was over and public school integration was accomplished, my father decided that perhaps he could make a contribution to the improvement of the racial situation. For three successive School Board elections he managed and financed the campaigns of the Rev. Daniel Hewlett, a black minister, for a seat on the School Board. Each election campaign his numbers went up to the pleasure of those observing this, but he never quite made it. My father also, to my very great pride and admiration, arranged in 1950 for Jackie Robinson to receive an award from the city of Louisville recognizing his contribution to baseball. (Robinson had been booed in Louisville in 1946 during the Triple A Little World Series between Louisville and Montreal—his first season in organized baseball.) Never was I prouder of my father—I had seen Jackie Robinson play in the famous 1947 World Series.

Early on at Princeton, I became interested in the Woodrow Wilson School of Public and International Affairs. Students had the option of doing their last two years of study and senior thesis within this school at Princeton. One advantage was that a Woodrow Wilson School major could take courses in any university department. With some effort (history, politics, and economics were the prerequisites; the first two were not difficult for me, but the third definitely was) I managed to be accepted. I decided that the politics of foreign policy was what interested me most and I resolved to become a diplomat. Professor Gordon Craig's course on diplomatic history from 1919 to 1939 made quite an impact on me. I still remember his tale of how Mussolini had a plan to place giant fans atop the Alps to blow the Central European cloud cover down over Italy and thereby make the Italians unhappy and gloomy and, as a result, as warlike as the Germans. During SALT II, I enjoyed telling this story to Soviet generals, who were unconvinced that it would have changed anything. My senior thesis was on American attitudes toward Soviet power, 1937–47, represented by editorials in *The Nation* and *The Wall Street Journal*, along with Gallup polls calibrated against the events of this period. A copy still sits on my coffee table at home today.

When I was a senior at Princeton, I applied to and was accepted at Harvard Law School, but I elected to go to L'Institut des Sciences Politiques in Paris for a year between college and law school. While at school in Paris I traveled to the eastern Mediterranean, including Syria, Lebanon, and Egypt in the spring of 1956. In Egypt I had myself photographed in a dark business suit sitting on a camel in front of the Sphinx. When I came home that summer my father, with his usual energy, had the *Louisville Courier Journal* do a story on me, which ran in their magazine section. The piece was entitled "Internationalist" and included the photo of me sitting on the camel. Although nothing in my resume up to that time could justify such an ambition, the article cites me as saying that I hoped for a career with the State Department or a U.S.–Middle East oil company. My year in Paris necessitated another application to Harvard, which was also successful. However, the Louisville Draft Board intervened, and in 1956 I was off to the Army for two years, voiding that acceptance as well. The Draft Board had not drafted anyone in fifteen months—the Korean War was over and Vietnam was some years into the future—but the president of the Draft Board was a political opponent of my father's and I was between deferments and, therefore, vulnerable.

I found my life as a recruit in the Army in those days to be somewhat less than satisfying and definitely ambition creating, but, in retrospect I am pleased that I served. It had an important effect upon me, one that was wholly beneficial. Nevertheless, I did feel time on my hands. My two-year term in the Army was set to end in September 1958, in time for me to enter law school with the class of 1961. I applied to Harvard Law a third time in the spring of 1958 and was successful once more. I also learned that the Army had a program at that time whereby an enlistment could be ended three months early if the applicant could demonstrate that failure to receive such an early out would delay his education by a year or more. But how to do this when my term in the Army ended approximately as the fall term at Harvard was beginning? Then I learned that Harvard Summer School was offering a special program that summer in Middle Eastern languages. Thus I applied for early release on the grounds that I intended to seek a career as a lawyer for a Middle East oil company (as the article had said) and wanted to study Islamic law while at Harvard Law School.

The Army accepted my application, even though Harvard Law School at that time did not offer a course in Islamic law, and in June of 1958, I left active duty in the Army and entered Harvard Summer School. Classical Arabic was my choice of study as it is the written language of the entire Arab world. It was a difficult course requiring study from early in the morning until late at night every day for most of the balance of the summer. Looking back this might seem to be a faintly ridiculous thing to have done, but it did spark a lifelong interest in and sympathy for the problems of the Middle East. I entered Harvard Law School on time in September, and when I reached the head of the registration line the clerk looked at my card and then at me and said, "At last!"

While at Harvard Law School, I signed up for then Harvard University professor Henry Kissinger's seminar on defense policy and administration, which was most interesting. We were required to read his book, *Nuclear Weapons and Foreign Policy*. Once a week the fifty of us in the seminar gathered around a large table to listen to Kissinger expound and interrogate his weekly guest, which included the likes of former French Premier Mendés-

France, retired Lieutenant General James Gavin, and the great French defense intellectual Raymond Aron. This course had been introduced to the law school curriculum some years before by a Harvard Law School professor named Barton Leach and later turned over to Kissinger. The theory was that most lawyers at some point in their careers likely would have to deal with the Department of Defense, but universities teach nothing about it.

I also took a particularly interesting course taught by Louis Sohn, one of the great men of the profession of teaching law. In the United States he is virtually a history of public international law. As I understand it, he was required to retire from Harvard Law School upon reaching the age of sixty-five. He then proceeded to the University of San Francisco, where he taught until required to retire at seventy-five. Next he went to the University of Georgia Law School, where he was allowed to teach until the age of eighty-five. He then taught at George Washington University Law School for ten years and at age ninety-five was given emeritus status. Someone asked him once upon a time how he remained so healthy. His reply was, "I never stop working all the time." He is on the Board of Directors of my current organization, the Lawyers Alliance for World Security (LAWS) and I have the pleasure of working with him still. I heard him say during a 1999 debate sponsored by LAWS on Kosovo and international law, "Don't tell me what the United Nations Charter says. I wrote it."

I enjoyed Louis's course in the spring of 1960 very much. It was a Christmas tradition that the Lincoln's Inn Society, a venerable club—largely social—at Harvard Law School, give a dinner for the faculty, at which a musical show lampooning the professors was a feature. There were of course favorite professors to make fun of, and I noticed in my first two years that no one wrote a song about Louis Sohn—public international law was just a little bit out of the way. My third year it came to my roommate, Bill Fitzgerald, and me to write the show. We recruited several of our classmates and wrote a show that turned out to be hugely popular. It closed with a chorus line with everyone singing to the tune of "It's a Long Way to Tipperary":

It's a long way to certiorari,
it's a long way to go,
climbing upward with certiorari,
to the highest court we know,
so long Second Circuit,
farewell Learned Hand,
it's a long, long way to certiorari,
but we'll see you on remand.

Our show was so popular that we were asked to put it on for the entire university, which we did. That was the end of our career together as a cast, however, as the show did not go over as well with this audience. The cast had made a decision to do a considerable part of the celebrating prior to the show rather than after, which had an effect on their performance. All of this was great fun, but a special part of the show for me was that I did write a song about Louis Sohn and his course, "Problems of World Order" (very relevant today, I might add), and sang it myself to the tune of "Home on the Range":

Oh, give me a home,
where the missiles don't roam
and the fallout stays far, far away;
Where everyone snubs
those nuclear subs,
and Nikita keeps his shoes on all day.
Sohn, Sohn at the fore,
outlawing nuclear war,
where there is never a quirk
from old Arleigh Burke,
and the fallout stays far, far away.

The song is somewhat dated, but not entirely so.

After graduating from Harvard Law School in 1961, with my father's help I was offered a clerkship with Chief Judge Wilbur Miller of the Circuit Court of Appeals for the District of Columbia. It was a great privilege to be Judge Miller's clerk. It was an interesting court with former Chief Judge Barret Prettyman—a great judge—still on it and Judge (later Chief Judge) David Bazelon and Judge (later Chief Justice) Warren Burger the rising stars. The nine law clerks held periodic luncheons during the year to which a notable guest was usually invited. One such luncheon guest in 1961 was Justice Felix Frankfurter. It was a most interesting discussion concluded by his wise counsel, "Gentlemen, do not spend your entire careers with one job objective in mind. You may never get there, and even if you do, you will likely find it not nearly as appealing as you had thought."

While clerking at the court I shared a house in Georgetown with my long-time friend John Rhinelander, who at the time was clerking for the great Justice John Marshall Harlan, grandson of John Harlan (from Kentucky), who was on the Supreme Court at the time of *Plessy vs. Ferguson* and had voted against the "separate, but equal" doctrine. John Rhinelander later was legal advisor to the U.S. SALT I delegation, general counsel of the Department of Health, Education, and Welfare (HEW), and undersecretary (now called deputy secretary) of Housing and Urban Development (HUD). He is recognized as a leading expert on the ABM Treaty, in that he prepared the drafts of the treaty during the negotiations, drafted a top-secret article-by-article analysis of it for the U.S. delegation, and co-authored a 1974 book entitled *SALT: The Moscow Agreements and Beyond*. Many years later, John and I were to work together on several arms control issues and teach together at Virginia and Georgetown for more than ten years. Among other things, he has been for a long time an eloquent defender of the ABM Treaty, which has been under siege for many years.

Two of my favorite political stories about John, however, do not involve arms control. In 1972, before he became general counsel of HEW, Congress passed Title IX of the Education Act, which required equal opportunity for men's and women's athletic programs in schools, including universities, that receive public funds, which is most of them. In typical fashion, Congress passed a generally written statement and left it to HEW—particularly its civil rights office and its large legal office—to define how it would be applied. In due course, John's office drafted and reworked the regulations, which were then put out for public comment. Ten thousand comments were received. Later John's office received a call from the White House to the effect that he was expected to attend a meeting in the Cabinet Room at the request of the president. When John went over to the White House, he was shown the way to the Cabinet Room. He opened the door and there on the other side of the table sat President Ford, flanked by the football coaches of Michigan, Texas, and Oklahoma. As John walked in, President Ford (who of course had played football at Michigan) said, "Well, John, what have you done to us today?"

John later went to HUD as deputy secretary, but resigned his position in December 1977 in a letter to President Ford effective January 20, 1977 (when Jimmy Carter was to take office) and eventually joined the law firm of Shaw, Pittman, Potts and Trowbridge, where he is still located in 2001. In early January, before the inauguration, Carla Hills's designated successor as HUD secretary, Patricia Harris, called John in his office at HUD. Secretary Harris said, "Mr. Rhinelander?" "Yes," said John. "Mr. Rhinelander, you're fired!" "But you can't fire me. You're not in office yet, and I resigned in a letter effective January 20." "It doesn't matter, you're fired!" It is a strange government.

Also during this time, I came to know Congressman Brent Spence from Kentucky, a friend of my father's. For thirty-two years, from 1930 to 1962, he represented the district centered on Covington, Kentucky (across the Ohio River from Cincinnati), the last fifteen as chairman of the House Committee on Banking and Currency. He was very popular and he once told me that one of his few difficult reelection challenges came in a primary from a man who earlier in his career had been charged with a serious crime, but had been found not guilty by reason of insanity. Congressman Spence said that he wrote to both the attorney general of Kentucky and the attorney general of the United States questioning whether his opponent should not be disqualified because of his insanity plea, but he received the same answer in effect from both—that there was nothing in the constitutions or the statutes of either the state of Kentucky or the United States of America that requires an individual to be sane to take office as a member of Congress.

Covington must have been quite a place in the old days when it was the gambling center of the eastern United States. In 1960 a gentleman named George Ratterman, formerly a star quarterback at Notre Dame, was the reform candidate for county sheriff. During the campaign he was lured by members of the opposition establishment to a meeting at a bar and given a drugged drink. He woke up unclothed in the bed of a striptease artist named April Flowers, with a photographer working for the incumbent sheriff flashing away. He was duly charged with something like indecent exposure and there was a trial. During the trial his lawyer challenged the credibility of the principal witness for the prosecution, April Flowers. She replied that, of course, she was a reliable witness; after all, she had been commissioned a Kentucky Colonel by the governor and thereupon she produced her colonel's commission.

At this time, I was a summer law clerk at the firm of Wyatt, Grafton, and Sloss, which later merged with another firm, to become Wyatt, Tarrant, and Combs, one of Kentucky's most prominent firms. (This was after returning from the 1960 Democratic Convention.) Wilson Wyatt—with whom I had attended the 1952 convention—was the senior partner of the firm and at the time he was the lieutenant governor of the state of Kentucky. Immediately following the courtroom incident involving witness April Flowers, it was disclosed in the press that none other than Lieutenant Governor Wyatt had signed her commission. After checking the date of the commission and verifying that he had been acting governor on that day, Wyatt responded to the newspaper reporter that he had signed eighty-six commissions that day and that he definitely did not know Ms. Flowers personally (Wyatt was planning to run for the Senate in the next election). Apparently, Ms. Flowers had been recommended to be a Kentucky colonel by a judge in Covington who had caught her act.

The next day the headline in the *Louisville Courier Journal*, in reporting Wilson Wyatt's revocation of Ms. Flowers's commission, read, "Wyatt 'Strips' April Flowers of Her Commission." And as I was driving to work, the radio disc jockey on the station I was listening to came on and said, "The next song is 'April Showers' in honor of Lieutenant Governor Wilson Wyatt." Everyone at the law firm that day, except Wilson, thought it was unbelievably funny. Politics was enjoyable in those days and Wilson Wyatt's distinguished career was in no way damaged. Incidentally, George Ratterman won the election and cleaned up Covington, forcing the eastern United States gambling headquarters to be moved to Atlantic City.

Near the completion of my clerkship in May 1962, Brent Spence approached me and asked if I would like to be counsel to the House Banking and Currency Committee for the balance of the year. He was eighty-seven years old and had announced his retirement for January. As a result, his counsel had taken a position with the Federal Reserve Board and Congressman Spence needed someone quickly to work for the next eight months.

I, of course, accepted and it proved to be a rich and rewarding experience. Congressman Spence, when he retired in January 1963 at the age of eighty-eight, was at that time the oldest man ever to serve in the House of Representatives. His mind was clear and quick, but he often needed someone with him to facilitate his getting around. As a result, I was able to accompany him in situations where I otherwise might not have been included. (I was also, at age twenty-eight, impressed by the fact that as I was about to leave home for the office on my first day at work, I received my first call from a lobbyist.)

One day in October 1962, during the Cuban Missile Crisis, but before it became public, President Kennedy called Congressman Spence and asked him to accompany him to Cincinnati where the president was scheduled to make a campaign speech. The Cincinnati airport, then and now, is located (not by accident) across the river in Kentucky in what was then Congressman Spence's district. Congressman Spence said yes, if he could bring an aide along, so I was able to accompany him on the trip. When we landed in Air Force One at the airport, the receiving arrangements for the president were not quite in place. Everyone but the president, Congressman Spence, and I left the plane. The president came back from his office on the plane and talked with us for about fifteen minutes while preparations were being completed. I do not recall what we discussed, but I remember well that when you spoke with President Kennedy, he looked you right in the eye as though he was intently listening to what you said—an important political attribute.

These were the halcyon days of the Kennedy presidency. But in the minds of some of us, at least, there was a small cloud on the horizon. President Kennedy was immensely popular, but it was almost as though he, his family, and his administration had reached for, and to some extent, attained too much. Some were saying that the Kennedy family plan was to have Robert serve as president for eight years after John F. Kennedy's eight years, followed by eight years for Edward Kennedy. And after that, who knew what? Was there an idea of some sort of dynasty? Perhaps Robert Kennedy should not have been attorney general, but who knows? It seemed to me that there was a sense, an intangible sense, of the Greek idea of hubris in the air, as though it was too much, that something would happen. Needless to say, what did happen was so terribly destructive to the American body politic, I am not sure that complete recovery has been attained even now, thirty-eight years later. In some ways, November 1963 led directly to the tragedy of Vietnam. This, of course, was already well advanced after the death of Vietnamese President Diem, an assassination in early 1963 in which the U.S. government was indirectly involved. Nevertheless, although his administration must bear much of the responsibility of Vietnam, had President Kennedy lived and been re-elected, he might have been able to pull us back. President Johnson, with all his culpability, probably could not have done that politically even if he had wanted to.

I must confess that in my own case I did not realize that the Vietnam tragedy was truly upon us until 1967. At that time I read an account of the war in the *New Yorker* magazine in which, among other things, an American pilot was explaining what a "free-fire zone" in South Vietnam was. Flying over such a zone one assumed anything that moved was an enemy. Upon reading that, it occurred to me that this war had to be unwinnable and that was what led me to support Senator Eugene McCarthy of Minnesota for president and ultimately work for the Republicans in 1968.

Congressman Spence retired in January 1963 and was succeeded by Congressman Wright Patman from Texarkana, Texas, a great booster of the savings and loan industry and an avowed foe of banks. Congressman Spence had always been a supporter of the banking industry. At one of his farewell luncheons, a longtime political supporter of Congressman Spence told him, "Brent, one of the many great services that you performed for the Republic during your career was that you kept Wright Patman out of the chair of the House Banking Committee for fifteen years."

I then went to work for Jim Saxon, the comptroller of the currency (the regulator of national banks) who was also a supporter of the banking industry and an admirer of Congressman Spence. It was his avowed goal to reverse some of the provisions of the Glass-Steagall Act of 1934, thereby increasing the opportunities for national banks and making them more effective. He hired me as his legislative assistant, hoping that I could help him with the committee. Chairman Patman, as the champion of savings and loans, proved to be an implacable foe. Comptroller Saxon's principal ally on the House committee where most of the battles were fought proved to be a young congressman from Rhode Island, Ferdinand St. Germain, who many years later became chairman of the committee. Several violent political confrontations took place in 1963 and pressure was put on Treasury Secretary Douglas Dillon to fire Jim Saxon. The secretary remained loyal, but in the end Wright Patman and the savings and loan lobby proved to be too strong and Saxon had only limited success in increasing the power of national banks.

The comptroller of the currency, as part of regulating the national banks, was the approving authority for mergers and new charters for national banks. Since Saxon favored expanding the powers of national banks, he also favored mergers to create more powerful entities and new charters to provide easier entry into the industry and more competition. In early 1964 Saxon was considering the application of a group in Texas to charter a new national bank. It seemed to be a routine matter until he received a call from a "judge" who wanted to come see him to talk about this application. During their meeting the "judge" said that he was a trustee of Lyndon B. Johnson's blind trust and that this new bank would be located near one of the banks owned by the trust. It could hurt the business of the trust's bank. He urged Saxon not to charter the bank, suggesting that otherwise there would be anger at the White House. Saxon chartered the new bank anyway and seemed to suffer no adverse consequences, although he did leave office the next year. This result reminded me of a remark that I remember a Harvard Law classmate, a young woman from a prominent political and commercial family from Dallas, making. She, as I recall, spent a summer working as an intern in the office of then Senator Lyndon Johnson. She once said that it was difficult to do that and retain one's faith in democracy. This matter caused me to reflect on that comment.

I certainly had a bias against the Johnson-Humphrey forces, but was more pro-McCarthy than anti-Johnson in 1968. With the Tet Offensive and the assassinations of Robert Kennedy and Martin Luther King Jr., that was a terrible year. It seemed we needed a new type of politician. The convention that year is famous for the violence associated with it, but what offended me was the treatment given to the McCarthy delegates by the dominant Johnson forces. It impressed me that the Chicago convention was more like what one would expect from the Soviet Politburo than a democratic process. The Johnson-Humphrey forces just steamrolled the McCarthy forces, leaving them little opportunity to even make their case. I came away from the convention so angry that I wrote to Mel Laird asking for a job with the Nixon campaign. He obtained a job for me for the last five weeks of the campaign with United Citizens for Nixon-Agnew (an organization designed to appeal to all citizens, not just Republicans) as special assistant to the chairman, Charles Rhyne, President Nixon's former roommate at Duke Law School. I did not have a lot to do, but it was an interesting experience for me. John Warner, now for many years Senator Warner, was Charles Rhyne's deputy in the organization.

Charles Rhyne fully expected to be selected as attorney general after the campaign. But following the coup by John Mitchell at the Republican National Committee (no doubt assisted by Haldeman and Erlichman), immediately after the campaign Rhyne was tossed aside with no job at all. In retrospect one wonders what would have happened if Charles Rhyne, a real leader of the bar, had become attorney general. Perhaps Watergate might not have been. I also came to know Lucy Winchester on the staff of the United Citizens for Nixon-Agnew, and after the campaign she became Mrs. Nixon's social secretary. She once obtained an appointment on my request with Mrs. Nixon for Hope Cooke Namgyal, the Queen of Sikkim, who was in town pleading the cause of the tiny Himalayan kingdom that was about to be absorbed by India. (Hope had been a college friend of my first wife, Clover Nicholas, and both she and the King—a wonderful man—had attended our wedding.) Essentially Sikkim wanted to be more like Bhutan, an Indian satellite, but a member of the United Nations. Indira Gandhi, with the 1962 war with China still on her mind, did not want this to happen and she crushed and absorbed Sikkim in 1973.

As I mentioned above, my experience at the 1968 Chicago convention caused me to seek a position in the Nixon campaign and then in the administration and, ultimately, to change my registration from Democrat to Republican in 1970. I have not always agreed with Republican Party positions—especially when they come from the Republican far right—but in our two-party system it seems to me important to pick one party and stay with it.

In March of 1969 my father died after an illness of some seven months, after which I resolved to leave New York, where I was working for the large law firm of Shearman and Sterling, and return to Washington to reenter government service. I visited with Mel Laird, by now secretary of defense, and he referred me to Robert Froelhke, a longtime friend of his, who was then a new assistant secretary of defense and later secretary of the Army. Bob referred me to John Steadman, Air Force general counsel, a holdover from the Johnson administration. John offered me a job as an attorney-advisor at the GS-14 level. On August 19, 1969, I reported for duty and spent one year in this office. Nineteen sixty-nine was, of course, a year of violent controversy concerning the Vietnam War, as was 1970. Even though protests swirled around the Pentagon, those of us working in the office of the general counsel of the Air Force were largely insulated. Mel Laird held up admirably, in my opinion, serving a president he did not like, prosecuting a war he, in general, opposed.

In January 1969, Paul Warnke, a senior official in the Johnson Pentagon (and in the late 1970s ACDA director), was asked by Mel Laird to stay for a while in his position of assistant secretary of defense for international security policy. Thus, he accompanied the secretary on his first Vietnam inspection tour in early 1969. As I understood it from Paul, Mel appeared to be convinced by this tour that the war was a mistake and unwinnable. On the return flight he drafted a long statement about the war which he cabled to the White House during a stopover in Honolulu. His plane arrived at Andrews Air Force Base near Washington, but before he could deplane several White House aides rushed on board and there followed a two-hour meeting. After the meeting the secretary deplaned, issuing only a terse arrival statement of a few sentences. One can only speculate on what was in his original statement and how history might have been different if President Nixon had allowed him to issue it and been influenced by its content.

In the early summer of 1969, I was informed by a colleague in the office that a small agency called the Arms Control and Disarmament Agency was looking for a lawyer with some Capitol Hill experience. Their assistant general counsel for congressional relations, Mel Christopher, had taken a job as the executive assistant to the director of ACDA, thus opening up the congressional job. From ACDA's creation in 1961 until 1985 the Office of General Counsel had the legislative liaison function in addition to its normal functioning as a legal office. In July of 1969 I met with the general counsel,

Bill Hancock, who expressed interest in me and invited me to demonstrate congressional support. I contacted the offices of the two Kentucky senators—both longtime friends of my father—John Sherman Cooper, a very prominent member of the Senate Foreign Relations Committee, and Thurston B. Morton, formerly Republican National Committee chairman. They both wrote letters on my behalf. A few weeks later, Bill Hancock called and informed me that I had the job. We agreed that I would start at ACDA in September of 1970.

When I moved to ACDA it was my sixth job in nine years, and I told myself that I should plan to stay for three years. As it turned out I stayed for twenty-seven. And I can honestly say that even during difficult times I looked forward to every day and wondered what it would bring. A favorite saying of mine while at ACDA was that, man for man, ACDA was the most controversial government organization in the history of the world. And it truly seemed as though it was—anything could happen and it usually did.

In my early years at ACDA, when I was asked where I worked, I replied by naming the Arms Control and Disarmament Agency. The response usually was, "Oh, I didn't know that you worked on gun control." In fact, many years later I did brush up against the gun control issue. When I was traveling the world in 1993–95 in search of votes for the indefinite extension of the NPT, I spent much time in Latin America. The nuclear non-proliferation part of the agenda was always quickly completed, often with an expression of support for indefinite extension, leaving the rest of my time with the foreign minister or the deputy foreign minister to discuss the issue of most immediate concern to them, which was usually the question of when the United States was going to stop the avalanche of illegal small arms that were flooding their country and going directly to drug organizations. It would seem that not only are gun manufacturers placing an ever-larger number of guns into circulation in the United States, but such weapons are spilling over to many foreign countries and finding their way into the hands of organizations inimical to the interests of the United States. It cannot be in our interest as a nation to permit the international drug cartels to be armed in effect by U.S. weapon production. Nevertheless, the United States leads the world with approximately $1.8 billion in international small arms sales annually.

When I joined ACDA in 1970 it was a quite vibrant organization. According to ACDA records, Director Gerard Smith had forty-six private meetings with President Nixon in forty-eight months. Subsequent directors never had more than three or four in total. My first assignment during my first week at ACDA in 1970 was to accompany Deputy General Counsel Charles Van Doren before the Senate Foreign Relations Committee during his testimony on behalf of United States ratification of Protocol II to the Treaty of Tlatelolco, which declares Latin America a nuclear-weapon-free zone. The Treaty of Tlatelolco was the first international agreement prohibiting nuclear weapons in a populated area of the globe. (Nuclear weapons had been prohibited in Antarctica pursuant to the Antarctica Treaty of 1959, and in outer space pursuant to the Outer Space Treaty of 1967.) It was negotiated in the mid-1960s in reaction to the Cuban Missile Crisis of 1963. Latin American countries—led by Mexico—wanted to ensure, to the extent possible, that they would not be drawn into any future superpower nuclear confrontation. The treaty was signed in 1967 with an elaborate approval system. The treaty provided that after signature and ratification a country still was not bound until all other Latin American states had ratified; until all territories in the area that were dependencies of foreign powers had been brought under the zone (e.g., Puerto Rico and the Virgin Islands) pursuant to Protocol I of the treaty; all the nuclear-weapon states had signed and ratified Protocol II; and until all the treaty states parties had concluded safeguard agreements with the International Atomic Energy Agency. (A safeguard agreement allows the IAEA to inspect a country's declared nuclear facilities for signs of diversion of fissile material to nuclear weapons programs.) However, a country could waive the entry-into-force requirements and bind itself under the treaty by depositing the waiver, along with the instrument of ratification, with the depository, Mexico. This permitted Argentina and Brazil, which had nuclear-weapon programs for many years, to sign and even ratify the treaty but not be bound. By 2001, all Latin American states had signed, ratified, and waived except for Cuba—which signed in 1995 but has not ratified—so the treaty is nearing full entry into force.

Protocol II of the treaty, which was before the Senate Foreign Relations Committee that day in late September, provides what is referred to as a negative security assurance. Pursuant to Protocol II, the nuclear-weapon states—the United States, the United Kingdom, Russia, France, and China—pledge that they will not use or threaten to use nuclear weapons against any of the parties to the treaty. By contrast, Protocol I of the treaty provides that out-of-zone states that have dependencies within the area of application of the treaty may place such dependencies under the provisions of the treaty. The United States ratified Protocol I in 1980, placing Puerto Rico and the Virgin Islands under the treaty.

The Treaty of Tlatelolco began the nuclear-weapon-free zone process. By 1998 all the nuclear-weapon states had ratified both protocols of the treaty. In 1986 the Treaty of Raratonga, the South Pacific nuclear-weapon-free zone treaty, was signed. It has the equivalent of Protocols I and II of Tlatelolco plus a third protocol prohibiting the testing of nuclear weapons in the area covered by the treaty. In 1996 the Treaty of Pelindaba, the African nuclear-weapon-free zone treaty, was signed. It contains the two protocols found in the previous two treaties. Following the indefinite extension of the NPT in 1995, the signatures of all the nuclear-weapon states were achieved with respect to the relevant protocols associated with these two later treaties. And all of the nuclear-weapon states, except the United States, have ratified these protocols.

The nuclear-weapon-free zone treaty process is the back-door route toward the elimination of nuclear weapons. Currently the entire land area of the Southern Hemisphere is subject to legally binding arrangements prohibiting nuclear weapons. In the September 1970 hearing, Charles Van Doren made the point to the committee that the United States understood the Tlatelolco Treaty not to prohibit port calls by U.S. Navy ships which might be carrying nuclear weapons, and not to prohibit transit of nuclear weapons through the area by air or by ship, as opposed to stationing of such weapons. Formal understandings to this effect were included by the executive branch in the draft resolution of ratification sent to the Senate. The Senate approved the resolution with the understandings in it. No Latin American treaty party ever objected. The Treaties of Raratonga and Pelindaba explicitly include these understandings in the text—U.S. experts had informally assisted in the drafting process of these two treaties.

The Treaty of Bangkok of 1996, which is now in force, established the Southeast Asia nuclear-weapon-free zone. Unfortunately, in spite of many discussions with the representatives of the nuclear-weapons states, the Association of Southeast Asian Nations (ASEAN) Working Group refused to make the point covered by the Tlatelolco understandings clear and, even worse, provided that the obligations of the treaty, as well as the negative security assurance provided in the protocol, extend to high seas areas of the Exclusive Economic Zone and continental shelf of the states parties. This means that the nuclear-weapon states effectively would be giving negative security assurances to anyone traversing these high seas areas, in addition to the land territory of the states parties as provided for in the previous three nuclear-weapon-free zone treaties. Thus none of the nuclear-weapon states has signed the protocol, nor do any appear likely to do so. As a result this regime lacks the credibility of the other three.

The nuclear-weapon-free zone process is an important one. Gradually the areas of the world where nuclear weapons are permitted can be reduced, making the task of proceeding to very low levels, and ultimately the prohibition of nuclear weapons, somewhat more achievable. Much progress indeed has been made since the Cold War peaks of around 35,000 nuclear weapons for the United States and perhaps as many as 45,000 for the former Soviet Union. Now the United States numbers are in the 10,000 warhead range, with at least some officials advocating significantly lower levels. But there still is a long way to go to reach very low levels for both the United States and Russia—the appropriate goal for U.S. policy and the direction which is required for the continued viability of the NPT regime.

I could not have realized it at the time, but my very first assignment would bear an important relationship to my work in the 1990s, when serious efforts toward the reduction of nuclear weapons to very low levels first began to be contemplated.

CHAPTER TWO **CHEMICAL AND BIOLOGICAL WEAPONS**

Chemical and biological weapons are two types of weapons of mass destruction that are closely linked historically and to which similar constraints were initially applied. Chemical weapons are essentially gas weapons, that is, chemical compounds that are in a gaseous state when activated, which are contained in shells, bombs, or spray tanks, and are delivered by aircraft, artillery, or ballistic missiles. During World War I, both chlorine and mustard gas weapons were used. Prior to World War II, far more deadly nerve gases were developed but gas weapons were not used between major combatants in that conflict. Toxin weapons are chemical compounds that are the product of processes involving biological organisms. The toxin that causes botulism is an example. Even though toxin weapons are inert like chemical weapons, they are considered to be biological weapons because they are the product of biological processes. Biological weapons are essentially types of bacteria that are intended to be delivered in such a way as to cause disease among enemy troops or in enemy cities. An example of a biological weapon agent is anthrax spores. Biological weapons make poor battlefield weapons but under some conditions could make good terrorist weapons. For example, former Secretary of Defense William Cohen used to say that a ten-pound bag of anthrax spores could devastate a large city.

Efforts to ban chemical and biological weapons began in 1899 when, at the invitation of Czar Nicholas II, an international peace conference was convened at The Hague with the avowed purpose of limiting the ever more destructive nature of warfare. This first Hague Conference resulted in a signed declaration that outlawed the use of asphyxiating gases in war. The second Hague Conference in 1907 prohibited the use of poison or poisoned weapons. Thus poison gas was declared to be an illegal weapon prior to World War I. Nevertheless, poison gas was put to widespread use in that war beginning at Ypres, Belgium, in 1915. Before the war was over, these weapons had caused more than

100,000 deaths and in excess of one million casualties. The public regarded poison gas as a particularly noxious weapon, which led to further efforts to ban it in the 1920s.

At the end of World War I, the victorious Allies reaffirmed in the Versailles Treaty the prewar ban on the use of poison gas in war and prohibited Germany from future manufacturing of such weapons. At the Washington Naval Disarmament Conference in 1922, the United States proposed that similar language prohibiting the use of poison gas in warfare be included in a treaty limiting submarines. The U.S. proposal was adopted, and the U.S. Senate subsequently approved the treaty without a dissenting vote— perhaps because a member of the U.S. Senate was included in the U.S. delegation. The treaty never came into force, however, because the requisite French ratification was never obtained as a result of French resistance to some of the submarine provisions. In 1925, at a conference in Geneva on the supervision of the international arms trade, the United States proposed a ban on the export of gas for use in war. At the suggestion of France, it was decided to negotiate a protocol prohibiting the use in war of poison gas, and, at the suggestion of Poland, this was broadened to ban biological methods of warfare as well.

The result of this negotiation was the Geneva Protocol—formally called the Protocol for the Prohibition of the Use in War of Asphyxiating, Poisonous, or Other Gases, and of Bacteriological Methods of Warfare—signed June 17, 1925. It banned the use in war of both chemical and biological weapons. As a rule on the conduct of warfare, rather than an arms control agreement, it does not contain verification provisions. Because of reservations adopted by many parties upon ratification, the Geneva Protocol is, in effect, an agreement prohibiting the first use of chemical and biological weapons in war among parties. The reservation adopted by France upon ratification in May of 1926 is instructive in this regard. France declared that it is bound to the structures of the Geneva Protocol only as regards relations with other states parties, and it is released from its obligations under the protocol with respect to any enemy state or states whose armed forces or allies do not observe its provisions. The Netherlands, in 1930, and the United States, when it finally did ratify in 1975, limited this first-use feature to chemical weapons. In other words, the Netherlands and the United States are bound by the protocol never to use biological weapons against a party in any situation and not to use chemical weapons as long as such weapons are not employed against them. Other countries, such as Germany (1929), Switzerland (1932), and Mexico (1932), entered no reservations at all.

Ratification of the Geneva Protocol by the United States was a special matter, however. Unlike the Washington Naval Agreement, the protocol encountered serious difficulties in the Senate, perhaps in part because there had been no representation from the Senate on the U.S. delegation in 1925. The Senate Foreign Relations Committee reported the protocol favorably, but because of strong lobbying against it by the Army Chemical Corps, the protocol was not brought to a vote on the floor of the Senate. Thus, although a significant number of countries, including most of the great powers, ratified the protocol in the late 1920s and the early 1930s, by the time of World War II the United States had not. Nevertheless, President Roosevelt announced on June 8, 1943, that use of the weapons covered by the Geneva Protocol had been "outlawed by the general opinion of civilized mankind" and that the United States would never be the first to use them. This statement by President Roosevelt could be interpreted to mean that the United States believed that the first-use constraint established by the Protocol had, by 1943, become part of customary international law in view of the widespread recognition of this rule over almost twenty years. However, the United States still did not ratify the protocol and, in 1949, the Senate returned to President Truman a number of older treaties that had not been ratified, including the Geneva Protocol.

In 1966, the United States was criticized in the United Nations for its use of riot control agents (tear gas) and chemical herbicides in the war in Vietnam. Riot control agents (RCAs) were used in part to drive enemy forces out of protected hiding places so that they could be attacked, and herbicides were used to defoliate forest areas so as to deny the enemy concealment. Hungary charged that the use in war of tear gas and chemical herbicides was prohibited by the Geneva Protocol—the obligations of which President Roosevelt had said the United States would respect—and introduced a United Nations resolution to this effect. The United States argued that the protocol did not apply to nontoxic gases and herbicides. In its final form, the Hungarian resolution simply called for strict observance by all states of "the principles and objectives" of the protocol and for universal adherence to it.

The debate over the interpretation of the protocol continued in 1969. In that year, in a foreword to a UN report on chemical and biological weapons, the secretary-general of the United Nations appealed for a "clear affirmation" that the protocol prohibits the use in war of all chemical and biological agents. Discussion in the Conference of the Committee on Disarmament in Geneva indicated that most countries represented there supported the view of the secretary-general on the interpretation of the protocol, although the United Kingdom argued that only the states parties to the protocol had the right to interpret it. (The Conference of the Committee on Disarmament began as the Ten Nation Disarmament Committee and was originally intended as a device to bring East and West together. Later, in the 1960s, it became the Eighteen Nation Disarmament Committee (ENDC) and included a few non-aligned states such as India and Egypt. In 1969 it expanded further and became the Conference of the Committee on Disarmament (CCD) and finally with further expansion became simply the Conference on Disarmament (CD) which currently has sixty-six members. For years it has been an operating multilateral negotiations body and nearly all of the multilateral disarmament treaties of the last thirty–five years have been negotiated there.)

This led to the introduction in the United Nations General Assembly of a resolution proposed by twenty-one countries that the use in war of all chemical and biological agents was contrary to international law. The United States argued its interpretation and also that it was inappropriate for the General Assembly to use resolutions to interpret treaties. Nevertheless, the resolution was adopted by a vote of 80–3 (the United States voted no) with 36 abstentions (including France and the United Kingdom).

While this debate was underway, President Nixon, responding to a proposal by Mel Laird, announced on November 15, 1969, that he would resubmit the Geneva Protocol to the Senate and request advice and consent to ratification. He reaffirmed the U.S. policy of renunciation of the first use in war of lethal chemicals (adding to this renunciation incapacitating chemicals but not riot control agents). He also announced a unilateral renunciation of biological weapons. In his statement, President Nixon described biological weapons as too unpredictable to be useful weapons. Some support for the U.S. interpretation on chemical weapons appeared. Although in 1930, during a discussion in Geneva, the United Kingdom had asserted that the Geneva Protocol covered tear gas, in 1970 the British foreign secretary stated in Parliament that this remained the British position, but that the riot control agent CS (which was what the United States had been using in Vietnam) was not harmful to man, unlike older tear gases, and therefore was not covered by the protocol. Also in 1970, during the debate in the Diet on ratification of the protocol, the foreign minister of Japan asserted that the protocol did not cover tear gas and herbicides. Japan was the first militarily significant state to ratify the protocol after the debate over its interpretation, and it did so with the U.S. understanding as to its coverage.

In the transmittal documents accompanying the protocol back to the U.S. Senate, the Secretary of State, under date of August 11, 1970, set forth a reservation which provided that the United States retained the right to retaliate in the case of a chemical weapon attack, and asserted an interpretive understanding that riot control agents and chemical herbicides are not covered by the protocol. The Senate Foreign Relations Committee, however, refused to accept the interpretation of the protocol as set forth in Secretary Rogers's letter. At the hearing in 1971, to my consternation, Professor Matthew Meselson of Harvard University—to this day one of the world's leading experts on chemical and biological weapons—strongly testified, with slide pictures showing the effect of Agent Orange, against approval of the protocol with the administration's interpretation. I encountered Matt coming into the State Department not long afterward and asked him why he had done this. Couldn't he change his position and urge ratification since it had taken twenty years to get the protocol back to the Senate? No, he thought stopping what the United States was doing in Vietnam with RCAs and Agent Orange was more important than U.S. ratification of the protocol, which already was part of customary international law.

This was the first example of a syndrome that I encountered often in the activist arms control community. Whatever has been done is not enough and therefore should not be accepted. (Objecting to the Stockpile Stewardship Program integrally associated with the U.S. signature of the CTBT is the most recent example of this.) Matt Meselson's argument was well taken, but U.S. ratification of the Geneva Protocol, for which the world community had been waiting since 1926, was far more important. Chairman J. William Fulbright stated after the hearing that, in his view and in that of many members of the Foreign Relations Committee, it would be in the interest of the United States to either ratify the protocol without "restrictive understandings" or to defer action until this became possible. The committee, as a result, took no action on the protocol and also held in abeyance approval of the Biological Weapons Convention, which was also before it.

The legal merits of this debate are unclear. There is no question that it was the use of poison gas in World War I that caused the Geneva Protocol to be negotiated, and that it was the prohibition on the use of poison gas in the Hague Conventions that the negotiators had in mind. Chemical herbicides were unknown in 1925, so the negotiators could not have had them in mind. Riot control agents and chemical herbicides were not used in Vietnam as weapons themselves but as adjuncts to other weapons; used alone they are generally not lethal. There is a distinction between the two in that the use of tear gas in conjunction with other weapons could lead to immediate casualties, somewhat akin to the direct effect of poison gas, but the use of herbicides normally would only cause casualties over time after concealment had been reduced. On the other hand, the Geneva Protocol, by its title, prohibits "asphyxiating, poisonous, or other gases," and the United Kingdom, in 1930, took the position that tear gas was covered (while later exempting CS). On balance, it would appear that the protocol is ambiguous on riot control agents but that it is difficult to sustain the argument that chemical herbicides are covered. In 1971, the Senate Foreign Relations Committee was responding to the politics of the day and the unpopularity of the Vietnam War. The Nixon administration was concerned that if it conceded the point to the committee, the United States could be accused of violations of international law in Vietnam, given that the first-use constraint of the Geneva Protocol was widely believed to have become part of international law binding on all states.

Later, the international community negotiated international conventions that not only prohibited all use of chemical and biological weapons, but also possession and production of those weapons. The Convention on the Prohibition of the Development, Production, and Stockpiling of Bacteriological (Biological) and Toxin Weapons and on Their Destruction, signed on April 10, 1972, and known as the Biological Weapons Convention (BWC), prohibits

Chemical and Biological Weapons

biological weapons entirely. A multilateral prohibition on chemical weapons, the Chemical Weapons Convention (CWC), was negotiated in the CD in Geneva beginning in 1983, with the intense concluding phase in 1992. The CWC was signed in Paris by 138 nations on January 13, 1993. The BWC entered into force on March 26, 1975, and the CWC entered into force on April 29, 1997.

In 1974, the Ford administration began a new effort to obtain ratification of the Geneva Protocol (and of the BWC). John Newhouse, who was then the counselor at ACDA, and I were asked by ACDA Director Fred Ikle early in 1974 to see if we couldn't work something out between the Department of Defense and the Senate Foreign Relations Committee to accomplish what President Ford wanted. John, a friend and colleague, was a distinguished journalist associated with the *New Yorker* magazine and the author of many books, including *Cold Dawn, the Story of SALT I*. Our interlocutor at the committee was Dick Moose, later assistant secretary of state for Africa in the Carter administration and undersecretary of state for management in the Clinton administration. The principal contact point at Defense was Assistant Secretary of Defense Robert Ellsworth, a longtime prominent Republican expert in defense matters. Essentially, the committee wanted our military to stop using RCAs in Vietnam to flush enemy soldiers from bunkers and caves and then killing them, and to stop defoliating Vietnam's forests with Agent Orange. The other effects of Agent Orange that damage human health were not understood at that time. Defense was willing to terminate these practices, but it wanted to be protected from war crime charges resulting from an alleged violation of international law.

In summary form, the compromise was that the committee would not rebut the interpretation of the coverage of the protocol set forth by the administration, and the administration by executive order would "renounce as a matter of national policy" the first use in war of RCAs and chemical herbicides. The first use of chemical herbicides in war would be renounced except to control vegetation on U.S. bases and around their immediate defensive perimeters. The first use in war of RCAs would be barred except in defensive military action to save civilian lives, such as when controlling rioting prisoners of war; when civilians are being used by the enemy as a screen; in rescue missions, for example, when a pilot is downed behind enemy lines; and in rear echelon areas to protect convoys from civil disturbances, terrorists, and paramilitary organizations.

In a carefully scripted question-and-answer session before the committee on December 10, 1974, ACDA Director Fred Ikle was asked what legal impediment there would be to the broadening of permissible use of RCAs and chemical herbicides by subsequent presidents. The director responded that there would be none, but that this policy is "inextricably" linked to Senate consent to ratification of the protocol. Therefore, such a change would be "inconsistent with the history of the ratification, could have extremely grave political repercussions, and, as a result, is extremely unlikely to happen."

The above-related concerns of the committee and the Department of Defense seemed to point to the compromise that John and I eventually worked out. It essentially allowed Defense to win on the law and the committee to win on the policy for the future. So we proposed the package basically as it was finally agreed. We had a number of meetings alternating between Dick Moose and a Defense Department committee chaired by Bob Ellsworth. We argued to Dick Moose, and through him to the committee, that the administration had the votes and was going to push the protocol with their understanding through the committee and the Senate. We argued to Defense that it looked hopeless, that we could not overcome the committee's interpretation, and that the committee would report out the protocol their way and see to it that it passed. Therefore, we argued to both sides that they should protect themselves by accepting the compromise and, eventually, they did.

On December 12, 1974, two days after Ikle's testimony, by unanimous vote, the committee reported favorably on the Geneva Protocol and the BWC. In its report, the committee indicated that it attached particular importance to this exchange between the committee and the ACDA director. The full Senate voted its approval, also unanimously, on December 16, 1974. President Ford ratified the Geneva Protocol and the BWC on January 22, 1975, and the United States' instrument of ratification of the Geneva Protocol was deposited with France on April 10, 1975, just two months shy of the fifty-year anniversary of its signature.

Thus, ratification by the United States in 1975 of the Geneva Protocol raised but did not settle some of the interpretive questions related to the now worldwide prohibition on the first use in war of chemical and biological weapons. As foreshadowed by the statement of President Roosevelt in 1943, because of widespread and longstanding adherence to the principles of the Geneva Protocol, its constraints, at least the constraints on first use, have become part of customary international law binding on all states without regard to whether they are states parties to the protocol. This is not to say that there have not been violations. Italy became a party in 1928 but it used poison gas against Ethiopia (a party) in 1936. Egypt also became a party in 1928 but it used poison gas against Yemen (a party) in 1967. Iraq has been a party since 1931 but this did not stop it from using poison gas in its war with Iran (a party) in the 1980s. Iran, of course, responded in kind. Iraq also used poison gas in internal struggles against the Kurdish people, but there is no evidence that the negotiators intended that the protocol apply to civil war, only international armed conflicts. On the other hand, it should be noted that the protocol did work effectively during World War II, even though all the warring great powers possessed chemical weapons, including deadly nerve agents that can kill in seconds.

In the long effort to ban the use of chemical and biological weapons, progress in prohibiting the manufacture and possession of such weapons came more slowly. During the 1932–37 Disarmament Conference, unsuccessful attempts were made to negotiate an agreement prohibiting the production and stockpiling of chemical and biological weapons. In the negotiations after World War II, chemical and biological weapons continued to be closely associated in various proposals. One hindrance to progress over the years was whether, in considering a ban on production and possession, chemical weapons and biological weapons should continue to be linked as they were in the protocol. A British draft convention banning biological weapons only was submitted to the ENDC in July of 1969, while a similar convention proposed by the Soviet Union and other Eastern European countries two months later covered both chemical and biological weapons. The Soviet representative argued that negotiation of a biological weapon convention separately could serve to intensify the chemical weapon arms race.

The United States supported the British proposal and argued that the two types of weapons are inherently different. Biological weapons have never been used in war, but chemical weapons have been. Without reliable assurance that other states are observing the ban, many countries, including the United States, would be reluctant to eliminate chemical weapons from their arsenals since such weapons are used to deter the use of chemical weapons against them, and to provide a retaliatory capability if deterrence fails. Meanwhile, the U.S. government had been conducting a comprehensive review of U.S. policy toward chemical and biological warfare. On November 25, 1969, President Nixon made the above-discussed announcement concerning chemical weapons and the Geneva Protocol and coupled it with a unilateral renunciation of biological weapons. The president asserted that biological weapons were inherently unreliable and declared that the United States would unconditionally eliminate from its arsenal all types of biological agents for use in war. In the future, the U.S. program would be confined to research on strictly defined measures of defense, such as immunization. The Department of Defense was directed to draw up a plan for the destruction of existing stocks of biological weapons and on February 14, 1970, toxin weapons were added to this unilateral renunciation.

The U.S. example was welcomed internationally and followed by several other states. Canada, Sweden, and the United Kingdom announced that they did not have any biological weapons and did not plan to produce any. However, conversion of these unilateral policy renunciations into a legally binding international agreement continued to be blocked by the insistence of the Soviet Union and other countries that chemical and biological weapons could not be considered separately. The Eighteen Nation Disarmament Committee in August of 1969 became the Conference of the Committee on Disarmament with twenty-six members. Discussion in the committee in 1970 produced no agreement until the Soviet Union and the states associated with it suddenly changed their position in order to break the impasse and on March 31, 1971, introduced a draft convention prohibiting only biological and toxin weapons. This shift permitted the co-chairmen of the committee, the representatives of the United States and the Soviet Union, to develop a draft convention and table separate but identical texts on August 5, 1971.

The BWC was opened for signature at Washington, London, and Moscow on April 10, 1972. This triple depository arrangement was a Cold War practice for multilateral treaties necessitated by the fact that the United States did not recognize states such as the German Democratic Republic, but it was important that they be bound. In the case of the NPT, the three depository states still are regarded as having a degree of administrative responsibility for the treaty regime. This practice was abandoned after the end of the Cold War; the CWC, for example, has the UN secretary general as depositary. In submitting the BWC to the Senate, President Nixon described it as "the first international agreement since World War II to provide for the actual elimination of an entire class of weapons from the arsenal of nations." (This honor for the nuclear weapons field was later claimed for the Intermediate-Range Nuclear Forces Treaty in 1987.) The Senate Foreign Relations Committee delayed action on the BWC, however, holding it for consideration until resolution of the debate over the interpretation of the Geneva Protocol. When this dispute was resolved in late 1974, it opened the way for ratification of both the BWC and the Geneva Protocol. The U.S. instrument of ratification of the convention was deposited on March 26, 1975.

Article I of the convention provides that the parties "never in any circumstances" will develop, produce, stockpile, or otherwise acquire or retain "biological agents or toxins" "of types and in quantities" that cannot be justified for "prophylactic, protective, or other peaceful purposes," as well as toxins "for hostile purposes or in armed conflict." Thus, the intent of the convention is to bind the states parties not to acquire biological weapons "in any circumstances," even if attacked by a hostile state with such weapons. There are no reservations to the convention permitted, meaning that the second-use reservation of the Geneva Protocol for biological weapons is void for parties to both agreements. Whether or not an agent qualifies as a biological weapon, and therefore whether its possession is prohibited, is judged on the basis of whether it exists in types and amounts that have no apparent justification for peaceful purposes. The effect of this article is to eliminate such agents and weapon systems from the arsenals of the states parties except when the agents can be shown to have a justifiable laboratory research purpose.

Article IV obligates the states parties to adopt implementing legislation to the extent this is required by their constitutional processes. In the United

States, there was a lively debate for many years as to whether this was necessary in view of existing regulatory legislation, but after fifteen years it was finally resolved that there would be merit in criminalizing possession, and thus legislation was sought. For years, for obscure reasons the Department of Defense opposed implementing legislation for the BWC, which would make it a crime for private persons to possess biological agents. (There was a rumor that circulated in the 1970s to the effect that an employee of the CIA—because he opposed President Nixon's decision to destroy stocks in 1969—took some biological agents home and hid them in his basement for a year until it was somehow discovered. I am unaware of any factual basis for this rumor.) ACDA urged such legislation almost every year, but the Office of Management and Budget would not approve it because of the opposition of Defense.

It was only when the Department of Justice concluded that such legislation would be a useful anti-terrorist measure that the legislation was finally sent to Capitol Hill with administration backing. Thus, legislation was passed in 1990 making it a criminal act for a private person to possess biological weapons in contravention of the convention. Much of the credit for successful congressional action should go to Senator Herbert Kohl of Wisconsin, who took a personal interest in the passage of this legislation. But even with the senator's personal interest and a supportive executive branch transmittal, the various agencies displayed little interest. In both the House Committee hearing and the Senate Committee hearing, I, as ACDA general counsel, was the only government witness.

Articles V, VI, and VII of the BWC provide the verification mechanism. The states parties are required to consult with one another in solving any problems that may arise as to the application of the convention. A party has the right to lodge a complaint of violation with the UN Security Council and all states parties are required to cooperate with any investigation that the Security Council may order. If the Security Council decides that a party has been exposed to danger as a result of a violation of the convention, upon request, all states parties are required to provide assistance to the party so endangered. But, in essence, the BWC has no verification provisions at all. The U.S. executive branch (both ACDA Director Ikle and chairman of the Joint Chiefs General George Brown) in the ratification hearings for the convention before the Senate Foreign Relations Committee in 1974 testified that the convention was not verifiable but remained in the interest of the United States in view of the U.S. unilateral renunciation. Ikle also stated his belief that biological weapons had no military utility.

Nevertheless, at the first Review Conference of the Convention in the 1980s, the United States at ACDA's insistence charged that an explosion in 1979 in the Soviet city of Sverdlovsk (now Ekaterinburg) revealed that an illegal biological weapons plant was in operation at that site. After the end of the Cold War, it was revealed that the Soviet Union had been engaged in massive violations of the BWC. The Soviet Union operated a huge biological weapons program that continued even after it became a party to the BWC. This points to the overriding importance of effective verification provisions for disarmament treaties, and the significance of the ongoing discussions in Geneva to develop a verification protocol for the BWC—an effort not welcomed by the U.S. biotech industry. The United States backed away from this negotiation in 2001, an unfortunate development.

It has been said that, as a country, the former Soviet Union spent more money on biological weapons than on pharmaceuticals. The Sverdlovsk issue was discussed again at the second Review Conference held in 1986. At that conference, the United States alleged Soviet involvement in the production, transfer, and use of mycotoxins (the so-called poisonous "yellow rain" in Southeast Asia), and that the Soviet Union maintained an offensive biological warfare program in violation of Article I. This assertion about Southeast Asia was never proven. Matt Meselson publicly claimed that the yellow rain was bee dung. This assertion was not proven either, and with all due respect to Matt and his genius, it seemed a bit on the bizarre side to me. This issue was left as one of the unanswered questions of the Cold War.

The companion agreement to the BWC, the Chemical Weapons Convention, was finally signed in early 1993. The CWC had long been of special interest to President George Bush, who was in office during the final push for completion of the CWC in 1992. (For many years only ACDA, led by Director Ron Lehman, had much interest in this negotiation, but by 1992 the full interagency was involved.) As vice president, Bush had introduced the U.S. draft in Geneva in 1984. This draft contained the famous "anytime, anywhere" inspection provision developed by some in the Pentagon to ensure that the Soviet Union would never accept it. However, after the 1986 meeting between Presidents Reagan and Gorbachev at Reykjavik, the Soviet Union began to show real interest in on-site inspection. Thus the United States rapidly began backing away from "anytime, anywhere." We did not want Libyan inspectors showing up at the CIA, for example. What was finally negotiated was a complex system of "managed access," which would at the same time provide for intrusive inspections while protecting sensitive facilities. In essence, the idea was to negotiate an inspection regime on an ad hoc basis where a sensitive facility was claimed.

Australia played a key role in this endgame by developing a text that many states important to the negotiation could accept. But much credit should go to the German chairman of the negotiating committee at the CD in Geneva, Ambassador Adolf Von Wagner. Based on the Australian draft text developed earlier, he produced a chairman's draft in June 1992 and pronounced the negotiations over. Five CD delegations refused to sign off on the text when it was forwarded to the United Nations in August, but did not attempt to block its transmittal as India did with the CTBT in 1996. In any case, the CWC was broadly endorsed by the UN that fall and ultimately signed by 138 nations in Paris in January 1993.

During the summer of 1992, the RCA issue moved front and center once again. The CWC draft text clearly included RCAs as chemical agents proscribed by the Chemical Weapons Convention. The Office of the Legal Advisor in the Department of State pronounced within the government that two of the four excepted uses in the 1975 executive order involved the use of RCA agents in warfare (rescuing downed pilots and separating civilians being used as a screen from combatants), and that they would not be allowed under the convention. This created a raging interagency debate as to whether the United States should raise this in Geneva. The Joint Chiefs wanted to raise it, but I argued for ACDA that it was certain to be rejected—perhaps better not to raise it and thereby not make it clearly illegal in case we had to do it someday. In the end it was raised in a half-hearted way and other delegations made it clear that these uses, in their view, would be contrary to the CWC. This issue dogged CWC ratification in the U.S. Senate almost to the end—the U.S. military cared about these exemptions—but nothing was done in the end to protect the exemptions. Presumably, the legal advisor's view in 1992 still guides U.S. policy.

Article I of the CWC to a degree mirrors Article I of the BWC. It provides that each party "never under any circumstances" undertakes to develop, acquire, or retain chemical weapons as defined by the convention. Article I extends this prohibition to the use of chemical weapons and to the engagement of military preparations for the use of such weapons. Like the BWC, the intent of the CWC is to bind states parties not to acquire and use chemical weapons even if attacked by a hostile state with such weapons. (Article XXII prohibits reservations to the convention—thus there can be no second use reservations.) Article I also requires each party to destroy all chemical weapons that it possesses or that it abandoned on the territory of another state (after January 1, 1925), and not to use riot control agents as a method of warfare—this last, as discussed, impacts on the four exceptions in the Ford executive order associated with U.S. ratification of the Geneva Protocol. Chemical weapons, defined in Article II as toxic chemicals or their precursors, are listed in an attached schedule along with associated munitions and equipment. Such toxic chemicals and their precursors are not considered chemical weapons, pursuant to Article II, if used for purposes not prohibited by the convention. These purposes are defined as industrial, agricultural, medical, etc., protective purposes against toxic chemicals, military purposes not connected with chemical weapons, and law enforcement, including domestic riot control, as long as types and quantities possessed are consistent with these purposes.

Article III provides for declarations by states parties as to their inventory of chemical weapons and production facilities, and Articles IV and V provide for the destruction of such weapons and facilities. The declarations and destruction are to be verified pursuant to the comprehensive Verification Annex, which contains detailed procedures for on-site inspection, including challenge inspections with managed access as required. Article VII requires the necessary national implementing measures, including implementing legislation to be adopted by each party. Pursuant to Article VIII, the states parties establish the highly important implementing body for the convention, named the Organization for the Prohibition of Chemical Weapons. Its Executive Council regulates the conduct of inspections, as it is the body that deals with compliance issues.

The CWC was submitted to the Senate in 1994, delayed by further interagency haggling over RCAS among other things, and approved by the U.S. Senate in the spring of 1997; there were twenty-six votes against, an unconscionable number given that banning chemical weapons is a cause close to motherhood and that the convention was supported by Presidents Reagan, Bush, and Clinton. The CWC, after pressure from the White House, had been scheduled for a Senate floor vote on September 26, 1996. Senator Richard Lugar was the floor manager and had done yeoman's service in achieving a favorable vote in the Senate Foreign Relations Committee, as he had done so many times with arms control treaties in the past, e.g., INF, START I, START II, and CFE. Majority Leader Trent Lott had agreed to a date for a vote in September. The American Chemicals Manufacturers Association supported the treaty, as they had throughout the negotiations as a result of careful ACDA cultivation. It was essentially the "permanent opposition to all arms control" faction that comprised the major part of those in the Senate against the CWC.

All was ready for a successful vote on the Senate floor. However, someone in this opposition group persuaded someone on presidential candidate Robert Dole's staff to put an anti-CWC letter in front of him, in spite of the fact that he had been favorable toward the CWC while still majority leader. This letter attacking the verifiability of the CWC and suggesting that the vote be put off came to light the morning of the vote. On September 26, 1997, ACDA Chief of Congressional Liaison Ivo Spalatin called me at home at the behest of ACDA Director John Holum and asked if I would fly to San Francisco that afternoon to deliver John's scheduled speech for him at the Commonwealth Club so that John could stay in Washington to try to save the CWC. Later that morning, before leaving for San Francisco, I saw John and he told me about the Dole letter. I urged him to press the case for holding the vote anyway.

Ever since my experience with SALT II, described later, I had been convinced that the Senate will never vote down a major treaty that the president wants. I was finally proved wrong in October 1999, with the Senate vote on the Comprehensive Test Ban Treaty. However, I believe we could have won—or at least not lost—the CTBT vote with more effective executive branch management. Prior to the CTBT vote, the Senate never had voted down a major treaty (at least in the twentieth century) that the president wanted—the Versailles treaty is not a true example of such a vote because President Wilson instructed his Democrats to vote against the treaty because

Chemical and Biological Weapons

of the Lodge Amendments. The trick is, of course, to get the Senate to commit to a vote. John told me that Secretary of State Warren Christopher had already called Senator Lugar and asked for a postponement, even though almost enough countries had ratified the CWC to bring it into force. I remain convinced that with the momentum created, a better vote could have been achieved in September 1996 than in April 1997. And, most importantly, it would not have been necessary to trade ACDA to get the CWC. This would have been so, I believe, even in the middle of the presidential campaign of 1996. In my judgment, when a vote commitment for a treaty is made by the Senate, no matter what the politics of the moment, it should be taken. In spite of the crisis over disarmament in the Senate, the audience at the Commonwealth Club that evening was not large, and none of the San Francisco newspapers mentioned the issue the next morning. This is an example of the problem that disarmament faces in the United States: strong government involvement but little interest from the public.

The United States did ratify the CWC on April 24, 1997, the same day as the Senate vote, and it entered into force on April 29, 1997. So the United States did slip under the wire to be an Original Party, which was essential if it was to participate in the development of the verification system. As of December 31, 2001, the CWC had 165 signatories and 145 ratifications.

CHAPTER THREE **SALT I**

Attempts to limit armaments and reduce the destructiveness of war go back at least to the Middle Ages. The medieval papacy outlawed the crossbow at the Second Lateran Council in 1139. The crossbow was soon surpassed in capability by the English longbow, which in turn was rendered obsolete by the destructive firepower of the cannon. Through the centuries there were further attempts at arms limitations, which also were largely ineffective either because of the advent of superior technology or because of lack of observance of the agreement. In 1819, for example, the United States and Canada reached an agreement to limit naval armament on the Great Lakes, referred to as the Rush-Bagot Agreement, but this agreement was honored far more in the breach than the observance. Similarly, the Hague Conventions of 1899 and 1907 effectively outlawed dum-dum (or expanding) bullets, but the agreement to ban gas warfare was completely ignored in World War I and this occurrence led directly to the Geneva Protocol as described in chapter 2. The Geneva Protocol of 1925 could be described as the first successful arms limitation agreement, although its success was not universal. And there were other attempts at arms limitation in the interwar period, such as the Washington Naval Treaty of 1922, which were complete failures.

Everything changed, however, on July 16, 1945 with the advent of the atomic bomb. J. Robert Oppenheimer, leader of the effort to build the atomic bomb at Los Alamos, wrote after witnessing the first nuclear weapon test at Alamogordo, New Mexico, (quoting from the Bhagavad Gita): "Now I am become Death, destroyer of worlds." James Conant, one of the principal Manhattan Project architects, noted in his diary that "the enormity of the light quite stunned me. My instantaneous reaction was that something had gone wrong and that the thermal nuclear transformation of the atmosphere, once discussed as a possibility and jokingly referred to a few minutes earlier, had actually occurred." And Brigadier General Thomas Farrell, also present at Alamogordo, described a "strong, sustained, awesome roar which warned of doomsday and made us feel that we puny things were blasphemous to dare tamper with the forces heretofore reserved for the Almighty." For the first time, humanity was in possession of the means of its own destruction. What over the centuries had been considered desirable—arms limitation—now, in the opinion of many, became essential to ensuring the survival of civilization. Even so, disarmament progress has been very slow.

The United States built nuclear weapons during World War II at the urging of Albert Einstein and other prominent nuclear physicists—many of whom had fled Europe—out of fear that Nazi Germany would develop these weapons and thereby ensure the worldwide triumph of fascism. It took a huge effort by the United States during the war to create nuclear weapons (in a program code-named the Manhattan Project)—during the peak years of effort, it consumed 2 percent of the electrical output of the entire country. The attacks by the United States on Hiroshima and Nagasaki with atomic weapons at the end of World War II were the culmination of this effort. The test at Alamogordo and the bombs dropped on Japan exhausted the U.S. arsenal, and no more weapons were fabricated for several years. In this sense, the drive to control nuclear weapons began almost with their creation. The first such serious proposal, called the Baruch Plan, came in 1946 and advocated the creation of an international authority to control nuclear weapons. This effort proved to be ill-fated with the onset of the Cold War, however, and later with the first test of a Soviet nuclear device in September of 1949, the nuclear weapons race began in earnest.

Once the Cold War began, it was inevitable that the Soviet Union would acquire nuclear weapons—especially given the extensive Soviet spy work at Los Alamos during the war years when the Soviet Union was ostensibly the ally of the United States. Soviet acquisition of the bomb in 1949 made British acquisition certain. The United Kingdom had been a virtual partner of the United States during the Manhattan Project. France, not to be outdone, and with the United States looking the other way, detonated its first nuclear device in 1960. China followed suit in 1964 with some initial help from the Soviet Union. This alarming proliferation of declared nuclear-weapon states was halted by the signing in 1968 and the entry into force in 1970 of the NPT—at least until the nuclear-weapon test explosions by India and Pakistan in 1998. By the 1960s, however, a vast bilateral nuclear arms race between the United States and the Soviet Union—one of the prime features of the Cold War—was underway. The former Russian Minister of Atomic Energy, Victor Mikhailov, said in 1996 that over the course of the Cold War the Soviet Union built 45,000 nuclear weapons and made enough fissile material for 90,000 more. The peak U.S. inventory was around 35,000 nuclear weapons. The United States spent more than $5.5 trillion on the nuclear arms race, an amount equal to its national debt in 1998, and the Soviet Union bankrupted itself. The narrow avoidance of worldwide thermonuclear destruction in 1962 during the Cuban Missile Crisis seemed only to spur the arms race on. It was this phenomenon of an all-out, uncontrolled, dangerous nuclear arms race that the Strategic Arms Limitation Talks (SALT) process was finally convened to address.

In 1969, negotiations began on possible limitations on the central strategic nuclear delivery systems of the United States and the Soviet Union. The efforts were bilateral and conducted in secrecy. The treaty between the United States of America and the Union of Soviet Socialist Republics on the Limitation of Anti-Ballistic Missile Systems (the ABM Treaty) is the most important of the two principal documents negotiated during SALT I, which lasted from 1969 to 1972. The other document is the Interim Agreement Between the United States of America and the Union of Soviet Socialist Republics on Certain Measures with Respect to the Limitation of Strategic Offensive Arms (Interim Agreement). The Interim Agreement is sometimes referred to as SALT I to go along with SALT II, START I, and START II as part of the series of agreements on strategic offensive arms. The SALT I negotiations were the first attempt through bilateral negotiations to limit the delivery vehicles of nuclear weapons. The objective of the SALT I negotiations was to place initial limits on the strategic nuclear offensive and defensive systems of the two superpowers.

There are three basic types of strategic offensive nuclear weapon delivery systems. First, intercontinental ballistic missile systems (ICBMs) are land-based ballistic missiles with a sufficient range to enable them to strike targets at intercontinental distances. (As defined in an Agreed Statement associated with the Interim Agreement, ICBMs are missiles with a range in excess of the shortest distance between the northeastern border of the continental United States and the northwestern border of the continental Soviet Union, or as later defined in the Treaty Between the United States of America and the Union of Soviet Socialist Republics on the Limitation of Strategic Offensive Arms [SALT II Treaty], more than 5,500 kilometers.) Second, submarine-launched ballistic missiles (SLBMs), although of shorter range and launched from under the sea, are considered capable of striking intercontinental targets. Third, certain heavy bombers were recognized by the two sides as capable of operating at intercontinental distances. Starting in the mid-1970s, long-range cruise missiles, highly accurate air-breathing systems that can be launched from sea, ground, or air, were a fourth type added to this list of strategic nuclear delivery vehicles.

On the defensive side, the key systems are anti-ballistic missiles (ABMs) that are designed to intercept strategic ballistic missiles (ICBMs and SLBMs) in flight trajectory. (Air defense systems, including surface-to-air missiles, have tactical and conventional, as well as strategic and nuclear, roles and have not been the subject of direct limitations.)

The SALT I negotiations began in November 1969 and culminated at the Moscow Summit in May 1972. The two agreements were signed on May

26 and entered into force on October 3, 1972. As the negotiations evolved, it became apparent that a relatively complete approach to strategic defense, but only a partial coverage for strategic offense, was possible. There was some discussion of a prohibition on multiple independently targetable re-entry vehicles (MIRVs), which are devices carried on ballistic missiles capable of directing a number of nuclear warheads (on a single missile) to widely dispersed targets. The United States first began to deploy MIRV systems in 1970. Negotiation of such a ban, however, was never seriously attempted. The Soviet Union commenced testing of MIRVs in 1975. With the advent of MIRVs on both sides, a first strike capable of destroying the other side's ICBMS became theoretically conceivable.

Pursuant to the terms of the Interim Agreement, the United States was permitted launchers of 1,054 deployed ICBMS and 656 deployed SLBMS, and the Soviet Union launchers of 1,608 deployed ICBMS and 740 deployed SLBMS. The limitations on ICBMS were achieved indirectly by a ban on construction of additional fixed, land-based ICBM silo launchers in Article I. The Interim Agreement and later the SALT II Treaty utilized missile launchers as the unit of account because the number of launchers could be verified by national technical means.

The term "national technical means of verification" (NTM) includes photographic satellites that the Soviets had claimed, in the 1960s, violated international law but which were implicitly recognized in the ABM Treaty and the Interim Agreement as operating in accordance with "generally recognized principles of international law." Both agreements contained further commitments not to interfere with or deliberately conceal activities from such satellites, again referred to as NTM. Launchers were also considered appropriate limits because neither ICBM silo launchers nor SLBM launch tubes were viewed as reloadable with sufficient speed to affect the outcome of a strategic nuclear exchange. Unlike the treatment of ICBMS, the SLBM limitations were explicitly set forth in the Protocol to the Interim Agreement. The initial limits, of 656 and 740 for the United States and the Soviet Union, respectively, could be increased to 710 and 950, respectively, if certain older ICBM launchers (i.e., Titan II for the United States and SS-7s and SS-8 ICBMS for the Soviet Union) were dismantled in what was described as a one-way freedom to mix.

Article II of the Interim Agreement provided a ban on the conversion of "light" ICBM launchers, or certain older ICBM launchers, to modern "heavy" ICBM launchers, thus fixing the number of deployed modern heavy ICBMS at zero for the United States and 308 for the Soviet Union. The sides were never able to negotiate a legal definition of heavy ICBMS—this, amidst much controversy, was left for SALT II—but the only modern heavy ICBM in existence in 1972 was the Soviet SS-9 missile system. The SS-9 had enormous lifting power and carried a huge 25-megaton warhead. In addition, as indicated, each side had a number of certain older ICBMS, defined as those first deployed prior to 1964: the 54 Titan II missiles (with nine-megaton warheads) for the United States and 210 SS-7 and SS-8 missiles (inaccurate systems with large nuclear warheads) for the Soviet Union. As stated above, pursuant to the terms of Article III of the Interim Agreement and the Protocol, these older missile launchers could be exchanged for SLBM launchers. However, at the Moscow Summit, President Nixon gave General Secretary Leonid Brezhnev a secret side commitment, undisclosed to the Congress, stating that the United States had no plans to exchange its launchers of Titan missiles for SLBM launchers.

Thus, the numbers ultimately were 1,000 ICBM launchers (plus 54 old Titan IIs) and 656 SLBM launchers for the United States, and 1,398 ICBM launchers and 950 SLBM launchers for the Soviet Union. The Interim Agreement had a five-year term. The United States considered acceptable the Soviet Union's approximately 50 percent advantage in strategic missile launchers in view of two factors: the ongoing U.S. MIRV deployment program, and the fact that the Interim Agreement did not limit heavy bombers, where the United States had a significant lead (approximately 450 to 150). Land-mobile ICBM launchers were not limited by the Interim Agreement; the United States made a unilateral statement at the close of the negotiations that it "would consider the development of land-mobile ICBM launchers during the period of the Interim Agreement as inconsistent with the objectives of that Agreement." Neither party deployed land-mobile ICBM launchers during the term of the Interim Agreement.

The reason for the indirect delineation of numbers in the Interim Agreement was Soviet unwillingness to disclose or even discuss its numbers of deployed ICBM and SBLM launchers. While the development and acceptance of the legality of photographic satellites under the rubric of "national technical means" made SALT I possible, this Soviet penchant for secrecy in military matters under negotiation made the agreements more controversial in the United States.

The achievement of equal numbers of treaty-limited strategic systems, a definition of heavy ICBMs, some limits on MIRVs, and the attainment of an agreed statement on data, all became major objectives for the United States in the SALT II negotiations. There was also concern in the United States over the greater size and lifting capability, or throw-weight, of Soviet missiles. Once the Soviet Union began to deploy MIRVs, these missiles would give it the capability to carry many more warheads than U.S. ICBMs. This disparity was due to the fact that the United States preferred to concentrate on light, miniaturized systems from the earliest days of the ICBM programs, whereas the Soviet Union preferred larger, cruder systems. "Throw-weight" was a controversial issue during SALT II, but even in the SALT II negotiations only initial steps were taken—a definition of heavy ICBMs in terms of throw-weight (and launch-weight) and a ban on increasing the throw-weight of heavy ICBMs, thus preventing any further growth in the capability of such missiles. Negotiations to eliminate the throw-weight disparity were left to the Strategic Arms Reduction Talks, or START, negotiations in the 1980s.

The ABM Treaty, unlike the Interim Agreement, is an agreement of indefinite duration. It originally limited strategic defense systems and components in ABM deployment areas to two sites for each party, later modified by a 1974 protocol to one site for each party. For purposes of the treaty, the three current ABM components are listed as ABM launchers, ABM missiles, and ABM radars. Article III limits the number of ABM interceptor missile launchers to 100 per site, or 200 for each party, and contains strict limits on the ABM radars deployed at each site. In 1985, an interpretation dispute arose within the U.S. government over the meaning of Article V, Paragraph I, of the ABM Treaty, which provides that "Each Party undertakes not to develop, test, or deploy ABM systems or components which are sea-based, air-based, space-based, or mobile land-based." This will be discussed in a later chapter.

Early on in my employment at ACDA I became involved with SALT. Within a few weeks of my arrival in September 1970, then General Counsel Bill Hancock took me over to see Larry Weiler, the special assistant to Ambassador Gerard Smith, the director and the chief SALT I negotiator. Larry gave us a briefing on the SALT I negotiations, including the air defense or surface-to-air missile-upgrade issue, which I found fascinating—I remain interested in the strategic arms limitation process to the present day. After all these years the issue I remember best from SALT I is that of SAM upgrade. Larry said that it lurked behind every other issue. The Soviet Union in 1970 had some 10,000 SAMs deployed around the country, which the United States feared could be quickly upgraded to an ABM capability. This issue was resolved ultimately by the radar limitations in the ABM Treaty and the prohibition on upgrades set forth in Article VI. As a result, SAM systems are not regulated by the ABM Treaty. This issue seems a bit ironic thirty years later with the quite capable systems under development that are asserted to be theater ABM systems, and therefore below the level of strategic ABM systems.

A word about Ambassador Smith, the ACDA director who hired me. He was a man of immense talent and integrity, and ideally suited for his position. The United States SALT I delegation that he headed was one of the finest ever fielded by the United States for any purpose. Paul Nitze—among many other assignments, a former Navy secretary and deputy secretary of defense and one of the great men of post–World War II U.S. foreign policy—represented OSD. Lieutenant General Royall Allison, a distinguished Air Force career officer, represented the Joint Chiefs of Staff. Ambassador Llewellyn Thompson, the prominent former ambassador to the Soviet Union and a Soviet expert, was the State Department representative. Phil Farley, the ACDA deputy director and an expert on arms limitation policy, was the ACDA representative and delegation deputy. Sid Graybeal, who had spent many years at the CIA and later was the first U.S. commissioner to the Standing Consultative Commission (SCC), the implementing body for the ABM Treaty and the Interim Agreement, and Larry Weiler, an arms control expert and subsequent Stanford professor, were key aides to Gerry Smith. Howard Stoertz represented the CIA (and at the same time was the national intelligence officer for the Soviet Union and therefore of high rank), although on paper he was listed as being from the State Department.

At first, Gerry Smith was the leader of the Washington interagency process supporting SALT, as well as the chief negotiator on the delegation. However, early on in 1969 then National Security Advisor Henry Kissinger circumvented Smith by creating something called the Verification Panel chaired by himself—ostensibly designed to consider verification issues—and by 1970 had drawn all power to it. The Verification Panel became the principals committee for SALT under Kissinger. Nevertheless, Gerry Smith continued to enjoy strong support from President Nixon. As I noted above, some years later when we did some research to support the nomination of Fred Ikle to be Gerry's successor as ACDA director, we discovered that Gerry had had forty-six private meetings with President Nixon in forty-eight months.

The first actual work I did on the SALT process was at the behest of Captain Dick Creecy, a retired naval officer and longtime ACDA official who was dedicated to disarmament. Subsequently, he was executive secretary (or chief of staff) of the SALT II delegation for a time. He asked me to draft some language in the fall of 1970 to extend the prohibition on the deployment of nuclear weapons on the seabed under the high seas, which was to be contained in the emerging 1972 Seabed Arms Control Treaty, to the internal waters (lakes and rivers) of the United States and the Soviet Union. I did so and the language was proposed to the Soviets by our delegation in early 1971. It was not included in the Interim Agreement but did find its way into the SALT II Treaty.

Other than the two matters of the briefing by Larry Weiler and working on the seabed provision, my work on SALT I was limited to reading the cables, reviewing texts, and doing congressional work related to the on-going negotiations. On a number of occasions I accompanied Gerry Smith and the rest of the delegation, along with General Counsel Bill Hancock, to Capitol Hill. As the assistant general counsel for congressional relations in the 1970–73 time frame, I did most of the routine legislative work and usually accompanied Bill at the higher-priority meetings.

In 1971 President Nixon announced an agreement with the Soviet Union to conclude in the first phase of SALT a treaty on strategic defensive systems to be accompanied only by "certain measures" limiting strategic offensive arms. Senator Henry ("Scoop") Jackson of Washington State, a hawk on defense and an ABM system advocate, had led efforts in the Senate in 1969 that ended with a one-vote margin, provided by Vice President Spiro Agnew, for approval of the Safeguard ABM system. Senator Jackson, who for years was a major figure on national security issues in the Senate, strongly favored limiting the strategic offensive arms of the Soviet Union as the first step. Thus, President Nixon's agreement turned things around from Senator Jackson's point of view.

The next time the delegation was in Washington, D.C., during a break in the negotiations, a briefing was arranged for Senator Jackson's subcommittee of the Senate Armed Services Committee. As usual, it was a closed-door, non-public session. Senator Jackson at one point in the proceeding said that he was only a country lawyer, but even he could see that the important thing to do was to control strategic offensive arms, which were what could destroy cities and populations, as opposed to defensive systems, which were designed to protect cities and populations. Gerry Smith replied that he was a city lawyer and he wanted to say that strategic defensive systems had to be limited first, to break the action/reaction cycle of the arms race and to provide a basis for strategic offensive arms limitation.

Thus, from the very first days the ABM Treaty was controversial. Some saw it as the essential basis for stopping the nuclear arms race, thereby permitting strategic offensive arms limitation. Others saw it as infringing upon the right of the United States to defend itself. Those who saw it as the underpinning of strategic arms limitation, I always thought, had the better of the argument. The theory of the ABM Treaty and its corollary, the doctrine of mutual assured destruction (referred to by its detractors as MAD), was that strategic offensive arms—thermonuclear weapons delivered in minutes by intercontinental ballistic missiles and in hours by heavy bombers—were so overpowering that each country had to be the hostage of the other in order to achieve strategic stability. If one side began to build strategic defensive systems, the other side would simply add more offense. MIRVs—permitting one missile to strike several targets—were originally justified by the Pentagon to overcome the Soviet ABM system initially being constructed around Moscow. After the ABM Treaty in 1972 limited each side to two ABM deployments, other rationales were created to support the continuing MIRV program, somewhat reminiscent of the changing rationales to support a U.S. national missile defense system.

There was a fleeting opportunity during SALT I to ban MIRVs but it was not pursued. Indeed, once deployments by the United States began in 1970 the bureaucratic momentum was too great to stop. And, of course, once the United States had MIRVs, that ensured that the Soviet Union would acquire them as well, which it did in 1975. In 1971, I accompanied Bill Hancock on a visit to the office of Congressman Felix Hébert. Congressman Hébert was then the chairman of the House Armed Services Committee, and the purpose of our visit was a briefing on SALT. The chairman was interested in the briefing and was positive about the negotiations, but as we were leaving he warned, "Don't come back here with a MIRV ban." Of course, the decision to go to MIRVs was most ill advised. Although the concept of the possible vulnerability of the Minuteman ICBM deployments to a Soviet disarming first strike predated the Soviet deployment of MIRVs (having been first given prominence by Senator Jackson during the SALT I ratification hearings), it was the deployment of MIRVs by both sides that led to Minuteman vulnerability becoming a dominant nuclear doctrinal issue, which negatively affected the politics of arms control for many years afterwards.

The U.S. negotiating position with respect to the emerging ABM Treaty frequently changed. In 1967 at the Glassboro Summit, it was the United States that was urging an ABM ban on a skeptical Soviet Premier Kosygin. At SALT I it was the Soviet Union that was pressing for limitations on ABM deployments. During negotiations in 1970, the United States told the Soviets that the United States could agree to zero ABM, one deployment location on each side, or two deployments on each side. The Soviets responded after a short delay that zero was their choice. Meanwhile, however, the bureaucratic battlefront in Washington had shifted again and the Soviets were informed that they had made the wrong choice. Their response was, "Well, what about one to one," and they were informed that they had chosen incorrectly again, and that the United States' proposal was one deployment for the Soviet Union and four for the United States. As stated above, the outcome in the 1972 ABM Treaty was two deployments on each side, one to defend an ICBM deployment area and the other the national capital, later reduced to one site for each side. In 1976 the United States completed its one ABM system deployment at Grand Forks, North Dakota, designed to defend the ICBM field there, at the cost of 6 billion dollars, a reasonable amount of money in those days. It was operated for four months and then was shut down because it was expensive and of no strategic value. The Soviet Galosh system became operational at Moscow in the early 1970s and it remains operational today—though only at partial capacity. Both the U.S. system and the Soviet Galosh system used nuclear-armed interceptors. The U.S. longer-range ABM interceptor, the Spartan missile, had a two-megaton warhead.

The SALT I negotiations ended on May 26, 1972, and the ABM Treaty and the Interim Agreement were signed that day by Presidents Nixon and Brezhnev. The ABM Treaty, to recapitulate, was a comprehensive agreement strictly limiting ABM systems. There were limits on large phased array radars (LPARS), recognized as the possible base for a nationwide defense. Space-based systems were also banned, as were all systems based on future technology—except in an Agreed Statement in which the two sides contemplated the possible amendment of the treaty to permit a land-based system based on future technology. This was designed to protect the Army's SAM-D air-defense system then on the drawing board and which contemplated such future technologies as lasers and particle beams. The upgrade of non-ABM systems (e.g., surface-to-air missile defense systems designed to counter aircraft) to ABM capability was prohibited in Article VI. In Article I of the treaty, the establishment of a nationwide ABM defense system or the base for such a defense was prohibited as a matter of principle. Although there is some dispute about this national defense prohibition, I have always believed that this was intended as a general prohibition supported by the other articles of the treaty, and that one could not violate this provision without breaking one of the other provisions of the treaty (as the obligation is not otherwise defined)—unless, of course, one announced that a nationwide defense was being built.

The Interim Agreement was simply a freeze expressed in rather general terms, particularly given the uncertainty about the numbers on the Soviet side. Both sides were to be frozen where they then were in terms of the number of ICBMs and SLBMs, as well as modern heavy ICBMs (i.e., the Soviet SS-9 ICBM). Missile capability growth was intended to be limited by the 15 percent limit on the increase in ICBM silo dimensions. The United States interpreted this to mean that either depth or diameter could be increased by no more than 15 percent, but not both, and if both dimensions were increased the two added together could not exceed 15 percent. When an attempt was made to clean up and include this provision in SALT II, we found that this was not the Soviet interpretation. The Soviets said that the increase could be up to 15 percent in both dimensions. As discussed earlier, the Interim Agreement also permitted a one-way freedom to mix, whereby the Soviet Union could eliminate up to 210 older heavy ICBMs (SS-7s and SS-8s) and replace them with SLBMs.

Since this was a freeze arrangement there were only a few agreed numbers. The SLBM limitations were based on their deployment on nuclear-powered submarines, but the Soviet Union was credited with more submarines and SLBMs than they actually had in 1972. The United States believed that they had fewer, but the Soviets insisted on, in effect, counting those under construction—even at a very early stage. By taking this position the Soviets gained an even greater advantage in the number of SLBMs in 1972, and later when they exercised the one-way freedom to mix and traded in the 210 older heavy ICBMs for modern SLBMs, their advantage grew still larger. The United States did not exercise that same right. In addition, Kissinger and Soviet Ambassador Dobrynin made a secret agreement two months after signature of the Interim Agreement, supporting the inclusion of modern SLBMs deployed on the conventionally powered missile submarines of the Soviet Union by defining a modern SLBM, which had been overlooked by Nixon and Kissinger at the Summit. Sid Graybeal, the U.S. commissioner for the newly created SCC—the implementing body for SALT I (and later SALT II) established by Memorandum Agreement in December 1972—was not informed of this last agreement for a year, and then he learned about it from his Soviet counterpart at a SCC session in Geneva during work on SALT I implementing procedures.

Thus, we had a well-drafted complete treaty limiting ABM systems, and a loosely drafted and incomplete agreement limiting strategic offensive systems. This was exactly the outcome that Senator Jackson opposed in 1971 in his response to the Nixon-Brezhnev agreement during the negotiations setting SALT I priorities. This set the stage for stormy ratification proceedings in the Senate, which led to other negative effects on the arms control process. Adding to the confusion is that in working out the final deals on the Interim Agreement, Nixon and Kissinger often met alone with Brezhnev and his aides, not even accompanied by a United States interpreter who could have verified translations and made notes.

The Senate ratification hearings began in June 1972 and continued into August. The House of Representatives was involved as well. The Interim Agreement on Strategic Offensive Arms was not a treaty and therefore was submitted to both houses for approval by majority vote, as required by the ACDA Act, while the ABM Treaty was sent to the Senate for advice and consent to ratification. The Arms Control and Disarmament Act of 1961, which established ACDA, explicitly recognized this alternative route for the United States to enter into binding arms control arrangements, to the later-expressed dismay of leading senators. In 1977 President Carter briefly flirted with submitting SALT II as an executive agreement, which would have required a majority vote in both houses, rather than as a treaty requiring a two-thirds Senate vote, because it was feared that the forty-one votes in the Senate against the confirmation of Paul Warnke as SALT II negotiator in 1977 indicated that a two-thirds ratification vote in the Senate for SALT II could not be achieved.

One of the first witnesses to testify on the ABM Treaty was Dr. John Foster, head of Defense Research and Engineering. One notable part of his testimony that influenced the ABM debate for many years afterward was his definition of a strategic ballistic missile target for ABM testing as a re-entry vehicle target that has an apogee greater than forty kilometers and a re-entry velocity greater than two kilometers per second. If an interceptor missile was tested against a target vehicle with characteristics exceeding either of these parameters (only the Soviet SS-N-5, among the missiles regulated by the Interim Agreement, had a re-entry speed of less than three kilometers per second), that interceptor missile was part of a strategic ABM system and therefore regulated by the ABM Treaty—as opposed to an unregulated tactical or theater ABM system. The ABM Treaty defines an ABM system as a system designed to counter a strategic ballistic missile in flight trajectory. Foster's definition, therefore, was important in distinguishing between regulated and unregulated systems. The Interim Agreement indicated which ICBM and SLBM systems were considered strategic, but after Soviet systems such as the SS-N-6 SLBM, modern in 1972, and the SS-11 ICBM, the backbone of the Soviet force in 1972, were retired there was only Foster's definition to go on. There was subsequent discussion between the United States and the Soviet Union in the SCC that, given the characteristics and test history of the Soviet SA-10 and SA-12 air defense systems, and given the characteristics of deployed strategic offensive arms in 1972, perhaps three kilometers per second re-entry velocity should be the line of delineation. (In the 1990s the United States pressed for a delineation of five kilometers per second, which was ultimately agreed to by the Russians. But in the 1970s and 1980s the United States wanted a tighter constraint and raised questions about the compliance of the SA-12 system with the ABM Treaty.)

My assignment at this time was to cover the SALT I ratification proceedings for ACDA and the State Department. I attended all of the open hearings and several of the closed hearings and wrote summaries of the proceedings. During the course of this work I became acquainted with Alexander Yereskovsky, who had a similar assignment for the Soviet Embassy. Shortly after we met at one of the hearings I asked him how many ICBM launchers the Soviet Union would have built if it had not been for the Interim Agreement. He replied, "Until our generals said we had enough." He introduced himself to me prior to a hearing before the Senate Foreign Relations Committee held in the Senate Caucus Room. Secretary of Defense Mel Laird was the witness and Senator Fulbright was in the chair. During the course of the hearing, the exchanges between Chairman Fulbright and Mel turned to the question of whether the Defense Intelligence Agency was inflating its estimates of Soviet military capabilities in order to support Pentagon budget requests. Senator Fulbright vigorously implied that they did and Mel stoutly asserted that they did not. After much back and forth Fulbright threw up his hands and proclaimed, "The only thing that saves us is that for every mistake that we make—and we make a lot—the Soviet Union makes a bigger one." Yereskovsky, who was seated next to me in the audience, leaned over and said, "That will be difficult to report to my government."

At a hearing before the Senate Armed Services Committee in July 1972, with the U.S. SALT I delegation as the testifying witnesses, Senator Jackson pressed with some vigor the issue of the lack of agreed data on Soviet systems. Ambassador Smith explained that we did not need agreement on the number of Soviet ICBM launchers because U.S. NTM could determine precisely how many there were in May of 1972, and whether there was any violation of the Interim Agreement freeze on the number of ICBM and heavy ICBM launchers. Senator Jackson responded in effect that that was not good enough: the U.S. government knows how many Soviet ICBM launchers there are; he, Senator Jackson, knows; and—after a quick word from Richard Perle, his long-time aide and later assistant secretary of defense, who was sitting behind him—there is a representative of the Soviet Union in the audience who knows (pointing in the general direction of Yereskovsky, who was again sitting next to me), but the American people do not know and this is not acceptable. All eyes of course briefly turned toward Yereskovsky.

As soon as the hearing was over the press representatives covering the hearing rushed up to Yereskovsky, who did not in any way want to be interviewed. The last I saw of Alexander that day was the sight of him running at top speed down the corridor of the Russell Senate Office Building, with ten to fifteen members of the press corps in hot pursuit. I did not see anything in the paper the next day so I assumed that they did not catch him. I had a number of other professional interactions with Yereskovsky over the years: when he was the executive secretary of the Soviet SCC delegation during the 1980s; at the time of my first visit to Moscow after the fall of the Soviet Union when he was participating in our discussions as one of the principal Russian experts on the ABM Treaty; and when he returned to Washington in the mid-1990s as counselor at the Russian Embassy. He retired in 1999 and was a capable and effective career diplomat.

The SALT I data issue lingered on through the ratification proceedings. When I became the legal advisor to the United States SALT II delegation in late 1974, I was determined to attempt to correct the SALT I deficiencies that had been raised during the hearings by Senator Jackson and others. In my first draft SALT II text, which I prepared with the U.S. delegation in 1975 in Geneva, I raised the issue of an agreed database, and over time this became a major U.S. objective—strongly resisted by the Soviets for a long time.

Another issue raised by Senator Jackson was the Interim Agreement limitation on increases in ICBM silo dimensions. He pointed out that the 15 percent limitation translated into a permitted silo volume increase of 32 percent or 52 percent depending on whether the permitted increase was in one dimension only either in diameter or depth, or a combination (e.g., 8 percent for one and 7 percent for the other), or whether both dimensions could be increased by up to 15 percent. The White House was confused when Senator Jackson first raised this issue, but after some internal consultations the White House insisted and all witnesses asserted that the negotiating record (which was nonexistent) clearly indicated that it was the former interpretation. As I indicated above, when we raised this for clarification in SALT II the Soviets said that theirs was the latter interpretation, although in practice they stayed within our interpretation when increasing the volume of the SS-9 silos to accommodate the MIRVed SS-18 ICBM, and the SS-11 silos to accommodate the MIRVed SS-19 ICBM. We settled this during SALT II with a simple limitation of a 32 percent increase in silo volume, as recounted later.

Another problem from the point of view of a lawyer was that the so-called common understandings associated with SALT I—which were sent to the Congress along with the ABM Treaty, the Interim Agreement, and the associated initialed Agreed Statements—were of dubious legal standing. They were not formal agreements at all, but simply statements plucked from the negotiating record by people in Washington to bolster the provisions of the treaty and agreement as part of the ratification effort. At SALT II we tried to fix that by requiring that Agreed Statements were to be used only for substantive obligations, Common Understandings only for questions of interpretation, and both were to be confirmed and formally agreed upon. At the end of the SALT II negotiations, in an abundance of caution, the White House insisted that all Agreed Statements and Common Understandings be treated identically, gathered together in a single document that would be signed by the heads of state, which is what was done. During the SALT I ratification, even unilateral statements by the United States were taken from the negotiating record, and in one important case where the Soviet Union had explicitly rejected the statement, legal force was claimed for them. This practice was dispensed with entirely in SALT II.

The problems and confusion surrounding the Interim Agreement (e.g., different interpretations, secret agreements, poor drafting)—contrasted with the lack of such deficiencies in the ABM Treaty—are a testimony to employing professionals rather than politicians when negotiating disarmament agreements. The Interim Agreement was largely negotiated by Nixon and Kissinger and it certainly shows it, while the ABM Treaty was negotiated by the two delegations led by Ambassadors Smith and Semenov, the Soviet SALT I negotiator.

One example of how the slapdash approach to the Interim Agreement created real problems came in June 1972: Secretary Kissinger asserted in his White House briefing for the Congress that month that, taken together, the Interim Agreement provision that launchers of light ICBMs could not be converted into launchers of heavy ICBMs (there was a freeze on the construction of new heavy ICBM launchers), the restraints on silo dimensions (about which there was a misunderstanding as to interpretation), and the U.S. unilateral statement that the largest Soviet light ICBM was the SS-11—and therefore any missile larger in terms of volume would be a heavy ICBM (explicitly rejected by the Soviets)—were an adequate constraint on the growth of Soviet missile capability. This proved to be a complete fraud and the Soviets vastly increased the capabilities of their ICBMs in moving to heavier MIRVed ICBMs, while not increasing their numbers of launchers and therefore remaining compliant with the Interim Agreement. The SS-11 was replaced by the SS-19 (already under development on May 26, 1972), which had triple the throw-weight or lifting power of the SS-11, while the replacement for the SS-9, the SS-18, had double the throw-weight.

The Interim Agreement was heard on the House side and the hearings before the House Foreign Affairs and Armed Services Committees generally were constructive. The House Foreign Affairs Committee staff prepared an excellent report. There was a memorable moment before the House Armed Services Committee when Ambassador Smith was questioned by Congressman Sonny Montgomery of Mississippi. The provision in the ABM Treaty for a national capital ABM defense proved to be quite unpopular. The ABM Treaty permitted two deployments, one to defend a deployment area, which we were planning, and one to defend the national capital area, which the Soviets already had in place. The national capital defense was particularly unpopular in the House because many congressmen were receiving letters from constituents wondering why billions were being spent to protect their representatives from Soviet missile attack but not them. Ambassador Smith was trying to explain the national capital defense to the House Armed Services Committee even though technically only the Interim Agreement was before them. Congressman Montgomery said that, in other words, because of this provision, under the ABM Treaty the Soviets could "squeeze off" a couple of ICBMs and it would be "OK under the treaty." Gerry Smith firmly replied that there was nothing in the treaty that authorized anyone to launch ICBMs.

Another fateful bit of testimony was that of Mel Laird before the Senate in setting forth the conditions of the Defense Department's support of SALT I. One condition was a continued vigorous research and development program on advanced (or futuristic) ABM systems. (This led directly to the Strategic Defense Initiative [SDI].) Support for the air-launched cruise missile (ALCM) and the sea-launched cruise missile (SLCM) was another. The issue of ALCMs and SLCMs was very difficult to resolve in SALT II. Deputy Secretary of Defense Bill Clements (later governor of Texas) was a staunch supporter of the ALCM and SLCM programs. These programs were not too popular in 1972 in the Air Force and the Navy, however, as it was feared they would replace pilots. Once, in 1976, I accompanied then ACDA Director Fred Ikle to the Hill to support Clements in an effort to persuade Senators Sam Nunn and Bob Taft, both Armed Services Committee members, to withdraw an amendment to the Defense Authorization Bill that called for a one-year slowdown in ALCM and SLCM development. Clements stormed around the room and announced to the two senators that it had taken him a year to ram the ALCM down the throat of the Air Force and another year to ram the SLCM down the throat of the Navy and he was not about to let anyone stop him now. On the way back Fred mused that he wasn't sure Bill was always the best advocate for weapons systems, but the two senators did withdraw their amendment. Ambassador Paul Nitze used to tell of his days with Bill Clements. Once in a debate between the two over a SALT I issue in front of Laird, Clements said, "Well of course Paul thinks that way, he's for the Russians." Nitze demanded an apology before he would continue.

Despite all these difficulties, SALT I did pass. The vote was 88–2 for each agreement in the Senate, with Senator Fritz Hollings voting "no" twice (against both the ABM Treaty and the Interim Agreement)—he used to say that he wouldn't let even Attila the Hun get to his right in South Carolina. Senator James Buckley voted no on the ABM Treaty, citing the ban on space-based futuristic ABM systems as the reason for his opposition (important in the later debate about the interpretation of Article V of the ABM Treaty). But in addition to the Laird price for DOD support there were other hidden costs. Lieutenant General Royall Allison, the JCS representative on the delegation, had angered Senator Jackson by publicly disagreeing with him over whether the SS-9 ICBM made the U.S. Minuteman ICBM vulnerable to a Soviet disarming first strike. Senator Jackson demanded Allison's removal from the delegation for SALT II and his replacement by Lieutenant General Edward Rowny (over the strong objection of the chairman of the Joint Chiefs who had already picked Admiral Tom Davies—later an assistant director at ACDA) because he apparently believed that Rowny would report regularly to him through Richard Perle and could be relied upon to represent his interests. Kissinger jumped into the fray here and sought a commitment from Nixon that ACDA—which he regarded as a threat to his power in the field of national security—would be substantially downgraded, its budget cut, and its reach reduced to a "research and staffing agency" (in the words of White House Press Secretary Ron Ziegler), and that the next director—after Smith was effectively forced out at the end of 1972—would be selected by him.

CHAPTER FOUR **SALT II, PART ONE: THE NIXON-FORD YEARS**

The ABM Treaty and the Interim Agreement were brought into force by the United States and the Soviet Union on October 3, 1972. The SALT II negotiations began at the end of November 1972 and continued in this first session until December 21. The SALT I practice of alternating between Vienna and Helsinki was abandoned and the negotiations were located at Geneva, where the strategic arms negotiations remained until the completion of START II in 1993. This first session was taken up entirely with drafting the Memorandum of Understanding that established the Standing Consultative Commission (SCC). Subsequently, Sid Graybeal was selected as the United States commissioner— at that time not a post subject to Senate confirmation.

The objective of the SALT II Treaty was the completion of the limitations on strategic offensive systems begun with SALT I. All arms control agreements beginning with the 1963 Limited Test Ban Treaty, which prohibited nuclear explosions everywhere but underground (except the Outer Space Treaty, which permits withdrawal on one-year notice for any reason), contain a "supreme national interests" provision permitting withdrawal if an "extraordinary event" related to the subject matter of the agreement should "jeopardize the supreme interests" of a party. At the close of SALT I, Ambassador Gerard Smith, the chief U.S. negotiator, stated formally for the United States that if a more complete agreement limiting strategic offensive arms was not achieved in the five-year term of the Interim Agreement, U.S. supreme interests could be jeopardized. The more complete agreement referred to in this statement was what the SALT II Treaty was intended to be.

When the SALT II Treaty had not been completed by 1977, the Interim Agreement was extended indefinitely by parallel statements of the states parties at the time of its expiration. This arrangement was objected to by many senators as violating Section 33 of the Arms Control and Disarmament Act, requiring congressional approval of arms limitation agreements if they are not submitted as a treaty. After a tumultuous debate, the Senate passed a resolution approving the informal extension of the Interim Agreement. The SALT II Treaty, which was signed in 1979 but never ratified, was similarly observed through an informal arrangement, this time by an exchange of oral statements between the U.S. secretary of state and the Soviet foreign minister. Citing Soviet violations, President Reagan terminated this informal arrangement for both agreements in the spring of 1986, some six months after the SALT II Treaty would have expired had it been ratified and nine years after the expiration of the Interim Agreement. From 1986 there were no limitations on strategic offensive arms until the START I Treaty entered into force in December of 1994.

The SALT II Treaty was signed in June of 1979, two years after the formal expiration of the Interim Agreement, and by its terms it was to continue in force until the end of 1985. It implemented the Vladivostok Accord of 1974 in which the United States and the Soviet Union agreed on the principle of equal aggregate limitations on ICBMs, SLBMs, and heavy bombers. The SALT II Treaty established an aggregate limitation of 2,400 ICBM launchers, SLBM launchers, and heavy bombers. This aggregate was to be reduced to 2,250 eighteen months after entry into force. Consistent with the Vladivostok Accord, limitations were placed on multiple warhead systems, ultimately to include heavy bombers carrying long-range (in excess of 600 kilometers) air-launched cruise missiles, and launchers of ICBMs and SLBMs equipped for MIRVs. The treaty eventually established a limit of 1,320 on all such multiple warhead systems, with sublimits of 1,200 on launchers of ICBMs and SLBMs equipped for MIRVs, and 820 on launchers of ICBMs equipped for MIRVs (viewed as the most threatening strategic systems).

The definition of a heavy ICBM, an issue that plagued the SALT I negotiations, was achieved in terms of launch-weight and throw-weight. Under the treaty, a heavy ICBM is an ICBM greater in either of these two measures than the largest light ICBM, now the Soviet SS-19, a MIRVed, substantially larger, and much more capable replacement for the less accurate single warhead SS-11, which had been the largest light ICBM in 1972. The provision codifying the Soviet monopoly in heavy ICBMs was carried over from the Interim Agreement. In Paragraph 7 of Article IV, a cap in terms of launch-weight and throw-weight was placed on missile growth beyond the parameters of the SS-18, a heavy MIRVed ICBM that was a much more capable replacement for the SS-9.

Two important verification counting rules were achieved. By national technical means it is not possible to determine how many individual warheads, below a maximum capacity for a particular missile type, are actually deployed on specific missiles tested with MIRVs. Likewise, by reconnaissance satellite, it is not possible to determine what type of missile, MIRVed or non-MIRVed, is actually deployed in a particular launcher. Hence, "type" rules were set forth in Paragraph 5 of Article II of the treaty: once a missile of a particular type has been flight tested with MIRVs, all missiles of that type are considered to be equipped with MIRVs, and once a launcher of a particular type has had a missile equipped with MIRVs flight-tested from it or deployed in it, all launchers of that type shall be included in the MIRV launcher aggregate total, regardless of the type of missile that is actually deployed in any such missile launcher.

Article IV of the SALT II Treaty contains many provisions that are important to the operation of the treaty. Paragraph 3 is the above-mentioned provision codifying the Soviet monopoly of heavy ICBMs, indirectly fixing this number at 308. This provision takes the form of a ban on the conversion of a launcher of a light ICBM and makes necessary the definition of heavy ICBMs found in Paragraph 7 of Article II. Article IV also contains the upper limit, in terms of launch-weight and throw-weight, on heavy ICBMs. In Paragraph 8, there is a prohibition on the conversion of medium-range ballistic missiles to ICBMs, which is accompanied by a Common Understanding banning the Soviet SS-16 ICBM. Since the Soviet SS-20 medium-range ballistic missile was simply the first two of the three missile stages of the SS-16 ICBM, this provision was designed to prevent breakout from the SALT II limitations by the deployment of a third stage on the then unregulated SS-20. A protocol to the SALT II Treaty of three years duration prohibited the flight-testing of land-mobile ICBMs and the deployment of land-mobile ICBM launchers, after which, pursuant to the treaty, such systems would be permitted and included in the limitations unless further constraints should be agreed. The protocol also provided for a three-year ban on the deployment of long-range sea- and ground-launched cruise missiles.

Paragraphs 9 through 11 contain elaborate provisions designed to limit growth in ICBM capability. Each party is limited to one new type of light ICBM, measured by a change in the propellant (liquid to solid) or a growth of more than 5 percent in the length, largest diameter, or throw-weight of the missile. The one permitted new type can have no more than ten re-entry vehicles, and each existing type of ICBM cannot be deployed with more than the maximum number of re-entry vehicles with which it had been tested. These numbers are listed for each ICBM type. An exception is made for the U.S. Minuteman III, which once was tested with seven very small re-entry vehicles but is capped at three. In addition, there is a prohibition on the testing or deploying of an SLBM with more than fourteen re-entry vehicles.

The SALT II Treaty was to be verified by national technical means. In a Common Understanding associated with Article XV, encoding (encryption) of telemetry signals from an ICBM to the ground during a test flight that impedes (not prevents, but impedes) verification is prohibited. The treaty also contains in Article XII a prohibition on the circumvention of the limitations of the treaty through a third state or states in any other manner. This provision, in a vague and general way, was designed to reduce the potential of the United States to evade the limitations of the treaty by transferring systems limited by the treaty to its allies, although the United States made clear its existing programs of cooperation with its allies would not be affected.

The SALT II negotiations began in a real sense in late January 1973. Gerry Smith had made it clear that after his treatment by Kissinger at the Summit in May 1972, he would finish out the year and then depart. (Gerry had been briefing the press on the two agreements after signature in Moscow, being properly careful about classified information, when Kissinger bounded onto the stage, grabbed the microphone, and announced that he would continue the briefing and was not bound by the same rules as Ambassador Smith.) U. Alexis Johnson was chosen as the new SALT negotiator. He was the most senior career diplomat at the time, having twice been undersecretary of state for political affairs, the number three job at State, and ambassador to a number of important countries. He was in his late sixties at this time. He was much the establishment diplomat, but was also a man who wanted to get things done.

Earlier I mentioned some of the effects of Senator Jackson's displeasure with the SALT I agreements. One effect had been what would have once been called the "cashiering" of General Allison for his defense of the agreements and rebuttal of Senator Jackson on the question of Minuteman ICBM vulnerability during the SALT I ratification hearings. Senator Jackson had argued that the codification of the Soviet monopoly in heavy ICBMs—the freeze at 308 for the Soviet Union and zero for the United States—threatened the survival of the U.S. ICBM force. This, in 1972, was a difficult case to make as the Soviets had not yet deployed MIRVs, so a two-nuclear-warhead attack on a single ICBM silo launcher was not yet possible. (Experts believed that two nuclear warheads arriving separately but in close proximity and attacking each ICBM silo were required to destroy a hardened ICBM silo. Of course the missile command centers—fewer in number in 1972 than later—could have been threatened.) The Soviet heavy ICBM threat consisted of 308 single-warhead SS-9 missiles (with very large nuclear warheads, to be sure), obviously not enough even to singly attack the entire 1,000 Minuteman ICBMs in the U.S. force. Even if the entire Soviet ICBM force was used against the 1,000 Minuteman ICBMs in 1972, a two-on-one attack was still not possible because of the numbers. The SS-9 was a modern heavy ICBM in 1972 and it did have considerable throw-weight and carry a very large nuclear warhead; nevertheless, this ICBM force did not have the capacity to threaten the survivability of the Minuteman forces.

The Soviet Union, because of the nature of its technology during the nuclear arms race, as indicated early, tended to build large, less accurate ICBMs, while the United States built smaller, highly accurate missile systems. In 1972, the light/heavy ICBM distinction was not a real one in terms of a true measurement of strategic capability. Of course, this changed with the advent of Soviet MIRVs, matching the earlier U.S. deployments. As I have said, there might have been a chance to ban MIRVs during SALT I, although there is some disagreement on this. Even if the negotiators had agreed, there probably never was a chance that the Senate would agree. Chairman Hébert's comment of "don't come back with a MIRV ban" likely reflected the majority view in the national security community on the Hill. This was typical of attitudes during the Cold War nuclear arms race. Once one side had the technology, it had to develop and deploy it. No one seemed to question whether we would be better off if both sides did not deploy this technology—or at least the assumption that we would not was never persuasively rebutted. The momentum of the arms race was such that simply no attention was paid to what the other side might do. The United States was certainly worse off with both sides deploying MIRVs. In retrospect, it was quite unwise for the United States to proceed in 1970 without considering a MIRV ban. A significant objective of the START process in the early 1990s was aimed at beginning to put this particular genie back in the bottle.

The United States began deploying MIRVs, first on the SLBM force, in 1970. In negotiating the Interim Agreement it was assumed that the Soviets could not possess MIRVs during its term of five years. That was how the numerical imbalances in the Interim Agreement freeze arrangement were justified: 1,656 ICBMs and SLBMs for the United States and 2,350 ICBMs and SLBMs for the Soviet Union (including the 308 modern Soviet heavy ICBMs compared to zero for the United States). The Soviet Union began deploying MIRVs in 1975, confounding this assumption. But it was worse than that. The Soviet Union exploited the loose and ineffective constraints on growth in missile capability, so touted by Kissinger in June of 1972, and fielded far more capable next-generation missiles with MIRVs. In place of the SS-11 and SS-13 light ICBMs, the SS-19 with six MIRVs and the SS-17 with four MIRVs were deployed. Most threatening of all was the replacement of the SS-9 with the very large SS-18 ICBM with ten MIRVs, each containing a warhead of around half a megaton. Now Minuteman was really threatened—the 308 SS-18s alone could lay over 3,000 large warheads on the U.S. ICBM force, 50 percent more than would be needed to destroy the force. Whether a first strike on Minuteman could ever realistically be considered anything other than an act of complete madness—with the SLBM force out there, not to mention the bomber force—is beside the point. After 1975, the theoretical capability existed to threaten Minuteman and this had significant political repercussions.

So General Allison was right to rebut Senator Jackson in 1972. The Soviet SS-9 force did not seriously threaten Minuteman, either actually or theoretically, but the failure to attempt a MIRV ban in SALT I and the resultant Soviet deployments ultimately did. However, Senator Jackson did not appreciate such an expression of a different viewpoint and demanded the replacement of General Allison for the SALT II negotiation by his man, Army Lieutenant General Edward Rowny.

Early in 1973, Admiral Moorer had selected Rear Admiral Thomas Davies to be the JCS representative on the SALT II delegation only to find to his dismay that the White House had decided that General Rowny would represent the JCS at SALT II. Ed Rowny was a dedicated soldier and a man who really cared about people and personal relationships. But it seemed that he never forgot during the SALT II negotiations who his sponsor was. A much-used route for information as to what was going on in Geneva was established: from delegation discussions in Geneva, Ed Rowny passed on information to his aide in Washington, Major (later Colonel) Sam Watson, who passed it on to Richard Perle and Senator Jackson. Ed Rowny opposed much of what Presidents Ford and Carter tried to do at SALT II, and he was an unflagging champion of the concept that the Soviet Backfire bomber (a heavy medium-range nuclear-capable bomber) must be included as a strategic bomber under the SALT II Treaty count. This was known throughout the negotiations to be a breakpoint for the Soviets. Rowny's assertion was that the Backfire was a heavy bomber that could carry a significant nuclear weapon capability to the United States, attack U.S. targets, and recover in Cuba. (Information on the Backfire's actual capability obtained near the end of the Cold War proved this assertion false.) Once during a U.S. delegation meeting in Moscow in 1978 to discuss SALT II, Marshall Ogarkov (formerly of the Soviet SALT I delegation and in 1978 Chief of the Soviet General Staff) offered Rowny a Backfire bomber that he could fly to Cuba. Ogarkov included in his offer "flowers for the widow Rowny." It was Ogarkov who had approached General Allison during a session in Vienna in 1970 after a presentation by Allison, in which he had included information on Soviet ICBM deployments in explaining the logic of the U.S. position. Ogarkov requested that Allison not make presentations like that in front of the civilian members of the Soviet SALT I delegation on the ground that they were not cleared for such information.

Rowny stayed on the U.S. SALT II delegation until the end of the negotiations in 1979. He refused to attend the signing ceremony at the Summit in Vienna, resigned from the Army, and testified against SALT II during the ratification hearings. He had wanted to delay his retirement long enough to be able to testify in uniform, but this was vetoed by Secretary of Defense Brown. Once, near the close of the negotiations, upset over some decision at a delegation meeting, he accosted several of us in the hallway outside the meeting room in Geneva and, waving his notebook in the air, said that he had everything that we had said during this and other meetings in his notebooks and we would have to answer for it. Also, in the spring of 1975, he complained to John Lehman, then deputy director of ACDA and later secretary of the Navy under President Reagan—who had been very much involved as a National Security Council assistant to Kissinger with the arrangements on ACDA made in 1972 with Senator Jackson—that I should be replaced as SALT II delegation legal advisor as I was not tough enough on the Soviets. However, Jim Malone, ACDA general counsel, strongly supported me and nothing came of this. But Rowny was in many ways a free spirit. He described his relationship with President Carter's national security advisor, Zbigniew Brzezinski, as "Poles apart" and he became somewhat of an arms control icon for many on the right. President Reagan tried to make him ACDA director, but this was blocked by Senators Baker and Percy in 1980. He was START negotiator from 1981 to 1983.

The part of the arrangement with Senator Jackson that involved the semi-destruction of ACDA was largely implemented by John Lehman acting for Kissinger. Jim Malone, who had been assistant general counsel, became ACDA general counsel under this plan. Jim's views were strongly on the conservative side, but he believed in arms control and was a public servant of the very highest quality. He played an important role in the resuscitation of ACDA after the 1973 downgrading. He was also one of the most delightful people I have ever worked with, and a faithful friend. Subsequent to his ACDA work he was assistant secretary of state for Oceanic, Environmental and Scientific Affairs (OES) in the first Reagan term. Tragically, he died after a long illness in 1998.

In the spring of 1973, White House Press Secretary Ron Ziegler announced that the ACDA budget was being cut from $10 million to $7 million and henceforth ACDA would be a "resource and staffing" agency, as opposed to the agency responsible for arms control policy development, which it had always been since its creation in 1961. This treatment, to put it mildly, was hardly appropriate for the agency that had pressed for and had negotiated the NPT, and whose director had been the chief of the United States SALT I delegation.

It is particularly ironic that the assault on ACDA in 1973 was in a sense compensation to Senator Jackson for his support of SALT I in spite of his objection to the terms of the Interim Agreement. Jackson had wanted limits on Soviet offense, not on U.S. defense, and ACDA helped implement the 1971 Nixon-Brezhnev agreement, which called for a treaty on strategic defense and "certain measures" constraining strategic offensive weapons. But in 1972 Jackson focused his objections on the terms, not the existence, of the Interim Agreement, which had been almost entirely masterminded by Kissinger, not ACDA. ACDA and the SALT delegation negotiated the ABM Treaty while making only relatively minor contributions to the negotiation of the Interim Agreement. And the Interim Agreement was a mess, as I have already indicated. But the blame for this should have been placed on Kissinger, not on ACDA. Considerable time was spent during the SALT II negotiations correcting the mistakes of the Interim Agreement.

Fred Ikle became the third director of ACDA in the summer of 1973. He was handpicked by John Lehman, presumably as part of the Jackson arrangement but he did much to restore the strength of the agency. He labored long and hard to revive interest in non-proliferation (which had flagged after the entry into force of the NPT) but only succeeded after the 1974 test by

India of a "peaceful" nuclear device. He also took on the entire government in an ultimately successful effort to block U.S. acquisition of binary chemical weapons—an attempt to modernize U.S. chemical weapons just as we were finally agreeing to join the rest of the world community and outlaw their first use in war. Ikle sponsored the compromise that permitted U.S. ratification of the Geneva Protocol that accomplished this. On the other hand, it was his opposition to the SALT II terms being negotiated in January 1976 that persuaded President Ford not to complete a SALT II agreement. Interestingly, after Henry Kissinger left the NSC and became secretary of state in 1974, John Lehman came over and joined Fred Ikle at ACDA as deputy director in 1975. In the end, ACDA was not downgraded at all. Fred Ikle proved to care about arms control and he rebuilt the budget. The entire Smith team was removed but they were replaced by other excellent people, including Tom Davies, Admiral Moorer's choice for SALT II, as assistant director.

So the SALT II delegation was put together during 1973, with U. Alexis Johnson as head of the delegation; Rowny representing the JCS; Mike May, former director of Livermore Laboratory, representing OSD (in place of Nitze, who left in 1974 shortly before the denouement of Watergate); Ralph Earle, a future ACDA director, representing ACDA (which no longer had the delegation chair); Boris Klosson, senior State Department Soviet specialist and former deputy chief of mission (DCM) in Moscow, representing State; and Howard Stoertz, the CIA National Intelligence Officer for the Soviet Union, continuing to represent the Central Intelligence Agency.

During 1973 and 1974, U.S. efforts at SALT II were largely focused on stopping the Soviets from deploying MIRVs, while protecting U.S. MIRV deployments. Proposals such as a freeze on MIRV deployments resulting in several hundred systems for the United States and none for the Soviets were put on the table to no avail. This stalemate continued from early 1973 until late 1974, and the negotiations were doing little more than just treading water. It was during this period that the U.S. SALT II delegation invented the concept of the "six-day weekend." The only accomplishment during this period was in the SCC. Sid Graybeal and General Ustinov, the Soviet SCC commissioner, negotiated the necessary detailed dismantling procedures to implement the ABM Treaty and Interim Agreement. These provisions detailed precisely what the sides agreed was required to dismantle an ICBM launcher, an ABM test and training launcher, an SLBM launcher, etc. Under the Interim Agreement, the Soviet Union could dismantle the older ICBM launchers, thirty H-class SLBM launchers, and those launchers on conventionally powered G-class submarines, which contained modern SLBMs, and replace them with modern SLBMs (then the SS-N-6) on modern nuclear-powered submarines (then the Yankee class). Also, the Soviets had to dismantle some ABM test and training launchers to reach the treaty limit of fifteen. The United States wanted to be sure that any dismantled launcher could not be rebuilt in less time than would be required to build a new one (some of the older SS-7 and

SS-8 ICBM launchers were above ground, as opposed to in silos, and in this case there was little to dismantle). Nevertheless, the procedures on dismantlement of ICBM launchers and H-class SLBM launchers effectively completed the Interim Agreement. And, most importantly, since the Interim Agreement permitted modernization and replacement, there were procedures for the dismantling of modern (e.g., SS-N-6) SLBM launchers to permit the dismantling of such launchers and their replacement by newer systems.

All of these procedures, particularly the dismantling and replacement procedures for modern SLBM launchers, established precedents for the dismantling provisions under the INF Treaty and START I and START II. The SALT I procedures, like all strategic arms draft treaties, were classified secret during their negotiation but, departing from usual practice, were not declassified upon signature. For no good reason they remained classified secret and were signed in that form by Nixon and Brezhnev at the 1974 summit. These were implementing procedures and thus entered into force upon signature. In this form they could be amended easily when necessary. During the hue and cry in the 1980s over alleged Soviet violations of the ABM Treaty, as well as the Interim Agreement and the SALT II Treaty (which were being informally observed), there was a demand from the Congress that all the verification provisions—including provisions comparable to those in the SALT I implementing procedures—be included in the treaty and made subject to Senate advice and consent. This was a significant departure from good treaty practice: it made implementing procedures virtually impossible to amend; it significantly lengthened and complicated the basic negotiations; it assured that no one would read the treaties in their entirety; it resulted in the 300–page START I Treaty monstrosity (where this departure from normal treaty practice was most pronounced).

The Interim Agreement and the SALT II Treaty limited ICBM and SLBM launchers because these were the large items that U.S. photographic satellites could actually see. The Reagan administration in its initial years, when it reformulated the strategic arms negotiations into INF and START, asserted the intent to limit the actual weapons, the warheads, "which are what kill people," as distinguished from the allegedly confused approach of the Nixon, Ford, and Carter administrations, which only limited the delivery vehicles—missiles and bombers. (When the Reagan administration entered office some of its appointees referred to career officials still employed as "Carter holdovers," "Nixon-Ford retreads," or, worst of all, both). It is true that the INF, START I and START II Treaties cast their limitations in terms of warheads, but the warheads are counted on the basis of their association with missiles and the missiles on the basis of their association with launchers, which amounts to the same approach as in the Interim Agreement and the SALT II Treaty.

It is perhaps worth mentioning that during the Nixon-Ford years the term "photographic satellite" was considered classified and these verification systems could only be referred to as national technical means of verification (or NTM). After a huge effort the Carter administration declassified this term so that photographic satellites used for verification could be referred to openly. It was the development of these systems in the 1960s, initially by the United States and later by the Soviets, that made strategic arms limitation possible. At first, in the early 1960s, the Soviets claimed that these systems violated state sovereignty—even though the prevailing international law rule was that national air space extended at most to the limits of the upper atmosphere, around sixty miles, and the satellites operated well over a hundred miles into space. The Soviets held to this position until they developed their own satellites. (There was a popular legend about these years that from time to time in the winter months the Soviets would write American expletives in the snow near their ICBM deployments for satellites to see.) The ABM Treaty and the Interim Agreement verification provisions state that the treaty/agreement is to be verified by "national technical means operating in accordance with generally accepted provisions of international law." What this means is that the Soviet Union agreed that verification satellites were legal but that the SALT I agreements were not to be verified by aircraft overflights such as the Gary Powers U-2 flight in 1960.

There was another verification issue in the early to mid-1970s that bears explanation. During this period, until about 1975, the United States was intercepting and reading radio broadcasts from Soviet test missiles in flight back to ground stations (referred to as telemetry) and thereby obtaining an accurate analysis of Soviet missiles. In about 1975, the Soviet Union began encrypting this data in some cases or storing the data in a capsule dropped off by the missile in flight. The CIA very much wanted an agreement with the Soviets at SALT II to ban telemetry encryption and related practices so we could continue to read their telemetry and continue to have an extremely accurate understanding of the capabilities of their missiles. But because of the sensitivity of this issue the U.S. SALT II delegation was prohibited from raising it directly with the Soviets and could only complain about deliberate "concealment" measures that were continuing but which must be prohibited under SALT II. In 1975 President Ford even issued a direct order that the phrase "telemetry encryption" was not to be used by the delegation with the Soviets. When in 1977 this was relaxed by President Carter, thus permitting direct discussion with the Soviets, Academician Shchukin, the representative of the Ministry of Defense on the Soviet SALT II delegation, noted that General Rowny had been discussing this with them for two years.

Academician Shchukin was a most interesting individual. Born around 1900, he was from an upper-middle-class family that owned a department store in St. Petersburg. French was the first language that he learned. He joined the Red Guards in 1917. He was educated in physics, and we understood that, along with Academicians Sakharov and Tamm, he was one of the fathers of the Soviet hydrogen bomb. A connoisseur of the classics, he was first Paul Nitze's opposite number and subsequently Michael May's. It was occasionally my privilege to be the third person present during post-plenary discussions in 1975 and 1976 between May and Shchukin, conducted in French.

It was the practice developed at SALT I and continued to the end of the strategic arms negotiations in 1993 to have formal presentations—usually written speeches delivered by the delegation head—referred to as plenary sessions, followed by informal discussions in a number of small groups following the plenary sessions, known as the "post-plenary." Meticulous records of these informal discussions were kept by both sides. There was usually, but not always, a junior officer taking notes for each side at these discussions. Some tended to give creative reports, while others were verbatim, but they were invariably detailed. Once, to illustrate a point, Soviet Ambassador Karpov, the deputy and eventually successor to Ambassador Semenov, the Soviet SALT I and SALT II chief negotiator until 1978, passed a Soviet Memorandum of Conversation, as these reports were called, in front of me and my interpreter to make a point—it looked as detailed as the U.S. reports.

Mike May, born in southern France, emigrated to the United States at the beginning of World War II in his early teens. He had lived in Indochina where, as I recall, his father had been a doctor and designer of Bach-Mai Hospital in Hanoi for several years before that. (U.S. B-52s destroyed the hospital during the Vietnam War.) He was educated in physics and rose to become director of the prestigious Lawrence Livermore National Laboratory, which, along with Los Alamos, is one of the two U.S. nuclear weapons design facilities. He resigned from Livermore, became director emeritus, and joined the U.S. SALT II delegation upon the resignation of Paul Nitze. Mike is a brilliant and thoughtful analyst of strategic arms and arms control issues. Paired with Academician Shchukin the conversation was always interesting, and unlike other post-plenary conversations, which would be in either English or English and Russian, these were conducted in French. With my rudimentary French, if I concentrated as hard as I could, I was just barely able to follow the conversation. The subject was usually strategic issues, arms control issues in general, nuclear weapons issues, or the plenary issue of the day. However, in one conversation I shall always remember, Shchukin recounted his life in St. Petersburg during the Russian Civil War and the years immediately following. It made a memorable impression.

It was in the context of the negotiations of the SALT I procedures that the Kissinger-Dobrynin secret agreement came to light. Ambassadors Smith and Semenov negotiated the memorandum establishing the SCC in December of 1972. Ambassador Semenov continued as Soviet SCC commissioner until General Ustinov was brought to Geneva to do this work in 1974. The submarine limitations in the Interim Agreement were the most hastily conceived element and were negotiated entirely at the Summit. As a result they were rather confusing. In particular, it became apparent that the agreement was not clear as to the definition of a modern SLBM. This was important because "modern" SLBMs on G-class submarines would be counted in the limitations. All SLBMs on nuclear-powered submarines (H-class and Yankee-class) were to be included in the totals, but only "modern" (not older) SLBMs on the diesel SLBM submarines, the G-class, would be counted. In July, while the Congress was considering the Interim Agreement, Kissinger and Soviet Ambassador to the United States Dobrynin reached agreement on a secret text on how to define a modern SLBM. This agreement was never communicated to the U.S. SCC delegation. As a result, in mid-1973 Ambassador Semenov informed U.S. Commissioner Graybeal to his surprise that the definition of "modern" SLBMs had already been agreed by the two governments. This incident was consistent with Kissinger's practice of conducting "back-channel" negotiations and not informing the U.S. delegation, not even the chairman, Ambassador Smith. This had created surprises for the U.S. delegation from time to time and led directly to the poorly drafted text of the Interim Agreement. The Carter, Reagan, Bush, and Clinton administrations did not follow this precedent.

From the beginning, the basic position of the Joint Chiefs at SALT II was straightforward and clear. They wanted the unequal aggregate limitations on strategic ballistic missiles of the SALT I Interim Agreement to be corrected. Instead, they wanted at SALT II an agreement providing for equal aggregate numbers of ICBM launchers and SLBM launchers, and the JCS were willing to include in the numbers to be regulated by SALT II heavy (or strategic) bombers (an area of U.S. advantage not limited by SALT I). Finally, they wanted full freedom to mix among these systems within the aggregate limitations.

President Nixon resigned in August 1974 as a result of the Watergate scandal. His last Summit meeting with Brezhnev had taken place the month before. There the SALT I procedures were signed, as well as an agreement limiting underground nuclear weapon tests to 150 kilotons (around twelve times the explosive power of the Hiroshima bomb), referred to as the Threshold Test Ban Treaty (TTBT). All above-ground tests had been banned by the 1963 Limited Test Ban Treaty. The TTBT had been hastily thrown together in a month in Moscow at Kissinger's urging, to give Nixon something to sign at the 1974 Summit. It did not cover so-called peaceful nuclear explosions (PNES) used to dig canals or perform oil and gas stimulation—always a pie in the sky. Including PNES under the limitations would require two more years of negotiations to complete the companion Peaceful Nuclear Explosions Treaty (PNET).

PNET took so long to negotiate because the Soviet nuclear bureaucracy had been wedded to the idea of using some 250 nuclear explosions to dig a canal between the Kama and Pechora Rivers in the north—undoubtedly it would not have required night lighting, as it would have glowed in the dark. The canal was originally Stalin's idea, though he wanted to use slave labor.

The TTBT gave rise to many claims of Soviet non-compliance. Its means of verification were simply inadequate, but were ultimately corrected by the highly detailed verification protocols to the treaty, negotiated during the Bush administration by Ambassador Paul Robinson, now president of Sandia National Laboratories, also an important and prestigious national laboratory. The protocols entered into force in 1990 along with the TTBT and the PNET themselves. The TTBT and PNET had been informally observed by both sides by an exchange of statements since 1976.

President Ford had been in office a little over three months when he journeyed to Vladivostok in November of 1974 to meet with Brezhnev. At Vladivostok the two presidents verbally agreed to a framework for SALT II. There was a U.S. interpreter present, Alex Akelovsky, who took notes. As I said, it had been Nixon and Kissinger's practice not to have a U.S. interpreter present during their discussions on strategic arms limitations with Brezhnev in order to preserve secrecy. Thus they were wholly dependent on the Soviet interpreter who was always present. In this case, at Vladivostok, the United States could reconstruct an accurate report of the discussion.

The verbal agreement provided for equal aggregates of strategic systems (ICBM and SLBM launchers, air-to-surface missiles, and heavy bombers) at the level of 2,400 with no limitation on the freedom to mix. There was a further limitation on MIRVed systems at 1,320 for both sides—the first agreement to limit MIRVs. The Soviet monopoly on heavy ICBMs was to be carried forward as well as the ineffective limitations in the Interim Agreement on the dimensions of ICBM silo launchers. The agreement was to last for roughly ten years, until December 31, 1985. Ford's White House spokesman Ron Nesson proudly announced that Ford had accomplished "in three months" what Nixon could not do in two years. This statement of Nesson's proved to be misleading. The negotiations took five-and-a-half more years to complete, the SALT II Treaty being signed in June of 1979.

After Vladivostok, Kissinger gave a press backgrounder on his airplane on the way to a meeting in Beijing. In this backgrounder he implied that the Soviet Backfire bomber was not included as a heavy bomber in the aggregate limitations for SALT II. The transcript of the press backgrounder was subsequently classified confidential to cover Kissinger's embarrassment after elements in the U.S. Congress turned up the heat on the Backfire issue. The Vladivostok Agreement was also unclear as to whether ALCMs were included in the newly limited category of "air-to-surface missiles." The United States said "no," that the clear understanding was that this term referred only to air-to-surface ballistic missiles, essentially a nul set; the Soviet Union said "yes," the term meant what it said. These issues remained in play until the end of the negotiations and were finally settled in the spring of 1979 (along with SLCMs and ground-launched cruise missiles, or GLCMs): Backfire was not to be limited; ALCMs were, but in a different and more complicated way. Richard Perle was interviewed on television shortly after Vladivostok, and when asked whether Vladivostok was a breakthrough, he responded, "Yes, but like the German victory at Tobruk, a breakthrough in the wrong direction." Kissinger and Dobrynin worked out an aide-mémoire to put the Vladivostok Understanding on paper, which was initialed in December 1974—it resolved nothing.

Jim Malone and I had worked closely together when we were both assistant general counsels at ACDA in 1971 and 1972. Jim had joined ACDA in 1971 as a White House recommendation. He became general counsel in April of 1973 at the White House's request, and asked Fred Ikle, when he became director, to remove Charles Van Doren as deputy general counsel. Charles was transferred to the Non-Proliferation Bureau, which he headed as assistant director in the Carter administration. I was then appointed deputy general counsel in July of 1973 and spent much of 1973 helping Jim remake rather than downgrade ACDA.

In early December 1974, I received a telephone call from Jack Mendelsohn, special assistant to Ambassador Johnson, who said that I would shortly be invited by Ambassador Johnson to a meeting at which I would be asked to be legal advisor to the U.S. SALT II delegation. Jack was a career foreign service officer who played a central role in SALT II and later was a principal on the Rowny START delegation in 1981–83. He went on to a distinguished career as an arms control expert outside of government. At this time, I had just finished up the work with John Newhouse on the Geneva Protocol. Ambassador Johnson also invited Mike Matheson, an attorney with the State Department Legal Advisor's Office, to the meeting. Mike had been a young attorney in the Office of General Counsel of the Department of the Air Force when I had been there, and subsequently went on to a distinguished career in State Legal, finally retiring in 2000 after many years as the principal deputy. Ambassador Johnson asked me if I would accept his offer to join the delegation as legal advisor and I said that I would. He asked Mike to take the lead in dealing with SALT II legal issues in Washington, which he said was equally important. I spent much of December and early January working with Jack Mendelsohn to develop a draft treaty text. It was then that I resolved to try to clear up some of the legal problems associated with the Interim Agreement in working out a SALT II treaty text. (I was careful to use the word "agreement" throughout the text to preserve the option of going to both Houses for a majority vote under the ACDA Act as with the Interim Agreement, but everyone was really thinking about an agreement resembling in structure the ABM Treaty.) The first thing that I wanted to do was regularize the use of Agreed Statements and Common Understandings, the former for additional obligations, the latter for interpretive matters, but both legally binding.

The SALT II negotiations resumed on January 30, 1975, with a meeting between the two chiefs. Right away I plunged into work with the entire delegation to complete a delegation draft text to submit to Washington for approval to table with the Soviets. Once I had a draft text available discussions with the full delegation were scheduled by Ambassador Johnson virtually daily. In the second week of February, the same week that my father-in-law died, Ambassador Stanley Resor, chairman of the United States delegation to the Mutual and Balanced Force Reduction (MBFR) talks in Vienna and former secretary of the Army from 1965 to 1971, invited me to come to Vienna to brief the U.S. MBFR delegation on the status of SALT II and the implementation of the Vladivostok Agreement. MBFR, a negotiation to reduce conventional forces in Central Europe and thereby ease the NATO–Warsaw Pact confrontation, lasted about a dozen years without showing any tangible result. I did go and do the briefing and formed a rather positive impression of MBFR. Stan Resor scheduled several dinners for me to meet and talk with other ambassadors from NATO countries as well as Warsaw Pact representatives. I concluded that substantive progress was unlikely but that MBFR was an important place for useful East-West contacts to take place.

The SALT II era represented a difficult time in my personal life as well. In 1968 I married Clover Nicholas, but unfortunately our marriage did not survive and we separated in 1980. My daughter Eliza was born in 1970, my son Tommy in 1972, and my younger daughter Clover in 1975. Eliza, Tommy, and Clover were wonderful children and are outstanding young adults now. They have always supported my work even though it often involved long absences. It is my life's greatest honor and pleasure to be their father.

In 1983, I married Christine Coffey Ryan, a young widow and lawyer whose husband, Tom, had been tragically killed by a drunk driver when her children (Thomas, born in 1972, and Missy, born in 1975—nine days after Clover in the same hospital) were both very young, aged five and two, respectively. Christine has been a tower of strength for her children, and Thomas and Missy also are outstanding young adults now. It has been equally a great honor and enjoyment for me to be their stepfather, and they both have shared my interest in international issues. Marrying Christine was my great good fortune. I am a better person as a result; she has added so much to my appreciation of the world and to my personal happiness. Christine's parents, Dr. and Mrs. Coffey, as well as all of the Ryan family, have been most kind to me. Dr. Coffey was one of Washington's great medical figures, chairman of the Department of Surgery at Georgetown University Hospital for twenty-five years and always delightful to be with; Mrs. Coffey was a solid source of strength behind him, remaining so for the family after his death in January of 1995.

Clover's parents were people I cared greatly about as well. Her father, R. Carter Nicholas, was for a long time interested in arms control, specifically arms control verification. He was also great fun to be around. In January of 1975 he was in Florida, dying of cancer. Before I left for Geneva for the first time on January 29, 1975, I went to Florida two successive weekends to visit him. He died in February 1975, by which time I was heavily engaged in Geneva with the SALT II delegation. Mrs. Nicholas insisted that I should not come home for the funeral, knowing of Mr. Nicholas's interest in arms control and the work I was doing. I took her advice and remained in Geneva but I have always regretted it. I tried to learn from this mistake and to be there more for people in the future, and I hope that I have at least to some extent succeeded.

Back in Geneva it was getting hot and heavy. Ed Rowny kept proposing additions to the text that went beyond Vladivostok and were substantively the same as proposals that President Ford had explicitly rejected for consideration at Vladivostok. One example was a provision limiting the rate at which MIRV systems could be deployed that of course applied only to the Soviets, not to the United States—U.S. MIRV systems were now fully deployed. The debate raged on through the next week with Rowny receiving little delegation support but consuming so much time that Johnson began to doubt that he could send a delegation text to Washington by the late February objective. Meanwhile the Soviets had tabled their draft text on February 1, and it included unacceptable proposals such as bans on ALCMs and SLCMs, and on nuclear weapons systems deployed in third countries (read "U.S. tactical nuclear weapons in Europe").

Jack Mendelsohn and I had been reporting the imbroglio in Geneva daily to Roger Molander, the senior arms control specialist on the NSC staff in the Ford and Carter administrations. Roger suggested we put Rowny's proposals in a separate cable and send it to the "SALT Action Officer" at the U.S. Consulate in Calcutta, India, and send the Vladivostok-based draft text to Washington. Jack and I adopted Roger's idea (but not the Calcutta destination), modified it somewhat, and discussed it with Ambassador Johnson. The next day Ambassador Johnson said at the delegation meeting that Ed Rowny's ideas are so important that they should be highlighted in a separate cable so as to focus Washington's attention. So the delegation will send two cables, one containing Ed Rowny's proposals, and one containing the Vladivostok draft text. The delegation agreed on this and the cable containing the Rowny proposals was known forever afterwards, by some at least, as the "Calcutta Cable."

Ambassador Johnson asked that I return home and help shepherd the draft text through Washington. This I did, returning to Washington in late February. Almost immediately I attended a NSC-chaired meeting in the Old Executive Office Building. Jan Lodal, Roger Molander's boss and the senior NSC staff official in the arms control area (and later an important OSD official in the Clinton administration), was in the chair. It was a large meeting containing many OSD officials, including Jim Wade, a senior hard-line bureaucrat who sympathized with Rowny's position. Lodal announced that there would be a review of the two cables and because of the importance of the second cable (the Calcutta Cable), he wanted special attention paid to that.

So two groups will be formed, he said, a "senior" group to consider the second cable, and a few technical experts to consider the draft Vladivostok text.

The meetings lasted all day. The technical experts reviewing the draft Vladivostok text included Jim Timbie, a longtime, dedicated, and most resourceful public servant and specialist in the arms control field, who had joined ACDA in 1971 as a nuclear physicist. He moved to the State Department in the early 1980s, where he remained. For years he was and remains the special assistant to the undersecretary for international security affairs (now arms control and international security affairs) and the Cardinal Richelieu of arms control. The technical experts group was chaired by Roger Molander. I was in the Vladivostok text group as well. There were about six of us, including OSD and JCS representatives, reviewing the draft Vladivostok text provision by provision. We went all the way through it with only one small change suggested by JCS, which was accepted. Lodal had chaired the second meeting, and just as we finished our work on the draft text, a number of officials who had gone to the meeting on the second cable rushed in the door, saying that Lodal, after a long desultory discussion, had just thrown out the entire second cable on the grounds that it was contrary to President Ford's wishes (likely having received word that the Molander-chaired group had just completed its work). They demanded to know what was going on here. Molander replied, "Sorry, we just finished," and walked out. Thus, the Washington detailed review of the draft Vladivostok text and the Calcutta Cable was history. It was a bureaucratic tour de force.

But OSD was not finished yet. The decision on the Calcutta Cable was appealed to the full Verification Panel, the cabinet-level national security review group (a principals committee today) chaired by Kissinger. At issue was whether the draft text would go to Geneva as approved (with the one JCS change) or whether some of the items in the second cable could be considered. In attendance and seated at the table were the secretary of state, the director of central intelligence, the chairman of the Joint Chiefs, the director of ACDA, and Deputy Defense Secretary Bill Clements representing OSD. Clements was seated right next to Kissinger, who sat at one end as chairman. I attended as the delegation lawyer, seated in the second row. The meeting was in the White House Situation Room, a very small room. The meeting was scheduled for one hour. Precisely on the hour, Kissinger walked in and sat down. He said that the issue was whether the SALT II text would go to Geneva for tabling or whether additional OSD recommendations could be considered. He then turned to Clements and said, "Bill, I made a speech last week in Dallas and I am making another next week in Houston. Are there any differences between audiences in Dallas and audiences in Houston?" Clements was from Texas, and a future governor of that state.

There then ensued what seemed to be an approximately 59-minute, 45-second discussion between Clements and Kissinger on the differences between Dallas and Houston audiences. Nobody else said anything. At the end of this discussion, Kissinger looked at his watch and said, "Time is up, I guess we are all in agreement; the draft text goes to Geneva as is." Then he stood up and walked out, end of discussion. The next day we were preparing the cable approving the text with the one change for transmission to Geneva when Bill Hyland, Kissinger's deputy, walked in. He said that there had to be some changes. They did not want to be vulnerable to an attack by Senator Jackson. So he inserted, on NSC authority alone, some extreme verification counting rules into the cable to be added to the text in Geneva. These additional provisions offended the Soviets, accomplished nothing, and could not be removed until the Carter administration arrived two years later. One can only speculate where they came from. But in the end, they did not confuse the text significantly or damage the negotiations, as some of the Calcutta Cable provisions might have. With the one JCS change and the Hyland provisions, the cable approving the draft Vladivostok text was sent to Geneva. The U.S.-proposed draft treaty was tabled in Geneva in the first week of March 1975. All in all, even with the Hyland additions, a brilliant performance by Kissinger, Lodal, and Molander.

I returned to Geneva shortly after the cable was sent. The two delegations formed a subgroup called the Drafting Group to work on the text, while the plenary sessions continued to debate the big issues. On the U.S. side, the Drafting Group was chaired by Boris Klosson with Ralph Earle as number two. I was on it as the delegation legal advisor and there were three other U.S. members, OSD and JCS representatives and an interpreter. The Soviets had a similar line-up, with Victor Karpov in the chair and Victor Smolin, a SALT I veteran with Karpov, as number two. As with the full delegation meetings, our sessions alternated between the U.S. Mission and the Soviet Mission. The U.S. delegation offices were on floors four to seven of the Botanic Building, formerly the offices of the Fund of Funds led by Bernie Cornfeld, which was looted by the international criminal Robert Vesco and went bankrupt—the building being then purchased by the U.S. government. Seven was the top floor of the Botanic Building. On this floor was our meeting room; perhaps once it was Robert Vesco's office. The U.S. trade representative had offices on the second and third floors. On the first floor was a lamp store named Zonka—with many electric lamps on display, but never any customers. I was assured by someone who should have known that it was not "ours," but that it was nothing to worry about—perhaps it was a Swiss government facility. Once during SALT II in the Carter years a call came from Secretary of State Vance for Ralph Earle, then chairman of the delegation, at about 11:00 P.M. Geneva time. The marine on duty referred the call to the executive secretary of the delegation, Norman Clyne, at his apartment. Ralph Earle was nowhere to be found; he was not in his apartment and the secretary of state wanted to speak with him. In desperation Norm called the Swiss police. Within ten minutes they called back and said that Ambassador Earle was at the Bat-a-Clan nightclub, table four. The Swiss carefully protect their neutrality.

In September 1975, when I was on my way back to SALT II, Hal Sonnefeldt, then State Department counselor to Henry Kissinger, asked me to come see him in his office, where he asked me to call him with regular reports on SALT II. But he said to use the open commercial line; too many people at the Pentagon have access to the recording of secure-line conversations, so in a way the open line is more secure. One has to learn the ropes, which are not always obvious.

The Drafting Group set as its objective the creation of a joint draft text—a joint document with English and Russian translations showing both sides' positions. Where there was agreement, the text would be unencumbered, and where there were differences in the English version, the U.S.-proposed language would be in brackets with the number 1 after it, and the Soviet proposed language would follow in brackets with the number 2 after it—the reverse in the Russian version. Sometimes the bracketed texts were long, encompassing a whole article where there was little convergence, and sometimes short, where the texts were beginning to come together.

The two sides in the Drafting Group met frequently between mid-March and May 7, when the negotiating session ended. They quickly approved the title "Agreement on the Limitation of Strategic Offensive Arms," a few preambular provisions, and, as in the ABM Treaty, verfication by national technical means. But there was agreement on little else. Much mechanical work was done piecing the two draft texts together. The SALT II Joint Draft Text formally was born on May 7, 1975, and went through many more versions until the completion of the negotiations in June of 1979. My daughter Clover was born on June 20, 1975, before we returned for our next session. "Baby Clover" became linked in the minds of the two sides with the progress of the SALT II Joint Draft Text. Smolin would say at a meeting, "How old is Baby Clover?" I would reply, "Two years." "Oh," he would say, "that means that we have been working on this Joint Draft Text for two years and we still have so much left to do."

The negotiations continued during 1975. Off and on I spent seven months that year in Geneva, the most time I ever spent abroad in one year. Agreement always seemed possible, but always elusive. We ground out an agreed text on Vladivostok matters, such as 2,400 ICBM and SLBM launchers. We also had useful discussions on issues which could not be resolved. For example, as I said previously, it turned out that the Soviets had interpreted the silo dimension provision to permit a 15 percent increase in both depth and diameter, thus permitting an increase in silo volume of over 52 percent. The U.S. interpretation was one dimension or a combination of both, adding up to 15 percent. The maximum volumetric increase under this interpretation was 32 percent.

In October of 1975, a thirty-five-nation Summit meeting took place in Helsinki, Finland, to sign the Helsinki Final Act. It had been under negotiation for three years and represented a long-sought Soviet goal of ratification of the post–World War II borders in Europe, providing that they could only be changed by peaceful means. But the Helsinki Final Act also contained the seeds of the destruction of the Soviet Union in its extensive human rights provisions. On the margins of Helsinki, Kissinger and Soviet Foreign Minister Andrei Gromyko held a SALT II meeting. Jan Lodal came through Geneva afterwards to report to us on it: the two had had an extensive discussion of the major issues with no immediate progress. Also, considerable time was spent on the silo dimension issue to no avail. "Neither one seemed to understand high school geometry," Lodal said. In the end, in 1976, during the discussions on missile throw-weight, the old silo dimension provision was dropped and a straight limitation on ICBM silo volume increase of 32 percent was agreed to and put in the text.

Peripheral matters were gradually agreed to. One such matter was the seabed provision, which Dick Creecy and I had worked on back in 1971. It had been tabled at SALT I but not included in the Interim Agreement. There was now a desire to include it in SALT II. The Seabed Arms Control Treaty, signed in 1972, banned nuclear weapons on the seabed under international waters beyond the twelve-mile territorial sea limit. As I have mentioned, the objective of this SALT provision was to extend the ban to the internal waters (e.g., coastal waters, lakes, and rivers) of the United States and the Soviet Union. In the summer of 1975 we quickly agreed on the substance but hit a snag in agreeing on unbracketed language for the Joint Draft Text. For some obscure reason, Washington instructed us to insist on the "bottoms" of internal waters, while the Soviets wanted to use "beds," as in the Seabed Treaty. A two-week wrangle ensued at the end of which the Soviets finally gave in and agreed to "bottoms." As we triumphantly reported our success in the Drafting Group to the full delegation, Mike May responded in horror, "I have just received a back-channel communication from OSD. The plan now is to base the MX missile in large concrete pools, like swimming pools, in the western United States (to protect it from counterforce attack). If you use 'bottoms' in this provision, you will ban MX, so you have to go back to 'beds.'"

With heavy hearts we returned to the Drafting Group the next day. Boris Klosson opened the discussion by saying to Karpov across the table, "We have reconsidered and now see the wisdom of the Soviet proposal; we want to use 'beds' instead of 'bottoms.'" Karpov regarded him very suspiciously and said, "Why do you want to do this?" "Because," said Klosson, "when we took the agreement back to our chief yesterday he could not understand whose bottom we were referring to." "Ho, ho, ho," replied Karpov, "we agree." An example of how humor can get you everywhere. The text was thus coming together as a result of the Drafting Group work by the end of 1975, but the major issues separating the sides remained unresolved: the Backfire bomber, cruise missile verification, and agreed data, or, in SALT terminology, an agreed database. The stage was set for one last effort by Ford and Kissinger in early 1976 to conclude a SALT II agreement during the Ford presidency.

Dick Creecy, who had been serving as the executive secretary of the SALT II delegation since mid-1974, decided to leave the delegation at the end of 1975. Ed Rowny always had first-class people working for him in Geneva, for example, Majors Sergei Chernay and Nick Minovitz, his interpreters. Another example was his chief staff assistant, Army Colonel Norman Clyne. Norm indicated to me that he would be interested in being Dick's replacement. I discussed this with Jack Mendelsohn, who strongly supported the idea, so I recommended Norm to Alex Johnson. He agreed and promptly offered Norm the job. Norm took over in January 1976, beginning a long and most distinguished career as executive secretary to delegations and ACDA directors. He was a "can-do" type of official, and he made a great contribution to arms control. He was executive secretary of the SALT II and INF delegations, executive secretary of ACDA under Directors Seignious and Earle, and special assistant to Ambassador Nitze when he was the special advisor to the secretary of state. One of his greatest gifts was for vigorous language, about which the stories are legion.

Richard Perle was a student of the conservative national security analyst Alfred Wöhlstetter and a longtime aide to Senator Henry Jackson. In the Reagan administration he served as assistant secretary of defense under Secretary Weinberger. To me he is one of the best examples of the adage that "the man makes the job," rather than the other way around. His job positions on paper were never exalted but he always had enormous influence. I do not think that I ever agreed with him on anything, but I always respected him as an individual of great ability. He commented in London in the mid-1980s on a long pro-arms control speech by the British foreign secretary, "this demonstrates that length is not strength." Reportedly, he is the author of the famous line in a Weinberger memorandum to President Reagan in 1986 describing the SCC as an "Orwellian memory hole into which today's concerns are brushed like yesterday's trash." Truly eloquent, bordering on the literary, which is unheard of in bureaucratic documents. Frank Gaffney was his aide in the Pentagon, and Frank went on to an influential career out of government as an effective organizer of conservative opinion, particularly on the Hill, and a frequent opponent of arms control agreements. Frank once introduced me to someone at an Embassy party shortly after introducing Richard Perle to the same person (Richard was sometimes referred to by admiring opponents as the "Black Prince of Arms Control" or the

"Prince of Darkness"—he claimed that this latter sobriquet was intended to apply to Robert Novak of *Evans and Novak* but the title stuck): "I just introduced you to the Black Prince, now I would like to introduce you to one of the White Princes."

John Lehman, Richard Perle's friend and colleague, became ACDA deputy director early in 1975 at Fred Ikle's urging after Kissinger became secretary of state. Like Perle and Gaffney, he was no particular friend of arms control. Lehman's coming to ACDA nevertheless did strengthen the agency when it really needed help—ACDA still was not long past the 1973 downgrading. Lehman was a very effective operator with a great sense of humor. In the Reagan administration, he subsequently spent a number of years as secretary of the Navy. In 1975, he had a tumultuous confirmation proceeding before the Senate Foreign Relations Committee. Senator Stuart Symington from Missouri, in particular, was out to get him, but he survived after several hearings. My best memory of John was in 1976 when Jim Malone came back from John's office saying that John had just written a piece about the beginning of Soviet SS-20 deployments, which he showed to me: "I am going to run it over to the offices of Evans and Novak so that they can print it," he said. And the next day it was printed virtually verbatim.

One of the most important issues during 1975 and 1976 at SALT II was the question of the definition of a heavy ICBM. At SALT I the United States had made a unilateral statement that any missile with a volume greater than the Soviet SS-11 missile was a heavy ICBM, and therefore subject to the relevant limitations. The Soviets, knowing of the advent of the SS-19, had explicitly rejected this statement. Despite the fact that there was no agreement, Kissinger touted it to the Congress in 1972 as an important constraint. Some measurement that could limit missile capability growth was essential for SALT II. The SS-19, with six MIRVs, was now replacing the SS-11 with triple its throw-weight, and another new light ICBM, the SS-17 (with four MIRVs), which was also replacing the SS-11, had substantially more throw-weight as well. And the SS-18, with ten MIRVs and twice the throw-weight, was replacing the SS-9.

The United States decided to attempt a comprehensive solution to this problem. Missiles would be defined in terms of their weight at the time of launch, "launch-weight," and what they could deliver on target, "throw-weight." The SS-19 would be the largest light ICBM permitted, and the SS-18 would be the largest heavy ICBM permitted. A heavy ICBM would be any missile with a launch-weight and throw-weight greater than the SS-19. Any missile with a launch-weight or throw-weight greater than the SS-18 would be prohibited. Eventually, after much effort and many discussions, the Soviet Union would agree to this by the end of 1976, with the entire year's work at Geneva largely focused on this issue. It would be the last contribution of the Ford administration and of Henry Kissinger to strategic arms control.

In January 1976, the Ford administration made its final effort to convert the Vladivostok Understanding into a treaty. Of course, President Ford was running for election, and the rumor was later that Chief of Staff Donald Rumsfeld had advised Ford to drop Vice President Rockefeller to forestall Ronald Reagan from running against him in the primaries and to go slowly on SALT II in order to maximize his election chances, two consistent pieces of advice. Allegedly, in December 1976, Hamilton Jordan, Governor Carter's aide, said to Ford that "the only thing that would have beaten us was a SALT agreement." And if Rockefeller had been on the ticket Ford would likely have won, as he would have carried the state of New York. So the White House atmosphere was not ideal for success at SALT II even though Ford very much wanted it. In addition, Fred Ikle, in league with then Army Chief of Staff General Meyer (but not the other chiefs), went to see Ford to inform him that he could not support a SALT agreement on the terms that were emerging. All of this made Kissinger's January trip to Moscow to talk SALT with Brezhnev and Gromyko an exercise in futility as far as completion of the negotiations were concerned, but they did reach agreement in principle that missiles would be defined in terms of launch-weight and throw-weight in the SALT agreement.

As noted, the entire year of 1976 was taken up with converting this agreement in principle to unbracketed language for the Joint Draft Text. George Schneitter, an outstandingly capable OSD official, came out from Washington in February with the idea of conducting a seminar on the subject of what the concepts of throw-weight and launch-weight meant. All through 1975, whenever the opportunity arose, the U.S. delegation had said that we needed a definition of a heavy ICBM. Now was the opportunity to accomplish this objective. Schneitter did conduct his seminar in the Drafting Group during many meetings in late winter and early spring of 1976. It was useful for the Americans who were fuzzy on these concepts, and essential for the Soviets, who did not understand them at all. For example, early on it was agreed in the context of the seminars that the exit shroud of an ICBM (the covering enabling it to exit the atmosphere at the beginning of its trajectory but which was jettisoned before mid-course) would not be included in throw-weight, since it did not reach the target—but it would be included in launch-weight.

One day in the summer of 1976, Boris Klosson, in the chair of the Drafting Group for the United States, was discussing a possible definition of launch-weight. "It is the weight of the fully loaded missile at the time of launch, free of anything attached to it, free of anything attached to it," he repeated for emphasis. Karpov, without waiting for the interpretation, immediately responded in English rather than Russian: "But I thought in America there was no such thing as a free launch." Karpov could be brilliant. He was enormously capable, understood the issues better than anyone on the Soviet side, and could always be relied upon to deliver once he made a commitment. Unfortunately, he had a sort of super-Russian love of drink, particularly Jack Daniels whiskey. Another memorable day in the Drafting Group was October 9, 1976, Karpov's birthday (and mine as well). We decided to bring a fifth of Jack Daniels to the Drafting Group meeting that morning as a present to Karpov. Victor was delighted. He opened the bottle, took a tall highball glass (used for water) off the table, filled it to the top with Jack Daniels, and drank it down as though it *was* water. He then sat down to chair the meeting on the Soviet side. It was one of the most productive meetings we had that fall.

Norm Clyne's opposite number, Vadim Chulitsky, the executive secretary of the Soviet delegation, was an impressive man who had spent many years on the delegation and who was also the deputy commissioner of the Soviet SCC delegation, which usually held its meetings while the SALT negotiations were in session. He said on one occasion: "Once you get on the Soviet SALT delegation, you never get off." In all my years in Geneva it was noteworthy to me that I almost never saw a non-Russian on their delegation, and never a woman other than an interpreter. Interestingly, the U.S. delegation had women in substantive positions, and the Soviets never quite knew how to deal with them. Chulitsky also would describe to us the horror of Stalin's times, when everyone feared the knock on the door in the middle of the night. He also said to me in an informal discussion when I was complaining about Soviet obduracy, "You Americans do not understand. If one of us displeases his superior, not only does he lose his job but his wife loses hers, he loses his apartment, his car, and his children are dismissed from school. Naturally, people are very careful."

I will say on behalf of the Soviets that they always seemed to have specific objectives at SALT that rarely changed, and that they tried to work toward gradually. They would hold to the same position for a very long time (Ambassador Semenov, not an expert in American slang, would often close his statements in 1975 by saying that the Soviets would give the American proposal "the attention it deserves"—until he was advised to stop that, probably by Karpov), and then they would make a sudden major change. By contrast, the United States was constantly changing its position and its objectives. A decision at the top in the interagency process in Washington was rarely a decision; usually it was the signal to begin the effort to circumvent the decision. There was the famous incident in 1970, recounted earlier, at SALT I in Geneva when the Soviets were told that the United States could agree to zero ABM, one site for each side, or two for each side. Another syndrome was for issues to switch sides. In 1967 at the Glassboro Summit, the United States was arguing for an ABM-only arrangement and the Soviets were arguing for limits on offense. In 1971 at SALT I, the positions were reversed.

It was the practice at SALT for the U.S. CIA representative to be under what was called "light cover." He would be listed on the U.S. delegation as being from the Department of State. This fooled no one, but it kept up appearances. In early January 1976, Howie Stoertz left the U.S. delegation after nearly seven years. Norm Clyne informed Chulitsky that the U.S. delegation would have a new member, Mr. John Whitman, at the next meeting. Chulitsky asked, "What agency is he from?" Norm replied, "State." "And whom is he replacing," Chulitsky asked. "Mr. Howard Stoertz," Norm said. "Oh, that wing of the State Department," Chulitsky rejoined.

In 1975, a very unpleasant man representing the KGB joined the Soviet delegation. The word was that he was a ruthless official who years before had interrogated the American RB-47 pilots shot down over the northwestern border of the Soviet Union. This incident involved an American reconnaissance plane alleged by the Soviets to be overflying Soviet territory in the northwest region of that country in 1960. Soviet fighters scrambled to intercept and shoot down the plane, and there were reports that captured crew members were subsequently treated roughly by their Soviet interrogators. Army Colonel Charles Fitzgerald, a brilliant Russian linguist, for many years a fixture of the U.S. SALT and SCC delegations, and a man who got more information out of the Soviets than anyone I ever met—he could empathize with them—let drop with one of the Soviets that the U.S. delegation understood that this official, named Finagin, was the son of Irish revolutionaries who had emigrated to the Soviet Union years ago. And wasn't that interesting? Finagin was gone in three days and afterwards there were occasional thankful hints from Soviet delegates. Another interesting member of the Soviet delegation was Victor Smolin, Karpov's deputy on the Drafting Group. A veteran of SALT I, he was a master with words, both in Russian and English, and although not legally trained, evolved into the lawyer for the Soviets in SALT II. For many years he was my opposite number and I liked him very much and respected his abilities, which were first-rate.

So the negotiations ground to a halt in October 1976, with the throw-weight/launch-weight delineations agreed upon but little else. One of the problems in agreeing on this had been terminology but that had been surmounted. For example, the Russians had no term for what the United States called the MIRV "bus," the device that carries the warheads and releases them beyond the atmosphere onto the correct trajectories. The Russians therefore invented the term "self-contained dispensing mechanism," which could be understandably translated into Russian to substitute for "bus." Throw-weight was thus the weight of the re-entry vehicles and the self-contained dispensing mechanism, and a Common Understanding associated with the definition of throw-weight made clear that what was referred to in the text as a "self-contained dispensing mechanism" corresponded to the U.S. term "bus."

Ambassador Johnson submitted a long report to President Ford in December 1976, which set forth the remaining major unresolved issues (Backfire, cruise missiles, verification and data) and attached a copy of the latest agreed Joint Draft Text. Also in December, Jim Malone was appointed ambassador to the Conference on Disarmament, a recess appointment to last until early 1977. Thus I became acting general counsel of ACDA on December 6. With President Ford having lost the election, all awaited the advent of the Carter administration.

CHAPTER FIVE **SALT II, PART TWO: THE CARTER YEARS**

The Carter administration took office on January 20, 1977. Since December 6, I had been acting general counsel of ACDA. Early on, President Carter selected Paul Warnke as director of ACDA, and at Warnke's insistence he was given a "second hat" as chief SALT negotiator. Walter Slocombe, a prominent member of the transition team in the national security area, came to see Alex Johnson and informed him that his report was appreciated and that he was summarily dismissed. Warnke, since he was being given two jobs, needed deputies both in Washington and in Geneva. For ACDA deputy director he chose Spurgeon Keeny, dismissed as assistant ACDA director with considerable vehemence by Kissinger in the 1973 purge. For his SALT II deputy, he chose Ralph Earle, who in 1973 had been brought as an ACDA representative on the delegation by Fred Ikle. Ralph had also been Warnke's deputy in 1968 when he was assistant secretary of defense for international security policy. Immediately the Carter team attempted to fashion a new SALT II policy. Zbigniew Brzezinski, the new national security advisor in the White House, wanted to move as close to Senator Jackson as possible. Accordingly, as the new proposal was being developed in February 1977, liaison with Richard Perle was maintained and many of his ideas found their way into the proposal that was presented to the Soviets in March at Moscow by Secretary of State Cyrus Vance.

In March Vance led a delegation to Moscow to meet with the Soviet leadership for the first time. The principal objective of this trip was to present the new SALT II proposal. Warnke, representing ACDA, was part of the delegation and looked forward to negotiations with the Soviets. The proposal fashioned by the White House in coordination with Richard Perle and Senator Jackson represented a significant departure from the Ford-Kissinger policy. It took direct aim at the Soviet monopoly in heavy MIRVed ICBMs, and generally at MIRVed land-based ICBMs. It leaked in Washington before the arrival of the delegation in Moscow and, of course, given its assault on the strategic strength of the Soviet

At White Sulfur Springs, West
Virginia, with my parents in 1942.

At the pyramids in 1956.

Return to the pyramids
in February 2000.

My hero, my father,
conferring a Louisville
civic award on my other
hero, Jackie Robinson,
in 1950.

Penn vs. Princeton, 1954. My
only picture in a race. Too
bad I was hitting the hurdle,
but I did finish second.

Summer vacation with
my parents, ca. 1954.

Visiting my cousin Mel
Laird in the Secretary of
Defense's office, with my
mother, in 1969.

ACDA senior staff with
Director Warnke in 1977.

SALT II negotiations in 1978.
Ambassador Earle in the chair, with
Ambassador Herb Okun to his left,
Dr. Gerald Johnson to my right and
Captain Ted Kramer.

Initialing of SALT II.

The 1980 NPT Review
Conference with Ambassador
Charles Floweree and
Ambassador Charles Van Doren.

Receiving my first government
award, the ACDA Silver Medal,
in 1979, with my daughter Eliza.

To Tom Graham
With best wishes,

Ronald Reagan

In the Roosevelt Room in the White House
after the successful effort to lift legislative
constraints to the Peacekeeper missile program.

McFarlane, Adelman, Nitze, Rowny, ACDA official Thomas Graham, Perle: Despite some deep differences, peace prevailed—for now

Shultz's Shaky Team

Newsweek

JANUARY 21, 1985

Can the harmony last once the bargaining begins?

At the Shultz-Gromyko meeting in Geneva that restarted arms control negotiations.

With Secretary Shultz as he signs papers sending the INF Treaty to the Senate.

Senior members of the U.S. CFE delegation with President Bush (Ambassador Woolsey is to his left; I am to his right).

Receiving a State Department award given to members of the START II delegation by Secretary Eagleberger (Ambassador Frank Wisner looking on).

Signing START II in the
Kremlin, January 1993.

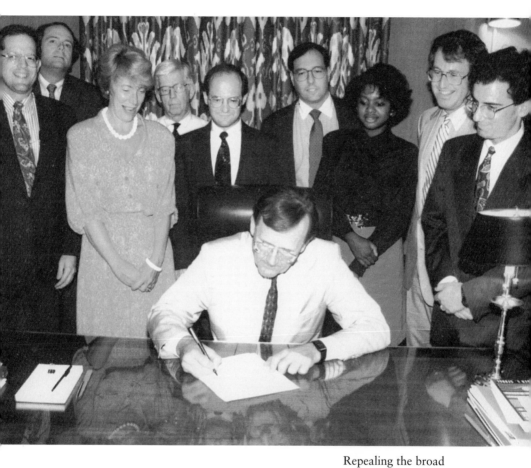

Repealing the broad
interpretation as acting
director. *From left:* Bernie
Seward, Dave Webster,
Mary Lib Hoinkes, Fred
Smith, Marshall Brown,
Rick Magnus, Bonnie
Jenkins, Dave Koplow, and
Steve Soloman.

With Harvard classmates at my sixtieth birthday celebration, October 9, 1993.
From left: George Daly, Larry Silverman, Al Purrington, Jerry Stern, and myself.

My swearing in as ambassador by
John Holum; Christine looks on.

The Washington Post

FRIDAY, APRIL 14, 1995   B

RETHINKING THE BOMB
Last of Six Articles

Next week, representatives of more than 170 nations will gather in New York to decide whether to renew the Nuclear Non-Proliferation Treaty, the world's most important statement about the control of nuclear weapons.

Arms control specialist Tom Graham worked hard to change U.S. policy to help win indefinite extension of the nuclear Non-Proliferation Treaty.

Mexico's Miguel Marin-Bosch wants to hold the United States and the other four nuclear powers to the letter of their NPT pledges.

A Hard Sell for Treaty Renewal

U.S. Campaign for Indefinite Extension Met With Skepticism

By David B. Ottaway and Steve Coll
Washington Post Staff Writers

Last May 19, President Clinton and P.V. Narasimha Rao, India's prime minister, concluded talks in Washington with a formal statement that attracted little attention—except in the office of Tom Graham, the administration's chief lobbyist for winning extension of the nuclear Non-Proliferation Treaty.

One sentence caught Graham's eye. It said the two countries "offered their strong support" for efforts to prevent the spread of nuclear weapons—"with the goal of elimination of such weapons."

Eliminating nuclear weapons was not something that U.S. presidents talked about publicly, even in this vague way. During the Cold War, when the United States and the Soviet Union had tens of thousands of nuclear missiles aimed at each other, it was hardly worth considering. Now, though, the Cold War was over, and the NPT was coming up for renewal. Graham seized on Clinton's statement as he sought to line up votes for indefinite extension of the 25-year-old treaty.

Last summer and fall, Graham traveled to more than 40 countries on nearly every continent. In meetings with diplomats, he repeatedly cited Clinton's statement as evidence of U.S. commitment to one of the treaty's central provisions: that the world's five nuclear powers would work toward the elimination of all nuclear weapons, including their own.

Back in Washington, diplomats read Graham's ca-
See NUCLEAR, A26, Col. 1

Washington Post front page immediately before the 1995 NPT Review and Extension Conference.

On the floor of the 1995 Review and Extension
Conference. *From left:* Mary Lib Hoinkes,
Larry Scheinman, myself, Ambassador Steve
Ledogar, Ambassador Ralph Earle, and
Ambassador Madeleine K. Albright.

With the First Lady of Ghana
at a presentation in Chicago
during the summer of 1995.

Last minute negotiations
on an Iranian objection to
the Middle East resolution,
May 1995.

Meeting with Indian
Foreign Minister Jaswant
Singh in New York, 1998.

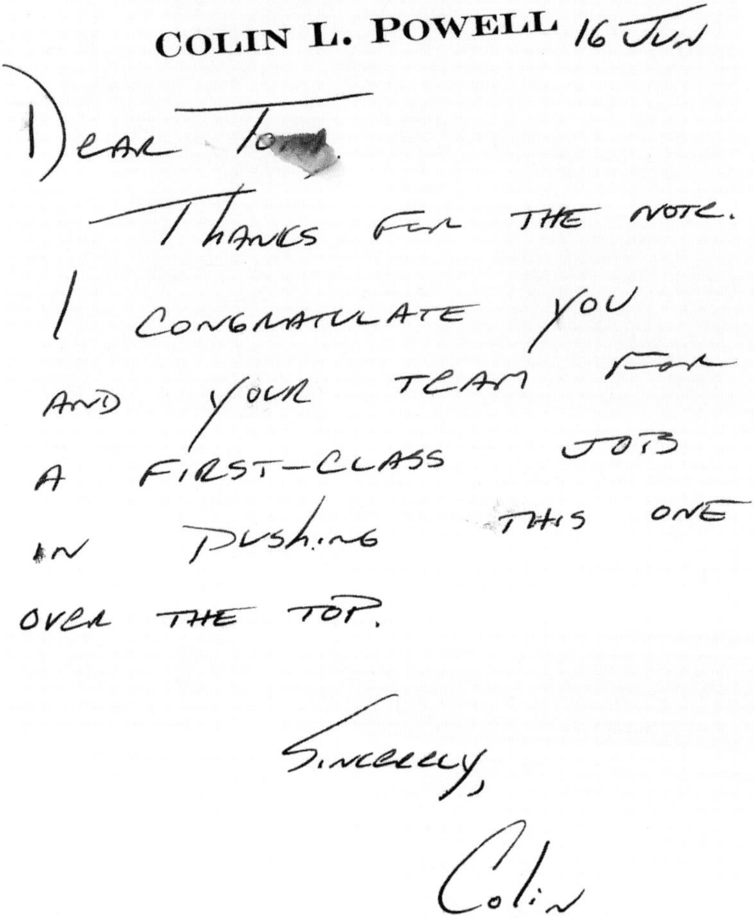

COLIN L. POWELL 16 Jun

Dear Tom,

Thanks for the note.
I congratulate you
and your team for
a first-class job
in pushing this one
over the top.

Sincerely,

Colin

Note from General Colin
Powell after the successful
1995 NPT Review and
Extension Conference.

Receiving the Trainor Award
for Excellence in the Pursuit
of Diplomacy from
Georgetown University, along
with Ambassador Jayantha
Dhanapala by Casimir Yost,
in October 1995.

At Sandia National Laboratory,
Albuquerque, New Mexico, in
April 1997. *From left:*
Ambassador Enrique Roman-
Morey (Secretary-General,
OPANAL), Ambassador Kamal
of Pakistan, Sandia President
Ambassador Paul Robinson,
Ambassador Sha Zukang of
China, and myself.

LAWS giving its annual Averell
Harriman Award to General Lee
Butler, 1998. From left: Pierce
Brosnan, Michael Donlan (head
of the LAWS Massachusetts
chapter), Butler, LAWS
Chairman Mark Schlefer, and
myself.

With Ms. Leonor Tomero of LAWS and
members of the Foreign Affairs Committee
of the British House of Commons in the fall
of 1998.

Meeting with Senator Alan Cranston and
South Korean President Kim Dae Jung,
1998. *From left:* Alex Slesar (LAWS director
of administration), Elizabeth Rindskopf,
myself, Cranston, Kim.

Meeting with Mikhail Gorbachev in Moscow, in the fall of 2001. *From left:* Damien La Vera, Robert McNamara, Gorbachev, and myself. Reviewing the past, looking to the future.

Cartoon by Signe Wilkinson given to me after a speech in Philadelphia in the spring of 2000.

On the top of Villarica
volcano in Southern Chile in
April 1995, with Christine,
after the OPANAL Conference.

After Missy's graduation
from Georgetown in
May 1998.

Union (MIRVed ICBMs), was summarily rejected, temporarily derailing the SALT II negotiations. Few at ACDA, including Warnke, were surprised at this. Its fundamental tenets were quickly abandoned by the Carter administration, but it did form the intellectual basis for the United States' approach during the START negotiations in the 1980s, and its objectives were largely incorporated in the START I and START II Treaties.

Since we had worked together on the Drafting Group in Geneva in 1975 and 1976, Ralph Earle recommended to Paul Warnke that he make my appointment as ACDA general counsel permanent. Paul said something about me being a Republican and Ralph replied that not all Republicans were bad. Ralph and I had become friends in Geneva. One act of kindness I will always remember occurred in December 1975. In the middle of one night, several distraught phone calls came through from Washington to the effect that little Clover, at the age of six months, had fallen off her changing table and fractured her skull. Extremely upset, I mentioned this to Ralph the next morning in his office. He motioned for me to sit down and explained how two of his children had had major skull operations, one at two weeks and one at two years. Both were now grown and were fine. "Babies' skulls are designed to be flexible, that is to enhance their ability to survive—don't worry." This calmed me somewhat and his advice was certainly good. Two weeks later, on December 24, after I returned home, Clover was given an EEG at Washington Children's Hospital, and all was fine.

Stan Resor, who was retained as MBFR negotiator by the Carter administration, also supported me and on April 6, 1977, Paul formally appointed me ACDA general counsel. George Bunn, the first ACDA general counsel, provided for a general counsel when he drafted the ACDA statute, but it was not included among the presidential appointments to be confirmed by the Senate. Thus, while the position of general counsel at ACDA was political—the ACDA general counsel served at the pleasure of the director—it did not require confirmation and one could serve as a career official in that position, which I did beginning in 1979 when the Senior Executive Service was established. This meant that I did not have to automatically resign when administrations changed—of course, I could be reassigned by the director. Further, this enabled me to serve as ACDA general counsel from 1977 to 1993 (with a hiatus from September 1981 to September 1983) in the Carter, Reagan, and Bush administrations and to be in place and able to serve as ACDA acting director in January 1993.

Paul Warnke's double confirmation as ACDA director and SALT negotiator proved to be very controversial, and was remembered for years afterward. The confirmation had joint management. There was a group working out of Paul's law office at Clifford and Warnke, which featured most prominently Tom Scoville, the son of Pete Scoville, a prominent former government official who had served as an ACDA assistant director in the 1960s. I was asked to head the government part of the effort by Doug Bennett, the new assistant secretary of state for congressional affairs. The final result was a decisive vote for ACDA director, 70–29, but the vote for SALT negotiator was only 58–41—thus the opponents were able to put down a marker that they had more than a blocking one-third vote in the Senate to stop SALT II.

Two mistakes were made with the Warnke nomination right at the beginning. First, Paul was not sent up to the Senate with the other cabinet and major sub-cabinet officials—his nomination did not go forward until February 8—thus he could be isolated. Second, two nominations rather than one were sent, thus permitting two votes. He could have been nominated to be ACDA director with his nomination papers stating that he was also to serve as SALT II negotiator with the rank of ambassador, thereby permitting only one vote. The two votes enabled the opponents to target SALT II directly and to claim that Paul's allegedly liberal views on arms control were acceptable for ACDA director but not to negotiate America's national security. Also, it permitted some senators, particularly conservative Democrats, to vote both ways.

The opposition to Warnke began suddenly during his confirmation testimony before the Senate Foreign Relations Committee. This opposition came in part from Paul Nitze, who was called in by the committee to comment on Warnke's testimony. I had a hand in Warnke's opening statement and tried to persuade him to back away somewhat from previous positions on weapon systems, for example, those expressed in the article on the U.S.–Soviet arms race "Apes on a Treadmill" in the spring 1975 issue of *Foreign Affairs*. Warnke was willing to include in his opening statement more conservative and centrist views on weapon systems, but he wanted to argue that these views were consistent with his past views. I argued that the better course would be to admit that they were different and say that one's views naturally changed upon coming into government from those expressed as a private citizen interested in arms control progress, but my argument did not prevail. A principal tenet of the subsequent attack on Warnke was that he was not being honest with respect to his views.

The rumor was that both Paul Warnke and Paul Nitze, among others, had been summoned to Plains, Georgia, during the summer of 1976 to talk with presidential candidate Carter about strategic policy. The rumor continued that Paul Nitze bored Carter at one of these sessions with a long lecture on Soviet throw-weight superiority and that this was the reason that president-elect Carter did not offer Nitze a position in his administration. Also, the rumor went, Warnke and Nitze had been close friends in the 1960s but had a severe falling-out in 1968 over Vietnam and related issues when Warnke, as assistant secretary, had aligned himself more with newly arrived Defense Secretary Clark Clifford than with his deputy, Paul Nitze. My guess is that the relationship was far more complicated than that and that both men in 1977 were expressing their honest—if somewhat defensive or frustrated—views. It was a tragic story; these two former friends and brilliant contributors to

United States national security ceased speaking to one another altogether as a result of the Warnke confirmation battle, and bitterness remained more than twenty years later. It was difficult for me. Paul Warnke formally appointed me ACDA general counsel, and I admired him (sadly he died in late 2001), whereas I worked extremely closely with Paul Nitze in the 1980s and came to regard him as one of the truly great men of the post–World War II era.

Initially, Nitze opposed Warnke only as SALT negotiator, not as ACDA director, but during the process his opposition developed its own dynamic, and he broadened his opposition to Warnke to include ACDA director. Former JCS Chairman Moorer joined the fray in the subsequent hearings before the Senate Armed Services Committee, but he opposed Warnke only as SALT negotiator, saying that an arms control advocate could be ACDA director but as negotiator the Soviets might use his public positions on various weapon systems against him.

Senator Jackson and Richard Perle seized on this controversy to turn the Warnke nomination into a full-scale debate on strategic policy, as well as a referendum on SALT II. They organized a series of hearings before the Senate Armed Services Committee in late February—unprecedented before or since for a nomination such as this. At the first hearing before the committee, Warnke testified for several hours in much the same manner as he had testified before the Foreign Relations Committee, essentially following the direction of his opening statement. His testimony was followed by that of Nitze and Moorer. Nitze opposed Warnke for both jobs, saying he was not honest as to his views, was always opposed to new weapon systems—such as the B-1 bomber, the F-14, the Trident submarine, and the M-1 army tank—always wanted to reduce the defense budget further, and implicitly was willing to concede strategic superiority to the Soviet Union. That these assertions were untrue or at best misinterpretations goes without saying, but there was a full-scale strategic debate now raging. Warnke had been critical of a number of weapons-system decisions in the past, and there was a real philosophical difference between the two men. However, both men were effective supporters of U.S. national security and world peace and stability as they saw it; it was the questions by the senators on both sides that forced the debate to become ever more polarized. A valid debate over philosophy degenerated into an *ad hominem* controversy over specifics. Senator McIntyre of New Hampshire even pressured Nitze into saying that he did in fact impugn Warnke's character as an American.

In the first part of February, I was called by Doug Bennet and asked to prepare a rebuttal of Nitze's February 8 testimony before the Senate Foreign Relations Committee, to be sent to the vice president. My office purchased a copy of the unedited transcript from the transcribing company, set to work, and in a few days we prepared a vigorous rebuttal of the Nitze testimony based on the unedited transcript, which did have a few errors in it. Nevertheless, what was produced was a comprehensive but fair adversary brief, which in part, however, made Nitze look a bit like an unguided missile. A copy was sent to the vice president's office on February 14 and copies were made available to Senators Culver and Cranston shortly thereafter. Senator Culver shared the paper with Senators Bumpers, Anderson, and Hart.

The paper was intended as an adversary brief to prepare senators for debate, and not at all for public dissemination. However, somehow Richard Perle obtained a copy, shared it with Paul Nitze, and it surfaced publicly at the Senate Armed Services Committee hearing on February 28, at which Nitze testified. Nitze was outraged, claiming that he had been denied access to the transcript and thus had no chance to correct it. He blamed Bill Ashworth, the senior arms control staffer of Foreign Relations for this and some days later a version of the transcript with Nitze's corrections did appear. Nitze insisted that the adversary memorandum be inserted in the Armed Services Committee record, which it was, but the majority staff did not include Nitze's comments penned on a copy of the document, claiming that they could not read them. Senator Cannon, a Warnke opponent and Jackson follower, said that he was shocked that the transcript of the Nitze testimony could be made available to the writer of this so-called anonymous memorandum but not to Nitze. Nitze claimed it had gotten wide circulation and Cannon claimed that it was full of errors. Obviously, the memorandum must have been effective if it aroused such opposition, but I doubt if it changed many views.

Through all this I was naturally anxious that the memorandum remain anonymous. Although many knew the author, it was not volunteered and the opposition did not try to have this disclosed. The last episode involving the memorandum occurred the day before the vote on Warnke. Tom Scoville prepared briefing books for seventeen senators, and he sent me a copy that afternoon. The memorandum was included in the book behind one of the tabs, and listed in the index for tab eight was "Graham Memorandum." I called Tom and said that the table of contents entry had to come out. About 10:00 P.M. that night I received a telephone call at home from Tom who said, "Operation Snipper is complete." He had spirited himself into seventeen senators' offices that evening and snipped my name out of the table of contents with a pair of scissors.

As the organizers had hoped, the attack on Warnke had far-reaching effects. On February 10, 1977, just as the campaign against Warnke was beginning, Senator Jackson was quoted by the *Washington Post* as saying that he was very pleased with the president's position on SALT so far. President Carter in a news conference on February 8 had said that he was amenable to a quick deal on SALT II, bypassing the issues of cruise missiles and the Backfire bomber, if the Soviet Union was willing to ban the land-mobile ICBM. At the time, two of these three points were unacceptable to the Soviet Union. There was an ideological propensity for Brzezinski to work with Jackson and this, combined with being on the defensive as a result of the Warnke nomination, led the Carter administration to go forward with the ill-fated Jackson/Perle-inspired March 1977 proposal to the Soviet Union.

But the Warnke nomination had further important consequences. By May 1977, as a result of the intervention of Secretary Vance, the SALT II negotiations were back on track. The vote on Warnke, however, led the White House to conclude that pressing forward on SALT II in 1978 was not wise, and Hamilton Jordan and Frank Moore (White House chief of staff and congressional liaison, respectively) recommended in a memorandum to President Carter, on November 17, 1977, that SALT II not be submitted as a treaty because the requisite two-thirds vote could not be obtained. They argued that the vote for SALT II negotiator was the best indication of the potential and philosophical divisions in the Senate on arms control, and noted that the vote was nine short of sixty-seven. SALT II should be out of the question for 1978 with the Panama Canal Treaty before the Senate, they advised. President Carter accepted both recommendations: 1978 became a dead year for SALT II with the big push to be in 1979 (thus SALT II was injected into the 1980 presidential campaign). And the delegation was to make clear to the Soviets (and change language as necessary) that SALT II was to be an Executive Agreement, in the United States submitted to both Houses by majority vote as was the Interim Agreement, as provided in the ACDA Act. Little needed to be changed as the SALT II Joint Draft Text from the beginning had used the term "agreement" rather than "treaty" in order to keep options open. However, once leading senators got wind of this latter decision in the spring of 1978, it was roundly denounced, with the majority leader, Senator Robert Byrd, implying that he would oppose SALT II if it was not submitted as a treaty. President Carter accordingly backed away from this plan, but no change was made in the text in Geneva for some months.

This seemed to me at the time an outrage. It was one thing to keep options open. It was quite another to circumvent deliberately the two-thirds rule in the Senate by declaring that one of the most important international agreements of the 1970s would not be submitted for approval in the United States according to our treaty-making process as provided in the Constitution. In retrospect, I am not sure that my in-the-trenches effort to provide that it would in fact be called a treaty in the text—so as to remove all doubt—was truly wise. I was the delegation legal advisor, and this appeared to me to be a basic, constitutional issue, given the importance of SALT II. Nevertheless, there was the precedent of the treaty admitting Texas to the Union. It was originally submitted as a treaty in 1836 and defeated, and the next year it was submitted to both Houses for approval and passed. Also, in 1789 George Washington, in referring to the two-thirds rule in the Senate (which essentially came from a protectionist arrangement for the South in the Articles of Confederation), said that it was a great evil but that it would soon pass. After a long effort of pressuring the bureaucracy to permit the word "treaty" to replace the word "agreement" in the text I finally obtained instructions to do so in January 1979, and we and the Soviets made the changes in the Joint Draft Text. The Soviets in Geneva did not have a strong preference but they did require me to make the international law argument for SALT II being a treaty before they would agree in the Drafting Group. So we made the change—in ninety-nine places. SALT II had grown to such a length.

In May 1977, the SALT II negotiations were put back on track. The March proposal had failed and was now history. The strategic debate in the Senate conducted on the back of the Warnke nomination was also over, but not without conservatives convincing the White House, as we have seen, that the 58–41 vote (the vote for ACDA director was 70–29, more than two-thirds) confirming Paul as SALT II negotiator demonstrated that there were not sixty-seven votes in the Senate for a SALT II Treaty along the lines of what President Ford had been attempting to negotiate. The White House in its analysis chose to focus only on the vote for negotiator, not taking into account at all the vote for director and ignoring the fact that members of Congress always relish the opportunity to vote both ways on a controversial issue. The opposition, led by Senator Jackson, had long focused on the perceived inequities of SALT I. The Jackson amendment to the SALT I Resolution approving the Interim Agreement called for a SALT II Agreement based on equal aggregates of strategic systems. This became a U.S. requirement from the beginning of the negotiations in 1973. Jackson also decried the throw-weight advantage presented by the larger Soviet ICBMs, but throw-weight was now controlled in the SALT II Joint Draft Text as a result of the agreements worked out in 1976.

It should be noted that the Joint Draft Text was classified secret, consistent with the practice established at SALT I when the Soviets, at least, regarded the SALT discussions as truly secret—traditionally, diplomatic exchanges are only classified confidential, mostly to avoid publicity. Thus, although it was never formally available to Congress as it went through draft after draft, interested congressional staffers never had a problem obtaining access. I used to invite cleared staffers to my office to read it. I and others urged more direct congressional involvement in SALT II in 1977. As a result, Secretary Vance formally invited the House and Senate to nominate observers who, when in Geneva, would be considered part of the U.S. delegation. This was favorably acted upon, and a House and Senate observer group was created, but it did not help SALT II. Among the most active in Geneva as official observers in 1977–79 were Senators Glenn, Mathias, Pell, Tower, and Baker.

All Senate and House observers were able to have private meetings with the Soviet chief negotiator (accompanied by the U.S. ambassador) and to attend a plenary meeting. Most members faithfully followed delegation instructions. However, Senator John Glenn, breaking with instructions, made a most controversial proposal to Soviet Ambassador Semenov. Senator Glenn proposed that national technical means (NTM) be defined in SALT II. Semenov was horrified—because these systems were in large part for the purpose of intelligence collection, this was the last thing either side would want to do. Semenov could only reply, "Minerva's owl flies only at night." No one wanted to publicly declare in a treaty text the type of NTM that was used nor the associated technology—least of all the United States.

Semenov also had the rank of deputy foreign minister and was usually referred to as "Minister Semenov." He was a veteran of Stalin's times and was married to a young wife whom we almost never saw. It was said of Semenov, a taciturn, classic Soviet diplomat, that in 1950, when he was the Soviet civilian representative in Berlin, a telegram arrived from Moscow abruptly recalling Semenov and his military deputy. The purpose of the recall was uncertain. The deputy was in the office when the cable arrived, returned to Moscow as ordered, and was shot. Semenov was away from the office that day for some reason, did not receive the telegram, did not return to Moscow as he guessed its purpose, and somehow survived. He served as the Soviet chief negotiator from the beginning in 1969 until 1978 and became known somewhat affectionately as "Iron Pants" because of his staying power in the chair.

Another noteworthy moment involving a member of Congress took place in 1978. Senator John Tower was the visitor and he was running for reelection in Texas. Ralph Earle, Warnke's SALT deputy and his successor as negotiator in late 1978, was the chair for the United States. He had taken Tower to his meeting with Semenov and then had a private meeting himself with Semenov thereafter. Upon his return, he debriefed the delegation (including Senator Tower) on this private meeting. He said, "Senator, Minister Semenov was very impressed with you. He said that you were a strong man and he wished you luck in your reelection campaign. You might say, Senator, that you have the endorsement for reelection of the Communist Party of the Soviet Union." Tower, who was leaning back in a chair puffing on a cigar, lost control of his cigar as it popped from his mouth. My impression was that he did not believe endorsement by the Communist party of the Soviet Union would improve his reelection prospects in Texas.

Another issue of major interest to Senator Jackson and Richard Perle was the cruise missile. It should be noted that in addition to specifics, both Jackson and Perle were deeply skeptical of détente and the SALT process, believing that it lulled the United States into a false sense of security. Cruise missiles, both air and sea, were essentially bargaining chips pressed on the Pentagon by Kissinger to ensure support for SALT I ratification. The Air Force and Navy in the mid-1970s did not like the programs that much. After all, they might replace Air Force and Naval aviators. As related above, in 1976, Senators Nunn and Taft, from their vantage point on the Armed Services Committee, introduced an amendment to the Defense Authorization Bill to delay both programs by a year, which, under pressure from Deputy Secretary Clements, was later dropped. As an aside, a vignette might serve to illustrate Clements's views on these kinds of issues. In November of 1976, Ambassador Johnson made a routine request to the Pentagon for an Air Force plane to bring the SALT II delegation home, which was the usual practice. It was denied. Johnson sent a cable to Clements expressing puzzlement and requesting a reversal. Clements sent a message back confirming the denial, in which he stated that the policy of the Department of Defense was to authorize the use of Air Force aircraft only for those missions that are in the national security interest of the United States.

The Vladivostok Accord was attacked by Jackson and Perle for ratifying the ballistic missile arms race and for drastically limiting cruise missiles. The 2,400 overall aggregate limit included ICBMs, SLBMs, heavy bombers, and air-to-surface missiles. It was higher than either side intended to build and thus simply capped the arms race. The Soviets claimed that air-to-surface missiles included cruise as well as ballistic missiles as part of this aggregate; the Ford administration claimed that the record, of which there was none, reflected that this term was intended to cover only air-to-surface ballistic missiles. Neither side had nor intended to have such missiles, although the Air Force had, shortly before Vladivostok, dropped a Minuteman ICBM out of a transport plane as a demonstration. Jackson wanted to proceed ahead and sign SALT II, leaving Backfire and cruise missiles out, and thus letting cruise missiles "run free." The Soviets remained adamant that there had to be limits on cruise missiles. President Carter mentioned favorably the Jackson approach as a possibility in February 1977. This thinking led to the failed proposal of March 1977.

The negotiations resumed in May. The Carter administration developed the idea of considering heavy bombers with air-launched cruise missiles the equivalent of MIRVed missiles, and rearranged the Vladivostok aggregates, retaining the principle of freedom to mix therein. The 2,400 included only ICBM launchers, SLBM launchers, heavy bombers, and the null set, air-to-surface ballistic missiles or ASBMs. The 1,320 would include heavy bombers with long-range cruise missiles (ALCMs), but 120 heavy bombers could "run free" with ALCMs and each ALCM bomber would count as a missile with MIRVs (although a limit of 20 ALCMs per bomber was subsequently negotiated). Within the 1320 "MIRV system" limit, there would be a 1,200 sublimit on MIRVed ICBMs and SLBMs, along with a further sublimit of 820 limit on MIRVed ICBMs, a new limit where the Soviets were potentially stronger. (It meant a reduction of about 100 in the Soviet MIRVed ICBM deployment plans but none in the U.S. plan, the overall number of which had long been fixed at 550 with the MX [Peacekeeper] intended as a replacement for Minuteman.) This was a brilliant reformulation, and the Soviets accepted it in principle at a Vance-Gromyko meeting in Geneva immediately before the resumption of the SALT II negotiations in May 1977. This reformulation was the central structure of the SALT II Treaty that eventually emerged.

Paul Warnke had formally designated me as ACDA general counsel in April of 1977. So, although I remained delegation legal advisor, I needed a Geneva deputy as I would not be able to spend as much time there as I had formerly. I asked Jack McNeill, one of the finest individuals and public servants that I have ever met, to take on this assignment. He had joined the office the previous year and up to this point had concentrated on nuclear non-proliferation policy. He and I worked together on the SALT II negotiations and ratification until completion. He was later legal advisor for the U.S. INF delegation before going on to a distinguished career as first assistant, later deputy, then principal deputy general counsel of the Department of Defense. Jack's untimely death in 1996 was a great loss for all of us. A day or so after his death, but before the funeral, I was driving to work and in relation to Jack the words of John Donne's poem suddenly came to me. Paraphrased, "no man is an island, entire unto himself, if a clod of dirt falls into the ocean it is as though a vast promontory were washed away. So ask not for whom the bell tolls, it tolls for thee." That afternoon Bronwyn, his daughter, called me and asked if I would give one of the eulogies. I based my eulogy in part on the poem by John Donne. It certainly depicted accurately the loss that we all suffered.

Most of 1977 was spent working out the new structure for SALT II and, in general, 1978 was a year of stagnation for SALT II as far as the major issues were concerned (e.g., Backfire and remaining cruise missile issues), but several verification issues are worthy of mention. There was now an open effort to obtain a commitment from the Soviet Union not to encrypt missile telemetry or otherwise conceal it, such as storing it in a capsule to be jettisoned. Telemetry includes signals from the missile as to how the various components are operating, to be analyzed by engineers at the launch facility. Our intelligence community had been intercepting these signals and reading them for years until the mid-1970s. So we had an excellent idea of the capability of the first and second generation Soviet ICBMs and SLBMs. Since about 1975 the Soviets, realizing what we were doing, began encoding these signals. We wanted this access to information back and therefore sought a ban on telemetry encryption and other forms of telemetry concealment under the "deliberate concealment from verification" concept. During the Ford administration this could not be discussed with the Soviets, but beginning in 1977, this ban was lifted.

As during the Nixon-Ford-Kissinger era, there were two tracks. The difference was that while Kissinger worked the big issues behind the scenes, not telling the SALT delegation what he was doing, Vance negotiated the major issues with Gromyko with a full interagency team that included the senior SALT delegation members. The negotiation of a ban on telemetry encryption was relegated to the Vance-Gromyko level with the Geneva delegations basically marking time on this issue. It was finally resolved at a second ministerial meeting in Geneva in December 1978, which set the stage for the final push on SALT II during the first six months of 1979.

Intervening between the Geneva ministerial meetings on SALT II in May

1977 and December 1978 were several Vance trips to Moscow to discuss SALT. Either Warnke or Earle always went on these trips, as well as Ed Rowny. The earlier trips included Les Gelb, who had worked for Warnke in the Pentagon and who was attending as the director of Political Military Affairs in the State Department. Subsequently, Les was managing editor of the *New York Times*. He was succeeded at State by Reg Bartholomew, a distinguished officer who later served as undersecretary of state in the Bush administration, as well as in many other posts. At these meetings there were always discussions on Jewish emigration issues, during which Vance and Gromyko would retire to a separate room to address specific cases. At this time the two delegations were left to mill around the inevitable green baize-covered table in the Kremlin meeting room.

During one of these sessions, as the delegations were awaiting the return of the ministers, Reg Bartholomew noticed a large, red button in the middle of the table. He looked at it for a while, but in the end his curiosity got the better of him and he leaned over and pushed it. Immediately, alarm bells and sirens began to sound. First Deputy Foreign Minister Korniyenko, a dour, long-time specialist in relations with the United States, who was standing next to Bartholomew, looked at him sadly and said, "There goes Washington!" It was a fire alarm.

At another such break in the action, at the same meeting, Marshall Ogarkov had his discussion on Backfire with Ed Rowny, mentioned above. In the early years after Vladivostok, the Soviets thought that the U.S. position on Backfire was a ploy, given Kissinger's statement in the Vladivostok post-meeting press conference in 1974 on the plane to Beijing that Backfire was not included as a heavy bomber under the Vladivostok aggregates, but by 1977 they had been disabused of that view. One thing to note concerning the long-running issue of Backfire: whereas the Backfire was a large medium-range bomber, the Soviets were never much interested in the bomber leg of the strategic triad. There was too much hostile territory to overfly to get to the United States, whereas the situation was the reverse for the U.S. bomber force. The Soviet weapon was the ICBM—big artillery.

In Geneva, for a long time the U.S. delegation had argued for the missile type rule and the launcher type rule for MIRV verification. These rules were considered essential for verification by satellite surveillance, and after years of discussion the Soviets finally accepted both of them. But the first hard case came in 1977. There were 180 ICBM launchers located at Derazhnia and Pervomaisk in what is now Ukraine. We knew they all had single warhead SS-11s deployed therein, but this type of ICBM launcher had been associated with the SS-19, a MIRVed ICBM, elsewhere. Therefore, the United States insisted that all 180 launchers be counted in the 1,200 and 820 MIRVed missile launcher subtotals. The Soviets were outraged. The delegations argued about this for a year and a half. Finally, the Soviets conceded in early 1979, and there is an Agreed Statement associated with SALT II that records this.

When the Soviets conceded on this point, Karpov said, "You know, we have been arguing with Moscow for a year on this; your presentations convinced us that you were correct on this point." This demonstrates the value of delegations; they can discuss issues and if they can agree on a point they can help one another to convince capitals and bring them together by employing sound arguments. Good arguments and effective presentations do in fact make a difference in diplomacy.

Another similar verification issue that dragged on for a long time was the matter of the 18 SS-9 test and training launchers at the Tyuratam Test Range. The United States had reason to believe that they were hooked into the operational force plan of the Strategic Rocket Forces and therefore should count in the SALT aggregates, not under the test and training launcher exception. This rather small issue dragged on for so long that by 1979 delegation staff were wearing T-shirts that said "Free the Tyuratam 18." Indeed it was the very last issue settled in June of 1979. Half of the launchers would be dismantled and the other half verifiably converted to space launchers. On the day the negotiations ended, Strobe Talbott, who was covering SALT for *Time* magazine and also writing what became an excellent book on SALT II, *End Game*, called me from Vienna, where he was awaiting the SALT II signing summit, and asked what was the last issue settled—I told him.

In November of 1976, an organization called the Committee on the Present Danger had been formed. It included, among others, Gene Rostow, ACDA director in 1981–82, Paul Nitze, and Max Kampelman, the nuclear arms negotiator in 1985–88. The organization was composed largely of conservative Democrats and its stated purpose was to point out the dangers of the Soviet build-up. Paul Nitze used it as a platform after the Warnke nomination battle to express his opposition to SALT II. It seems as though continually throughout the latter stages of SALT II, important information was leaked which made his attacks more effective. Rowny was involved in the provision of information to Senator Jackson's office through his Watson/Perle channel. This opposition was effective, constantly creating negative press. Two congressmen very active in arms control and constantly showing up in Geneva beginning in 1977, Democrats Bob Carr of Michigan and Thomas Downey of Long Island, wrote to President Carter urging Rowny's removal. However, he was protected by Brzezinski because of the Jackson relationship. Dr. Gerald Johnson, Defense Secretary Harold Brown's representative on the delegation (replacing Mike May), once called Brown using the telephone outside the conference room and demanded Rowny's removal. In a large delegation meeting Rowny had referred to Johnson's views as making Rowny unsure of which side Johnson was on. For that matter, Mike May spoke little to Rowny during his last two years on the delegation. Nevertheless, Rowny stayed on the delegation until the end of the negotiations.

Verification was an important issue in the negotiations from start to finish.

When Fred Ikle became ACDA director he reformulated the bureaus of the agency and established a Verification Bureau to be sort of the watchdog on SALT. The head of the Bureau was Amron Katz, a conservative on verification issues. His deputy was Fred Eimer, who was even more conservative. When Warnke came in as director he abolished the Verification Bureau, locating its functions among other bureaus. At this time Richard Perle called me and said that on the Hill they were going to observe the fate of Fred Eimer, whom he had never met, as a bellwether, which would indicate whether Paul Warnke was behaving as he should and pursuing the national interest. Several months later, Earle was talking with Karpov in Geneva and brought up the subject of verification. Karpov replied, "But I thought that you Americans had abolished verification." The Verification Bureau was reestablished in the Reagan administration, and it remained part of the table of organization at ACDA until the end of ACDA in 1999, with Fred Eimer serving as assistant director through most of the Reagan and Bush administrations.

Another long-running issue that bedeviled the negotiations was the question of how to deploy the MX missile so that it would not be vulnerable. Earlier, I mentioned the swimming pool idea of 1975. What emerged in the Carter administration was the idea that MX, a very large missile with ten extremely accurate warheads, each with around a 500-kiloton yield, would be deployed in Utah pursuant to a plan that would involve what was called a "racetrack." The missiles would be moved on a huge transporter from hardened shelter to hardened shelter—200 missiles in all—in a widespread deployment area to be located in the Utah desert. If built it would have been the largest public works project in the history of the world, joining the Great Wall of China in being visible with the naked eye from the moon. The MX, later named the "Peacekeeper," barely fit under the SS-19 launch-weight and throw-weight numbers to qualify as a light ICBM. Of greater difficulty, since land-mobile ICBMs were to be banned by SALT II, was how to characterize the MX as a fixed ICBM launcher that was just moved around. This was the argument that the Pentagon made to the Hill to justify the program. The proposed deployment was never constructed, so this concept never became an active SALT problem. Once the Utah public became aware of this program and how this deployment would be considered a great "sponge" that would soak up Soviet reentry vehicles fruitlessly trying to destroy MX missiles that were constantly on the move, they became somewhat disenchanted, to put it mildly. Senator Jake Garn, a rock-solid Armed Services Committee conservative, made it clear that this would not happen in his state, and the Reagan administration quietly abandoned the idea.

Thomas Watson, former chairman of IBM and later ambassador to Russia, was appointed chairman of the General Advisory Committee on Arms Control and Disarmament, supported by ACDA. This concept of a fixed ICBM launcher that could move was first presented outside DOD by Assistant Secretary of Defense Walter Slocombe, later undersecretary in the Clinton administration, in one of the committee's early meetings under Tom's chairmanship. Coming from the business world, he found it all rather astonishing. Watson was a great breath of fresh air for the arms control process during his time as chairman.

An important organizational step was made in 1977 at SALT. The Drafting Group had been formed in 1975 along with the Military and Verification Subgroups. The latter two went away after a short time as being essentially of little utility, which meant that all operational power in the delegation flowed to the Drafting Group (except what was discussed in the Head of Delegation meetings—plenaries had become very formalized). By the end of 1977 the Drafting Group had become quite formalized as well. Therefore, I suggested that a subgroup of the Drafting Group be formed which would be called the Conforming Subgroup, as innocuous a name as possible. Allegedly, it was formed for the purpose of conforming the English and Russian texts. It consisted of the delegation lawyer (Smolin on the Soviet side), usually a foreign service officer, and an interpreter. Avis Bohlen, a distinguished foreign service officer (later Max Kampelman's executive director during the negotiations in the mid-1980s, DCM in France, Ambassador to Bulgaria, and assistant secretary of state for arms control from 1999 to the present) filled in ably for a considerable time. During the last two months it was Jack McNeill and me, along with an interpreter, on our side. In actuality, the subgroup became the place where all the difficult textual negotiations took place and were resolved.

One morning toward the end of the negotiations, I brought in to a full delegation meeting a list of twenty issues that I wanted to address in the subgroup meeting that afternoon. They all had relatively obvious solutions, but some of the issues were important. I listed the issues more or less in descending order of importance. And so I started through the list. "For issue number one," I said, "I propose we do this." "Yes," said the delegation, "we agree, you are authorized to do that." Number two, we do this; "yes," said the delegation, "we agree." Number three, yes. Number four, yes. And so on down the list. The delegation was agreeing on all points. But as we came to numbers fourteen, fifteen, and sixteen, I could sense a degree of restiveness in the air, as though they believed they were being too easy, too compliant. By issues eighteen and nineteen, it was palpable. The twentieth and final issue was simply a reordering of part of one article of the treaty. I was recommending that the third paragraph logically should be second and vice versa. The delegation practically rose as one from their chairs: "Never," said many voices. "Never will we agree to put the third paragraph before the second." So I lost that one, but I had my nineteen other points and left the room.

In these last months the pressure was intense and some unpleasant things happened. I was directed to approach Smolin and pass to him the idea that if the Soviets conceded on one point of interest to us, we would concede on another of interest to them. I approached Smolin, who said that he would consult Karpov and get back to me. The next day Smolin reported that Karpov had agreed to the trade and would make his move, which he did the next morning. Later the first day I had been informed that Secretary Vance had decided for other reasons that we should now stonewall on our half of the deal. I was in agony as to whether I should inform Smolin before Karpov made his concession. I was strongly advised not to. The next day, when we failed to deliver, Smolin was mortified. After the meeting, he accused me of deception. I said that I was sorry, but I had had no choice. He said that he would never be able to work with Karpov again.

Karpov was the quintessential Soviet negotiator, on top of the issues, fluent in English, and on excellent terms with the Army and the KGB. You could always count on him to deliver when he gave his commitment. Smolin, his longtime number two going back to SALT I, was not gregarious like Karpov. Karpov was very witty, but he had a serious drinking problem. I once saw him at the airport greeting a Soviet general who was joining his delegation. It was 10:00 A.M. and he was dead drunk. At one point he was sent back to Moscow for a month to dry out. We wondered if he would return, but he did. On another occasion he was caught by the KGB (witnessed by "someone" on our side) in the garage of his apartment building late at night dancing naked around his car, which had a woman in it whom he had picked up at the local Pickwick Bar. None of this seemed to affect his career. He succeeded Semenov as Soviet chief negotiator in 1978, he was the first Soviet START negotiator, and he later was head of the Arms Control Directorate in the Foreign Ministry, but according to the Russians the alcohol eventually did lead to his premature death.

Smolin, as I have said, was in a sense my opposite number from the beginning of the Drafting Group in 1975 until the end of the negotiations, although our direct relationship was more clearly defined in 1977. At the very first meeting of the Drafting Group in April 1975, he turned to us and said, "Well, gentlemen, are you ready for strategic battle?" I worked closely with him for nearly five years. In the final weeks of the negotiations, with the June Summit date set, Karpov approached Earle and said that he had been ordered to be in Vienna several days before the signing date to meet with Brezhnev. There were sixteen unresolved issues remaining. We now knew when Karpov had to finish the negotiation and we had a word processor (an early one) and the Soviets did not. Accordingly, we refused to move on any of the sixteen issues, which drove the Soviets crazy. In the end we did compromise on one and the Soviets had to concede to us on the other fifteen.

Smolin was always the diplomat, a real professional and a great wordsmith for our textual discussions. And he had a sense of humor. Once, we were proposing a mid-stage in the dismantling process to be reached early, which we called "assured inoperability," but in theory not yet at the stage where the particular weapon system could not be reconstituted. For bombers one wing was to be cut off to reach the stage of "assured inoperability."

Smolin commented that he was sure that if there was a desire to reconstitute the bomber in question that the pilots would have to be volunteers.

After the negotiation was completed and the treaty text initialed, but before we went to Vienna, Smolin, Jack, another Soviet, and I went out to lunch. Smolin proceeded to drink a large amount of cognac. Previously I had seen him at gatherings so drunk he could not speak (not uncommon for a Soviet), but this was beyond that. He began telling Jack and me that the United States was arrogant, always arrogant. When he was a boy during World War II, he was starving. He received a lend-lease package from Iowa. Inside were a knife and fork but no food. "You Americans have so much, you are arrogant, you do not try to understand others." This behavior was shocking to Jack and me; it was like Dr. Jekyll and Mr. Hyde. We wondered if Smolin all along had been possessed with these feelings. Later, he worked on the early stages of CFE for Ambassador Mendelevich in Moscow and became Soviet Ambassador to Colombia. In Bogotá, I understand, roughly in the time frame of the abortive coup attempt against Gorbachev, Smolin committed suicide by hanging himself. It was a real tragedy.

Another clear rising star on the Soviet SALT delegation in those days was Vitaly Churkin, who joined the delegation as an interpreter right out of school at age twenty-one. The Soviets often trained diplomats as interpreters and then moved them on to substantive work. The Soviet delegation had many excellent interpreters, but we found Churkin's flair for English exceptional. He captured not only the meaning, but the mood as well. One could tell jokes through him. My few words of Russian were mostly SALT terms like "bomber" and "missile." I once asked Churkin what would happen to me if I arrived in the Soviet Union and started using those words. He replied, "You would be moved quickly to the East." Earle once told Karpov how much the Americans liked working with Churkin. A few months later Karpov told Earle that Churkin had been promoted, "But not because of anything that you said," he said with a smile. Nearly twenty years later, Churkin was a prominent Russian deputy foreign minister, representing Russia on the Yugoslav issue, and by 2000 was the Russian ambassador to Canada.

In an assertion of bureaucracy, the State Department Legal Advisor's Office sent a lawyer, Art Rovine, the capable assistant legal advisor for treaty affairs, over to Geneva to witness the initialing of the text and to carry the treaty to Vienna for signing at the Summit. Ralph Earle had tried to get an Air Force airplane to take us to Vienna, but his request was denied. We wondered if Presidents Carter and Brezhnev would mind traveling to Tripoli to sign SALT II in the presence of Colonel Gadaffi if our commercial flight were hijacked at the airport. Rovine was carrying the completed original of the treaty in a small black Samsonite briefcase. Ralph saw it come through the X-ray machine, lifted it off and put it behind him. Rovine walked through and Ralph pointed to three other identical briefcases that had come through the machine and asked Rovine if he knew which one was his. I had never seen someone actually turn first green then gray before. Then Ralph handed Art the real briefcase. Art opened the briefcase every thirty minutes thereafter in order to see if the treaty was still there, all the way to Vienna.

After two months in Geneva, Vienna was a culture shock. Jack and I set up a small office there for a few days, in case any last-minute legal work was necessary before the signing ceremony. As it turned out, there was legal work to be done. On the margins of the first Summit meeting it was decided to put titles into the signature blocks for all the treaty documents. Now the situation was reversed from Vienna. This was easy for the Russians because they were using manual typewriters. It was difficult for us because we were using a word processor, and doubly difficult in that we discovered there was only one word processor of the type we were using (made by Exxon) in all Vienna, which we obtained with some difficulty. And the number of treaty documents had grown. Washington had decided that all Agreed Statements and Common Understandings, whose legal status we had carefully clarified over the years, had to be signed by the presidents. So we collected them all in a lengthy legal document—there were around 100 statements and understandings by now. There was also a Protocol and a Joint Statement of Principles, all in both English and Russian with *alternats* (i.e., direct translations). In the English version, U.S. comes first and USSR second where named, the reverse in the Russian. In the Russian language *alternat* U.S. would come first, in the English language *alternat* USSR would come first, so that each side could have a direct translation of their text. This made for four originals of each document, thereby requiring sixteen signatures by each president.

Someone decided that in his state of deteriorating health, sixteen signatures was too many for Brezhnev to do in the signing ceremony, therefore only the four signatures on the treaty itself would be done at the ceremony. As a result, it fell upon me to obtain the other twelve signatures the day before the ceremony. First, I went to the Soviet Vienna Embassy with the four originals of the Protocol, Agreed Statement and Common Understandings Document, and the Statement of Principles in hand. There was no problem there as Smolin was available and he promptly returned with the signed documents. Then I had to find out where President Carter was. After several hours of inquiry at the U.S. delegation I was informed that the president soon would be at the residence of the U.S. ambassador, where he was staying, for a tennis game. I went there, was passed through by the guards, and went to the front door of the residence, rather than down by the tennis court where the guards said they believed the president was. I was greeted at the front door of the residence by a beautiful young woman who said that she was an assistant to the president, and who explained that the president was not playing tennis, but rather was taking a nap. I described my mission and she said that I could not visit the president now, but if I would put paper clips where I wanted him to sign she would endeavor to obtain the requisite signatures.

I did so and she disappeared with the documents, slightly to my dismay as I did not know who she was, but assumed she was who she said she was. After about forty minutes she returned with "Jimmy Carter" in all the right places, done with a felt-tipped pen, as was his trademark. So I returned happily to our office.

The next morning the treaty was signed by the two presidents in a brief ceremony. Congressmen Carr and Downey were present, as they had been so often during SALT II even though they were not formally part of the House Observer Group, and they were recognized by President Carter from the podium. Brezhnev gave a short speech about peace. Carter gave a longer speech, obviously aimed at the U.S. Senate, about how arms control and military strength go hand in hand. Also, in order to prepare for the coming ratification debate, there had been a formal discussion the day before between Carter and Brezhnev about some of the thorny issues, particularly Backfire. In this discussion Brezhnev undertook not to give Backfire—which in the end was not included as a heavy bomber—in-air refueling capability. This became a contentious point during the ratification proceedings.

After the signing ceremony, we all climbed into buses to proceed to the airport to return to Washington, D.C. Both Air Force One and Air Force Two (the backup to Air Force One) were there, and they left within fifteen minutes of one another. I had with me the signed English original with the signed Russian *alternat*. These documents were transmitted to the Senate the next week, and to the best of my knowledge at the end of 2000 there they still lay, as SALT II was never ratified, even though it has expired by its terms and has been superseded by a ratified START I Treaty.

On board Air Force One, Roger Molander was working on the president's speech on SALT II, which he was to deliver that night to the Senate. In it he wanted to say that the treaty would be sent to the Senate the next day. I was on Air Force Two with Jim Timbie, and Jim was in telephone contact with Roger. I urged Jim to have Roger put "a few days" in the speech so we would have time to draft, complete, and negotiate with all the interested agencies the article-by-article analysis, providing the government's official interpretation of all the provisions in the treaty documents that must accompany the documents to the Senate—a monumental task. This is a job that was always done by the ACDA General Counsel's Office, and it was in this case, but only after a number of days of round-the-clock work.

The SALT II Treaty was signed on June 18, 1979, and submitted to the U.S. Senate for advice and consent to ratification on June 22, 1979. Hearings began in July. A hot reception awaited it because of the vagaries of U.S. domestic politics, but it was a treaty richly deserving ratification. After seven years, Gerard Smith's insistence at SALT I on a more complete agreement limiting strategic offensive arms had been redeemed. And even though he opposed the treaty, Senator Jackson had his agreement limiting Soviet strategic offense. Critics charged that it did little more than cap the strategic arms race. In a broad sense this was true, but that was very much worth doing. But SALT II did more than cap the arms race. It put the first limits on MIRVs, freezing the parties where they were as to the missiles they had and permitting only one new type of ICBM (the Soviet's strong point) with up to ten warheads, thereby accommodating the MX. And there were significant verification advances with the type rules and the ban on telemetry encryption. The Soviet ICBM building program was significantly retarded with the 820 MIRVed ICBM limit and the inclusion as MIRVed ICBM launchers of the 180 missiles at Derazhna and Pervomaisk.

In response to Senator Jackson, the U.S. ALCM program was not at all limited by the inclusion of ALCM bombers under the 1,320 aggregate and the limit of twenty ALCMs per bomber. And the protocol did not significantly limit the U.S. sea- and ground-launched nuclear cruise missile programs— the latter was limited, indeed abolished, by the INF Treaty. Sea-based nuclear cruise missiles are prohibited by the START I Treaty but their conventional counterparts, which are externally indistinguishable, run free—witness the frequent use of the sea-launched Tomahawk missile against Iraq. But it is right to want some limits on cruise missiles—they can carry nuclear weapons, they can fly under radar detection systems, and they are accurate to within a few feet. The Backfire bomber was left out of the treaty, except for the Brezhnev commitment in Vienna but information which became available after the demise of the Soviet Union demonstrated conclusively that Backfire was not a heavy bomber.

Lloyd Cutler, who had been brought in as White House counsel, was put in charge of the SALT II ratification effort. Ralph was made his deputy, and Madeleine Albright was very involved as the congressional liaison for the NSC. A major campaign to secure ratification was launched, both with respect to supporting witnesses at hearings and attempting to persuade senators, but also to attempt to persuade the public. Governmental officials were dispatched in teams all over the country to make presentations on behalf of SALT II—this was derided as "SALT-selling" by the opponents. Paul Warnke was brought back to head this program.

Shortly after the treaty was sent to the Senate, I was called by Hoyt Purvis, the chief assistant to Majority Leader Robert Byrd. I was informed that Senator Byrd was planning a trip to the Soviet Union in late June to discuss SALT ratification with Brezhnev and Gromyko. Hoyt asked if I would go along as the majority leader's SALT advisor. We went first to Rome where Senator Byrd could do some intensive preparation away from the Senate and then on to Leningrad for a little sightseeing and further preparation. Finally, we arrived in Moscow, where Gromyko was expecting us.

My assignment in accompanying Senator Byrd was to give him advice on SALT II. I attended some of the lower-level meetings, but not the meeting with Gromyko at the Foreign Ministry (I sat outside the door), or the meeting with Brezhnev, which was conducted at his summer home at Sochi on the Black Sea. These meetings were restricted to Senator Byrd and his staff. The meeting in the Crimea involved only Senator Byrd and Hoyt, flown there from Moscow on Brezhnev's personal plane. One of Byrd's principal purposes was to urge Soviet leaders not to react to strong statements made in the Senate in the course of the debate over the ratification of SALT II. There will be strong statements made in the heat of debate, but it would be counterproductive should the Soviet Union respond to them, he told Gromyko. Gromyko responded that if he were to read a strong anti-Soviet statement made during the debate and he should reach for a pen to write a response, his other hand would grasp his wrist. If he were to call his secretary to prepare a letter, she will have been given the day off. If he reaches for his telephone, it will have been disconnected. The meeting with Gromyko was more issue-oriented, while the one with Brezhnev was general in nature.

The SALT II hearings began in a big way after our return. As with the SALT I hearings, the SALT II Senate Foreign Relations Committee hearings were conducted in the Senate Caucus Room, with Senator Frank Church in the Chair. Unfortunately, Senator Church had a liability which could not help but affect his management of the hearing process for SALT II. He was in a hard fight for re-election in Idaho against a strong conservative, Steve Symms. Also, he had made a trip to Cuba a few years earlier which had engendered criticism. As a result, he was always looking over his right shoulder as the hearings commenced.

General Rowny testified against the treaty. Secretary of State Vance, Secretary of Defense Brown, JCS Chairman Jones, and ACDA Director Seignious were all eloquent speakers for the treaty. George Seignious had succeeded Warnke in the fall of 1978, after Paul had resigned. George had been a lieutenant general in the army and director of the Joint Chiefs, and had retired early to become president of the Citadel. He was Brzezinski's personal choice to succeed Warnke and early on was objected to by Senators Culver, Kennedy, and others on the grounds that it was improper to have a retired general as ACDA director. George, however, was a strong supporter of SALT II and had succeeded Harold Brown as the public member of the SALT II delegation in 1977. After he was announced as the prospective nominee, he and I met and planned out his confirmation campaign. I noticed that he was listed as a member of an organization called Peace through Strength, which was an avowed opponent of SALT. I pointed this out to George and he promptly resigned. This outraged some of the more extreme conservatives. Thus, when George and I met with Senator Tower in the course of his pre-nomination consultation rounds with key senators, Senator Tower commented as we were sitting down, "Well, George, you are being attacked by both the right and the left, so you must be right where you should be." Subsequently, we met with Senator Kennedy and, after asking a few questions about SALT, he pledged his support of the nomination. His aide said as he was showing us out, "You didn't really think that the Senator was going to oppose the general, did you?"

Under Paul Warnke, ACDA had been a significant player in part because of Paul's relationship with Secretary Vance. Under George, ACDA retained influence as a result of the relationship between Seignious and Brzezinski. A strong ACDA was important to the proper functioning of the arms control interagency process. Having ACDA on the figurative left end of the spectrum with the JCS on the right, State left of center, and OSD right of center makes for the best policy. I remember hearing many complaints from JCS officers in the mid-1970s that ACDA was trying to get to their right and that was wrong. Harold Brown told me in 1975 that he had upbraided Kissinger over the ACDA purge and downgrading, telling him that he now had State exposed on the left, which is not where the secretary of state should be. This view of the interagency process, with which I agree, was to my mind one of the strongest arguments against merging ACDA into the State Department.

In July, the hearings were gradually strengthening the case for SALT II. At the beginning of the process, indeed before SALT II was submitted to the Senate, Chairman Church had contrasted the SALT II and Panama Canal treaties for Ralph Earle and me. The Panama Canal treaty was one that the country opposed but that the senators supported, and a way was found to achieve ratification. SALT II is more difficult; it is a treaty that the country wants but one which many senators personally oppose. Nevertheless, steady progress was being made in July and early August, senator by senator. One memorable moment in July involved Secretary Brown answering questions from Senator Thurmond before the Senate Armed Services Committee. Brown was asked—the senator reading from a list of questions—"Mr. Secretary, does the Soviet Union have an ACDA?" (as though to suggest that evil imperialists unlike us are not that stupid). Brown answered that the arms control function was located in the Soviet Ministry of Foreign Affairs. Senator Thurmond did not follow up the answer; he did not follow up on any of his questions, but continued reading from his list of questions. After a while he lost his place and asked again in stentorian tones, "Mr. Secretary, does the Soviet Union have an ACDA?" Brown replied, "Well, whatever they've got, it hasn't changed in the last five minutes."

The issues were for the most part old ones: the Soviet monopoly on heavy ICBMs, the Backfire bomber, and verification (compounded by the recent loss of our monitoring stations in Iran as a result of the Iranian Revolution in January 1979). Then came the Cuban crisis.

After the end of the Cuban Missile Crisis in 1962, the Soviet Union decided to retain a small detachment of troops in Cuba indefinitely as they were gradually withdrawing their principal deployments of personnel. Over time, this number dwindled to about 2,500 to 3,000 men with no offensive arms capability. By 1979 this unit of Soviet troops had been in Cuba for seventeen years. Suddenly, in August of 1979, Soviet troops in Cuba were "discovered." Senator Church, given his situation in Idaho, had to react violently and denounced this deployment. President Carter, in an even greater overreaction, went on national television to assure the nation that there was no threat of imminent attack. Senator Stone of Florida, a conservative Democrat considered important to SALT ratification, who had built his brief political career in part on anti-Castroism, also reacted strongly. Chaos resulted, the momentum of SALT II was thrown off track, and what had been looking bright began to look dim. However, after a few weeks of hand wringing, the disrupted and now damaged ratification process was back on track and the Senate Foreign Relations Committee began its mark-up of the treaty. In a virtually unprecedented procedure, the committee went through the treaty article by article, receiving, considering, and voting on amendments to many of the treaty articles.

Such amendments were placed against a three-level scale. Category one did not require that the amendment to the resolution of ratification be communicated to the Soviets. These usually involved some obligation on the president, such as spending more money on a specific weapon system, and they were usually not opposed by the administration. Category two had to be communicated to the Soviet Union but did not change a provision of the treaty, and usually consisted of statements of policy. The administration tried to discourage these. Category three involved a change in one of the provisions of the treaty and had to be agreed to by the Soviet Union. All of these were considered "Treaty breakers" given the delicate balance between the two sides in many of the treaty provisions, and the administration opposed all such proposals. After many days of mark-up, in October the committee finally voted on the resolution itself, festooned with many category ones, a few category twos, but no category threes. The vote was nine to six, with Senator John Glenn of Ohio in the negative but Senator Charles Percy, Republican of Illinois and the next chairman, in the affirmative. This was difficult for Percy because his minority leader and colleague on the committee, Howard Baker, had announced for president at the beginning of the SALT ratification process, with virtually his only issue being opposition to SALT II. Upon return to our office after the vote, one of my assistants, Kathy Crittenberger, wrote on the blackboard, "Christians-9, Lions-6," and that was close to how we all felt.

So by October, SALT II was out of committee. The committee report was of major book length and covered all the principal issues in a comprehensive fashion. Combined with the six volumes of committee hearings, it certainly could be said that the issue of SALT II Treaty ratification was fully documented. But whereas during the summer there had been rising expectations with respect to approval of the treaty by the Senate, the Cuban matter had definitely eroded support. It was not clear after committee action that a two-thirds majority was really there for the treaty. Many, however, remained optimistic, including myself. In the last two years, I had briefed many senators on SALT, close to a majority of the Senate. In addition, I had participated in public presentations on SALT in Des Moines and Phoenix, and I believed that I had some understanding of the public view. And, lastly, I had stayed in touch with the office of Senator Byrd and I knew how determined the majority leader was. Increasingly, though, senators were beginning to look ahead to the 1980 presidential campaign, and more and more opposition to SALT II had become potentially a part of the Republican position. Nevertheless, it seemed to me at this juncture that there were perhaps fifty votes for SALT II and twenty to twenty-five on the fence.

Among the many senators that I briefed on SALT II was Senator Dale Bumpers of Arkansas, who had succeeded to Senator Fulbright's seat. Over the years I briefed Senator Bumpers quite a few times on strategic arms control, as he was very interested. The first time that I participated in a briefing of Senator Bumpers on this subject I was in his office with Ralph Earle. After we had completed our presentation on the status of the negotiations, Senator Bumpers said to us, "Did I ever tell you how I became interested in this subject?" "No," we said. "Back in the 1960s," said Senator Bumpers, "I was elected governor of Arkansas, the youngest governor in the country—I was known as the 'Boy Governor of Arkansas'—and I was brought up to Washington to meet with the Great Man, Lyndon Johnson. We had a one-on-one meeting in the Oval Office and he referred to me as 'Boy' throughout the meeting. At one point he said: 'Boy, do you see that small black suitcase over in the corner?' 'Yes, Mr. President.' 'Boy, do you know what is in that suitcase?' 'No, Mr. President.' 'Inside that suitcase is a big red button and, Boy, do you know what would happen if I went over there and opened that suitcase and pushed that big red button?' 'No, Mr. President.' 'Not a damn thing! I would just get a call from some general in the Pentagon who would say, 'Mr. President, have you lost your mind?'" There is virtue in bureaucracy, said the Senator.

On November 4, 1979, before a floor date was scheduled, Iranian militants seized the U.S. embassy in Teheran and took all U.S. diplomats in the embassy hostage. Thus began the hostage crisis that was so devastating to the Carter presidency. A floor vote on SALT II that fall became an impossibility. But the majority leader had not given up. His plan was to schedule a floor debate on SALT II in late January and force senators to vote. He was convinced that if forced to vote the Senate would not fail to approve the SALT II Treaty—the votes would somehow be found. The United States Senate in the twentieth century had never voted down a major treaty that the president wanted (and didn't until 1999), if forced to vote; the tactic always used by those opposed to a treaty was to prevent a vote. The Senate did not like to be seen as formally rejecting a major foreign policy initiative. Thus, it seemed to me, Senator Byrd was on solid ground.

Senator Sam Nunn, already a leader in the Senate Armed Services Committee, was playing a significant role in the SALT debate as the leader of the moderate, uncommitted conservatives. He eventually developed into one of the greatest of senators, and already in 1979 his positions were taken very seriously by all. I remained in regular touch with his office as well, and in mid-January 1980 I had what I considered to be a most interesting meeting with a member of his staff. Senator Nunn had been arguing since the beginning of the SALT II Treaty debate in the Senate the importance of fully integrating defense policy and arms control policy, thereby making both more sound and more effective. In the January meeting I was shown a draft speech stressing this theme and explaining how the SALT II Treaty would fit into this integrated policy and thereby strengthen U.S. security. I was also shown a list of nineteen uncommitted senators, including Senator Nunn, who would have announced their support for SALT II in the wake of Senator Nunn delivering that speech. I was told that this had been planned for January, shortly before Senator Byrd would schedule SALT II for floor action. If this had happened, there is no doubt that the SALT II Treaty would have received advice and consent to ratification. I never mentioned this to anyone. By the time I was made aware of these facts, the fate of SALT II had been decided. With the perspective of nearly twenty years, I am not sure how seriously to take this. Were the facts correct; did I understand it all properly? If so, was this a plan that had been considered, but not decided upon, or would it in fact have been carried out had not President Carter, in a most ill-advised decision, requested on January 3, 1980, that the Senate not consider SALT II? I cannot say, but it is an interesting might-have-been.

On December 26, 1979, the Soviet Union invaded Afghanistan, killed its president, and took over the country. This was considered by many to be the coup de grâce for SALT. Gromyko long afterward said privately, it has been rumored, that the Kremlin had decided that they had little to lose with SALT. It seemed to them, according to the rumor, that the Cuban issue was obviously a non-issue, given that the troops had been there for seventeen years, and that it must have been a ruse by the administration to permit the United States to back away from SALT II. President Carter was advised by White House officials in the wake of Afghanistan, with opposition to SALT II virtually certain to be a Republican Party campaign issue, to back away from SALT. This was reminiscent of the equally bad advice given to President Ford in January 1976.

On January 3, 1980, an extraordinary National Security Council meeting was held to consider appropriate retaliation for Afghanistan. Item number four on the list was a proposal to put SALT II aside. On that day George Seignious had just resigned as ACDA director and Ralph Earle had not yet been sworn in as his successor. Spurgeon Keeny was acting director for a short time but was not invited to this historic meeting. Thus, ACDA had no representation. At the meeting, a short draft letter from the president to the majority leader requesting that SALT II not be considered by the Senate was produced by the NSC staff and approved. It was sent the same day and the fate of SALT II was sealed.

This letter came as a complete surprise to Byrd. He had not been consulted beforehand. He was still planning a floor vote in late January and he continued to believe he could win, and he still believed that limiting the strategic arms race between the United States and the Soviet Union was in the national security interest of this country, no matter what the Soviets did in Afghanistan. Byrd believed he could find the necessary votes; however, when the letter arrived this was no longer possible. Senators were let off the hook, and they were glad of it. Senator Byrd tried for a week or two to hold things together, but it was of no avail. He reluctantly had to concede. This ended SALT II as a ratified treaty, even though there was some talk from the White House about the desirability of ratifying SALT II later in the year during the campaign. Even so, SALT II was informally observed by the United States and the Soviet Union from 1981 until 1986, actually past the time that it would have expired by its terms, pursuant to policies adopted by President Reagan in 1981, in spite of his opposition to SALT II during the presidential campaign.

Very little happened in arms control in 1980. SALT II was on the shelf. There was discussion about beginning theater-missile arms control talks with the Soviets and preliminary discussions of the subject did take place in Geneva in October under the rubric of the theater nuclear force (or TNF) negotiations. Also, in March, it was learned that there had been an explosion in a laboratory in Sverdlovsk (now Ekaterinburg), which apparently released deadly anthrax spores and caused a number of deaths. The United States learned of this from defectors. Anthrax is a prime biological weapon agent and this information strongly suggested that the Soviets were in violation of the BWC. The BWC, as discussed in Chapter 2, has no verification provisions, but the United States learned of this violation through essentially intelligence means—the interviewing of defectors. This form of information is referred to as HUMINT (human intelligence). This became a big issue. The first Review Conference of the BWC was held just a few weeks later and the United States raised this issue with vigor. I remember looking at this report with Keeny, and subsequently ACDA insisted that the issue be raised at the Review Conference. I wrote a legal memorandum to that effect. This was the first great Soviet treaty violation political issue which was to become so familiar in the 1980s. This led directly to the situation where the Senate took the position that in the future, with respect to bilateral U.S.-Soviet arms control treaties, separate, subsequent implementing agreements concerned with verification issues were no longer acceptable. All verification provisions, including procedural ones, had to be included in the text of the treaty or associated protocols, thereby creating lengthy, almost indecipherable documents and ensuring long negotiations. Other than charge and countercharge, not much was accomplished at the BWC Conference, but the issue was joined and the United

States had considerable support from other BWC parties at the Review Conference. And indeed this was true evidence of a violation, which was pursued long past the end of the Cold War until well into the 1990s. Indeed, to some degree the vast Soviet-built underlying infrastructure for their biological weapons program still exists. This issue opened the door to eventual discovery of a massive and systematic violation.

The era of SALT was ending. Nevertheless, the Reagan administration did put the strategic arms limitation process back on track in 1981 and 1982 with the INF and START negotiations.

CHAPTER SIX **THE REAGAN REVOLUTION AND THE INF AND START TREATIES**

Ronald Reagan ran for president on a platform that included opposition to SALT II. But he was for real arms control, he said, and he wanted to limit the things that mattered—the warheads. He claimed that he did not want simply to ratify the arms race. Thus, early in the Reagan presidency there was an effort to withdraw SALT II from the Senate. It was thought that all the president had to do was to send a letter to the new majority leader, Senator Howard Baker, whose own anti-SALT II presidential bid had gone nowhere, and the treaty would be extracted from the Senate Foreign Relations Committee where it was then languishing, and returned to the executive branch. Desires to do this cooled somewhat when it was learned that it took a majority vote of the Senate to return a treaty. Senior White House staff official Ed Meese said publicly in mid-1981 that the United States was in no way bound to observe SALT II. I had just written a legal memorandum to Gene Rostow, the newly confirmed ACDA director, stating that under international law as reflected in the Vienna Convention of the Law of Treaties, the United States was bound not to defeat the object and purpose of the treaty—that is, not to do something that would make the treaty regime impossible, such as testing a second new type of ICBM—as long as the United States did not formally decide it would never ratify SALT II. This is the international law rule for a treaty that has been signed and whose ratification is pending. Needless to say, Mr. Meese was not happy with me as my memo was leaked by someone to the newspapers. This produced a brief flurry that soon passed.

In February 1981, Secretary of Defense Caspar Weinberger, Director of Central Intelligence William Casey, National Security Advisor Richard Allen, Secretary of State Alexander Haig, Chairman of the Joint Chiefs General David Jones, National Security Agency Director Bobby Inman, and President Reagan met to decide whether to attempt to have SALT II withdrawn from the Senate. The three civilians advised the president to withdraw it, while the three military officers (Haig, Inman, and Jones) opposed withdrawal. Secretary Haig opined, "You can't beat something with nothing." Thus, SALT II was not withdrawn and the first step was taken toward agreeing with the Soviets informally to observe SALT—it was proposed by President Reagan in a statement in the spring and agreed to by Haig and Andrei Gromyko in the fall—and to begin to reconstitute the SALT negotiations, renamed START, in early 1982.

The change in administrations initially was hard on ACDA. John Lehman, soon to be Navy secretary, saw several ACDA employees in the State Department dining room in early January 1981 and asked them if they were "ready for the revolution." It did appear ominous. Reagan had after all run on a platform that opposed SALT II, and during the campaign he had belittled the issue of nuclear proliferation. Ed Rowny was the first choice of the White House for ACDA director but his nomination was objected to by Majority Leader Baker and Foreign Relations Chairman Charles Percy. Rowny's name accordingly was withdrawn, to surface somewhat later as START negotiator. After a few weeks passed, Gene Rostow, former undersecretary of state in the 1960s, dean of Yale Law School, and senior member of the Committee on the Present Danger, was chosen.

In the meantime, my old friend Jim Malone, head of the ACDA transition team for the incoming administration, was selected as acting ACDA director pending his confirmation as assistant secretary of state for OES. Mike Pillsbury, from the staff of Senator Orrin Hatch of Utah, was named acting deputy director. David Sullivan, a former CIA employee who had been fired for allegedly leaking intelligence information to Richard Perle, was named acting ACDA counselor. At this time he was on Senator Jesse Helms's staff. Not long after Sullivan's arrival, a memorandum from the CIA arrived over the signature of Director Casey, which in effect said that as long as Sullivan was employed at ACDA, the agency would receive no highly classified intelligence information from the CIA. A fourth individual from the transition team, Brett Sciaroni, a capable lawyer, joined the General Counsel's Office.

Under Jim Malone's temporary leadership, everything went reasonably smoothly for a few weeks until the Rowny nomination faltered and Rostow was selected. Rostow asked Bob Grey, a respected State Department career officer and much later ambassador to the CD, to be his advance man to ACDA. Rostow's desire that Grey be his deputy after he was confirmed became known apparently to the consternation of Pillsbury, who hoped to become confirmed as deputy director. Pillsbury had gone to see Rostow in New Haven after he was selected and suggested to Rostow that Pillsbury's contacts on the Senate Foreign Relations Committee could either help or hurt Rostow. Rostow was singularly unimpressed. Pillsbury then approached Jim Malone and urged him to dismiss Grey as Rostow's advance man. He indicated to Malone that he, Malone, would soon be going before the committee in connection with his nomination and that he, Pillsbury, could help him or hurt him with some of the conservative Republicans on the committee. After a few days of this, Jim concluded that the better part of valor would be for him to leave ACDA and proceed upstairs to the seventh-floor office of State/OES and prepare for his confirmation hearing. This effectively left no one in charge of ACDA, although Mike Pillsbury remained the acting deputy and Bob Grey was on the scene as advance man for Rostow.

About this time, in March 1981, Pillsbury decided that he would help some conservative senators oppose President Reagan's decision to sell AWACS aircraft to Saudi Arabia. First, he attempted to have a negative ACDA arms control assessment of the proposed sale, required by the law, prepared. Mel Christopher, the man I succeeded as assistant general counsel in 1970 when he became Gerry Smith's executive secretary, and a long-time key ACDA employee, was head of the section assigned the task of drafting this assessment. He came to me for advice and I urged him to go slowly. Second, Pillsbury wrote a letter as ACDA acting deputy to Senator John Glenn critical of the sale. Third, he made a trip to Israel in an attempt to heighten Israeli opposition to the proposed sale. I assumed, but did not know, that Pillsbury may have been working with Senator Helms on this as it was my understanding that it was with Senator Helms's possible opposition that Pillsbury had threatened Rostow and Malone (Senator Helms did not try to hold up either nomination).

By now it was April and all this was too much for the Reagan White House. I was standing in the doorway of my GC office one morning when Jim Hackett, the director of administration at ACDA since 1973, walked by. He said, "Tom, if you have nothing pressing right now please come with me, as I need a witness for what I am about to do." As we proceeded to the empty director's office and sat down on the sofa, he informed me that he had just been appointed acting director. After a few minutes Pillsbury, Sullivan, and Sciaroni filed in. They sat down and Hackett said, "Well, gentlemen, I assume that you have by now all found something else to do." Pillsbury asked what Hackett meant by this, and Hackett said that as he had been appointed acting director, it was necessary to prepare for nominee Rostow's arrival, and the three of them were fired. Pillsbury claimed that Hackett had no authority to do this. Hackett replied that he had been called at home that morning by the national security advisor, the secretary of state, and the secretary of defense directing him to do what he was now doing. A thirty-minute debate between Pillsbury and Hackett on the subject of Hackett's authority ensued during which neither I nor Sullivan nor Sciaroni said a word. Hackett made the point that the three constituted what remained of the transition team (Sciaroni was there more by accident than anything else; the essential transition team had been Malone, Pillsbury, and Sullivan). Other agencies had long since dispensed with their transition teams and it was time for ACDA to do so, given that it had a new director coming soon. After this discussion ended, the three filed out and left ACDA shortly thereafter. Hackett remained acting director for about six weeks, doing a credible job holding the fort for the advent of Rostow.

Rostow's confirmation proceeding was relatively uneventful. Senator Helms did vote against him in committee and for a time Rostow was worried that Senator Christopher Dodd, a Democrat from Connecticut, might do so as well. Rostow had campaigned for Senator Buckley against Dodd in the 1978 election, and he feared that Dodd might still harbor some resentment. Fortunately, there was a secretary then at ACDA, one of whose best friends was Senator Dodd's then lady friend. We arranged to have the lady friend ask the senator in a diplomatic way what his position on the Rostow nomination was. The message came back by this circuitous route that he would not vote against Rostow. In the end, he did not vote and the nomination cleared the committee with only one negative vote (Senator Helms). It passed the full Senate by voice vote shortly thereafter.

Gene Rostow was a statesman and he did a good job as director. Once, early on in his tenure, we were discussing SALT II around the conference table in his office in the midst of many skeptics—including the designee for chairman of the ACDA General Advisory Committee, William Van Cleave, a very strong conservative on arms control issues. I was speaking about a provision of the treaty, which was already being observed informally pursuant to President Reagan's policy at this time, in mid-1981. I said that under this particular provision the United States is obligated as follows. Then I thought I caught something in Rostow's eye and I hastily said, "What I meant, Gene, was the United States would have been obligated to do this if SALT II had entered into force." Rostow said, "No, no, Tom, don't worry, SALT II will be with us forever. As the French say, 'nothing is so permanent as the provisional.'"

Van Cleave's nomination as chairman was abruptly withdrawn when, not long after the meeting, President Reagan, responding to strong objections from the Utah and Nevada senators whose constituents were not pleased at the thought of being the "sponge" that soaked up Soviet RVs, cancelled the shelter-based moveable MX ICBM. At a press conference in California, Van Cleave indicated that he thought Reagan was playing loose with U.S. security. Naturally, the White House was not pleased. Even in 1981, as the Pillsbury and Van Cleave affairs indicated, the extremists on strategic nuclear policy questions were falling by the wayside, and on these issues Reagan was developing into the centrist president that he became.

Gene Rostow duly proposed Bob Grey to be ACDA deputy director and Norman Terrell, a career State Department official and then NASA employee, to be assistant director for non-proliferation. Bob wanted his friend and carpool mate, Rich Richstein, a nice man with no arms control background, appointed general counsel. Rostow agreed to do this and as compensation put my name to the White House for assistant director for congressional relations. All went well with my nomination for the first review or two, but then my name was discovered on a list of government officials who had made speeches on behalf of SALT II (three to be precise) and the White House said no. I was then removed as general counsel, but was made head of an Office of Congressional Relations and Public Affairs with the same rank that I had as general counsel.

The Grey and Terrell nominations ran into heavy sledding in the Senate. They were reported from committee but held by conservative Republicans on the floor. A long political stalemate through 1982 ensued and contributed to Rostow's firing in January of 1983. Senator Roger Jepsen of Iowa appeared to be the leader of the anti–Grey/Terrell forces. Rostow and I met with him several times in an attempt to resolve the stalemate. In the second meeting, he made it clear that the Right wanted some satisfaction here— probably a reaction to the blocking of Rowny as director—and if Rostow would just drop Terrell, Grey could go through. In the third meeting, Senator Jepsen made the same offer but said Terrell could be renominated for something else, ambassador-at-large, for example. In the car on the way back to the office, I urged Rostow in the strongest possible terms to accept this offer, and he was initially inclined to do so. However, on our return, Terrell persuaded Grey not to move and Grey turned Rostow around. So the decision was made to make no compromise, with fatal results. Grey and Terrell were not confirmed, and after Rostow's firing Grey went to SHAPE as political advisor and Terrell left the government. This was tragic for Bob Grey, who deserved confirmation, and something could have been done for Terrell. Rostow was a good director who could have done more had he been able to stay longer. My deputy for congressional relations was Mel Christopher and my deputy for public affairs was Joe Lehman, younger brother of John, now Navy secretary, and Chris, who was on the NSC staff. Joe was so superbly capable that I ended up spending most of my time on congressional matters when I was not in Geneva with Paul Nitze.

The major arms control focus in 1981 was the Intermediate-Range Nuclear Forces (INF) negotiations, which became the centerpiece of Reagan's strategic policy. In the fall of 1977 Chancellor Schmidt of Germany had made an epochal speech at the International Institute of Strategic Studies in London observing that in all of the efforts to reach a strategic arms agreement with the Soviet Union, Eurostrategic weapons (primarily the SS-20, which was destabilizing the balance in Europe) were being overlooked. Also, there was negative reaction in Europe resulting from President Carter's precipitous decision to cancel the enhanced radiation tactical nuclear warhead (the neutron bomb). Thus was sparked a two-year negotiation within NATO, headed by Reg Bartholomew on the U.S. side, with assistance from John Newhouse, who was an ACDA assistant director in the Carter administration. Long negotiations with the British, Germans, Belgians, Dutch, and Italians ensued. It was envisaged that the United States would base two new medium-range missile systems in those countries to offset the Soviet SS-20: the extremely accurate Pershing II medium-range ballistic missile and the highly accurate land-based version of the Tomahawk cruise missile (a GLCM). The upshot of all this was that NATO adopted the famous two-track decision in December 1979. Arms control would be attempted for four years to try to remove or contain the threat of the SS-20s. If after four years, in 1983, satisfactory results had not been achieved on the arms control track, then NATO would proceed with the planned deployments of Pershing II and GLCM, which would be ready for deployment by that date.

The Reagan administration moved slowly to meet this commitment. Preliminary technical discussions had taken place in the fall of 1980 under the rubric of the TNF discussions, referred to as "preliminary exchanges." When the Reagan administration finally turned to this issue a dramatic proposal was made. Speaking at his alma mater (Eureka College in Illinois) in June 1981, President Reagan proposed the so-called "zero option," i.e., if the Soviet Union would destroy its 1,000 or so SS-20s and other medium-range missiles already deployed opposite Europe, the United States would not deploy the 108 Pershing IIs and 476 GLCMs it planned to begin deploying two years hence. This was a proposal claimed to be inspired by Dutch peace groups, but in actuality it was devised by Assistant Secretary of Defense Richard Perle and was intended to be unacceptable. It was derided by some as an insincere offer to trade nothing for something. But history sometimes plays tricks on us, as it did here on both proponents and opponents of the "zero option."

The principal U.S. objective when the negotiations began in November 1981 was the limitation of the growing Soviet modern, highly accurate, road-mobile, MIRVed, medium-range ballistic missile force (the SS-20s), which replaced the older, less accurate, single-warhead, fixed, medium-range ballistic missiles (SS-4s and SS-5s—missiles deployed in Cuba during the 1962 crisis). For the United States, the principal objection to Soviet replacement of the older SS-4s and SS-5s with the SS-20 was that, with the mobility and improved accuracy of the SS-20, the Soviet Union appeared to be replacing large, inaccurate city-busters with a war-fighting weapon and many more deployed nuclear warheads. The same could be said for the Pershing II and the GLCM, which looked to the Soviets like war-fighting weapons. The Soviets eventually agreed to eliminate all SS-20s (as well as all SS-4s and SS-5s) in exchange for the elimination of the U.S. Pershing II missiles and GLCMs, which began to be deployed in Europe in 1983. The INF Treaty contains a ban on intermediate-range missiles (with ranges of 1,000 to 5,500 kilometers) for the parties worldwide (including beyond the Urals outside of European Russia). In the INF Treaty the United States and the Soviet Union also agreed to ban, worldwide, shorter-range missiles (with ranges of 500 to 1,000 kilometers), in particular the Soviet SS-12 and SS-23 ballistic missiles and the U.S. Pershing I ballistic missile, deployed in Germany for some years.

At the Reykjavik Summit meeting in 1986, the Soviet Union agreed to the principle of intrusive on-site inspection for the INF Treaty. This was a true breakthrough in nuclear arms control agreements. Ironically, in 1990, almost two years after the entry into force of the INF Treaty, it was learned that in the mid-1980s the Soviet Union had transferred SS-23 missiles to the German Democratic Republic, Czechoslovakia, and Bulgaria, creating a serious diplomatic problem. The Soviet side maintained that the transfer did not involve an INF Treaty violation because these missiles were not "possessed" (the treaty term) by the Soviet Union as of the time of its entry into force. However, given the fact that during the negotiations the Soviet Union had insisted on the elimination of the U.S. Pershing I missiles transferred to the Federal Republic of Germany, not to have mentioned during the negotiations that it had transferred INF missiles as well was, in the view of the United States, indefensible.

The United States did not want to agree to a non-circumvention provision in this negotiation because the lack of clarity of the meaning of such an obligation in the SALT II Treaty had received much criticism in the U.S. Senate. However, the issue of the 72 Pershing I missiles that the United States had transferred to the Federal Republic of Germany was strongly asserted by the Soviet Union to be a problem that needed to be addressed in some way by the INF Treaty. The United States did not want these missiles included under the treaty as they belonged to a sovereign third state, even though the United States controlled the nuclear warheads. Eventually, the Federal Republic of Germany unilaterally announced that it would destroy these missiles prior to the completion of missile elimination under the INF Treaty, and the United States agreed to destroy the associated reentry vehicles after these missiles had been eliminated. A similar arrangement, in the view of the United States, should have been developed for the transferred SS-23 missiles, but this issue was overtaken by the collapse of the Warsaw Pact and the fall of the Soviet Union.

The Treaty between the United States of America and the Union of Soviet Socialist Republics on the Elimination of Their Intermediate-Range and Shorter-Range Missiles, known as the INF Treaty, was signed on December 8, 1987, and entered into force on June 1, 1988. In addition to the complete elimination of a whole class of nuclear-weapon delivery systems, the most notable feature of the INF Treaty is the far-reaching verification regime which includes intrusive on-site inspections.

Article IV of the INF Treaty provides that all intermediate-range missiles, launchers of such missiles, and all support structures and support equipment of the parties shall be eliminated within three years of entry into force in two phases, the first of 29 months duration and the second up to 36 months. This article also provides for the elimination of all shorter-range missiles, launchers of such missiles, and associated support equipment of the parties within 18 months of entry into force. Article IV was regarded during the negotiation as, in fact, the strongest bulwark of verification in the treaty.

This article prohibits the production and flight-testing of the missiles to be eliminated under the treaty. Thus, even if the national technical means and on-site inspection verification regimes miss a significant number of covert missiles, their value will dramatically decline over time due to the lack of flight-testing, which is verifiable by national technical means.

Article VIII, Paragraph 1 of the INF Treaty, to assist the operation of the verification regime, requires that all intermediate-range missiles and launchers of such missiles (including stages of missiles), after entry into force, may be located only at deployment areas or missile support facilities or be in transit. Paragraph 6 further requires that 30 days after entry into force, intermediate-range and shorter-range missiles (including stages) and launchers of such missiles may not be located at missile or launcher production facilities or at test ranges.

Article IX provides for a comprehensive exchange of data on systems subject to the treaty to be contained in the Memorandum on Data. It is provided that this data shall be updated as of the date of entry into force, 30 days after entry into force and 30 days after the end of each six-month period thereafter. The data to be exchanged includes the number of missiles, launchers, support structures, and equipment for all missile systems subject to the treaty. In addition, Article IX, Paragraph 5, requires notification of the elimination of a deployment area, missile operating base, or missile support facility 30 days in advance; changes in the number and location of elimination facilities and of the scheduled date of elimination (except launches for purposes of elimination) 30 days in advance; a launch or series of launches for purposes of elimination 10 days in advance; changes in the number of missiles, launchers, support structures and support equipment as a result of elimination pursuant to the Protocol on Elimination 48 hours after they occur; and transit of intermediate-range or shorter-range missiles or launchers of such missiles, as well as training missiles and launchers of these types no later than 48 hours after it has been completed. "Elimination" is the INF Treaty term meaning removal from the aggregate numbers covered by the treaty. Elimination is to be accomplished primarily by destruction. However, in limited numbers and for a limited period, SS-20s could be launched to destruction under the treaty. Elimination could also be effected by accidents and in small numbers under strict regulation as static display in museums.

Article X requires that missile systems subject to the treaty be eliminated in accordance with the Protocol on Elimination, with on-site inspection thereof pursuant to the Protocol on Inspection. The Protocol on Elimination in general provides for elimination by explosive demolition, cutting, crushing, or flattening, depending on the nature of the piece of equipment being eliminated. Paragraph 5 of Article X provides the detail for destruction by launch and permits a party in the first six months after entry into force to eliminate by launching up to 100 intermediate-range missiles. The purpose of this provision was to permit the Soviet Union to meet the time schedules set forth in the treaty given the large number of ss-20s it possessed. Experimental missiles, never deployed, of which each party had one type, must be eliminated within six months after entry into force. Paragraph 7 provides that missile systems are considered to be eliminated under the treaty once all the requirements of the Protocol on Elimination are met and notification given pursuant to Article IX.

Article XI, along with the greatly detailed Protocol on Inspection, sets forth the on-site inspection regime of the treaty, truly a new beginning in arms control. Paragraph 2 provides that such inspections may be conducted on the territory of the parties as well as within the territories of third party basing countries (permitted by associated Basing Country Agreements); that is, the United Kingdom, the Netherlands, Belgium, Germany, Italy, Czechoslovakia, Poland, and the German Democratic Republic. Paragraph 3 of Article XI provides that no later than 30 days after entry into force each party shall have the right to conduct on-site inspections at all missile operating bases and missile support facilities (other than missile production facilities) listed in the Memorandum on Data, and at all missile elimination facilities contained in the first data update called for in Paragraph 3 of Article IX. These inspections must be completed 30 days after entry into force. This is the so-called baseline inspection for the purpose of verifying the initial data.

Paragraph 4 provides for on-site inspection of the elimination of missile operating bases and support facilities, which must be conducted within 60 days of the scheduled date thereof. This has been termed the closeout inspection. Paragraph 5 contains the right to conduct inspections, beginning 90 days after entry into force, of missile operating bases, missile support facilities (other than elimination sites), and missile production facilities to verify the numbers of missiles, launchers, support structures, and support equipment located at such sites, as well as former missile operating bases and support facilities that have been eliminated. This right of periodic inspection was to exist for thirteen years under the INF Treaty—the three-year elimination period and for ten years thereafter—and therefore expired in the year 2000. A declining number of inspections is provided, that is, twenty per calendar year during the first three years after entry into force, fifteen such inspections during each of the subsequent five years, and ten per year in the last five years. No more than half of these inspections by each party in any one year may be in the territory of one basing country.

During the negotiations, the United States learned that the first two stages of the ss-25 land-mobile ICBM are identical ("outwardly similar" in the language of the treaty) to the two stages of the ss-20. The United States insisted upon the right of continuous inspection of the ss-25 final assembly plant (which had also built the ss-20)—the Votkinsk Machine Building Plant, located in the town of Votkinsk in the Ural Mountains—to assure itself that only ss-25s and not covert ss-20s are produced there. Paragraph 6(a) of the

Protocol on Inspection grants the United States this right. A reciprocal right was granted the Soviet Union at a former U.S. Pershing II production facility at Magna, Utah, in Paragraph 6(b), much to the surprise of the Hercules Corporation, whose site it was. This right was granted to the Soviet Union only for purposes of reciprocity, as the similarity problem did not exist in the United States. In spite of the fact that the company only learned at the last minute that they would have a continuous and permanent presence of Russian inspectors at their plant, they were always cooperative. The parameters of the inspection are governed by the protocol, which, in summary, establishes a perimeter with portals through which the missiles must leave the plant and, in appropriate cases, grants imaging of the missile canisters and the right to open up to eight missile canisters a year. (Unlike U.S. ballistic missiles, Soviet ballistic missiles leave the final assembly facility and are subsequently deployed inside canisters.) This right is effective six months after entry into force and would terminate at any time after the end of the second year after entry into force if there has been no final assembly at such plant for a previous period of twelve months.

Paragraph 7 sets forth the right of on-site inspection of the process of elimination, including elimination by means of launching pursuant to Article X, Paragraph 5. Inspectors conducting these inspections are required to confirm that the process of elimination has been completed in each specific case before the data may be changed. The final principal part of the verification regime is Article XIII, Paragraph 3, termed national technical means enhancement. Up to six times a year, for the three-year reduction period, the United States may, upon six hours notice, request cooperative measures at deployment bases of SS-25 ICBMs that are not former SS-20 operating bases (where a right to inspect would already exist under Paragraph 5 of Article XI), whereby the roofs of all fixed structures for SS-25s shall be opened and all missiles displayed on launchers in the open, so satellites can see them.

By the summer of 1981 it had become clear that President Reagan was committed to the INF negotiations when he proposed the zero option. Since it was clear that there would now be a negotiation, a negotiator was needed. The State Department candidate was Maynard "Mike" Glitman, a career diplomat and former deputy chief of mission at NATO. Rostow, who wanted to have his own candidate, settled on his colleague from the Committee on the Present Danger, Paul Nitze. I was dispatched to Nitze's summer home in Maine to help persuade him to accept. I spent two days at the Nitze household discussing INF with Paul and enjoying the Maine summer. In the end, Paul did accept and the settlement with State was that Mike Glitman would be his deputy, an arrangement that worked very well.

In October, Nitze began to assemble his negotiating team. He asked me to be the senior ACDA representative on his delegation. Bob Grey urged me to accept ("Tom, many are called, few are chosen") and I did. So I was now wearing two hats, chief of congressional relations and public affairs and senior ACDA representative on the INF delegation. Norm Clyne was asked by Paul to be his executive secretary and Jack McNeill his legal advisor. Major General Bill Burns of the army, a future ACDA director and subsequently a most important influence outside of government, was his JCS representative, and John Woodruff, a capable career official, represented OSD. In the first meetings we speculated on what we wanted to call the negotiations. The Soviets wanted to call them the medium-range missile negotiations, so we certainly could not accept that. Someone suggested that we use the word "intermediate" as meaning the same thing but different from the Soviet word. So that was agreed, and our proposal was to refer to the negotiations as Intermediate-Range (probably the same word in Russian) Nuclear Forces (INF). After about a year the Soviets gave up and accepted our title. With respect to other subjects that Nitze raised in the first two or three meetings, all of us were so in awe of the great man that we limited our responses to "Yes, Paul," "That's right, Paul." After the third meeting Norm Clyne telephoned each one of us on behalf of Paul. "If you are not prepared to speak up and challenge Paul's ideas in these meetings, then you should leave the delegation. Paul doesn't want to be surrounded by a bunch of 'yes men,'" he told us. I always admired this in Paul; he wanted you to challenge him, but you had better be sure of your ground when you did.

As a result of my SALT II work, I had become a bit controversial. As recorded above, as early as the spring of 1975 Ed Rowny had complained to John Lehman that I had become too personally involved in the success of SALT II and therefore should be removed as SALT II legal advisor. Jim Malone backed me, however, so I stayed. In September of 1981 Rowland Evans of Evans and Novak interviewed Gene Rostow, and since I was now head of the Office of Congressional Relations and Public Affairs I sat in on the interview. As I was walking to the elevator with Evans afterwards, he said, "You know you're pretty controversial up there" (referring to Capitol Hill). This surprised me a bit, as I was unaware that many on the Hill paid much attention to me.

Accordingly, I was a little concerned when I was informed in Geneva the day before the INF negotiations began that I had been listed in a right-wing publication as one of the "communists" on the INF delegation. So I obtained a copy of the publication. I was relieved when I saw that the list of the alleged "communists" on the U.S. INF delegation included three others—Jack McNeill, Norm Clyne, and Paul Nitze. I am always happy to be included on any list with Paul Nitze. Of course, Paul Nitze certainly encountered much controversy during his career, which, I suppose, goes with the territory. Senator Joe McCarthy accused him of being pro-communist because of his work under Dean Acheson; Bill Clements said he was "for the Russians"; he was denounced as right wing because of his work with the Committee on the Present Danger; and Richard Perle in 1982 leveled perhaps the ultimate charge when during a debate over INF negotiation policy he publicly referred to him as an "inveterate problem solver."

The INF negotiations opened on November 30, 1981. The first session, which lasted only two weeks, concerned itself with preliminaries. It was agreed that the delegations would return in January and operate roughly on a two-months-on, two-months-off schedule. The Soviet chief negotiator, Yuli Kvitsinski, was considered an expert on Europe in general and on Germany in particular. In his forties, he was a rising star in the Soviet diplomatic service and was deputy foreign minister when the Soviet Union collapsed. In the late 1980s, at a meeting in Bonn, he made the memorable statement that it was the nuclear arms control process that convinced Soviet leaders that they no longer needed the protective cloak of secrecy for security and, therefore, could agree to intrusive on-site inspection in the INF Treaty.

Early in the January round, Ambassador Kvitsinski made clear that the Soviets wanted to take account of British and French systems in establishing the balance in the treaty to be negotiated (the Soviets as yet had not come around to calling the negotiations the INF negotiations). Kvitzinski urged that the United States act in its own interests. He said that Germany would never develop its own nuclear weapons because if it did it would "quickly disappear." But Britain and France did have nuclear weapons, along with missile delivery systems, which they would never aim at the United States, so the Soviet Union had to consider these systems as part of the European missile balance. Thus, the Soviet Union wanted to call the negotiations those on medium-range missiles in Europe—by now anathema to the United States—as they were intended to implicitly include British and French systems.

Kvitsinski argued that the United States should deal with its allies the way the Soviet Union dealt with its allies. To illustrate this he told Nitze a story. A bear was traveling on a train and a rabbit entered the compartment, having just gotten on board, and he asked the bear if he could join him in the compartment. The bear said, "Yes." After a few minutes the conductor could be heard proceeding down the passageway. Suddenly, the rabbit discovered that he had forgotten his ticket and asked the bear for help. "No problem," said the bear, "I will hold you by the ears out of the window, and the conductor will not see you. I will give him my ticket, the conductor will leave to go to the next compartment and then I will pull you back in." "Great," said the rabbit, and the bear held him out the window with his left hand, holding his ticket in his right hand. The conductor came into the compartment and took the bear's ticket. He then said, looking suspiciously at the bear, "What is that in your left hand?" "Nothing," said the bear as he pulled his arm in the window and showed the conductor his empty left hand.

The Soviets tabled one inequitable formula after another for the INF missile balance, all based on either inclusion of or compensation for British and French systems. (Both the United Kingdom and France had ballistic missile submarines, and the French also had eighteen medium-range, land-based missiles. The Soviets did not try to include the nuclear-capable bombers or the short-range French nuclear missile Pluton.) The United States was strongly opposed to any compensation for British and French systems, in part because the United Kingdom and France were strongly opposed. They regarded these systems as strategic weapons for themselves, not theater weapons.

Kvitsinski had a somewhat conspiratorial way of operating. Once, his special assistant invited me to a private dinner at his apartment. For a while we discussed literature, Kvitsinski's assistant memorably remarking at one point that Dostoevsky was not truly Russian as he was "too emotional." After a while the talk turned to the negotiations and I was pressed for what the real bottom line was for the United States. At this point Kvitsinski suddenly materialized at the door and began asking questions himself as though he had been listening in on the conversation. Needless to say, it made one suspicious—a very different style from Karpov and Smolin.

The Soviets were pulling out all the stops in 1982, insisting on compensation for British and French systems so as to preserve a large advantage for themselves, while at the same time launching a huge propaganda campaign in Europe, led by a senior official, Victor Fallin, working directly for the Politburo. The objective, partly successful, was to try to whip up the European peace movement to a frenzy to make it as difficult as possible for the United States to deploy Pershing II and GLCM. Undoubtedly, the Soviets did hope to have a degree of political *diktat* over Western Europe with their large SS-20 deployments. For their part, the Soviets argued that Pershing II and GLCM were so accurate that they must be designed to decapitate the Soviet leadership in time of crisis as a prelude for all-out war. As 1982 proceeded, the peace movement opposition, particularly in the United Kingdom, the Netherlands, and Germany, grew more and more intense. The Soviets were determined to stop the Pershing II deployment in Germany scheduled for November 1983. The first GLCMs had arrived in Europe at Greenham Common in the United Kingdom a few months earlier.

Nitze, of course, was adamantly opposed to any form of direct compensation for British and French systems and any arrangement that would leave the Soviet Union with a missile preponderance in Europe. Nevertheless, he was concerned by the Soviet propaganda war being conducted in Western Europe and feared possible erosion of the commitment to deployment. He concluded that perhaps some kind of settlement based on U.S.–Soviet equality in INF missile systems in Europe, coupled with a limited concession to the Soviets in British and French systems, might be worth exploring. After all, there also were the U.S. Poseidon SLBMs offshore, which were dedicated to the European balance but which were not part of the negotiations. Nitze once told me that he thought the essence of this type of negotiation was to try to imagine in advance that narrow strip where both sides could stand comfortably and then try to steer the negotiations in that direction. In the spring and early summer of 1982, Nitze began meeting with Kvitsinksi privately. In their first meeting, they took a drive to Saint Cergue above Geneva and took a walk in the woods together. They sat down on a log, and Nitze, making clear to Kvitsinski that he had no authority to do this and was acting on his own, sketched out his idea. Each side would have equal numbers of INF systems in Europe, but the United States, as a concession to the Soviets, would deploy only GLCMs and not the Pershing II, which the Soviets regarded as the most threatening system. Thus, in politico-military terms, the SS-20 would be offset by equal numbers of U.S. GLCMs.

In a number of subsequent meetings this idea was refined into an agreement in principle. It was a brilliant move. On the U.S. side only Bill Burns, the JCS representative, and Gene Rostow in Washington knew what Nitze was doing. Who knows about the Soviets, but it was our belief that Kvitsinski had kept Gromyko informed. Nitze and Kvitsinski each returned to their capitals in August, and it was left that Kvitsinski would let Nitze know at the next meeting the reaction of the Soviet government.

Nitze returned to Washington and made a forceful presentation at the first NSC meeting held to consider the "Walk in the Woods" proposal, billed as a joint proposal by the two ambassadors but nothing more than that. Secretary of Defense Weinberger appeared to be neutral, the JCS were comfortable, and Reagan appeared interested. Perle, however, was out of town and urged delay and a second meeting to consider the proposal. In the interim, he persuaded Weinberger to oppose the deal on the ground that the United States could not give up the Pershing II, the equal numbers sweetener for the Soviet Union. Reagan was turned around by Weinberger's opposition and concluded the second meeting by deciding that he would not accept the deal. He said to tell the Soviets if they demonstrated continued interest in this idea that the answer from the United States was "no" and "that I am just one tough son of a bitch." When Nitze returned to Geneva, Kvitsinski did not mention the proposal again but many of us thought that if Nitze had been able to say that this arrangement would be acceptable to the United States, the Soviet Union would have had to accept. To do otherwise would have been to risk the immediate and total loss of the propaganda war it was still pursuing in Europe. Although the final INF Treaty was a better result, the "Walk in the Woods" formula, for its time, was a tour de force.

One of my personal rewards for being on the INF delegation was working closely with Paul Nitze, and since I was now concentrating on congressional relations when in Washington this meant that I accompanied Paul on all his Hill trips to report on INF. Thus I had many taxicab rides with Paul in 1982 and 1983, to and from Capitol Hill. During these rides I often was treated to a Paul Nitze story. One of the stories that especially impressed me was how in 1953 he was held over for a time as head of State Policy Planning (until attacked by Senator Joe McCarthy), and in the spring Paul had called his former boss, Dean Acheson, and invited him to lunch. Acheson accepted with pleasure and noted that this was his first luncheon invitation since he had resigned as secretary of state in January, *sic transit gloria mundi.* Paul also related at some length how he came to be a co-founder of the Aspen Ski Corporation and a skiing pioneer in American West—originally primarily to find a place to ski comparable to what he knew in Europe.

He was truly indefatigable—in Geneva we would work all day and sometimes I would accompany him to speak with students at one of the universities in Geneva in the evening. Later in the Reagan administration, when he was no longer INF negotiator, he was special advisor to Secretary Shultz for arms control. He would go to an INF decision meeting in Washington and be assigned the task of briefing the allies. Thence to the airport after the meeting, he would fly all night, meet with Prime Minister Thatcher in the morning, Chancellor Kohl in the afternoon, go to Italy that evening for a meeting with the prime minister and foreign minister, meet with the president and prime minister of France the next morning, and conduct a North Atlantic Council briefing at NATO at mid-day. On his way back to Washington he would stop at The Hague in the afternoon to brief the Dutch government, and be back in his office in Washington later that day. And he was in his late seventies. There was a story about him, probably apocryphal but which I choose to believe. In his middle sixties, while in Geneva at the SALT negotiations, he played a game of tennis against Roger Molander of the NSC, then about thirty years old and a good player. Paul won easily and was asked how he could play tennis like that at his age. He allegedly replied, "My body does what I tell it to." To my mind, that sums up the man.

The strategic arms negotiations finally began again in June of 1982, renamed the START negotiations, with General Rowny as chair of the U.S. delegation. As billed, this negotiation was going to limit warheads, which kill people, rather than missile launchers, which do not and which had been what the effete people at the SALT negotiations focused on. It turned out that the warheads were counted by means of their associated ballistic missiles, which in turn were counted by means of their associated missile launchers. The end result was the same; the only difference was public relations. This first phase of the START negotiations was characterized by propagandistic U.S. positions. Rowny had a good team with him. Ambassador Jim Goodby (later the "loose nukes" negotiator during the Bush and Clinton administrations) represented State and Jack Mendelsohn (of Calcutta Cable fame) represented ACDA. Nevertheless, this phase of START went nowhere in its year and a half of life between June 1982 and December 1983, when the negotiations were terminated in the wake of the Soviet walkout from INF in November.

In January 1983, Gene Rostow was abruptly fired as ACDA director by the Reagan administration. Among the rumored reasons was the long stalemate with the Right over the Grey nomination and Rostow's inability to refrain from offering unsolicited advice on the Middle East at interagency meetings. In addition, by his support of the "Walk in the Woods," Rostow had demonstrated that he also was a "problem solver," an attitude anathema to some in the Reagan administration, particularly in the early days. Perhaps the other issues were the means and this was the real reason. In any case, Jeanne Kirkpatrick's deputy at the U.S. United Nations mission, Ken Adelman, was chosen to replace Gene. Ken was then thirty-six years old and was perceived by many as a reflexive Reagan right-winger whose mission would be to destroy ACDA and arms control. History proved Ken to be anything but a reflexive right-winger. He was supportive of ACDA and arms control policy and did not lack personal courage. He was somewhat skeptical about the effectiveness of some arms control policies but he was a constructive force. And no one backed his people better than Ken Adelman.

His lack of arms control experience and apparent lack of interest in the subject did make him vulnerable to an all-out attack from Democrats in the Senate during confirmation hearings. Initially, the State Department managed his confirmation and Joe Lehman and I were excluded from the process. His confirmation became a cause célèbre. There were many minor issues, such as whether or not he improperly brought back African art to the United States while accompanying his wife, Carol, in Zaire for several years while she was on an Agency for International Development posting. The real issue was whether he did or did not have the assigned mission of destroying arms control. The point at which his confirmation changed from mildly difficult to very difficult came before the Senate Foreign Relations Committee. Senator Claiborne Pell, Democrat of Rhode Island, asked, "Would you resign if you became convinced that President Reagan had turned his back on arms control?" Ken had never experienced a show like this before and he understandably did not want to say he would resign at his confirmation hearing. While the simple and correct answer was "yes, of course," to dismiss the question, Ken replied that this would never be an issue because that could never happen. He thus sounded evasive and this enabled Pell and other Democratic senators to ask the question again and again with the same answer.

In all, the question was asked seven times and each time put Ken in more trouble. Joe and I, sitting behind the State Department managers, tried to pass a note to Ken that read, "say, yes," but the State managers refused to let it be passed through. Joe and I then went to a pay telephone in the hallway and called Bud MacFarlane, then deputy national security advisor. There was little he could do on the spot since the damage was already done but I was made co-manager of the confirmation the next day. However, at this point it was largely a rearguard action. Ken received a negative vote in committee, but with effort his nomination did pass on the floor with a fifteen-vote margin (57–42), not a ringing endorsement, but Ken turned out to be one of the few nominees in history to lose in committee and win on the floor.

Into this maelstrom came the Rowny "hit list" controversy. For the incoming ACDA director in January 1983, Ed Rowny decided to prepare some unsolicited advice on personnel. He had his assistant in Geneva, Colonel Sam Watson, who was his conduit to Richard Perle during SALT II, prepare comments on key personnel, which he reviewed and then forwarded to Adelman in Washington. Adelman maintained that he never really looked at the document, but routinely passed it on to Robin West, a friend who was helping him with the transition. As the storm broke, given Adelman's precarious position in the confirmation process, this was a good position to be able to take.

There were some fourteen people on the list. The comments on Jim Goodby and Jack Mendelsohn of Rowny's own delegation were that they supported "progress at any price," and Joe Lehman was described as incompetent. I was described as "smart, quick, left-leaning," and had to be carefully watched. And it implied that I spent too much time with Senator Howard Baker—my job was congressional relations. Furthermore, the way it was worded, it appeared that I was left-leaning *because* I spent too much time with Howard Baker—by anyone's measure a real stretch. There were also scurrilous remarks about other people. Somehow—Washington works in mysterious ways—a copy of this memorandum found its way onto Gene Rostow's desk in New Haven, where he had returned after his firing. He then commissioned Joe Pressel, a career State Department officer who had served as his executive secretary, and Bob Grey to make its contents known to those on the list. Joe Pressel came to see me, and he also visited Joe Lehman, who was quick to come counsel with me—he was outraged and immediately so informed Bud MacFarlane. (With one brother at this time on the NSC staff and the other secretary of the Navy, Joe was a very poor choice for an ad hominem attack.)

My first act was to call Cran Montgomery on Senator Baker's staff, my good friend and later ambassador to Oman. He thought the whole thing was insane, of course, and, unbeknownst to me at the time, his first act after hanging up the telephone was to call Pam Turner, White House aide for the Senate, and brief her on this. The memorandum soon found its way into the hands of the press, the expected cause célèbre followed; Strobe Talbott wrote an article in *Time* magazine entitled "Memo Misfire," and it all tended to further tar Adelman with the suspicion that he really did intend to dismantle arms control once confirmed.

As the furor increased, the Senate Foreign Relations Committee demanded an explanation from Rowny. He returned from Geneva to prepare for a hearing date before the committee. As Rowny was on his way back, I was called by Pam Turner and asked to be Rowny's coach to prepare for the hearing and appear with him before the committee—me, the "had to be carefully watched" guy. Needless to say, I was surprised but not dismayed. I had been on the Hill a few times after the memo leaked and found that senators thought that the suggestion that I was left-leaning because I spent too much time with the majority leader uproariously funny. Also, people at ACDA began appearing at work wearing Rowny hit list T-shirts, complete with bull's-eye, so there was humor about this even in the executive branch.

Rowny arrived and I spent two days coaching him before we appeared before the committee in executive session in their small hearing room. Nobody pressed Ed too hard and his explanation that this was prepared by his staff without his direct participation was not challenged. I had counseled him to be apologetic and he was. Thus the hearing ended with no real damage to anyone. After the hearing ended I walked over to the side of the room to say hello to Cran. While we were talking several committee staffers came up and said, "Aha, we caught you" (spending too much time with Senator Baker's staff). Later that day I accompanied Paul Nitze to a briefing of the Senate Intelligence Committee on INF, and at the conclusion of the hearing, the chairman, Senator Moynihan, said, "And Mr. Graham, I hope that you keep your job." As I was walking out of the hearing room I ran into Senator John Chaffee, the late Rhode Island Republican, in the hall. "Tom, oh ho-ho, you Baker left-leaner, oh ho-ho," he said. Disarmament is a crazy subject.

So, as 1983 ground on, INF in its post–"Walk in the Woods" mode went nowhere, just like START. The first deployment of Pershing II and GLCM grew nearer and nearer. As I said, the first INF deployment was to be GLCM at Greenham Common in England in September, but the real deadline for the Soviets was the Pershing II deployment planned for November in Germany, the only one of the five NATO basing countries that would receive the Pershing II—the others got GLCMs. Ambassador Kvitsinski kept dropping hints that the Soviets would walk out if the November deployment took place. As the months went by, the situation became more and more tense. The rhetoric from the Soviet Union became more shrill, the demonstrations by the peace groups in Western Europe became more strident, but the United States and NATO stood firm. The negotiations continued to make no progress, November arrived, and the first Pershing II missile systems arrived in Germany. A few days later at the regularly scheduled INF plenary meeting, Kvitsinski told Nitze that he was leaving and that the negotiations were suspended. He then went outside, told the press the same thing, and departed. A week or two later, Soviet Ambassador Karpov said the same thing to Rowny and START was suspended as well.

So by December 1983, arms control did appear dead, not because of anything that Ken Adelman did in Washington, but rather because in 1982 the Reagan administration would not accept the brilliant deal on INF that Paul Nitze had brought them on a silver platter. Even though it would later prove to be the dark before the dawn, 1984 was a dangerous time. The Cold War was at one of its worst points. Disarmament negotiations had collapsed, military build-ups continued on both sides, the nuclear arms race was in full swing, and early in 1984 the Soviets shot down a commercial airliner—Korean

Air Lines 007 bound for Seoul—with a U.S. congressman on board. It was a bad time. Secretary Shultz and Foreign Minister Gromyko could hardly speak to one another.

The only significant issue I worked on in 1984 was as part of a team operating out of the White House to persuade Congress to lift the legislative "fence" around the MX (or Peacekeeper) ICBM and allow its deployment to be funded. After several weeks of work—we met daily in the Roosevelt Room in the White House—we were successful. At our last meeting someone from the president's personal staff entered the room as we were disbanding and asked us to wait a moment. President Reagan then entered the room and congratulated and thanked each one of us individually. He was good that way. But there was nothing to do in the disarmament field in 1984—at least with respect to nuclear weapons—except the work on MX deployment.

In December 1981 I had noticed a poster on the side of a number of buildings in Geneva. It was a proclamation of the newly elected Geneva City Council. In the proclamation good wishes were given to the INF negotiations—probably because there was nothing else available at the time that the newly elected city council could comment on as it took office. Nevertheless, it was the only official acknowledgement by Geneva or Switzerland of the many important disarmament negotiations that had been held (and would be held) there that I had ever seen. I mentioned this to Jack McNeill and he went to the offices of the city council and asked if there were any copies remaining of the proclamation. He was given the last three copies. He gave one to Paul Nitze and one to me. We all framed the proclamation and hung it on our office walls. The Geneva nuclear arms negotiation process appeared incomplete and dead in 1984 but we looked at the 1981 proclamation on our walls and hoped.

After the disaster of KAL-007 and the stalemate and stagnation of 1984, and with Gorbachev soon to take power, both the United States and the Soviet Union began to attempt to move away from this truly confrontational period of the Cold War. Brezhnev had died in 1982 and had been succeeded by two successive long-time Communist Party leaders, Andropov and Chernyenko, each of whom lived only about one year after taking office. President Reagan, for his part, began to distance himself somewhat from the harsher rhetoric of his first years in office. Of course, no one could know, and indeed no one suspected, that the situation was about to turn dramatically for the better with the advent of Gorbachev and that the Cold War itself had only about six or seven years to run.

Early in 1985, Senator Edward Kennedy of Massachusetts made a trip to the Soviet Union and was one of the first western politicians to meet with the newly installed Gorbachev. Before he went to Moscow, Senator Kennedy asked to be briefed on several aspects of Soviet policy. I was asked to do the briefing on arms control and spent several hours with the senator, bringing him up to date on START, INF, and other arms control issues. As I recall, there were three others who briefed Kennedy on various subjects, including Mark Palmer, a senior Soviet expert and later U.S. ambassador to Hungary. Kennedy went to Moscow, met with Gorbachev, and returned and briefed the administration. A few days after his return I received a dinner invitation from Senator Kennedy. He invited his four briefers to his house for drinks and dinner and gave us a lengthy debrief of his meeting with Gorbachev, along with his personal assessment of the new Soviet leader, which was quite positive. It was an unusual courtesy and greatly appreciated.

Secretary Shultz and Foreign Minister Gromyko met in Geneva in January 1985 with the objective of attempting to put the arms control process, suspended since December 1983, back on track. I wrote the secretary a memorandum explaining the relationship between SDI and the ABM Treaty (the broad interpretation debate was to come later that year) and briefed him on it in Geneva, for which I received a nice letter from the secretary. It was a stellar delegation that Shultz led to Geneva. It included Paul Nitze, now the special advisor to the secretary of state for arms control, ACDA Director Ken Adelman, Deputy National Security Advisor Bud MacFarlane, Ed Rowny (who was still listed as the START negotiator), and Richard Perle from the Pentagon. Our first morning in Geneva we met in Shultz's hotel room at the Intercontinental. He greeted us in his dressing gown and we had a general run-through of our strategy with the Soviets. As part of the discussion, I presented the conclusions of my memo to the secretary that SDI was consistent with the ABM Treaty as long as it remained a research program but that compliance problems began once the development and testing stage began, in particular the development, testing, and deployment of space-based ABM systems based on any technology that was prohibited by Article V of the treaty. No one expressed any objection to this conclusion.

Gromyko, in the discussions, expressed strong objections to the SDI program, claiming that it was illegal under the ABM Treaty, and he said the objective of the Soviet Union was to forestall an arms race in space. Shultz asserted that what the United States wanted was to revive the START and INF negotiations, and that the United States could not accept any formal link to limitations on arms in space. In the end, it was agreed that strategic arms negotiations would begin again, that the negotiations would be called the Nuclear and Space Arms Talks (NST), and that there would be three sub-negotiations, which would not be linked: START, INF, and Defense and Space. The Soviets expected that their concerns about SDI would be responded to in the Defense and Space Arms sub-negotiation, while INF and START moved forward. The Soviets indicated that INF and START could proceed but could not be completed and signed until there was agreement on space arms issues. It was agreed that the negotiations in this new format would reopen on March 12, 1985. *Newsweek* magazine, among other publications, did an article on this meeting and published a picture with the article. The picture showed Nitze, MacFarlane, Rowny, Adelman, Perle, and me standing side by side, with a caption that read, "Shultz's Shaky Team." After the delegation returned to Washington there was an NSC meeting in the Cabinet Room at the White House attended by both the president and the vice president. Secretary Shultz brought me along as the delegation lawyer and introduced me to President Reagan as such. The president was very cordial, but he expressed skepticism as to whether the Soviet Union cared about law.

The United States had a new delegation to form. It was decided that Max Kampelman, also a former member of the Committee on the Present Danger, a prominent former colleague of Hubert Humphrey, an outstanding lawyer, and the former U.S. representative at the Helsinki Final Act follow-on conference in Madrid in 1980–81 (where he greatly distinguished himself), would be asked to head the U.S. delegation to the Nuclear and Space Arms Talks. He was to have Executive Level II rank, sub-cabinet level, and was to be supported by seven other ambassadors: the negotiator and deputy in each sub-negotiation and his deputy Warren Zimmerman, former DCM in Moscow and Paris and later the last U.S. ambassador to Yugoslavia, who would be his executive secretary. I was the legal advisor for the entire delegation, although as a practical matter at that time I spent most of my time with the Defense and Space Arms Group.

Rowny was not continued as START negotiator; he was made a special advisor to Shultz but, unlike Nitze, had little to do and therefore was effectively shelved. John Tower, later President Bush's first choice as secretary of defense, blocked by Senator Nunn and others, was asked to be START negotiator. Tower asked Ron Lehman, who had been on his Senate staff and was then at the NSC (and a future START negotiator and ACDA director), to be his deputy. Mike Glitman, Nitze's former number two, would head INF, and Hank Cooper, a future head of the SDI Office (SDIO), would head Space. All told the delegation had about a hundred members.

The Soviet delegation was not quite this large, but it was sizable and most of the old standbys were there. Karpov was overall head as well as START negotiator. General Starodubov, formerly of the Strategic Rocket Forces and now the SCC Commissioner, headed their Space Group, and Alexander Obukhov, an old SALT hand, INF. Obukhov later succeeded Karpov as overall head of delegation and START negotiator and Lem Masterkov succeeded him as INF negotiator. In the Bush administration, after the NST structure was abandoned, Yuri Nazarkin succeeded Obukhov as START negotiator.

The leadership of this huge U.S. group left Andrews Air Force Base by Air Force plane on the morning of March 11, 1985. The senior members for the most part had their wives with them. I had an aisle seat, Christine was next to me, and Dan Gallington, an OSD colonel, was against the wall; "wall" is the right word—there was no window seat as this was one of those converted tanker planes often used by delegations, which had no windows. Dan was one of the point men for SDI, a lawyer, Air Force colonel, and long-time bureaucrat in OSD. Later he went on to outstanding service in the Intelligence Unit at the Justice Department. During our time together at the negotiations we agreed on little but became good friends. He leaned over—we had not met before—and asked me why I had become involved in arms control. I replied sarcastically, "to work for peace." I think he took me seriously, and perhaps he mentally noted me as one to watch.

As the negotiations began it became quickly clear that the United States was going to stonewall in the Defense and Space Arms Group—to the great disappointment of the Soviets—but would try to plow ahead in START and INF. The Defense and Space Arms discussions sank into what were essentially polemics on both sides. The Soviets were accusing the United States of violating the ABM Treaty with SDI, and the United States responded with various breach of ABM Treaty compliance charges against the Soviets. The U.S. intra-delegation Defense and Space Group discussions were a different matter. For whatever reason huge arguments occurred among the dozen or so men in our small secure conference room almost every day. I am not really sure why: perhaps it was the personalities—Dan and Hank (Cooper) often got into it; perhaps it was the intensity of the issue—the Group was sharply divided between those who were pro-SDI and those who were pro-ABM Treaty. The pro-ABM Treaty numbers were smaller, and I was always thankful that one of them was State Representative Greg Suchan, for many years and still a distinguished officer. Greg, in those days, looked as though he could easily—and might actually—take on two or three of the other side at once. The ABM Treaty always seemed to bring out high emotion; perhaps it was the cramped space in our small conference room; or maybe we needed a few women present for leavening—there were no women on the Defense and Space Group delegation at this time. In any case, all through the spring and summer there were huge battles over how to characterize Soviet ABM performance, how to characterize SDI, etc. Several of our discussions quite literally came close to blows. Perhaps it was the subject matter.

A year or two later, there was a Defense and Space Arms negotiation backstopping meeting at ACDA. Lou Nosenzo, assistant director for strategic affairs, was in the chair for ACDA. During the meeting the OSD representative, who had just spent two weeks with the delegation in Geneva, was pressing for a particular course of action. The State Department representative, who had spent the better part of a year with the delegation and who was a Soviet specialist, was opposing the idea on the grounds that it would be counterproductive. The OSD representative retorted that if the State representative only understood Russians he would know that the Soviets would be comfortable with the proposal. This went on for a time and the meeting ended inconclusively. Afterwards, the State representative walked up to the OSD representative and said, "I may not know Russians, but I do know assholes, and you're one," whereupon the OSD representative attempted to punch him; they were quickly pulled apart by others at the meeting.

There was another meeting the next day and everyone was in their places except the State representative. He opened the door and saw the OSD representative sitting in his seat and refused to come in. Whereupon Lou, the chairman, stood up, took the OSD representative by the arm, went into the hall, took the State representative with his other arm, and shepherded them down the hall to an empty room. He put them both inside, shut and locked the door, and said through the door that there was a telephone inside and when they were prepared to behave like civilized human beings they could call him and ask to return to the meeting, but not before. About forty-five minutes passed, and finally the call came. They returned to the meeting and after that everything proceeded normally. I guess it was the subject matter.

The INF and START negotiations made little progress in 1985. The real progress in START was made during the Bush administration with first Richard Burt (former assistant secretary of State/PM and ambassador to Germany) and subsequently Linton Brooks (a former NSC senior staff member) as negotiators.

The INF negotiations were a bit different. After the failure of the "Walk in the Woods" initiative, there had been a stalemate until the suspension in November 1983. This stalemate largely continued in 1985, with the United States pressing for its zero solution and the Soviets rebuffing this and complaining about the nuclear forces of the United Kingdom and France. This state of affairs carried on more or less until the turning point of the Reykjavik Summit in October 1986. During 1985 and 1986 there was progress on subsidiary issues—the issue of the lower range INF systems was discussed, those missile systems with a range of 300 to 1,000 kilometers—but there was no progress on major issues such as numerical limits, verification, and the Soviet demand for compensation for third-country systems.

Max had successfully proposed to the Soviets a two-month-on, two-month-off negotiating schedule. I spent the first two sessions in 1985 in Geneva with the delegation and two weeks of the third session in the fall. Given the state of affairs and also the debate now raging in Washington over ABM Treaty interpretation, I did not return again to the delegation until early 1987, after the Reykjavik Summit, although I kept in close and regular touch by telephone.

In my judgment, the Reykjavik Summit was the true watershed of modern arms control. The proposal to meet came unexpectedly from Gorbachev, and plans were hastily made. Only Ken Adelman attended for ACDA. It is well known that by the end of the meeting in Reykjavik Ronald Reagan was discussing with Mikhail Gorbachev a proposal to eliminate all strategic nuclear arms as a progression from the U.S. proposal to eliminate all ballistic missiles. Perhaps something might have happened if Reagan had not been pulled back by his advisors, who urged him not to continue because his dream, SDI, would not be protected. Gorbachev wanted SDI limited to the laboratory. Of course, SDI would not have been needed if President Reagan had been allowed by his advisors to try to realize his real dream: the elimination of the strategic nuclear threat. But nevertheless Reykjavik did represent an arms control sea change. At that meeting Gorbachev agreed to the principle of intrusive on-site inspection for the INF Treaty. Nothing thereafter was ever the same. This fundamental change in position permitted INF to be signed in 1987, CFE in 1990, START I in 1991, START II in 1993, CWC in 1993, and CTBT in 1996. All of these treaties have provisions for intrusive on-site inspection.

It had been traditional for the Russian State to hide its military weakness behind a veil of secrecy. Russia has been successfully invaded five times from the West in the last four hundred years. I have recounted how General Ogarchev asked General Allison not to talk about Soviet ICBM deployments in front of the civilian members of the Soviet SALT I team because they were not "cleared for that information." The Soviets would agree to no numbers applicable to their forces in SALT I, as we have seen. In December 1978, at a Vance-Gromyko meeting in Geneva on the margins of the SALT II negotiations, a rather contorted paragraph was finally agreed to with the Soviets to the effect that they would not impede verification by encoding or any other form of deliberate concealment of telemetric information. In June of 1978, when Ambassador Semenov agreed to the principle of a simple agreed data base setting forth the numbers possessed by each side of the systems being limited (e.g., number of ICBM launchers, the number of SLBM launchers, etc.), he remarked to Ralph Earle, "Today we are repealing four hundred years of Russian history."

After the Reykjavik Summit it was a changed situation. In 1987 the Soviets at INF were prepared to exchange more data on their systems than the JCS wanted, as there was a limit to what the JCS was prepared to turn over. In the last week of the INF negotiations the Soviet officer making the presentation said, "a week ago I would have been shot for what I am doing today" (he really meant a year ago). Gorbachev agreed to the U.S. proposal, pressed during 1986 in Geneva, of double zero. These were, first, a ban on all intermediate-range, ground-launched nuclear missiles (both ballistic and cruise) of ranges from 1,000 to 5,500 kilometers and a ban on all short-range, ground-launched nuclear missiles of ranges 500 to 1,000 kilometers. The higher range ban captured the U.S. Pershing II and GLCM as well as the Soviet SS-20. There were no systems between the range of Pershing II (1,800 km) and Pershing I (950 km). The Soviet SS-23 had a 500-km range and was caught by the lower range ban. In 1981 Richard Perle had urged Ronald Reagan to propose a zero solution for INF. It looked good. Dutch peace groups had proposed it, but it was virtually out of the question that the Soviet Union would accept it given their advantage of about 1,200 to zero in INF systems. But lo and behold, five years later Gorbachev was accepting not one, but two zeros, the famous INF double-zero solution.

When I returned to the delegation in 1987, all was different. I continued to work with the Defense and Space Arms Group, although little was happening there. I worked occasionally with the INF Group. Karin Lawson from my office was the INF attorney and had been so for the last two years. Normally she was the only delegation officer that Mike Glitman took with him when he went to Shultz-Shevardnadze meetings on INF. She knew the whole text. INF was in high gear, with much of the effort spent on working out the data to be exchanged and agreement on the parameters of inspections. One issue that I worked on in Washington was obtaining the consent of the five allied governments (Belgium, Germany, Italy, the Netherlands, and the United Kingdom) to Russian inspectors conducting inspections of U.S. bases on their sovereign territory. This agreement had to be obtained in a legally binding manner. The Soviets claimed they had the same problem with East Germany, Czechoslovakia, and Poland. Therefore, protocols had to be worked out and signatures obtained so this could be done.

After about six weeks I returned home at the insistence of Norm Clyne to begin ACDA general counsel work on the INF article-by-article analysis, as it was now clear that INF was going to happen. As soon as the summit signing date was announced I returned to Geneva about two weeks before the conclusion of the negotiations. When I arrived several senior delegation officials said, "It's impossible, we cannot possibly finish by December 8; INF will have to be signed later." I replied, "INF will be signed on December 8, the two presidents have willed that it be so." This time I was heavily involved in INF issues, although Karin appropriately kept the lead on the most complicated issues. We worked ahead often until the wee hours, sometimes all night. Some delegation officials cracked and couldn't work any more, but the delegation kept going.

There were four INF documents: a treaty, a protocol, a verification protocol, and a database document. The meeting in Washington at which Reagan and Gorbachev would sign INF was set for Tuesday, December 8. We had a large converted Air Force transport plane standing by. On Saturday two of the four documents had been completed and the two negotiators, Glitman and Obukhov, initialed each page, signifying their attestation that these documents were complete and ready for signature. But the other two documents had many issues remaining. The delegations worked around the clock Sunday and Monday, but as we were preparing to leave for the airport one major issue remained. The U.S. delegation was waiting around the U.S. Mission. Most of the arms control function had been transferred over to the newly completed, fortress-like U.S. Mission in Geneva in 1984. Nuclear and Space Arms and SCC went to the Mission, multilateral—the Conference on Disarmament—stayed at the Botanic Building, where it still remained in 2000. Karin was dispatched down the hill to the Soviet Mission to try to resolve this last issue with Mr. Kryuchkov, the son of the then head of the KGB. About an hour later she returned with agreement.

Since we knew that we would not have time to initial the texts, we had persuaded Obukhov and his deputy for INF Lem Masterkov (Masterkov's name allegedly is not a real name, but an acronym name given to him by his parents standing for Lenin, Engels, Marx), to go with us on the plane. So we initialed the many pages in the cavernous Air Force transport plane, with seats set up like a movie theater, on our way to Washington on December 7. Not surprisingly, we found an error on one of the pages the next morning, so I had to find Obukhov at Gorbachev's arrival ceremony at the White House to get him to initial the corrected page, and then find Mike in the State Department and get his initials. But a complete agreed, conformed, and accurate treaty text, page by page, was before the two presidents that afternoon.

European peace groups had put on massive demonstrations, sit-ins, indeed all kinds of civil disobedience campaigns as the November 1983 deployment date grew near. Hundreds of thousands marched in Germany and the Netherlands. There was unrest in the other basing countries. And the nuclear freeze movement was growing stronger in the United States. Nevertheless, the European governments and NATO stuck to their guns and went ahead with the deployments as planned pursuant to the 1979 two track decision—if an INF agreement was not reached four years after the NATO decision of December 1979, NATO would begin offsetting missile deployments. After the deployments were underway the opposition gradually faded away. And by the time of signature the INF Treaty was secondary news. It was important on the day it happened but little noticed afterward. But it is a landmark agreement. It provided for intrusive on-site inspection and it eliminated a whole class of nuclear weapon systems, two important firsts.

Ratification of the INF Treaty was organized in the classic way. The ACDA Office of General Counsel wrote the article-by-article analysis to accompany the treaty to the Senate. It was drafted in a literalist way, without any special insights or conclusions, to ease its passage through the bureaucracy, an unfortunate trend in recent years. Max Kampelman, the overall NST negotiator, and Mike Glitman, the INF negotiator, were put in charge of ratification, with Max serving as the overall head and Mike as his deputy. This was the normal pattern and it usually achieved success.

All agencies supported the treaty during the hearings and much was made of the fact that this was the first arms control treaty in history to completely eliminate an entire class of nuclear weapon systems. And indeed it was historic and precedent setting. The only significant problem that arose was the effort of Senator Dan Quayle to achieve some prominence. He raised with great fanfare a Philadelphia lawyer-like issue as to whether the INF Treaty covered systems based on other physical principles. He could not be persuaded to put aside this largely irrelevant point, so we went back to the Soviets to confirm that this was their understanding as well as ours—that such technology, should it ever appear and be relevant to medium-range systems, was covered. Somewhat perplexed, the Soviets confirmed that this was their understanding as well. Fortunately for INF ratification, a Reagan-Gorbachev Summit meeting was scheduled for June 1988 in Moscow, and the White House very much wanted to achieve Senate approval by the summit. With this deadline, the Senate did act promptly and the INF Treaty was brought into force in June 1988.

During the run-up to entry into force, initial discussions had been held with the Soviets on the implementation of the INF Treaty on-site inspection regime. Early on in late 1988 it had to be decided in what agency the United States on-site inspection function would be placed. The new national security advisor, General Colin Powell, would make the decision. My first contact with Powell was during an attempt (one of many) on the ABM Treaty, also in 1988. He had recently become national security advisor after Frank Carlucci left for Defense. Powell, who had been Carlucci's deputy at the NSC, was regarded even then, before he became prominent, as a most capable and steady leader who was a very quick study. Carlucci's and Powell's arrival at NSC had resulted in more creative and effective arms control policies. We were preparing for the 1988 ABM Treaty Review Conference, which was held in Geneva in August. Some in Defense wanted the United States to declare at the Review Conference that the Soviet Union was in material breach of a central provision of the ABM Treaty because of the Krasnoyarsk radar deployment. That they were in material breach of the treaty was beyond question, but such a declaration from the United States would be tantamount legally to saying that we were severing treaty relations with them and that would be the end of the ABM Treaty. Powell, although not a trained international lawyer, quickly grasped the point and ruled in the negative despite long, complicated arguments on both sides at the decision meeting.

Powell and Adelman were friends, so I believed that there would be a good chance for the INF inspection function to be given to ACDA if Ken pushed for it. Max Kampelman, from his position as counselor to the secretary of state and NST negotiator, supported ACDA for this assignment. Others proposed OSD, as most of the inspectors would be military officers. But this function was, it seemed to me, Ken Adelman's for the asking. A long debate ensued in Ken's outer offices. Mike Guhin, Ken's executive assistant, and Lou Nosenzo believed this would be too large a function—in terms of both people and money—to graft onto ACDA. Fred Eimer and I argued that arms control verification/inspection was integral to arms control treaty-making and it was essential to place this function under the control of ACDA. Ken decided, not long before he resigned as ACDA director, to side with Mike and Lou and decline this role for ACDA, a fateful decision in my view, since five years later, with much of the arms control negotiating agenda completed and the emphasis shifting more to implementation, verification, and compliance, it became easier for opponents of an independent ACDA to argue that the agency had outlived its usefulness.

The on-site inspection function was therefore located in OSD as the On-site

Inspection Agency (OSIA), to be headed by a general—the first director was General Roland LaJoie. ACDA was permanently given the deputy position and was one member of the interagency committee that oversaw OSIA activities, but it never had any real influence over OSIA. OSIA (later part of the Defense Threat Reduction Agency) has done a superb job under its most capable directors; nevertheless, the end result was a negative one for arms control.

I want to mention one special memory I have of INF that took place in the summer of 1988, about a month after INF entry into force. General LaJoie came to brief then ACDA Director Bill Burns, myself, and a few others on the results of the first INF on-site inspection. The Soviets had established a counterpart to OSIA in the Foreign Ministry headed by an army general, General Medvedev, who had been a key figure on the Soviet INF delegation. General LaJoie described how he met General Medvedev in Moscow and traveled with him to the first SS-20 site to be inspected. When they arrived, the Soviets offered several members of LaJoie's team the opportunity to drive the transporter-erector-launcher (TEL) of the SS-20 around. Then a rain shower came up and the two generals ducked inside an empty SS-20 canister for cover. We listened with amazement; we all still thought in Cold War terms, accustomed to Soviet secrecy. No U.S. official had ever seen, even via satellite photography, an SS-20 missile outside its canister, as the Soviets had never exposed one. Yet, here were U.S. officials not only seeing the missile but hiding in its canister and driving its TEL around. For the first time we understood emotionally the scope of the arms control sea change resulting from the verification revolution agreed to by Gorbachev at Reykjavik.

The Bush administration, upon taking office, put major emphasis on arms control. Indeed, in my judgment, this administration did more than any other to further the cause of arms control. Ron Lehman, former NSC official, START negotiator, and assistant secretary of defense, became director of ACDA and he selected his successor as START negotiator, Read Hanmer, as his deputy. Ron was someone who really cared about ACDA as an institution as well as arms control and he fought hard against the first attempts to eliminate ACDA in 1992. Rick Burt was appointed START negotiator and he chose Linton Brooks as his deputy. Burt was given the full support of Jim Baker, the new secretary of state, and he proceeded ahead with vigor. Marshall Brown, the ACDA/GC lawyer assigned to START, continued to grind out the treaty text.

Early in 1989, I became centrally involved in the CFE Treaty negotiations, the subject of a later chapter, and thus from March 1989 to June 1991, I had only limited time to give to START. Marshall Brown was in place virtually full time in Geneva doing a superb job as delegation lawyer. The START text grew and grew, eventually reaching several hundred pages in its joint draft text because of compliance concerns, which required that all of the verification/inspection/data implementing provisions had to be included as part of the treaty or protocol text. Many useful agreements were being reached, the entire SALT II compilation of constraints was revived and improved upon, a comprehensive on-site inspection regime was developed, and provisions for extensive data exchange were agreed. Nevertheless, the negotiations proceeded ahead only slowly, and Rick Burt finally left as negotiator at the end of 1990. Lint Brooks took over and did an excellent job until the completion of the negotiations in July 1991, also serving as the START II negotiator in 1992.

I suppose that the START negotiations might have ground on forever had not President Bush imposed a deadline—arms control negotiations usually need a deadline in order to conclude. Most expected Bush to propose to Gorbachev a September Summit in Moscow for the purpose of signing START, but in June of 1991 Bush and Gorbachev agreed that START would be signed in Moscow on July 31. Amid cries that there was not enough time, that it was impossible, the U.S. delegation prepared to put on the full court press in Geneva. This date was insisted upon by Bush, so the story went, because he wanted to begin his Maine vacation on August 1, with START behind him. In any case, it represented great prescience on the part of the president as the Moscow coup attempt began on August 19 and the Soviet Union collapsed on December 25. July 31 was probably close to the last date that START could have been signed. If it had not been signed then, it likely never would have been signed and the process of strategic arms reduction would have been destroyed. It is one thing to negotiate a relatively simple START II Treaty with Russia based on the comprehensive START Treaty, and to multilateralize the existing START Treaty; it would have been quite another thing to attempt to negotiate the huge and complicated text of the START Treaty with the four START successor states at some reconstituted strategic arms process in 1992 or 1993. We were lucky.

As part of the crash effort to get the START Treaty to Moscow in time for the summit signing on July 31, I greatly augmented the GC presence in Geneva. In addition to Marshall Brown, I asked Steve Solomon, who then had the SCC portfolio and was just finishing a session, to stay on. I went over on July 17 and brought with me Paul Lembesis, the START interagency lawyer, Bernie Seward, an additional recruit from Virginia who became our CWC lawyer, and another junior lawyer, Ed Joseph. Deputy General Counsel Mary Lib Hoinkes effectively held down the fort in Washington. Martha Kaulaity, my long-time secretary, also came over for the endgame, as was invariably the request of every U.S. disarmament-negotiating delegation for many years. She was an outstanding secretary and also a master at putting treaty texts in final form.

So GC had six lawyers, including the general counsel, and the senior office secretary in Geneva for the START Treaty endgame. Nevertheless, even given this unprecedented legal effort, there was almost too much work. All of us worked virtually around the clock. I divided the START Treaty package among the six of us, but there were so many agreed statements, verification provisions, data exchange provisions, and the like that it was just overwhelming.

I went to Moscow a day ahead of time to address problems created by the State Department assistant legal advisor who had come with the secretary's party—he had suggested taking certain liberties with the legal structure of the treaty package, which might have been agreeable in most cases, but not in the START process. For example, he had proposed having the protocols and subsidiary documents signed by the negotiators rather than the presidents—anathema if one wants to argue to the Senate that all the documents have equal legal force.

This was quickly set right in Moscow, but meanwhile the endgame crisis continued in Geneva. The last few agreed pages of treaty text were handed out the car window to Soviet officials in front of their Geneva Mission as the delegation sped to the airport. But still much work remained to be done in Moscow. All of us, most especially Martha, stayed up all night on July 30 at the U.S. Embassy in Moscow, putting the treaty texts in final form for signature the next day. To ease the tension, the six of us (leaving Martha at the word processor) took a break about 3:00 A.M. and played a game of pick-up basketball in the Embassy gym for about half an hour. Even with all this effort, nearly a hundred errors, minor in nature, were found after signature in various parts of the voluminous treaty package and Marshall had to return to Moscow and clean these up by letter agreement about a month later (after the coup attempt had been suppressed). Notably, on his way home from the START summit, President Bush stopped in Kiev and included an important passage in his speech arguing against breaking up the Soviet Union.

The START I Treaty, a lawyer's dream, is the ultimate example of the 1980s approach of arms control conservatives that everything had to have the same status as the treaty text and that subordinate implementing agreements were just not acceptable. This approach gave rise to the doctrine that "technical changes" (as opposed to amendments) to the treaty text are to be authorized by the treaty regime—as we will later see—in case of doubt as to whether they are actually technical changes and not amendments with the approval of the Senate Foreign Relations Committee leadership; otherwise even minor inspection procedural changes, such as whether inspectors could carry flashlights or whatever, would be treaty amendments requiring Senate and Duma (as well as the national legislatures of Ukraine, Belarus, and Kazakhstan) approval.

There is a dizzying array of documents in the START I package. There is, of course, the treaty text proper; then there are thirty-eight Agreed Statements on such subjects as non-transfer of strategic offensive arms, SS-11 reentry vehicle attribution, strategic offensive arms operations outside national territories, the relationship between the START and INF Treaties, throw-weight of new types of missiles deployed before the eighth flight test, and reimbursement of costs for telemetry tape exchange. In the START I Treaty—being post-Reykjavik—there is a simple flat ban on the encryption of telemetry and provision for the exchange of telemetry tapes in some cases, a far cry from SALT secrecy. There is an annex that contains the definitions of 124 terms for the purposes of the START Treaty. There is a highly complex protocol on procedures governing conversion or elimination of strategic offensive arms. There is the even more complex protocol on inspections and continuous monitoring activities—the verification protocol (with twelve Annexes on various technical issues and activities.) There is the protocol on notifications to assist verification. There is the protocol on ICBM and SLBM throw-weight—procedures to determine and attribute a throw-weight value to missiles and to verify this. There is an entire protocol on telemetric information—ensuring access to missile telemetry for verification purposes. There is a protocol on the Joint Compliance and Inspection Commission that created the implementing body. There is a very lengthy memorandum of understanding on the establishment of a database.

And then there are other related agreements, letters signed by the two negotiators containing certain commitments, correspondence on various important issues setting forth commitments signed by the U.S. secretary of state, the Soviet foreign minister, the Soviet defense minister, and in one case both the foreign minister and defense minister of the Soviet Union (this latter statement is on the subject of the relocation of heavy SS-18 ICBM silos, and contains assurances that any new silos built will be solely for the purposes of replacement—no more freeze, but a fixed number). There are joint delegation statements as well as statements and declarations by one or the other of the delegations.

All of these letters and statements address important subjects, but perhaps one deserves special attention. On June 13, 1991, the Soviet deputy foreign minister—Obukhov, the last NST negotiator—in a meeting with U.S. Ambassador Lint Brooks, read a statement on the interrelationship between the START and ABM Treaties. It says that the Soviet side states that the START Treaty is effective and viable under conditions of compliance with the ABM Treaty and the extraordinary events referred to in the supreme national interest withdrawal provision (treaty Article XV) include withdrawal by one of the parties from the ABM Treaty.

Article II of the START Treaty sets forth the central limits, which are: 1,600 deployed ICBMs and SLBMs and their associated launchers, including 154 deployed heavy ICBMs and associated launchers (halving the long-time Soviet total); 6,000 warheads attributed to deployed ICBMs, SLBMs, and heavy bombers, with 4,900 attributed to ICBMs and SLBMs, 1,100 attributed to mobile ICBMs, and 1,540 to heavy ICBMs (ten warheads each, the existing number). Article III sets forth the counting rules. For example, if an ICBM is maintained in stages, the first stage shall count as an ICBM; for the United States up to 150 heavy bombers equipped for long-range nuclear ALCMs (conventional ALCMs and conventional SLCMs, although externally identical, are exempt from treaty limits—elaborate verification arrangements address this issue) shall be counted as ten warheads each (U.S. bombers can carry twenty) and beyond 150 with the number of nuclear ALCMs with which they are actually equipped (this arrangement potentially exempts 1,500 U.S. nuclear ALCMs), and other heavy bombers are counted as one in the warhead totals no matter how many non-ALCM nuclear bombs and missiles they may carry (so much for limiting warheads). Other articles set up the relationship to the various protocols, annexes, and the memorandum on database. All in all, a tour de force.

The Soviet Union passed into history on Christmas Day, 1991. The Baltic states had already become independent and the Soviet Union was succeeded by twelve new states (referred to as the NIS, newly independent states). Fortunately, Bush and Gorbachev made a very important informal agreement in October 1991 pursuant to which the United States eventually eliminated 95 percent of its tactical nuclear weapons and the Soviet Union/Russia was to do the same, although even today it is unclear how much of this has been accomplished by Russia. It was agreed that nuclear weapons would no longer be deployed on surface ships, strategic bombers would be taken off alert, and strategic missile systems in excess of the START limits would be deactivated. Most significantly, in light of the breakup it was agreed that all tactical nuclear weapons scattered throughout the Soviet Union would be brought back to the territory of the Russian Federation, which was accomplished by January 1992. Because of these farsighted measures, the nuclear question was limited to only four of the successor states. Strategic offensive arms remained deployed on the territory of Russia, Belarus, Ukraine, and Kazakhstan. It was concluded in January that these were the relevant START successor states. Several alternatives were considered as to how to deal with the START Treaty given the new situation, but after some prodding by senators to include Ukraine, Kazakhstan, and Belarus in START, these four states were regarded as replacing the Soviet Union—no one wanted to renegotiate the START Treaty.

Secretary of State Baker made a brief tour of these four new states early in January 1992, shortly after which an arms control delegation visited Moscow, Kiev, Minsk, and Almaty beginning in the second week of January. The purpose of the trip was to speak with officials primarily about succession for START and CFE, and to urge adherence by Ukraine, Belarus, and Kazakhstan to the NPT as non-nuclear weapon states, Russia having been accepted as the successor to the Soviet Union for the NPT. This latter was most important as the United States wanted to avoid the creation of additional nuclear weapon states in the wake of the collapse of the Soviet Union.

The delegation was led by Reg Bartholomew, undersecretary of state for international security, the lead position at State for disarmament. The delegation included Jim Timbie, always the man you wanted to have involved; General John Shalikashvili, then J-5 and responsible for disarmament and later the outstanding chairman of the JCS; Steve Hadley, the most capable assistant secretary of defense for international security (later deputy national security advisor in the second Bush administration); and Doug MacEachin, senior CIA official, later deputy under Jim Woolsey. I attended as ACDA general counsel.

The first stop was Moscow, where we spent several days. I remember Alexander Obukhov, whom I had known so well during SALT II and who was the successor NST negotiator for the Soviets, greeting us at the Russian Foreign Ministry with the phrase "Welcome to the *Russian* Foreign Ministry." There was not much disagreement between the sides; we told the Russians that the United States recognized Russia as the successor to the Soviet Union for the NPT, and we discussed the need to provide for succession for START and CFE. The Russians mentioned the importance of all of the NIS becoming NPT parties as non-nuclear weapon states. They also unequivocally stated the importance of the continued viability of the ABM Treaty in its relationship to START. The U.S. delegation agreed.

The discussions with the Ukrainians were difficult from the beginning. Early on they indicated their ambition to be considered a nuclear power; they wanted to be a START nuclear state and they had problems with joining the NPT as a non-nuclear weapon state. One Ukrainian official said that Ukraine wanted to be the France of the East and France has nuclear weapons. It was clear to me that we would have a long road to travel with Ukraine.

We moved on to Minsk, where we stayed and had our meetings at Brezhnev's former hunting lodge outside of town. There was deep snow everywhere; it was very beautiful. Our discussions with Belarus officials were positive. They would cooperate on START and they would join NPT as a non-nuclear weapon state. Early on in our stay in Minsk our advance man called from Almaty and informed us that the Kazakhstanis had taken the position that, unless we gave them $20,000 in cash in small bills, they would not give us gas for our airplane. They would not accept credit cards, the billing for which went through Moscow, where a cut was taken. They had accepted a check from Secretary Baker the week before, but they would not take one from us. In fact, we had encountered a somewhat similar problem in Kiev, where our hotel wanted cash and not credit cards for the same reason.

We left Minsk for Almaty late at night, the five-hour flight bringing us in not long after dawn. As we stood on the tarmac at the airport in Minsk waiting to leave, a small plane pulled up alongside us. It contained Ambassador Jack Maresca, our CSCE ambassador, arriving from Frankfurt where funds were deposited. He walked up to Reg Bartholomew and without comment handed him a briefcase that contained the $20,000 cash. For a moment I wasn't sure if I was doing disarmament or running drugs.

When we arrived in Almaty, the last stop on our disarmament consultation, Reg went off to meet with the prime minister and later with President

Nazerbaev. We called the Foreign Ministry in an attempt to get discussions going. We said we wanted to discuss NPT, CFE, and START. The response from our contact at the Foreign Ministry was that the only people at the ministry who worked on substance were the foreign minister and the deputy foreign minister. Everyone else worked on protocol; did we want the minister or his deputy? Kazakhstan, of course, had never been an independent state and was then about two weeks old. Therefore, our discussions with various individuals were arranged in a somewhat haphazard fashion. Although they were to a degree in a learning mode, the Kazakhstanis indicated that they wanted to cooperate on START, NPT, and CFE as well.

Toward the end of our stay, the urgency of what we were doing was brought home to us when Reg told us that President Nazerbaev had told him that he had already received offers from several Middle Eastern nations to purchase the 500-kiloton nuclear warheads on the 108 former Soviet SS-18 strategic missile systems deployed on the territory of Kazakhstan. He had refused all offers, he said. The last night we were there the foreign minister hosted a traditional banquet and gave Reg the honor of distributing the sheep's eyeballs, ears, tongue, etc. Appropriately he gave one eyeball to Doug MacEachin as our CIA representative and he gave the other to Liz Verville of the State Department. Liz adamantly refused to eat it and was prepared to risk a diplomatic incident to protect her right not to eat the eyeball. So it was given to Doug, who took a nibble out of each one. We left the next morning, stopped in Brussels for a debrief at NATO, and returned home in the afternoon.

As I said above, various concepts for dealing with START were advanced, but reasonably early in 1992 it was decided to multilateralize the treaty by having the four states where strategic arms were deployed be the successor states for the START Treaty. A difficult negotiation ensued, particularly with Ukraine, which led to the Lisbon Protocol of May 1992. By means of this protocol Russia, Belarus, Ukraine, and Kazakhstan agreed to assume the START obligations of the former Soviet Union, and Belarus, Ukraine, and Kazakhstan agreed not to have strategic arms deployed on their territories and to join the NPT as non-nuclear weapon states.

Persuading Ukraine to do these last two things was like pulling teeth. President Kravchuk agreed to provide President Bush a letter on the question of eliminating strategic offensive arms from the territory of Ukraine, so it was agreed that the elimination obligation would be adhered to outside the text of the protocol. The draft letters from Belarus and Kazakhstan were straightforward, but there was much back and forth between Washington and Kiev on the text of the President Kravchuk letter, which was ambiguous. Finally, it was agreed that the five states would meet in May in Lisbon to complete and sign the protocol making START multilateral. The signing ceremony was to be on a Saturday. I arrived in Lisbon on Thursday to work out any last minute details, and Secretary Baker's party arrived in London, where he had other business, on Friday and planned to come to Lisbon Saturday morning.

The protocol was to be in five languages and, whereas there was not much worry about being able to achieve Ukrainian and Belorussian texts, the Kazakh language was a concern. I asked the State Department to find a Kazakh linguist for me; I was informed that there were only two in the United States. One of them ran a Turkic language program at the University of Wisconsin, and I invited him to come with me to Lisbon where he was most helpful. In Lisbon I made the rounds of the delegations. Belarus was no problem. When I finally found the Kazakhstanis, they were not a problem either. I had a long meeting with the Russians, who made it clear that NPT membership for the other three was a *sine qua non* for them and that such membership would be a Duma condition to ratification. The Ukrainians were another matter. I had three meetings with them on Thursday and Friday, and they said that maybe they could sign, maybe they could not, and they were unsure about providing a signed copy of the Kravchuk letter. It was quite frustrating. Finally, on Friday evening, after my third meeting with the Ukrainians, I called Jim Timbie, who was with Baker in London, and reported on the situation. He said he would speak with the secretary and that he would call me back later that night or in the morning.

Early the next morning, Jim called me at my hotel in Lisbon. He said Ukraine was going to be all right. The previous night he had relayed my message to Baker in his hotel room. Baker was sitting there in athletic attire, having just come from the exercise room. He promptly telephoned Ukrainian Foreign Minister Zlenko and Jim said, "I will tell you later what he said, but suffice it to say that I have never heard one man speak to another in quite that way."

The signing of the Lisbon Protocol on Saturday did go forward as planned; the Ukrainians were cooperative after all. I was asked by Secretary Baker's staff to brief the four foreign ministers as to the procedure to be followed during the signing ceremony. In a small holding room, off the room where the documents were awaiting signature, I carried out the assignment. Present were Secretary Baker and three or four of his staff; Kozyrev, the Russian foreign minister, with two or three aides; Zlenko, with one or two aides; and the Belorussian and Kazakhstani foreign ministers, also with one or two aides. I explained how each was to enter the room, where to sit, what documents would be passed for signature in what order, and finally what would indicate the conclusion of the ceremony. Baker interjected at that point "and then you will all leave"; he did not want any Ukrainian or Russian speeches. The signing went off without a hitch and the small audience composed entirely of the delegations applauded.

The Lisbon Protocol provides that Russia, Kazakhstan, Ukraine, and Belarus all became parties of the START I Treaty in place of the former Soviet Union. It obligates the four states to make the necessary arrangements among themselves to implement the treaty's limits and restrictions, to allow the proper functioning of the verification systems of the treaty and to allocate those costs that would have been borne by the Soviet Union. It also clarifies how certain treaty terms will be applied now that there are four states in the place of the former Soviet Union. All provisions of the treaty not explicitly addressed remain the same and any additional procedures required will be worked out in the Joint Compliance and Inspection Commission (JCIC)— and many have been.

Additionally, the Lisbon Protocol obligates Belarus, Ukraine, and Kazakhstan to adhere to the NPT as non-nuclear weapon states in the shortest possible period of time. Letters associated with the protocol from these three states obligate them to eliminate all nuclear weapons and strategic offensive arms from their territories within seven years of the entry into force of START I treaty. (It entered into force in 1994.) The treaty was signed on July 31, 1991, and submitted to the Senate on November 25, one month before the Soviet Union dissolved. The Lisbon Protocol was signed in Lisbon on May 23, 1992, by the United States, Russia, Ukraine, Kazakhstan, and Belarus, as I have just described. The Lisbon Protocol is an integral part of the START I Treaty and it was submitted to the Senate in June of 1992 to become part of the START treaty package. The treaty, including the new protocol, was approved by the Senate in the fall of 1992.

Meanwhile, the White House was not wasting time. In mid-June, a month after the Lisbon Protocol was signed, Presidents Bush and Yeltsin held a summit in Washington where agreement in principle was reached between the United States and the Russian Federation to further reduce the START I levels. This agreement, which came to be known as START II, reduced the warhead levels from 6,000 to 3,000–3,500 and put additional limitations on strategic bombers. The Russians wanted a level of 2,500, and if the Russians were willing to go that low, so was JCS. This would have avoided the great expense of overhauling four Trident submarines. But OSD would not have it, and the Russians eventually accepted the 3,000–3,500, a level they could not support for their own services. This became one of the obstacles to Duma ratification of START II until the 1997 Clinton-Yeltsin agreement on a START III level of 2,000–2,500, to be negotiated promptly after START II entry into force.

The idea of START II was that it could be a short agreement in that it was based on the comprehensive START I Treaty. Also, the parties were limited to the United States and Russia. Pursuant to the START I agreement, strategic offensive arms would be eliminated from the territory of Belarus, Ukraine, and Kazakhstan. Draft texts were exchanged through diplomatic channels, moving the START II negotiations along during the summer and fall. Some problems developed. The Russians wanted tighter constraints on U.S. bombers and for their SS-19 they wanted to be able to download (that is, to reduce the number of warheads on a missile, which is not verifiable), just as the United States was going to download the D-5 missile on its Trident submarines in order to reach START II warhead levels. There would be on-site warhead inspection to attempt to verify this, although everyone recognized the breakout potential. Also, for economic reasons, the Russians wanted to continue to use the SS-18 silos for a single warhead missile. One of the strengths of the START II deal from the U.S. point of view was that land-based MIRVed ICBMs (the Russians' strong point) would be eliminated, and one of the weaknesses of the agreement from the Russians' point of view is that MIRVed SLBMs (the U.S. strong point) would not be severely impacted. Thus, the United States would have to eliminate its MX or Peacekeeper ICBM, but could keep the D-5 SLBM, perhaps with fewer warheads, but not as a single-warhead missile. The Russians would have to eliminate (or download in the case of the SS-19) their SS-17, SS-18, and SS-19 ICBMs, the backbone of their strategic force. They could keep their single-warhead mobile SS-25 ICBM. The Russian Duma saw this as an unequal deal, but only through U.S. reduction could the Russians hope to maintain parity. Eliminating MIRVed ICBMs, particularly the huge SS-18 ICBM, was a good deal for the United States. How to write a provision that would permit the Russians to keep SS-18 silos but verifiably prevent them from using such silos for SS-18 ICBMs and to write the restrictions on the U.S. bomber force were sufficiently complicated that it was clear by the fall that there would have to be a negotiation using delegations.

On Christmas night 1992, Lint Brooks called me at home and asked if I could go to Geneva on December 27 as legal advisor on a START II delegation. I agreed to go and asked if I could bring Bill Parsons, my right-hand man on ABM and CFE and a key figure on the SCC delegation (but not a regular START lawyer) with me. Lint assented and I asked Bill to go. Paul Lembesis was not available, as he was planning to leave government in early 1993, Marshall Brown was on a well-deserved vacation, and I had great confidence in Bill. The negotiation had to be short and intense, as the summit for signing START II was set for January 3, 1993. President Bush wanted START II finished on his watch.

Larry Eagleburger, Baker's number two, had succeeded him first as acting secretary of state and then in early November, pursuant to a recess appointment, as secretary, after Baker left for the White House in late August to run the Bush reelection campaign. Larry was very popular, with one of the sharpest wits I have ever encountered. We traveled to Geneva on his plane and he stayed on the first day to discuss START II with Grachev, the Russian defense minister. All together the Geneva negotiation took less than a week. We broke into several working groups. For the United States Doug MacEachin headed the working group on verifiably converting SS-18 ICBM silos into single-warhead missile only silos. This was accomplished in large part by shortening the depth of the silo by adding layers of concrete on the bottom, combined with inspections. With Bill's superb assistance, a sound

START II package was quickly developed. Eagleburger's plane came back and picked us up on January 2 to take us and the START II text to Moscow. We had had only a few days in Geneva, but they had been very long ones and the text was complete. I did notice at the Moscow airport the signature of an American president at a foreign meeting—the airport seemed filled with huge American planes: the president's Air Force One, a 747, the back-up 747, the secretary of state's 707, the press plane, etc. The cost must have been immense.

At the START I signing, ACDA, backed by the NSC, had strongly pushed for Marshall Brown, as delegation lawyer, to hold the treaty book for President Bush at the signing ceremony. In the end, Marshall was bumped by Joseph Reed, the State Department chief of protocol. In the START II case, the same effort was made, accompanied by a vigorous push by Susan Koch, formerly of ACDA and then on the NSC staff. This time the effort succeeded, in part because there were no State Department lawyers or chief of protocol at this summit, and I was designated to hold the book.

Since the assistant legal advisor for treaty affairs was not present at this summit, there was no one to seal the treaty, that is, to run the special ribbon through all the pages and then seal the ribbon with wax and the U.S. seal. This job also fell to me and I asked Sally Horn of OSD, their verification expert, to help me. Together we spent several hours in my hotel room the night of January 2, struggling with the U.S. original treaty pages, the ribbon, the wax, and the seal. Finally, with Sally's indispensable assistance, we completed our task successfully, but that was more nerve-wracking than anything during the negotiations—we had to succeed.

The next day it was agreed that Bush and Yeltsin would sign the subsidiary documents beforehand and only the treaty itself in front of the cameras. Accordingly, I and my Russian counterpart, who had been in Geneva, went to a small conference room off the Alexander Hall, where the public signing was to be. Bush and Brent Scowcroft entered just after having had a walk around the Kremlin grounds in the freezing weather. The president looked very happy. The room gradually filled up, and Yeltsin arrived. Bush and Yeltsin then conducted a bilateral discussion with about a dozen aides on each side. One of the agenda items was the preliminary signing. I stood behind the president and he began to sign above the line "for the United States of America." I said, "No, Mr. President, below the line." He left a small mark above the line on the first document and signed the remaining documents below the line. I noticed Yeltsin was quite taciturn, while Bush made a quip or two. After obtaining the necessary signatures and completing the bilateral, the two presidents, my Russian counterpart, and I walked out of the room and onto the stage in Alexander Hall. The two presidents sat at the table, each of the two of us stood behind our president. The two delegations sat in seats just off the stage. I was holding the correctly sealed U.S. treaty book, with bookmarks where Bush and Yeltsin were to sign.

The light was very bright in the large room to accommodate the television cameras. In front of the stage where the signing table was situated there was a virtual sea of reporters, cameras, and TV cameras. Flashbulbs were constantly flashing and shutters were clacking. The signing began promptly. I put the book in front of President Bush, opened to the correct page. Once again he began to sign above the line and once again I said, "no, Mr. President," and pointed my finger at the proper place. The cameras were going crazy by now and all tried to simply ignore them—at least that is what I did. I turned the page to the place for the second signature, and after that was executed my counterpart and I exchanged the books and the two presidents exchanged pens. At this time there was a loud "whoosh" from the audience as I guess every camera in the place recorded this moment. In a few more moments the signing was complete. I took the U.S. treaty book and took a seat with the rest of the U.S. delegation while the two presidents made speeches. A member of the NSC staff, offered to carry the treaty book back to Washington and I passed it to her. The deed was done.

Article I of the START II Treaty provides for reductions from START I levels, in two stages, to a level of 3,000–3,500 for warheads attributable to deployed ICBMs, SLBMs, and heavy bombers. Within such limitations there is to be a limit of 1,700–1,750 on SLBMs, zero for MIRVed ICBMs, and zero for heavy ICBMs (thus the feared SS-18 would be eliminated). Article II provides for the elimination or conversion to a single-warhead ICBM of all MIRVed ICBMs. Article III indicates that START I rules are to be used for warhead attribution. Article IV eliminates the 150 nuclear ALCM bomber special treatment in the START I Treaty and the special treatment for bombers not carrying ALCMs. It also requires that the number of warheads attributed to a heavy bomber in all cases must be the number with which such a bomber is actually equipped, as set forth in the associated Memorandum on Warhead Attribution and Heavy Bomber Data.

Up to 100 heavy bombers may be reoriented for a conventional role (that is, taken from their nuclear assignment), but must be deployed separately from other heavy bombers, used only for non-nuclear missions, and have differences observable to NTM that would differentiate them from other heavy bombers of that type that have not been reoriented. These differences must distinguish such bombers from reoriented bombers of the same type that have been returned to a nuclear role, as well as heavy bombers of the same type that were never reoriented. If not all bombers of a type are reoriented, one reoriented bomber must be exhibited in the open, to demonstrate to the other party the observable differences that distinguish it from other bombers of its type. Likewise, if not all reoriented bombers of a type are returned to a nuclear role, one such bomber returned to a nuclear role shall be exhibited in the open to demonstrate to the other party the observable differences distinguishing it from other bombers of its type that were never reoriented, and those which have been reoriented but not returned to a nuclear role.

These exhibitions are to be carried out pursuant to the Protocol on Exhibitions and Inspections. These elaborate provisions are designed to permit the United States, its military being more dependent on bombers, to live with the tighter rules on bomber armament.

Article V provides that the START I Treaty verification provisions are to be used for implementation of the START II Treaty except where otherwise explicitly provided. The Protocol on Elimination and Conversion of Heavy ICBMS sets forth the rules on removing heavy ICBM launchers and missiles from the Russian inventory. The first section provides for complete elimination of the launcher and the missile and the second section provides procedures for those cases where Russia desires to retain the launcher for a single-warhead ICBM. It provides, among other things, that concrete is to be poured into the silo up to a height of five meters from the bottom of the silo launcher, and that this is measured and verified. Thus, should the START II Treaty come into force, the heavy ICBM will finally be eliminated after all these years.

START I was approved by the U.S. Senate in the fall of 1992, with Lint Brooks, as the treaty's chief negotiator, appropriately taking the lead. It was a relatively problem-free ratification as the Lisbon Protocol went down fairly well. There was some skirmishing on ABM, and Senator Richard Lugar's chief staff man, Ken Myers, told us he had had to step between Lugar (the floor manager of the treaty) and Senator Malcolm Wallop on the Senate floor to prevent a fist-fight—something about missile defense. Other than that it went smoothly.

START II was dealt with differently. There was concern that senators might speak too favorably about the treaty and cause a negative reaction by the Duma, so there was uncertainty about whether to proceed ahead in 1993, once the Clinton administration took office. After some debate, it was decided to send the treaty forward and to have the ratification hearings, but to hold off floor consideration until gauging the reaction in the Duma. At this time I was acting director of ACDA and gave the principal treaty ratification testimony at a hearing in May 1993.

The U.S. Senate finally gave its advice and consent to START II by an overwhelming vote in 1994. Because of many things, including the perceived one-sidedness of START II, the fact that Russia did not want to spend the money to go up to START II levels because its forces were deteriorating, NATO expansion, the U.S. bombing of Iraq, the war in the Balkans, and Russian domestic politics, the Duma did not approve START II until April 2000. But, pursuant to agreement in Helsinki in 1997, the START II Treaty has amendments extending the reduction timeline to accommodate Russia. Thus it has to go back to the U.S. Senate for approval of the amendments before it can enter into force. As of the end of 2000 and the Clinton presidency, START II had not been resubmitted to the Senate. The concern was that since the administration was committed to sending the 1997 ABM Demarcation Protocol and Memorandum on ABM Treaty Succession (referred to in Chapter 7) to the Senate at the same time, this could engender a huge new debate on national missile defense.

The campaign for START I entry into force was somewhat happier. Kazakhstan ratified START and joined the NPT in 1993 and Belarus did the same. The Rada in Ukraine, after several false starts, approved START in the spring of 1994 but held back on NPT. In September of 1994, Rose Gottemoeller on the NSC staff, responsible for arms control issues in the NIS, asked me if I would go to Kiev and make a pitch for NPT. At the time I was totally involved in the NPT extension effort, which is covered in a later chapter. I agreed to go and in mid-September I did so.

My old friend Bill Miller, former long-time aide to Senator John Sherman Cooper of Kentucky, was ambassador in Kiev, and at our first meeting we discussed our continuing joint interest in the ABM Treaty. My principal pitch with the Ukrainians was that the NPT is the "Club of Civilization and it is time that Ukraine joined." I had a good reception in the Foreign Ministry, where I met with Ambassadors Tarasuk and Hryschenko, the key figures in their government for this subject. I was to meet with the Rada International Security Committee, but only the chairman was there to see me. On the other hand, I was to have a one-on-one with the deputy leader of the Rada, but when I walked into the very large room where he was to meet me, klieg lights went on and I found myself giving a speech to and answering questions from about twenty Rada members in front of television cameras. All of my discussions were positive, and the Rada approved the NPT about two weeks later, but they were probably ready to do so. START was formally brought into force in December 1994, on the margins of the CSCE Summit in Budapest. We finally had a complete strategic offensive arms agreement in force after twenty-two years of trying.

Seven years later, on December 5, 2001, the United States and Russia formally announced full implementation of START I. As of December 2001, the START II amendments had not been submitted to the U.S. Senate, and on December 13, President Bush gave formal notice of withdrawal from the ABM Treaty pursuant to Article XV thereof. Although Russian President Putin promptly stated his continued commitment to the START I and II treaties, this action by the United States made their futures uncertain. When the Russian Duma approved them, the resolutions of ratification conditioned Russian adherence to each treaty on the continued existence of the ABM Treaty. Only time will tell.

CHAPTER SEVEN **THE ANTI-BALLISTIC MISSILE TREATY**

The ABM Treaty from SALT I, unlike the Interim Agreement, is an agreement of indefinite duration. It originally limited strategic defense systems and components in ABM deployment areas to two sites for each party. For the purposes of the treaty, the three current ABM components are listed as ABM launchers, ABM interceptor missiles, and ABM radars. Article III limits the number of ABM interceptor missile launchers to 100 per site and a total of 200 for each party. It contains strict limits on the ABM radars deployed at each site. One site may be located to defend the national capital and one may be located to defend one ICBM deployment area. The two sites must be at least 1,300 kilometers apart to prevent them from having overlapping coverage that could create a base for a national or territorial defense.

Article I of the ABM Treaty enumerates the object and purpose of the treaty by including the fundamental obligation not to create an ABM defense of the national territory or the base for such a defense. The creation of an ABM defense of a region is prohibited except for such deployment as permitted by Article III. Agreed Statement D provides that if fixed land-based ABM systems or their components based on future technology or "other physical principles" (not defined in the treaty) such as lasers or particle beams should be created in the future, such systems or components cannot be deployed absent amendment of the treaty. Article IV provides an exception to the deployment limitations of Article III for ABM launchers and ABM radars for the purpose of testing an ABM system or its components at ABM test ranges.

Article V of the ABM Treaty prohibits the development, testing, and deployment of ABM systems or components that are not fixed land-based (i.e., sea-based, air-based, space-based or mobile land-based). This sweeping prohibition on ABM systems or components except fixed land-based is designed to reinforce the objectives of Article I.

Further to this same objective are two constraints in Article VI. One prohibits the upgrade, or improvement, of air defense or theater missile defense systems to ABM capability. The second, in conjunction with another Agreed Statement applicable to the deployment of large phased array radars (then the relevant modern technology), covers radars that are not ABM radars, but that are deployed in the future for the purpose of early warning of ballistic missile attack (as opposed to an ABM role of directing missiles to intercept the incoming weapons). They must be located on the periphery of the national territory and oriented outward so as not to contribute to the creation of a base for a nationwide defense by means of the location of large ABM-capable radars throughout the country. This provision was the subject of a much-discussed Soviet violation when a large phased array radar with the characteristics of an early-warning radar began to be constructed near Krasnoyarsk in Siberia. It was neither located on the periphery nor oriented outward. After years of argument the Soviet Union finally agreed to dismantle the radar. Allegedly it was to be converted into a shoe factory.

The objective of the ABM Treaty, in essence, is to prohibit the deployment of large-scale ABM strategic defense, thus making each party a hostage of the other. This concept is known as assured destruction or mutual assured destruction, often referred to as MAD. Each party to the ABM Treaty assures the other side of the effectiveness of its deterrent. If one side were to build up strategic defense, the other side might have to increase its strategic offensive weapons to overcome the defense. Further, the building up of strategic defense could be seen by the other side as an attempt to gain a first-strike capability, with defensive systems deployed to blunt a retaliatory second strike, thereby adding to instability. By keeping strategic defense at a low level the ABM Treaty therefore establishes the basis for reductions and reinforces strategic stability. It is accurately referred to as a "cornerstone of strategic arms control" and plays as important a role today as in 1972, a fact recognized by President Clinton in his September 1, 2000, speech announcing the deferral of any plans to announce the authorization of deployment of a national missile defense.

The ABM Treaty was amended in 1974 by a protocol reducing the two permitted deployment areas for each party to one, thereby reducing strategic defense deployments to a level just short of abolition. The entire structure of the ABM Treaty is designed to interact so that all provisions operate to reinforce the fundamental goal set forth in Article I.

In 1985, an interpretation debate arose within the U.S. government over the meaning of Article V, Paragraph 1, of the ABM Treaty, which reads, "Each party undertakes not to develop, test, or deploy ABM systems or components which are sea-based, air-based, space-based, or mobile land-based."

One side of this debate argued that a "broad" interpretation of the language of this provision would be legally permissible. Such an interpretation would limit the application of this provision to ABM technology actually in being at the time of signature of the treaty in 1972. Thus, it was argued that the only limitation on ABM systems employing future technology is the deployment ban in Agreed Statement D. In this view, the definition of ABM systems set forth in Article II, Paragraph 1, limits all the subsequent Articles of the treaty to then existing technologies.

Article II, Paragraph 1, the key definitional section of the treaty, is critical to this dispute. It reads as follows: "For the purpose of this treaty, an ABM system is a system to counter strategic ballistic missiles or their elements in flight trajectory, currently consisting of: (a) ABM interceptor missiles . . . (b) ABM launchers . . . and (c) ABM radars. . . ." Further, Agreed Statement D provides that:

> In order to assure fulfillment of the obligation not to deploy ABM systems and their components except as provided in Article III of the treaty, the states parties agree that in the event ABM systems based on other physical principles and including components capable of substituting for ABM interceptor missiles, ABM launchers or ABM radars are created in the future, specific limitations on such systems and their components would be subject to discussion in accordance with Article XIII and agreement in accordance with Article XIV of the treaty.

This so-called broad interpretation argument essentially holds that there was no agreement in 1972 to limit the development and testing of ABM components that use future technologies. The "currently consisting of" language in Article II means that the list of ABM components in Article II was intended to be complete, and thus all subsequent articles limit only 1972-vintage ABM launchers, ABM interceptor missiles, and ABM radars. Therefore, there are no treaty limits on ABM systems based on future systems except in Agreed Statement D, which contains only a deployment limitation. Because there are no testing limits on ABM systems based on future technology, the testing of future technology ABM systems, whether based on the ground, in the air, on the seas, or in space, is allowed.

The other side of this debate adhered to the traditional interpretation of Article V, which was that it applies to all types of mobile ABM systems, regardless of technology. This came to be known as the "narrow" or "traditional" interpretation. Those arguing for this interpretation asserted that the broad interpretation is inconsistent with the structure and purposes of the treaty, starting with the basic obligation of Article I not to deploy a nationwide ABM defense or to "provide a base" for such a defense. Future ABM systems based on technology such as lasers and particle beams could be capable of much wider area coverage than 1972-vintage ABM launchers, ABM interceptor missiles, and ABM radars. Article V, containing a ban on development and testing, as well as on deployment, of all mobile-type systems, thereby reinforces Article I.

The proponents of the traditional interpretation maintained that an ABM system is defined as a system to counter strategic ballistic missiles or their elements in flight trajectory, with the treaty noting that it only *currently* consists of ABM launchers, ABM interceptor missiles, and ABM radars. There is a comma before currently to make it clear that what follows modifies the definitional clause. The words of this phrase, as interpreted by accepted rules of English grammar, could be read, it was argued, in no other way than that future ABM systems were contemplated by both parties to be included within this definition of an ABM system. Agreed Statement D reinforces the limitations on the deployment of fixed land-based ABM systems that are set forth in Article III and is intended to ensure that these strict limits cannot be undermined by the deployment at one of these sites of, for example, ABM laser interceptors covering a wide area in lieu of conventional ABM interceptor missiles.

The U.S. executive branch officially adopted the broad interpretation in 1985, but the U.S. Congress enacted legislation that in effect denied any funding for tests or the purchase of long lead-time items inconsistent with the traditional interpretation. After this debate became public, the Soviet Union publicly stated that it adhered to the traditional interpretation. The Clinton administration repudiated the broad interpretation in 1993.

On March 23, 1983, President Reagan, catching not only the world but his own administration by surprise, announced plans to develop a nationwide ballistic missile defense utilizing futuristic technology and based in space. Quickly dubbed "Star Wars" after the movie, it was immediately apparent that it was on a collision course with the ABM Treaty. It was self-evident then as it is now that the ABM Treaty prohibits space-based missile defense no matter what the technology. Within days, State Department Legal Advisor Davis Robinson advised Secretary Shultz in a memorandum drafted by Mike Matheson, then assistant legal advisor, of this fact.

To a degree the issue receded for a time as first the INF negotiations and then the START negotiations broke down in the fall of 1983. Reportedly, at least to some extent, Reagan may have been influenced not long before his announcement to pursue "Star Wars" or the Strategic Defense Initiative (SDI), its official name, by Dr. Edward Teller, the inventor of the hydrogen bomb. President Reagan may have been susceptible to Teller's arguments and those of others because, it was widely rumored, he believed that nuclear weapons should be abolished, considering their continued existence as threatening to the United States, but he was told by his advisors that this was impossible.

The issue began to resurface in 1985. The Reagan administration had declared that SDI would be compliant with the ABM Treaty—the NATO allies insisted on it and the newly revived strategic arms control process with the Soviet Union was dependent on it. In the spring of 1985, an article printed by the Heritage Foundation argued what would become the essential points of the broad interpretation. The national security community did not pay much attention to it at the time, however.

In late September of 1985, I was home from the newly revived strategic arms control negotiations, the Nuclear and Space Arms Talks, with the Soviet Union. I attended, with Paul Nitze, an SDI interagency working group meeting co-chaired by General Abrahamson, the director of the Strategic Defense Initiative Office (SDIO), and Richard Perle. The first half-hour or so of the meeting was routine, and Paul Nitze left because of another meeting. He asked me to sit at the table in his place and represent him. When he left, there were perhaps two dozen senior policymakers, most at the assistant secretary level, sitting around a long rectangular table with the two co-chairs at the far end of the table from me.

Without forewarning, Perle brought up a new subject, interpretation of the ABM Treaty. He said he had not given much credence to the Heritage Foundation thesis, but had turned it over for analysis to a young, recently hired attorney, a Mr. Phillip Kunsberg, who worked for him and who had no previous arms control experience (so he could look at this in a fresh light). Perle said he was "bowled over" when the attorney not only told him that the Heritage Foundation thesis was correct, but produced an impressive legal memorandum to back this up. He then asked the author of the memorandum to state his case to the working group, which he did. Seeing me at the table, Richard then asked me to state the traditional view, which I did, making more or less the above argument for the narrow interpretation. Richard then asked that I submit my views promptly in writing to the group, which he would forward to the NSC for review, coupled with the memorandum supporting the Heritage Foundation thesis that he already had. On the way out of the meeting, I stopped to speak with him and said, "Richard, why are you doing this? The SDI program can go forward for several years on the basis that only sub-components are being tested." He replied, "I want all the flexibility that I can get." With the help of Ray Waters, an attorney in ACDA/GC who left the office early the next year, I submitted a few days later the requested memorandum to Richard in his capacity as co-chair. Thus was the ABM interpretation debate born.

National Security Advisor Bud MacFarlane scheduled a senior arms control policy group (referred to as SACPG, quickly corrupted to SACK-PIG for a time until later changed for aesthetic reasons to SAC-G) meeting a few days later on October 4, to address this new issue coming from the SDI working group. Adelman at that meeting declared himself to be at the "fifty-yard line." Nitze had come to this meeting with a memorandum stating that the legal interpretation might be open to debate, but it was unwise to raise the issue after all these years. However, when he saw how aggressive the Pentagon was in presenting his case and how little opposition there was to the broad interpretation, he decided not to distribute the memorandum.

Perle then sent the proposed new ABM Treaty issue directly to the NSC for decision. The Perle-proposed interpretation at this time was quickly named the broad interpretation, or later by its partisans as the LCI, or "legally correct interpretation." In the approximately two weeks between the SDI working group meeting and the October 11 NSC meeting there was much activity. I had several meetings with Ken Adelman, discussing with him the impending controversy, both before and after the October 4 meeting. Ken had no background on this important but arcane and technical subject, but by the time of the NSC meeting, given the circumstances, I thought that he had the best position of all the NSC principals. He was the only NSC principal to even question the broad interpretation, asserting that he was on the fence. It was assumed that the State Department legal advisor would take a formal position against the broad interpretation and hold to the traditional interpretation for general reasons, but particularly in view of legal advisor Davis Robinson's memorandum two years earlier.

But there was a new legal advisor in place in October 1985. Judge Abraham Sofaer, recently from the U.S. district court in New York, where among other assignments he had presided over the libel action brought by former Israeli Defense Minister (now Prime Minister) Ariel Sharon against *Time* magazine for their report on his role in the massacres in Palestinian refugee camps in Lebanon. Sofaer was brilliant, highly capable, and energetic. With no background in arms control he succumbed to Perle's influence and embraced the broad interpretation. More surprisingly, Sofaer also, in several long conversations, somehow persuaded Paul Nitze, who knew better, to go along with the broad interpretation. The only explanation I can offer was that Nitze had been the subject of several recent vicious public attacks as being too liberal for the hard men of the Reagan administration, so perhaps he was caught in a weak moment. But also Sofaer had the reputation of being very persuasive. Nitze's subsequent positions on the issue would tend to suggest that early on he regretted being drawn to support the broad interpretation. For example, Nitze later coined the phrase that for SDI to be deployed it should be "cost effective at the margin," a requirement that could never be met. This criterion meant that it would have to be demonstrated that it would be cheaper to add additional defenses than to add additional offensive reentry vehicles.

When Adelman reported Sofaer's position I was surprised, but when he reported Nitze's position I was alarmed. I could see now that we were really in for it. Sofaer's position as legal advisor and Nitze's as special arms control advisor to the secretary—which he had become after the suspension of INF in 1983—virtually guaranteed that the secretary of state would support the broad interpretation. Perle could already deliver Secretary of Defense Weinberger. The NSC meeting was to be on a Thursday and on the Sunday before the meeting, October 6, MacFarlane appeared on the television show *Meet the Press* and virtually declared for the broad interpretation. Nitze tried to stop the steamroller a bit by sending a memorandum to the NSC that urged that while the broad interpretation was a permissible reading of the ABM Treaty text, it likely would be so disruptive to the NATO alliance that, Nitze argued, the United States should declare for the broad interpretation in principle, but also state that it was unnecessary now and that for the time being the United States would, as a matter of policy, adhere to the traditional interpretation. Nitze was furious with himself and McFarlane and urged Shultz to try to limit the damage and persuade the president to support the Nitze compromise.

The day before the NSC meeting I prepared a revision of the paper that I had sent to Perle, with the objective of presenting as simply and briefly as I could the arguments for the traditional interpretation. My memorandum was one-and-a-half pages long. Adelman prepared a memorandum of his own directed to all NSC principals, in which he said that he was on the fence, the arguments on both sides were persuasive but that all principals should read the attached memorandum by his general counsel before taking a position on the issue. Adelman's memorandum and its attachment went to all NSC principals the night before the meeting, so the arguments contained therein were available to all in advance. It should be noted that at this time I was using what I believed to be strong, virtually irrefutable arguments based on the actual text of the treaty, the negotiating history, and the ratification record. It was over a year later that Nitze commissioned my study of U.S.-Soviet subsequent practice in the SCC, which in my opinion proved to be utterly destructive of the broad interpretation.

Jack McNeill wrote a similar memorandum at Defense, but it was blocked by the then DOD general counsel. A few weeks earlier in the buildup to the beginning of this debate, Jack had argued in a Pentagon meeting, in response to a question as to why we did not give to Congress an ABM Treaty interpretation response that suits our interests on SDI, that it also suits the interests of the United States "to obey the law and honor our treaty obligation," the key issue here.

At the NSC meeting, a decision was taken to have the president declare that the broad interpretation was the correct interpretation of the relevant provisions of the ABM Treaty. All the principals agreed to this except for Mike Guhin who, sitting in for and under instructions from Ken, urged further study before a decision was taken. For a country that believes in the importance of international law and the sanctity of contract, in my opinion, this was a black day—an act much more typical of the former Soviet Union, which essentially believed in force, not law, as the arbiter of human relations. In the end, the Nitze formulation was also approved by the president: the United States would declare for the broad interpretation but for the time being adhere to the traditional interpretation for the sake of the sensitivities of our allies—even so, Shultz had some fence-mending to do.

But this action was not the resolution of the matter; it was merely the first battle in a long war, which ended at least in part only in June of 1993. As I said, Ken Adelman had proved to be the only NSC principal who even raised a question about the broad interpretation at the NSC meeting. However, there never was any real legal basis for the broad interpretation. Its only basis was politics, but even for political reasons it was unnecessary. As I had said to Richard Perle, SDI testing for the foreseeable future could be called testing of sub-components and therefore not a violation of the ABM Treaty. But proponents of the broad interpretation wished to dramatically sweep away the ABM Treaty. Of course, the ABM Treaty has a withdrawal clause, but the SDI advocates knew that the president would never exercise the right of withdrawal set forth in this provision. It would have wrecked strategic arms negotiations with the Soviet Union, which had just begun again pursuant to the January 1985 agreement, and our European allies would have violently objected. Most of NATO would have regarded such an action as provocative in the extreme—which it would have been—and Britain and France would have considered their nuclear deterrent degraded. As it was, under the ABM Treaty regime, the British and French nuclear weapon delivery vehicles enjoyed essentially a free ride into the Soviet Union. Even partially effective strategic defenses constructed by the former Soviet Union in the absence of the ABM Treaty regime might have largely nullified the small British and French nuclear forces.

Therefore, the SDI advocates decided to try to destroy the ABM Treaty through the back door by creating an interpretation of the treaty that essentially nullified its basic purpose. The central objective of the ABM Treaty set forth in Article I is to prohibit a nationwide ballistic missile defense. Advocates of the broad interpretation argued that a nationwide missile defense could be developed and tested under the ABM Treaty as long as new or futuristic technology based on other physical principles was used. It is not possible to square this assertion with the language of Article I. Thus, it seemed that the motive of the advocates of this "interpretation" was to destroy the ABM Treaty—apparently not so much for the purpose of promoting the SDI program that did not need help like this for many years, but to eliminate arms control as a viable policy objective with the former Soviet Union. Those in State and the NSC who supported this effort appeared largely to do so to gain favor with what they perceived as the dominant political forces, centered in DOD. But, in addition to being wrong and misguided—and harmful to the SDI program in the end—it seemed to me that the whole exercise questioned the honor of the United States of America, a country that stands for the rule of law. Here we were, taking one of our most important international legal obligations and standing it on its head. In 1988, after all of this was largely over, I encountered Senator Sam Nunn, chairman of the Armed Services Committee, at a book-signing gathering and we discussed the subject briefly. Senator Nunn had led opposition to the broad interpretation in the Senate. I said that I did whatever I did because I regarded the episode as a blot on the honor of the United States. Senator Nunn replied that that was his motivation as well.

Since the SDI advocacy contingent knew they could not win the national missile defense debate if it meant abrogation of the ABM Treaty, they decided to convert a legitimate policy debate into a misguided legal debate. In effect, it was argued that the U.S. negotiating delegation in 1972 did not understand that they failed to achieve the one central thing the ABM Treaty was designed to do—ban national missile defenses in the United States and the Soviet Union—and that national missile defenses could be developed and tested as long as futuristic technology is used. In the over-heated national security interagency process in the Reagan administration at the time, such a concept was accepted. It was my impression throughout that the Reagan administration had limited regard for the law—Iran/Contra demonstrated this. The concern was policy and if the law got in the way, it should be ignored, repudiated, or reinterpreted. So in a sense it seemed that the actions of the Reagan administration with respect to the broad interpretation were consistent with attitudes and actions existing elsewhere, at least in the national security part of the Reagan administration.

The initial phase of the ABM interpretation debate focused on the text of the treaty itself, the negotiating record, and the ratification record. The all-important area of subsequent practice was ignored until later. Keeping in mind the prohibition on national missile defense set forth in Article I, one turns to the definition of ABM systems found in Article II. The definition, which was carefully developed during the negotiations, defines an ABM system as a system "to counter strategic ballistic missiles in flight trajectory, currently consisting of ABM launchers, ABM interceptor missiles, and ABM radars." In my judgment, there is no other way to read the first phrase, followed by the comma and the "currently consisting of" phrase, than as intending to encompass all systems capable of countering strategic ballistic missiles in flight, regardless of the technology used. The comma in this sentence functions in a manner similar to a period but permits modification of the all-inclusive definition set forth in the first phrase with a phrase indicating that at present ABM system technology comprises launchers, missiles, and radars, leaving the basic definition open for components based on future technology. To argue that this straightforward definition covers only current technology when the words and grammar indicate otherwise and in light of the central objective of the treaty set forth in Article I is, in my judgment, sophistry. Once the integrity of the Article II definition is upheld, there is no room left for the broad interpretation. The ban on sea-based, air-based, space-based, and mobile land-based ABM systems becomes comprehensive automatically because of this definition.

Since the language of the treaty predominates over everything, and the authority of the negotiating and ratification records is of secondary importance in any case, one need not even look to these sources to judge the broad interpretation. But even so, there is nothing in the negotiating record that in any way supports the broad interpretation. Several exchanges confirm the traditional interpretation, however, such as the September 15, 1971, exchange between Victor Karpov and Sid Graybeal in which Karpov acknowledges that space-based ABM systems, regardless of the technology used, are prohibited. And throughout the history of ABM Treaty implementation, Soviet officials acted consistently with this interpretation—but that is subsequent practice to which I shall turn later. Further, the U.S. negotiating instructions directed the negotiators to ban all ABM systems in whatever basing mode except for fixed land-based. There was a desire to keep development and testing open for futuristic systems in a land-based mode to accommodate the army's SAM-D advanced air defense system that was under development and was being designed to use laser beam weapons. Also, the ratification record contains several assertions by government witnesses that ABM systems in all basing modes are banned regardless of technology. One of the two senators who voted against the ABM Treaty, Senator Buckley, based his opposition on the fact that space-based futuristic ABM systems are banned by the treaty. Senator Buckley was never refuted by another senator or by an administration spokesman.

Finally, in the one place in the treaty where futuristic technology based on other physical principles is mentioned—Agreed Statement D—the language simply reinforces the traditional interpretation. Article III of the ABM Treaty states that ABM systems and their components may not be deployed—except at two permitted deployment sites set forth in the Article and with certain constraints on the location, number, and capability of launchers, missiles, and radars—and there are no limits on the development and testing of fixed land-based ABM systems, unlike the Article V limitations on sea-based, air-based, space-based, and mobile land-based ABM systems. Agreed Statement D provides that, should ABM systems based on other physical principles—futuristic technology capable of substituting for fixed land-based launchers, missiles, and radars permitted under Article III (this is a reference to SAM-D)—be developed in the future, appropriate limitations will be discussed in the treaty's implementing body, the Standing Consultative Commission. If agreement is reached, necessary amendments to the treaty permitting such deployments will be negotiated and agreed pursuant to the amendments article of the treaty.

Under generally accepted rules of international law on treaty interpretation, treaties are interpreted on the basis of the language of the text, and where the treaty language is ambiguous the treaty language should be understood as reflected by the practice of the parties in implementing the treaty, referred to as "subsequent practice." Recourse can be had to the negotiating record only on a secondary basis to help clear up issues that the treaty text and subsequent practice do not resolve. Subsequent practice under international law is considered far more authoritative than the negotiating history, since practice reflects the understanding of states as they carry out their obligations, while all negotiating records are by their nature somewhat confusing. As the ebb and flow of the discussion goes on, different people record this or that in their own way.

In their initial assault on the ABM Treaty, the advocates of the broad interpretation tried to muddy the text of the treaty by pulling random statements from the negotiating record and claiming that even though the U.S. negotiators believed that they had banned space-based ABM systems regardless of technology, the Soviet Union never agreed, and therefore they failed. Of course, the excerpts they pulled from the record did not establish their claim but it was an irrelevant issue in any case. The text of the treaty is unequivocal and Soviet subsequent practice is equally unequivocal, as was the United States' practice until the announcement of the broad interpretation. Thus, both parties were and are bound to the traditional interpretation.

For whatever reason, the initial debate did not address the all-important issue of subsequent practice. Later I will discuss the sequence of issues in the debate, but first some general comments on United States and Soviet subsequent practice under the ABM Treaty.

For its part, the United States had never done anything that is contrary to the traditional interpretation. Indeed, year after year, the United States published in its Annual Arms Control Impact Statement—written by ACDA but cleared interagency—the flat statement that space-based ABM systems are banned regardless of the technology involved. And there was a whole series of statements in SCC discussions of various implementing issues, and also during development of provisions for the SALT II Treaty, that space-based ABMs are banned regardless of the technology involved. Some of these statements were made by U.S. representatives, concurred in by the Soviets, and some were made by Soviet representatives, concurred in by U.S. representatives.

In the early 1980s, a series of formal exchanges in the SCC between the United States and the Soviet Union took place. These exchanges annually reaffirmed the traditional interpretation and culminated in an exchange in May 1985 that began with the Soviet commissioner complaining about certain ambiguous statements made by Ambassador Nitze in a congressional hearing. He followed this complaint with a clear reaffirmation of the traditional interpretation. The U.S. commissioner responded by saying that Nitze's comments were wholly consistent with the traditional interpretation, and then he unequivocally reaffirmed the traditional interpretation. Marshall Akhromayev, the chief of the Soviet General Staff, made a public statement in June 1985 reaffirming the traditional interpretation. And the Soviet Union, from 1972 onward, had never done anything contrary to the traditional interpretation.

And so the issue was joined in the fall of 1985 with the Perle impetus, the Sofaer articulation, and the MacFarlane rush to judgment. However, there was some mitigation as a result of the Shultz-Nitze intervention that for the present the United States would continue to observe the traditional interpretation, even though it was declaring that the broad interpretation was justified. About this time I met Sofaer for the first time; he told me that I was a famous man—I do not think that he meant this in a flattering way.

With the outbreak of the broad interpretation, Congress became energized. The Senate Foreign Relations Committee conducted hearings on the subject. John Rhinelander, the SALT I legal advisor, declared that the broad interpretation had no basis in fact or law. In *SALT: The Moscow Agreements and Beyond*, which he had co-authored in 1974, Rhinelander sets forth the traditional interpretation of Article V of the ABM Treaty. John had written an article-by-article analysis of the ABM Treaty and the Interim Agreement while he was the delegation lawyer. Consistent with the practice of the day, the document had been classified top secret so John had not had access to these documents for over ten years. (It was finally declassified in 1999. In his analysis written from the vantage point of the delegation lawyer as the negotiations unfolded, John made clear that the ABM Treaty applies to all technologies, not just 1972 "current" technology, and that ABM systems based on other physical principles, such as lasers or particle beams, are prohibited.) He said in public testimony based on his recollection that his analysis made clear that space-based ABM systems were prohibited regardless of the technology used and that all members of the U.S. SALT delegation agreed. That was my recollection also in 1985. When I had done the first draft of the ABM Treaty official unclassified article-by-article analysis to accompany the treaty to the Senate, I had based the draft on John's memos and this point was unequivocally made. Unfortunately, in 1972 the ACDA Deputy General Counsel Charles Van Doren and ACDA Deputy Director Spurgeon Keeny decided to rewrite my draft and this point was lost in the revised official government submission.

Ralph Earle testified in these hearings on behalf of the traditional interpretation, pointing out the significance of the comma in Article II after the word "trajectory" and before "currently." A number of former SALT I negotiators stepped forward and stated that the broad interpretation was without any substantiation whatsoever. These included the chairman of the delegation, Ambassador Gerard Smith, my old boss; Ray Garthoff, the executive secretary of the delegation and a key negotiator; retired General Allison, the JCS representative; and Sid Graybeal, also a key negotiator and from 1973 to 1977 the U.S. SCC commissioner.

In the winter of 1985, Graybeal and Colonel Charles Fitzgerald, the longtime advisor to the U.S. SCC delegation and brilliant Russian linguist, had been commissioned by OSD to do an analysis of the negotiating record of SALT I in the hope that they would conclude that the traditional interpretation was not supported by the record. Instead, their report came out with precisely the opposite result, to the dismay of those in OSD who had requested the study. Perle had turned to Mr. Kunsberg, the young Defense Department lawyer I mentioned earlier. Kunsberg, of course, came up with the conclusion Perle wanted. This was announced at the fateful interagency meeting in September, and the rest is history.

In the fall 1985 Senate Foreign Relations Committee hearing, Sofaer and Nitze stuck to their guns, Sofaer referring to selected portions of the negotiating record as well as the record of the ratification process to support his case. This aroused an interest among certain senators to be able to review the record themselves. The principal activists on this issue in the Senate were Democrats Joseph Biden and Claiborne Pell of the Senate Foreign Relations Committee and Carl Levin and Sam Nunn of the Armed Services Committee. Senator John Warner of Virginia appeared deeply troubled, man of principle that he is. Senator Nunn led the Senate investigation and eventual rejection of the broad interpretation by the Congress (by means of the banning of any funding to implement the broad interpretation), but Senator Levin played an important role as well, because he collided with Judge Sofaer directly on the interpretation issue. At one point when Levin questioned Sofaer on an issue, Sofaer replied that he had not reviewed the memorandum in question carefully, but rather it had been prepared by the "young lawyers" on his staff. After a strong letter from Nunn and others, it was decided early in 1986 to send the entire ABM Treaty negotiating record, still classified secret for diplomatic (not security) reasons, to the Senate. It was housed in a special vault and access was restricted to senators themselves and a few key staffers. Nunn and Levin did review the record themselves, as did Bob Bell, Nunn's indispensable aide and later a key figure on the NSC staff of President Clinton.

In the early spring of 1986, three things of note took place that affected this process. First, Bill Sims, one of the "young lawyers" on Judge Sofaer's staff who, since the fall of 1985, had been almost entirely dedicated to supporting Sofaer on the ABM debate, approached me. He said that he could no longer in good conscience work for the Legal Advisor's Office on this subject. He said that he had brought forward evidence in October of 1985, as he was preparing his first legal memorandum justifying the broad interpretation, which proved that it was false. In particular he had presented evidence of subsequent practice, including the aforementioned SCC exchange regarding Nitze's statements, which had simply been ignored. Bill was a former Air Force officer who put a great emphasis on honor and integrity. He was concerned that he might be charged with misconduct by Bar Association authorities because of his participation in the broad interpretation exercise. As a result, he was thinking of leaving government, reluctant as he was to do so. I urged him to come to work at ACDA in the General Counsel's Office instead of leaving government. I thought very highly of him, as did my colleague Bill Parsons, who, with the departure of Ray Waters in January of 1986, was my partner in ABM Treaty interpretation work. Bill Parsons had been a student in John Rhinelander's course on arms control, which we subsequently taught together at the University of Virginia Law School on weekends in the spring from 1984 to 1991. He came to ACDA not long after graduation. He was brilliant, intense, sometimes difficult, but his work was always of the highest quality. His recommendation to offer Bill Sims a job carried great weight with me.

Bill Sims thought it over for a week or two and then accepted. He then informed Sofaer, who was furious. Judge Sofaer called me to his office and accused me of deliberately undermining his effort by stealing Bill Sims from him. It was one more example of my lack of loyalty to the administration and to the broad interpretation, he said. I pointed out that Sims approached me rather than me him, but that cut no ice with Sofaer. He concluded the conversation by noting that Sims was a young lawyer so he chose not to hurt him. Nevertheless, he condemned the whole thing.

Judge Sofaer also decided about the same time to write his definitive broad interpretation justification memorandum. He had written three memoranda in October 1985, one on the negotiating record, one on the ratification record and one on post-ratification statements. He now decided to draw it all together in a memorandum he completed in August 1986. He circulated a draft of this memorandum to me in June 1986 before going final. I pointed out several serious flaws in his argumentation in a memorandum to Adelman, who authorized me to transmit these thoughts to Sofaer. I then wrote Sofaer a memorandum in July, stating that I was not trying to reopen a debate that I had already lost, but was pointing out some errors in his analysis from the standpoint of advocacy of the broad interpretation. My suggestions were not accepted.

Also in the spring of 1986 Paul Nitze called me to his office and said that he would like to have a memorandum that analyzed arguments that a supporter of the traditional interpretation, such as Sid Graybeal, might make on behalf of his view. With Bill Parsons's help I laboriously analyzed the negotiating record and rebutted the Sofaer arguments one by one and set forth the unequivocal support for the traditional interpretation that existed both in the negotiating record and the ratification record. Bill Parsons, the drafter of the memorandum, referred to it as the "monster memo" (only to be surpassed by the memorandum on subsequent practice of January 1987), which was completed in June of 1986 and contained some relevant references to subsequent practice. These came from the SCC in the late 1970s (during the negotiation of the 1978 Memorandum of Understanding on Testing in an ABM Mode) and from SALT II. But, even though Bill Sims had drawn my attention to it, the memorandum did not examine the conclusive SCC record of the 1980s, nor did it emphasize the transcendent importance of subsequent practice under international law. Since the charge was to set forth and examine potential Graybeal arguments—Nitze's excuse for a traditional interpretation advocacy memo—the 1980s were seen as not relevant because Graybeal was out of government then. Thus, it concentrated on the negotiating record, the ratification record, and the SCC proceedings of the 1970s, in which Graybeal participated or which occurred shortly after his departure from government. I furnished the memorandum to Nitze, who was pleased with it, with copies to Adelman and to Sofaer, who did not appear pleased with it.

Meanwhile, the Senate review of the negotiating record continued through 1986. One of the Sofaer arguments, later referred to as the Sofaer Doctrine, that particularly rankled the senators was that the U.S. government had believed that it had achieved the traditional interpretation in the negotiations but had failed because the Soviets never agreed—this against the fact that the Soviets never said that they adhered to the broad interpretation, that they made many unequivocal statements that the traditional interpretation was correct between 1975 and 1985, and they never took any action contrary to the traditional interpretation. Nevertheless, Sofaer argued that the government mistakenly represented to the Senate during ratification the traditional interpretation of Article V but that this was not binding on the executive branch because the representation was in error. Therefore, a subsequent administration could come along, discover the true facts, and declare that the treaty meant something other than what the Senate believed that it meant. Many senators saw this as a direct derogation of the Senate's constitutional right of advice and consent. This ultimately led to the Biden Resolution that burdened future ratifications of arms control agreements. This resolution declared that the executive branch was bound by any "shared understanding" as to the meaning of a treaty provision that ran between the Senate and the executive branch. The Senate regarded this—and it was—as a direct repudiation of the so-called "Sofaer Doctrine," which I have set forth above. Thus, to say the least, a majority in the Senate were becoming increasingly skeptical of the broad interpretation.

Toward the end of 1986 Bill Sims decided that he simply had to distance himself from this process. He continued to be deeply concerned that he might be cited for professional misconduct because of his work in the Legal Advisor's Office on the ABM Treaty interpretation issue, and he just wanted to get away. He had an offer from a prestigious Phoenix, Arizona, law firm and decided to accept it. I hated to see him go, as he was a capable and highly effective colleague. But he was just too tarred by it all.

Near year's end the attitude in the Senate was hardening, leading ultimately to the Biden Resolution and further down the road to the congressional denial of funds to any strategic defense program inconsistent with the traditional interpretation. The 1989 SDIO Report was correct when it said the greatest burden that the SDI program had to carry was the broad interpretation. The Senate's frustration was effectively expressed in a December 1, 1986, letter from Senator Carl Levin to Secretary Shultz, which captured the emotions of those times. In this letter, Senator Levin stated that in October of 1985, the government announced that it had arrived at a "new interpretation" of the ABM Treaty, which, in essence, would allow for testing and development of space-based "exotic" defensive systems like those envisioned in the Strategic Defense Initiative. This interpretation, he said, reversed a view held for thirteen years: that the treaty banned everything other than research on so-called exotic systems that would use future technologies in anything other than a fixed, land-based mode. He noted that until recently, most discussions of this issue were restricted to idle speculation. Since no one outside the administration had access to the negotiating record on which the new interpretation was based, it was difficult to review the basis for this new view of the treaty. Similarly, until the meeting in Reykjavik in October 1986, questions about the relationship between SDI testing, the ABM Treaty, and future arms control agreements were being asked in more or less a vacuum.

Now, however, members of the Senate have had an opportunity to review the negotiating record and the United States may have an opportunity to reach an historic arms reduction agreement with the Soviet Union, he said. In this environment, questions about the ABM Treaty and SDI take on a new significance. After all, no matter how one views the value of SDI, it is clear that the U.S. claim that it can test and develop such a system (a claim that can be made only by virtue of the new interpretation of the ABM Treaty) has been, and remains, a major obstacle to any meaningful arms control agreement with the Soviets.

Based on his review of the negotiating record, Senator Levin concluded that Judge Sofaer's interpretation of the treaty was incorrect, and that the process he used to develop and justify that interpretation was "fatally flawed." Specifically, Senator Levin said that he believed that Judge Sofaer had provided the Congress with an incomplete and misleading analysis of the record in an effort to justify his interpretation of the ABM Treaty and that our national interest requires that the administration authorize a new and independent review of the ABM Treaty.

Senator Levin went on to amplify these points. He noted that, while ambiguity can be found in the text and context of any treaty, Judge Sofaer had sought to find areas of uncertainty and to magnify their meaning in order to advance a specific policy interest, specifically, making it possible for the United States to test and develop SDI. And the Senator noted that the ratification debate in the Senate on the ABM Treaty contains a number of statements in support of the restrictive view. In fact, he added, one of the two members voting against the treaty, former Senator Buckley, did so precisely because he believed it would prohibit the development and testing of a laser type system based in space.

Senator Levin then continued on at length questioning Sofaer's unwillingness to meet with members of the U.S. ABM Treaty negotiating team—except for Ambassador Nitze who, Levin noted, had said that his agreement with the new interpretation differed from his earlier opinion. If, Levin said, Judge Sofaer thought it important to obtain Nitze's views, why did he not also seek the views of, for example, Gerard Smith (the chairman of the delegation), John Rhinelander (the delegation lawyer), Sid Graybeal and Ray

Garthoff (key members of the delegation), or General Royal Allison (the JCS representative on the delegation), as Levin had done? Levin noted that Allison had helped him to understand what General Palmer meant when he told the Senate in 1972 that the prohibition on exotic weapons "was a fundamental part" of the final agreement. Senator Levin concluded in his letter that, in his view, Judge Sofaer

> had an ax to grind—and after he sharpened it, he buried that ax in the back of the ABM Treaty. The process he used was one of an advocate, not an objective judge. He clearly wanted to stretch the fabric of the treaty to allow for SDI testing and development. Judge Sofaer's approach, if sanctified by our government, would weaken respect for international law and the regime of treaties as well as threaten the possibility that a reasonable arms control agreement could be reached in the near future.

In March 1987, Judge Sofaer was called to testify before the Senate Foreign Relations Committee. During the hearing, Senator John Kerry, Democrat of Massachusetts, accused him of creating a constitutional crisis by breaking with the interpretation that the Senate had in mind when it approved the ABM Treaty, as reported by Strobe Talbott in "The Master of the Game." Senator Biden asserted that Sofaer had effected an "inconceivable politicization of his office." At about the same time, Senator Nunn concluded an exhaustive review of the negotiating history material supplied to the Senate. He announced his conclusions in March in a series of detailed and strongly worded reports. Nunn asserted that in his view most of Sofaer's work was based on "a complete and total misrepresentation of the record" and warned that if the administration insisted on pressing its view on the ABM Treaty interpretation, it would risk provoking a "constitutional crisis." On May 5, the Senate Armed Services Committee voted to prohibit funding for any SDI tests that would violate the traditional interpretation. Later, this constraint was adopted by the Congress and became law.

January 1987, to my mind at least, represented the turning point of the ABM debate. (It also began the personal assaults on me by broad interpretation supporters, in an attempt to discredit my views rather than continuing to rely on Sofaer's memoranda.) In the second week of January, Paul Nitze became aware for the first time of the May 1985 SCC exchange of views evoked by his congressional testimony. Commissioner Ellis sent the text of the May 1985 exchange to me on January 5, 1987. On January 12, I briefed Adelman and Nitze on it. On January 9, I had briefed their staffs, and Norm Clyne discussed it with Sofaer, who admitted that it was "highly significant."

This was the first time I had directly focused on this question. Nitze asked Sofaer about it, and Sofaer said that he had been unaware of it—even though Bill Sims had stated that he had brought it to his attention in October 1985.

Both Adelman and Nitze urged me to immediately write a comprehensive memorandum on the relevance of subsequent practice in general and the impact of the Ellis-Staradubov exchange of views in particular. I talked it over with Jim Timbie, saying that I thought the Ellis-Staradubov exchange was dispositive of the broad interpretation, given the importance of subsequent practice. Jim urged me to draw no conclusions in my memorandum, but simply set down the law and describe the relevant SCC exchanges. Mike Guhin also urged me to set forth no conclusions. This turned out to be good advice. Norm Clyne told me around the middle of January that Perle had told him that Sofaer initially had been inclined to concede in the face of the Ellis-Staradubov exchange, but that he had ultimately decided otherwise.

As usual, I turned over the drafting to Bill Parsons, and I did the editing. Bill did a magnificent job of presenting the law—largely customary international law as reflected in the Vienna Convention on the Law of Treaties. He grouped the SCC exchanges in chronological order—explaining each one—and presented them in ascending order of dispositiveness. The memorandum explained that under international legal rules treaties are interpreted on the basis of the plain meaning of the text in light of any subsequent practice. These two sources are considered to be on an equal basis. Reference to preparatory work (the negotiating record) is provided for in a different provision of the Vienna Convention and is clearly secondary, and subordinate, to subsequent practice. Subsequent practice can be statements, action, or lack of action. Not taking action contrary to a particular interpretation of a treaty for a period of, for example, ten years, could be argued to be conclusive. Certainly, statements as to a state's view on an interpretation after the treaty enters into force, if consistent, are dispositive. The Soviet SCC statements began in the early 1980s in response to a speech by then Secretary of the Air Force Hans Mark, and were responded to by the United States. Even these first statements by both sides effectively asserted the traditional interpretation. The exchanges became more and more precise over the years until the spring of 1985, when Staradubov (the Soviet commissioner), in commenting on Nitze congressional testimony, unequivocally and directly supported the traditional interpretation and Ellis (the U.S. commissioner) did the same in his reply. Even without a conclusion, no one could read the law as set forth in the memo side by side with the SCC exchanges and come to any other conclusion but that the broad interpretation was incorrect.

Thus, in January 1987, the last intellectual underpinnings of the broad interpretation fell away. There never was any real support for it in the negotiating record, but as in any such record there was some confusion as negotiators were working their way through problems day by day. But there was no confusion as to what the objective of U.S. negotiators was with respect to all types of ABM systems other than fixed land-based, regardless of technology. And the one or two times this issue was directly addressed by the negotiators, the record was clear that both sides agreed that the development, testing, and deployment of such systems would be prohibited by the ABM Treaty, particularly the September 1971 exchange between Graybeal and Karpov. However, Judge Sofaer was able to draw on other parts of the record, which were not directly on point, to support his brief for the broad interpretation.

The ratification record was less ambiguous, but even here there were presentations that arguably could be made consistent with either interpretation primarily because the issue of mobile ABM systems was not being addressed. But there was really no doubt that Senator Buckley, in casting his vote on the floor of the Senate, unambiguously was voting "no" because of the ban on the testing and deployment of future technology ABM systems that were other than fixed land-based. The following (truncated) exchanges left little doubt as well. The first is part of a Department of Defense response of June 6, 1972, to questions from Senator Barry Goldwater in connection with Secretary Laird's testimony before the Senate Armed Services Committee. The second is excerpts from the June 22, 1972, testimony of Dr. John Foster, director of Defense research and engineering, before the same committee, with a subsequent addition for the record. I reprint both here.

6 June 1972—DOD Responses to Prepared Questions from Senator Barry Goldwater

QUESTION: The ABM bit does not bother me too much, although I have not seen the fine print. For my money, we should have long since moved on the space-based systems with boosting phase destruction with shot, nukes, or lasers. I have seen nothing in SALT that prevents development to proceed in that direction. Am I correct?

ANSWER: With reference to development of a boost-phase intercept capability or lasers, there is no specific provision in the ABM Treaty that prohibits development of such systems.

There is, however, a prohibition on the development, testing, or deployment of ABM systems which are space-based, as well as sea-based, air-based, or mobile land-based. The U.S. side understands this prohibition not to apply to basic and advanced research and exploratory development of technology which could be associated with such systems, or their components.

There are no restrictions on the development of lasers for fixed land-based ABM systems. The sides have agreed, however, that deployment of such systems which would be capable of substituting for current ABM components, that is, ABM launchers, ABM interceptor missiles, and ABM radars, shall be subject to discussion in accordance with article XIII (Standing Consultative Commission) and agreement in accordance with article XIV (amendments to the treaty.)

22 June 1972—Exchange between Senator Henry Jackson and Dr. John S. Foster, Director of Defense, Research and Engineering.

SENATOR JACKSON: I couldn't agree with you more, but, you see, the problem is that we are creating a climate of confusion. I want to—before we conclude here—is there anything in these arrangements that impinge on our right to research those areas that bear on both our defense and on defense capability? Specifically, there is a limitation on lasers, as I recall, in the agreement and does the SALT agreement prohibit land-based laser development?

DR. FOSTER: No sir, it does not. (Deleted, meaning the subsequent comments remain classified.)

SENATOR JACKSON: (Deleted.)

DR. FOSTER: (Deleted) What is affected by the treaty would be the development of laser ABM systems capable of substituting for current ABM components.

SENATOR JACKSON: If it is sea-based, air-based, space-based, or mobile land-based. If it is a fixed land-based ABM system, it is permitted; am I not correct?

DR. FOSTER: That is right.

SENATOR JACKSON: What does this do to our research—I will read it to you: section 1 of article 5—this is the treaty: "Each party undertakes not to develop"—it hits all of these things—"not to develop, test or deploy ABM systems." You can't do anything; you can't develop; you can't test and finally, you can't deploy. It is not "or."

DR. FOSTER: One cannot deploy a fixed land-based laser ABM system which is capable of substituting for an ABM radar, ABM launcher, or ABM interceptor missile.

SENATOR JACKSON: You can't even test, you can't develop.

DR. FOSTER: You can develop and test up to the deployment phase of future ABM system components which are fixed and land-based. My understanding is you can develop and test but you cannot deploy. You can use lasers in connection with our present land-based Safeguard system provided that such lasers augment, or are an addendum to, lasers as an ancillary piece of equipment but not as one of the prime components either as a radar or as an interceptor to destroy the vehicle.

SENATOR JACKSON: The way I read this—but I may be wrong; it depends upon the interpretation here—but it says each party undertakes not to develop, test or deploy ABM systems or components which are sea-based, air-based, space-based, or mobile land-based.

DR. FOSTER: That is correct.

SENATOR JACKSON: Now, it could well be read into this that even though you are conducting research you have not deployed it, that you cannot do that either. The way I read this, Mr. Chairman—you might take a look at it—I think it raises a real question here whether you can actually engage in research.

(The information follows:)

Article V prohibits the development and testing of ABM systems or components that are sea-based, air-based, space-based, or mobile land-based. Constraints imposed by the phrase "development and testing" would be applicable only to that portion of the "advanced development stage" following laboratory testing, i.e., that stage which is verifiable by national means. Therefore, a prohibition on development—the Russian word is "creation"—would begin only at the stage where laboratory testing ended on ABM components, on either a prototype or bread-board model.

For whatever reason, the record of subsequent practice was not fully examined until January 1987; although there had been a review of such practice in the Standing Consultative Commission in the 1970s, that occurred relatively soon after ABM Treaty ratification, as well as in the SALT II record, in the mid-1986 memoranda by Judge Sofaer and by me. This was all consistent with the traditional interpretation but not dispositive. But the record of practice in the SCC in the 1980s was dispositive, and this was examined closely for the first time in January 1987.

In the second week of January 1987, as I said, Paul Nitze became directly aware of the May 1985 Ellis-Staradubov exchanges in the SCC on the subject of Article V of the ABM Treaty, prompted by testimony that he had given. In addition, Judge Sofaer had written a memorandum to Paul Nitze in mid-January in which he stated that in an exchange in May 1985, the U.S. commissioner adhered to the traditional interpretation of the ABM Treaty and that the Soviet commissioner made a substantively identical statement and thus an understanding emerged. This was misleading, as this had always been the interpretation and in addition to the negotiating and ratification records there was ample material in the SCC record and the SALT II record going back to 1973 to support this. Indeed, a very similar exchange of statements by the two commissioners had been made in 1984, and there were rather clear statements virtually every year going back to 1980. But there is no doubt that the May 1985 exchange was dispositive.

Judge Sofaer, in his January 1987 memorandum to Nitze, complained that he had never seen these exchanges and that I had not included them in my June 1986 memorandum (revised and reissued in early July) on possible Graybeal arguments as I had done for Nitze. Sofaer did admit in his mid-January memorandum that there was "substantial overlap" between the Staradubov and Ellis statements. However, it was my understanding that Mark Siegler, a State Department advisor to the SCC, had brought them to the attention of Sofaer's staff in November 1985, and that Bill Sims had directly informed Judge Sofaer in October 1985 of these exchanges. With respect to my June-July 1986 memorandum, it was intended to be limited in scope, focused on possible Sid Graybeal arguments. As I've already noted, Sofaer had written several memoranda in October 1985, one a textual analysis, the second an analysis of the negotiating record, and the third an analysis of post-negotiation statements as well as a self-styled comprehensive analysis in August 1986.

In his memorandum of August 1986, Judge Sofaer does make some reference to subsequent practice, but in the first three he made none. Indeed, in his third October 1985 memorandum he stated that statements made during the treaty's negotiations are given more weight in treaty interpretation than statements made later in time. This reverses the accepted international law rule set forth in Articles 31 and 32 of the Vienna Convention of the Law of Treaties that in interpreting a treaty one uses the language of the treaty on its face and subsequent practice of the parties (Article 31). The negotiating record (or "preparatory work") can only be used to clear up any remaining ambiguities (Article 32). The ratification record is, of course, subsequent practice, but international law puts a higher value on statements and actions more distant in time as reflecting the understanding of the parties as they implement the treaty. This is considered to be the best basis on which to judge the meaning of a treaty other than the language of the treaty itself. In his August 1986 memorandum, Judge Sofaer did make some reference to subsequent practice but it received only a brief reference in an otherwise lengthy and detailed memorandum. Moreover, he asserted that those SCC statements from 1973 through 1980 that he did review formed no part of his basis for concluding that the broad interpretation was the correct interpretation of Article V of the ABM Treaty. Thus, it could be said that subsequent practice was not used in asserting the correctness of the broad interpretation and that the 1980s SCC record, which eliminates any intellectual support for the broad interpretation, was not even reviewed.

As an aside, I might note an interesting issue that came up at the Geneva NST negotiations. As part of a SDI test referred to as the Homing Overlay Experiment, a missile was launched to a predetermined point where it could intercept a simulated reentry vehicle. It then closed and impacted the simulated reentry vehicle being guided by its on-board infrared sensor. In Geneva, the Soviets raised the question of whether such a kinetic (or collision) kill vehicle was a device based on "other physical principles" in the meaning of Agreed Statement D of the ABM Treaty, and likewise was the interceptor missile with the on-board homing device an ABM component based on "other physical principles." Hank Cooper asked me to confirm in a memorandum, if I could, his initial response of "no" on both questions to the Soviets. I did write such a memorandum and distributed it in February 1986. In the memorandum, I concluded that kinetic kill vehicles did exist in 1972 and thus were not based on future technology or "other physical principles" and that the infrared sensor was a permitted adjunct under the treaty, not a component based on "other physical principles." This is worthy of note, because it was kinetic kill vehicles that formed the backbone and most promising part of the SDI program and, since they were based on 1972 technology, were not liberated by the broad interpretation—thus demonstrating the irrelevance of the broad interpretation to anything other than the destruction of arms control.

Meanwhile, Bill Parsons was working away on the memorandum on subsequent practice. On January 29, I took my last look at the newly completed memorandum and left for a wedding in California. It was duly completed later that day by Bill and my deputy, Mary Lib Hoinkes. On January 30, Bill and Mary Lib called and said that Nitze was insisting on the memorandum by February 2. I asked Mary Lib to clean up any typos, date it January 29, sign it for me, and send it out. It was sent out the afternoon of January 30, 1987. It was sent to Ken Adelman, Paul Nitze, Judge Sofaer, and Commissioner Ellis, among many others. It did not contain a conclusion. It simply set out the law of treaty interpretation under Articles 31 and 32 of the Vienna Convention and compiled the SCC record of subsequent practice under Article V of the ABM Treaty. The reader was left to judge for himself or herself.

With respect to the law, the January memorandum stated that Articles 31 and 32 of the Vienna Convention on the Law of Treaties represent the most authoritative guide to the interpretation of treaties under international law; the State Department Office of the Legal Advisor, the *Restatement of Foreign Relations Law*, and several U.S. federal courts have recognized the authority of the Vienna Convention, particularly Article 31 as it relates to subsequent practice; under the convention subsequent practice has greater legal authority than the negotiating record; the convention requires the interpreter of treaties to examine all evidence of subsequent practice before turning to the negotiating record; and the interpreter should not turn to the negotiating record at all as a means of interpretation unless the procedure of examining the text of the treaty and all subsequent practice would lead to an ambiguous or manifestly absurd result. Of course, the negotiating record can always be used to confirm an interpretation based on the treaty text and subsequent practice. And discussions held during the SALT II negotiations and in the SCC constitute subsequent practice that is highly relevant to the ABM Treaty interpretation issue.

The memorandum then included a compilation of all relevant statements in the SCC from September 1974 to May 1985. The memorandum noted that in May 1985 in the SCC (five months prior to the promulgation of the broad interpretation) the Soviet Union had complained that Ambassador Nitze recently had asserted in congressional testimony that the ABM Treaty permitted the development of space-based ABM components based on other physical principles, when in fact any activity to develop, test, or deploy space-based ABM systems is prohibited by the treaty. The United States responded around two weeks later that Ambassador Nitze, in the testimony referred to, did not say what the Soviet commissioner had alleged and never stated that the development, testing, or deployment of space-based ABM systems were permitted under the ABM Treaty. Nitze had in fact been discussing permitted research and the procedure set forth in Agreed Statement D. In addition, said the U.S. commissioner, the United States does not contend that the development, testing, or deployment of ABM systems that are sea-based, air-based, space-based, or mobile land-based is permissible under the ABM Treaty; and that there is no question that the ABM Treaty prohibits the development, testing, and deployment of space-based ABM systems, including those of the type referred to in Agreed Statement D—those based on other physical principles. But the United States does assert that the treaty does permit research into possible advanced ABM systems and components, including those covered by Article V. Following this up, on June 4, 1985, Marshall Akhromayev, chief of the Soviet General Staff, likewise complained in an article in *Pravda* about Nitze's testimony and affirmed that the ABM Treaty prohibits space-based ABM systems based on any type of technology and that future technology ABM systems can only be tested and deployed pursuant to Article III and Agreed Statement D, that is, fixed land-based in the designated deployment area.

In my view, Paul Nitze had long before January 1987 begun the process of backing away from the broad interpretation. He commissioned the "Graybeal" memorandum in 1986 and he is the one who initiated the process that led to the memorandum on subsequent practice. Also, in May 1987, he wrote a memorandum to Secretary Shultz about a proposed SDI experiment that was scheduled to involve only sensor tests but which the SDIO had proposed to be modified to involve a kinetic kill intercept and thus implement the broad interpretation (mistakenly, as I have mentioned). Nitze questioned correctly whether such a test can in fact be implemented even under the broad interpretation. Thus, by implication, but not directly, he opposed going ahead with this test, which, at least in the minds of some, would have implemented the broad interpretation—contrary to declared U.S. policy. In February of 1987 some had been arguing within the U.S. government that the United States should move ahead and implement the broad interpretation. This prospect spread widely around town, and in short order I received calls from Jeff Smith of the *Washington Post*, Charlotte Sarkowski of the *Christian Science Monitor*, Warren Strobel of the *Washington Times*, and Bob Bell of Senator Nunn's staff. I could say nothing about the subject, and as a precaution I had Mary Lib sit in as a witness that I did not. On February 10, Jeff Smith published an article in the *Washington Post* entitled "Legal Hurdles Remaining for Key SDI Tests" in which he addressed this issue.

On the weekend of January 29–31, 1987, as I said, I had gone to California for a wedding. On Thursday, the 29th, after approving the memorandum in general before departing, I received a call from Michael Gordon of the *New York Times*. Since this came out of the blue and the memorandum had not yet been distributed, I took the call, thinking he had some other reason for calling. I was authorized to talk to him about the U.S. ABM radars located in other countries, i.e., Fylingdales in the United Kingdom and Thule in Greenland. And in the first part of the discussion that is what he addressed. Then he said he understood that I was writing a new memorandum on the ABM interpretation issue focused on the SCC and what could I tell him about it. I replied that I could not discuss it at all and on that note our conversation ended. I reported this to Ken Adelman and Sig Cohen, our public affairs officer, by memorandum. My understanding was that Gordon then called Judge Sofaer and they talked for some time. Later in the evening of the 29th, after I had arrived in California, Bill Parsons called to tell me that he had heard that there was going to be big trouble concerning the memorandum, and that I should be prepared for it the next week.

On Monday, February 2, I was having lunch with a friend in the State Department eighth-floor dining room. Sofaer walked by my table and asserted that I had leaked classified material to the press. Gordon had published an article in the *New York Times* that morning in which he mentioned the existence of my memorandum with no details. He did mention the May 1985 exchange, which by now was widely known, as well as an Earle-Karpov exchange at SALT II that was also widely known. He also included six other exchanges that were not included in my memorandum. But Gordon did cite one official as saying that there was "overlap" between the May 1985 statements using the phrase in Sofaer's mid-January memorandum to Nitze. At the door of the State Department dining room I encountered Sofaer again and asked him if he had received my January 29 memorandum. He said he had but wished he had reviewed it before the *New York Times*. I denied telling Gordon anything and asked Sofaer to call me.

The same day, however, rather than first calling me, Judge Sofaer wrote a memorandum to Secretary Shultz, with a copy to Ken Adelman and many others, saying that we are in for a new round of unfair attacks with respect to the ABM Treaty based on an analysis of subsequent practice, which some will say established the "narrow" interpretation. He implied in his memorandum that I had leaked this information to the press. Naturally, he did not discuss his memorandum with me in advance. I responded to Sofaer on February 4, indicating my resentment of the offensive insinuations in his memorandum. I said that his statement suggesting that this latest "round" of attacks was "triggered" by my January 29 memorandum could not be taken seriously since he knew that I had been asked by Ambassador Nitze and Director Adelman to prepare the memorandum. I also objected to his implication that I had leaked all or part of my memorandum to the press. I said that neither I nor any member of my staff had ever discussed this matter with any member of the press and that we were all prepared to make sworn statements and to take lie detector tests to this effect.

At a National Security Council meeting a few days later, Secretary Shultz, reflecting the contents of the Sofaer memorandum, declared that one of the problems the administration faced in the arms control field was that Ken Adelman's general counsel, Thomas Graham, had been leaking classified material to the *New York Times*. Ken replied, "Mr. Secretary, that is an irresponsible statement. There is no proof of any such thing." I am told that all this went on in front of President Reagan, without him being too perturbed. Ken had asked me when he reviewed the February 2 Sofaer memorandum whether there was any truth in it. I replied that there was none and I sent him a copy of my response to Sofaer. He said to Mike Guhin, his executive assistant, when he returned from the NSC meeting that he sure hoped that I was telling the truth because he had really gone out on a limb that day. Meanwhile, Jim Timbie and Paul Nitze spoke with Secretary Shultz and explained the real situation. About a week later Shultz called Adelman and apologized, a rare event for the secretary, I understand. That same day Adelman complained to Sofaer about his February 2 memorandum, and Judge Sofaer asserted that he had not actually said that I had leaked my memorandum. Gordon's short article referred only to the existence of the January 29 memorandum (not mentioning a date) and referred to two SCC passages which had been in the press several times before. There is no evidence that the memorandum ever did leak in fact. And it should be noted that half of the memorandum, the description, that part describing the international law rules, was unclassified. The other half, the compilation of statements by the United States and the Soviet Union in the SCC, was classified secret solely for diplomatic protocol reasons. This never was a question of state secrets. The response to my memorandum, as well as the nonexistent leak, was just one effort among several to discredit my views.

On February 24, Senator Helms wrote to Adelman stating that he was in possession of the February 2 Sofaer memorandum and complained about my leaking my memorandum to Gordon. Two weeks later Adelman responded in a letter to Helms, stating that he and Nitze had requested my memorandum. He said that I had been authorized to speak with Gordon about Fylingdales and Thule, that I had not leaked the memorandum, and that, in fact, there was no evidence that it had ever been leaked. Adelman also noted that my memorandum was a research memorandum which had no conclusions. On March 24, at the ACDA authorization hearing, Senator Helms raised again all the points in his letter and Adelman repeated all the points in his response. Helms read the Sofaer memorandum into the record and asked Adelman if he should have people working for him who disagreed with the president. Adelman replied that he always asked his staff to tell him what they really believed and he made the decisions.

Earlier I mentioned Bill Sims of Sofaer's office. Bill had finally left Washington and joined a law firm in Phoenix, Arizona. Early in 1987, the Senate Foreign Relations Committee and the Senate Judiciary Committee decided to do a joint hearing on the ABM interpretation issue. They called Bill Sims to testify on what happened in the Legal Advisor's office. Jack McNeill and I were called as well. We both declined.

On April 23, John Ritch of the committee staff had called and asked me to testify at this hearing. I said that I would only do so as an authorized government witness. On April 28, I called John back and told him I would not appear at the hearing the next day. John said that was all right, they would just say that I was "muzzled." Dave Sullivan, now Senator Helms's assistant for national security issues, called later that day and asked if I was going to testify and I said I would not. He said that was preferable as it could have been uncomfortable for me. He said that he admired me for holding to my views and that there was nothing wrong with holding views contrary to the administration as long as they were kept "in school." I said, "Of course." He said, "Tom, each of us has a role to play in life. You probably have noticed that the Senator has attacked you publicly. Right now you represent something that the Senator hates [opposition to the broad interpretation]. But he doesn't hate you, in fact he likes you. So don't take all this personally." If only it didn't hurt so much. Dave went on to say by way of a "heads up" that Congressman Dornan was planning something "nasty with respect to the Strang case," which will be discussed below.

Bill Sims agreed to testify. On April 13, 1987, ACDA received a letter from Chairman Pell and Senator Biden asking that Bill be allowed to review his own work while at ACDA/GC in preparation for his testimony. They noted that as a major in the Air Force Reserves he still had a security clearance. Their letter specifically referred to an August 1986 memorandum that he authored. A similar request came from Bill's law firm, from an attorney who had agreed to represent him with respect to the forthcoming hearing. I responded on behalf of Ken Adelman that since Bill had a security clearance ACDA had no objection to his reviewing files comprising his work while he was at ACDA—in particular the August 1986 memorandum—on the assumption, of course, that he would give only unclassified testimony in open session. Bill came to the office and reviewed his files prior to his testimony on April 29. At the hearing he testified to the effect that he had had strong reservations about the process that led to the broad interpretation, as well as about the conclusion reached. Chairman Pell noted that Jack McNeill and I had been muzzled. Senator Biden quoted from the Sofaer memorandum denouncing me for holding 'heretical' views with respect to the ABM Treaty.

"What were those 'heretical' views?" asked Biden. Namely that the ABM Treaty is clear on its face and supports the narrow interpretation. "We can understand," said Biden, "why the ACDA general counsel is not here. Perhaps his absence is more eloquent than his presence would have been." That was the last I heard of the February 2 Sofaer memorandum.

Bill wrote me a very nice letter on November 11, 1987. He said that he realized that by speaking out and relying on his DOD clearances for help, he ran the risk of never making lieutenant colonel in the Reserves. He attached a letter from the Air Force informing him that there had been a congressional inquiry asking whether his clearance had been used improperly in connection with access to files at ACDA and subsequent testimony. The Air Force had responded that there was no question of Bill's clearance being used improperly. The letter concluded that this inquiry was now something of a "witch hunt" emanating from "political bias" on Capitol Hill. The letter went on to wish him well in his new Reserve assignment. Bill said in his letter to me that he stood ready to continue to help in any way that he could, and "I hope that you, and those who are aligned with you, are successful in your defense of arms control." Not a bad epitaph for the whole ABM interpretation war.

About this time, as predicted by Dave Sullivan, Congressman Bob Dornan began to whip up a frenzy about a security case at ACDA involving a woman named Kathleen Strang. The case had begun in mid-1985. Strang was a longtime ACDA employee whom Ken and Mike Guhin had commissioned to be sort of a watchdog on State Department NPT enforcement. There was concern among Ken and Mike that State was not adequately policing material that could be used in a nuclear weapons program being exported from various European countries with a destination of Iraq or Pakistan. In the course of her work, Kathleen had secreted a large number of highly classified intelligence documents in her own office safe, cleared for top secret but nevertheless outside the secure storage area for intelligence materials. Allegedly someone found such an intelligence document on her desk during working hours with her not in the room. He immediately reported this to Berne Indahl, the ACDA security officer, who launched an investigation.

The ACDA deputy director at this time was David Emory, a man of strong right-wing sympathies with no love for Adelman. (For his own reasons, Adelman had cut Emory out of just about everything and relied on Mike Guhin as his de facto deputy.) Emory intervened in this case in what appeared to be an attempt to make the situation look as bad as possible. Working initially with the security officer and later with Dornan's staff, one of whom was lodged, unbeknownst to everyone, on a semi-permanent basis in the ACDA administration office, Emory, at least to a degree, rode herd on the investigation. Later, some of Kathleen's co-workers began coming to my office asserting that the deputy director had threatened them with security violation prosecutions of their own should they have the temerity to write character letters in support of Strang. The ACDA Chief Administrative Officer Bill Montgomery convened a panel of three security experts who recommended the removal of Strang's security clearance and separation from the agency. Montgomery confirmed this finding and according to regulations sent this recommendation to the director. Strang had hired former Assistant Secretary of Defense Dave McGifford of Covington and Burling as her lawyer, and he appealed to me for a hearing before the director. The document was discovered on Strang's desk on July 1, 1985, and by this time it was the spring of 1986. Although I had almost nothing to do with the case up to that point, I had been concerned by what seemed to me procedural irregularities in the form of the threats against possible character witnesses for Strang. On the other hand, the National Security Agency, whose intelligence was involved, and the State Department Intelligence and Research Bureau, were deeply concerned. Even though there was no allegation of any of the material from her safe falling into the wrong hands, Strang, it seemed to me, had committed a most serious security violation. Finally, I agreed with McGifford to recommend a hearing to Ken, who duly granted the request.

The hearing took place in November 1986. NSA was invited to send an observer, which they did. Before the hearing Ken asked several of us to review the record for him. On June 25, 1986, Ken sent an unclassified memorandum stamped "eyes only" to three assistant directors—Fred Eimer (Verification and Intelligence), Lou Nosenzo (Strategic Affairs), and Lew Dunn (Non-Proliferation)—and myself. He asked that each of us separately review the record of the Strang appeal and give him our views by July 25 as to what, in our judgment, constituted the most important factors in this case and what we believed should be the outcome of the appeal.

We each submitted our private views to Adelman by July 25th and were subsequently asked to disclose these views for the record by Adelman, who was responding to a request by Strang's lawyers at the hearing on November 3. Nosenzo and Dunn advocated a reversal of Montgomery's decision and its conversion into a six-month suspension, after which Strang could return to work—she had been on administrative leave since July 1985. Eimer advocated upholding Montgomery and the resultant firing of Strang, who could not work without a security clearance. I also supported upholding Montgomery but narrowly. The next morning before announcing his decision, Adelman asked me informally, as his lawyer, whether I believed procedural irregularities had occurred during the investigation and I responded that yes, I thought such had been the case. I also said to Adelman that although I believed that the record supported upholding Montgomery, the procedural irregularities were sufficient to support a reversal of Montgomery if he was inclined to do so.

Adelman, in agreeing to grant Strang a hearing on my advice, limited the scope of the hearing to whether to uphold or reverse Montgomery's decision. The hearing lasted all day. In the morning an NSA deputy director testified. Thereafter, Strang testified, followed by six colleagues who testified on her behalf. The four of us gave our views at the end of the day. In addition to Mary Lib, myself, and Strang's lawyer, the NSA observer, a senior lawyer, sat in all day. Mike Guhin was also present, in addition to Adelman, who chaired the hearing. It was unclassified and informal, and witnesses were not sworn.

Adelman decided to reverse Montgomery and suspend Strang's clearance for six months, after which she could return to work. Also, she would be placed on probation for a year, meaning that she would be fired if she committed another security violation. And he recommended that she never again be granted intelligence clearances. Adelman, in explaining his decision, stated that although her security violations were serious, there were mitigating factors. He stated that Strang had a good record of twelve years of service prior to this case, the investigative file was filled with gossip and innuendo, and the security officer had done an inadequate investigative job. A later GAO report done on this case seemed to essentially support this judgment by Adelman. Congressman Dornan had requested this GAO study in connection with the next ACDA authorization request, and Chairman Dante Fascell and ranking Republican William Broomfield commissioned the investigation by GAO on June 29, 1988, the report being submitted on August 10, 1988. The report noted that the investigative file included letters that commented negatively on Strang, attacking her emotional stability and stating that she was a serious security risk. The report noted, on the other hand, that letters submitted on Strang's behalf to the security panel, in a memorandum submitted to the panel, were judged to be not valid; it was asserted that the writers did not have all the facts, Strang gave them erroneous information, and they appeared to be "coached."

After the decision by Adelman, Strang's lawyers urged that a decision be taken promptly concerning the commencement of her suspension and eventual return to work. McGiffert told me that they planned to advise Strang to return to work for one day and then resign and seek work elsewhere. This was good advice that should have been taken. Strang's suspension began at the end of the year and she returned to work in early July 1987. She was assigned to the Historian's Office in the Public Affairs Office in our Rosslyn, Virginia, office, as far removed from the agency's work as possible. She stayed there for three years and subsequently resigned and went to law school at the University of Georgia. First from the Historian's Office and subsequently from law school, Strang waged a long, unsuccessful effort to have her suspension overturned. But McGiffert's advice had been wise, for everyone. Immediately upon her return to ACDA in July 1987, Congressman Dornan decided to use her case as a vehicle to attack ACDA, Adelman, my views on ABM, and arms control in general, as well as others such as Mike Guhin, and in the process he damaged Strang as well. The reason that I have mentioned this case in this volume is that it led to a long shadow being cast over the agency and a most negative atmosphere. I have never known the whole picture of this case and have gone into detail concerning the part with which I was familiar: the background of the Adelman hearing, the hearing itself, and the political aftermath.

On July 9, 1987, Dornan wrote to Adelman saying that he understood Strang had been reinstated and assigned to Public Affairs. Since PA by its very nature deals with every aspect of the agency's business, he asked for, among other things, a detailed job description and measures taken to keep her away from intelligence information. Adelman replied that she was assigned to the Historian's Office as a research analyst, and that she would have no contact with the media and would have no access to intelligence information.

A month previous, Dornan wrote to Secretary Shultz saying that he was investigating a serious security situation at ACDA. He said that on a regular basis Strang had provided Mike Guhin with extremely sensitive State Department intelligence information, some of which came from memoranda and notes written by staff in Shultz's own office and also the office of Ambassador Richard Kennedy, the secretary's advisor on non-proliferation issues. Given, Dornan said, Strang's disclosure of NSA intelligence to foreign nationals, he believed this individual should never hold a security clearance again and he simply could not understand Ken Adelman's arrogant decision to reinstate Strang's top secret clearance. Dornan went on to say that he had discussed this matter with General Odom, director of NSA, who said it was NSA's position that Strang had forfeited her right to a security clearance; a frustrated Odom had done all he could. Dornan said that given the security revelations at our embassy in Moscow, ACDA top management must be responsible for its actions and that deliberate security violations could not be condoned. He found it difficult to believe that ACDA had no inspector general (IG) (a decision remedied by Congress after the GAO report) and that Adelman's decision thus could not be overturned. Nevertheless, he urged Shultz to put his own IG on the case and deny Strang a building pass.

It is difficult to know what to make of the Strang case in retrospect. At issue was proper supervision of nuclear-related exports from Europe to Iraq and Pakistan. History has proven Adelman and Guhin to be justified in their concern about this matter. Strang had a good record at ACDA but made a number of enemies. In my opinion, she showed bad judgment in improperly keeping a large number of intelligence documents in her personal safe outside the designated secure storage area for such documents. NSA as an institution and General Odom personally were very upset over this case, but there was no proof or assertion of the material held in her safe being disclosed to persons outside the United States government. State Intelligence and Research (INR) was understandably upset, but an official from Ambassador Kennedy's office testified at the hearing on behalf of Strang. There appeared to have been some procedural irregularities. Emory's pressure on Strang's supporters is hard to understand, but he was angry with Adelman and may have become Dornan's man in ACDA. Montgomery just wanted it all to go away. I believe that on the basis of the requirements of due process and basic fairness, Adelman's decision was supportable, but it did bring a firestorm upon ACDA.

So this was in the background as the battle over subsequent practice continued in the spring of 1987. Once the situation with Shultz was set right with respect to Judge Sofaer's assertions, as I said, somehow Sofaer's memorandum found its way into the hands of Senator Jesse Helms. Senator Helms made two floor speeches denouncing me for leaking classified information to the *New York Times* and wrote to Ken demanding an explanation. Evans and Novak had a somewhat derogatory column on me with respect to this issue, linking it to the emerging Strang "scandal" in mid-1987. Adelman duly answered Helms's letter, stating that there was no leak and in fact there was no evidence that anything ever leaked. Helms repeated the complaint at the ACDA authorization hearing in the late spring and Adelman gave the same answer. But this was not the end of the matter. Using the Strang case as a lever, Dornan demanded an FBI investigation of my case.

The agent came to interview me, read me my rights, and said that he was investigating my case and D.C. Mayor Marion Barry's many problems. He asked me a series of straightforward questions about the subsequent practice memo. He also asked why SCC exchanges were classified secret. I explained that it was to maintain the confidentiality of diplomatic exchanges and in the case of the SCC it was pursuant to specific agreement with the Soviets. Subsequently I heard that the agent had interviewed members of the current U.S. SCC delegation and had been informed that there was no evidence that anything ever actually leaked. I heard no more of this matter.

In the summer and fall of 1987, Dornan decided to put his campaign against ACDA into high gear. His motivations were never entirely clear. He seemed to be opposed to arms control generally and to want to discredit my views on ABM, and he seemed to want to attack Ken directly for being a selection of the conservatives but performing in entirely too liberal a manner with respect to policy, with Mike Guhin portrayed as his Rasputin. Dornan may have merely sought right-wing notoriety. The Strang case was his vehicle for all of this. He claimed that several of us—Adelman, Guhin, myself, and others—were guilty of obstruction of justice. He demanded an FBI investigation. Adelman dispatched Guhin and me to talk with him. Our meeting with Dornan and Jerry Gideon of his staff, a surreal experience, failed to come to grips on any specific issue.

The FBI did send an agent to ACDA to investigate obstruction of justice charges by Dornan. But he found nothing. Dornan demanded that he be replaced by another more aggressive agent, which also led to nothing. In this atmosphere, part of the investigative file of the ACDA security officer was destroyed; ACDA demanded an investigation by State INR, but that never happened. Berne Indahl's three years at ACDA were nearly complete at this time and he was duly given a significant overseas assignment in the fall of 1987 and replaced by Bruce Tully, also from State Diplomatic Security. About this time I was scheduled to go to Geneva to work on the NST negotiations—I did some work on INF, a bit more on Defense and Space. I had not been to Geneva for over a year and I wanted to reengage.

I should note that rumor had it that the standard leak route in those days was from the ACDA Intelligence Office to the ACDA Bureau of Verification and Intelligence and from there to cleared members of the staff of Senator Helms (all technically legal) and finally to Evans and Novak or similar publications (not controllable). At the time there was a debate over whether a Soviet ABM radar at a place called Gomel was a prohibited mobile ABM radar. Since the Krasnoyarsk case there had been many charges of Soviet ABM violations in order to cast the ABM Treaty in as bad a light as possible. The Krasnoyarsk case was a gross violation, but most of the others varied from borderline to spurious. Michael Gordon asked to see me to talk about ABM issues. I received permission from Sig Cohen at Public Affairs to talk with him, and Sig sat in with me for the interview. During the discussion Gordon did ask about Gomel and I answered him based on the cleared guidance that we had.

The next day there was an article in the *New York Times* written by Gordon on the Gomel issue and containing intelligence information. Possibly to cover tracks someone in the Bureau of Verification and Intelligence apparently blamed it on me, which I of course denied and Sig Cohen backed me up. I was leaving for Geneva that night and as I was walking down the hall Bruce Tully popped out of his office and advised me to be careful, telling me that there were people around who did not like me. Sure enough, the first thing that happened when I arrived in Geneva was that the regional security officer for the U.S. mission called me in, read me my rights, and questioned me about the Gordon article. This too came to nothing.

Dornan, by now, was escalating his attack on me. Mary Lib, my deputy general counsel since July 1, 1985, had taken over the day-to-day legal defense relative to Strang, Dornan, et al., and was doing a superb job. As a result, all the claims of obstruction of justice and the like were proving to be dead ends. But now, Jerry Gideon from Dornan's office, perhaps alerted by Emory, was secretly stationed in Montgomery's office and was doing as much damage as he could. I was seated at my desk in Geneva in October 1987 when the telephone rang. It was John Barry of *Newsweek* who said, "Tom, it's all over the Hill, the reason for Adelman's leniency with Strang is that you and she are having an affair and also once a week you go over to the Soviet Embassy and meet with Vitaly Churkin to pass classified information." I replied, "John, as to the latter charge I have met with Churkin twice in the last five years, both cleared in advance and both reported afterwards. As to the former charge, I would have to be one of the fastest guys around as, in the last nine years, the only time that I have been alone with Kathleen Strang was for a minute and a half several years ago in the hallway of the State Department." I reported this to Sig Cohen and he said, "Yeah, Barry was in here with the story and I told him to forget it." Nothing came of this either.

So the Dornan campaign continued through 1987 on into the early part of 1988. Ken Adelman resigned as director at the beginning of 1988 and was replaced by Major General Bill Burns, the former JCS representative on the Nitze INF delegation and, since retirement from the Army a year or two previously, a deputy in the Political-Military Bureau of the State Department. He is a man of cool, sound judgment and great courage, a real leader. He ended the Dornan campaign against ACDA abruptly. In his first week in office in March 1988, he went to see Dornan and told him that he was a former major general of the U.S. Army and did not want his command tampered with. That was the last we heard of Dornan directly, but some of the things he set in motion continued on through 1988. The GAO investigation that he called for at a hearing on the security practices of ACDA conducted by the House Foreign Affairs Committee ground on to a conclusion. The idea was created that ACDA was somehow lax on security, even though it was much better than State. George Murphy, former chief security officer of the Senate, was imposed on Burns as his deputy to clean up ACDA security practices. And at the ACDA authorization hearing in June of 1988, Fascell and Broomfield commissioned the GAO report, which, as indicated above, was completed in August of 1988.

The period from July 1987 to March 1988, the intense period of the Dornan campaign, was hard on ACDA. Gideon was popping up everywhere and there was a steady stream of leaks to Bill Gertz of the *Washington Times* about the security risks at ACDA. The principal targets of these attacks were Adelman, Guhin, and myself, for somewhat different reasons, with Mary Lib occasionally getting caught up in the attacks on me. It was wonderful to have her as my deputy and colleague during this time. She could see things that I couldn't, and vice-versa. As a team, I believe that we dealt with this situation effectively.

Earlier I mentioned the telephone call in Geneva. I had met with Churkin twice. Whoever had accused me falsely with respect to Churkin had to have access to the memorandum of conversation record. The first time we met in Washington was in 1982 and it was largely social. The second time was in January of 1986 and we had a most interesting discussion. We met at the Astor Restaurant and first Churkin went into a long thing about SDI and how the United States said it was compliant with the ABM Treaty as traditionally interpreted, and we should develop some criteria so this could be demonstrated with respect to specific tests. I replied that this was virtually impossible; each test had to be judged on a case-by-case basis. But then he turned to INF and

The Anti-Ballistic Missile Treaty

said he thought there was a good opportunity for progress, that we could have an agreement by the next summit, and it would not be linked to progress on space arms limitations, the standing Soviet position since March of 1985. The policy of the Soviet Union was that if the substantive issues were settled, verification would not be allowed to be a problem. The Soviet Union could accept on-site inspection as long as the United States accepted it on an equal basis. This conversion foreshadowed the Reykjavik Summit and the memorandum of conversation received wide circulation and attention. Adelman put a note on it that said the memorandum of conversation was most interesting.

If one was opposed to arms control these Churkin suggestions should be discredited. When I returned from Geneva I went to see Dave Emory and complained about what had been passed to *Newsweek*. He said, "Well, if you are innocent I am sure it will come out." I was not impressed with this comment.

In the wake of the furor over the subsequent practice memorandum, Ken decided to hire John Norton Moore of the University of Virginia Law School to do an impartial review of the entire ABM interpretation matter. Moore began work in February of 1987 and was to give Adelman his judgment by April 15. I asked Bill Parsons to be the liaison with Moore, as he had once been Moore's student and later student assistant. Bill made his second top-secret qualified safe available to store Moore's materials, much of which were classified. He also gave Moore's several secretaries the combination to that safe. And otherwise he serviced Moore's many requests.

On March 16, Adelman, in an official ACDA press release, stated that he had hired one of the country's top international lawyers, from outside the administration, to do a "zero-based" review of the entire ABM interpretation matter. Adelman asserted that "his [obviously referring to Moore] tentative conclusion was that the broad interpretation was not only fully justified but had the better of the argument." Moore must have orally reported this preliminary judgment to Adelman in the first month or so of his review. By September, however, Moore still had not completed his study, and about that time reported that he needed several more months to do so. He worked on the study through the fall and in December proposed a contractual arrangement to continue his study into 1988, to be signed on December 11, the day Adelman was scheduled to resign from ACDA. The contract was not signed by Adelman before he left, and Emory, who was acting director until Burns arrived in March, refused to sign it, saying he was not familiar with the issue.

In January and February of 1988, it became clear that GAO, pursuant to the ongoing Dornan campaign, would do a search of all of ACDA's files to look for improperly stored classified material. It was important to do something about Moore's safe, as he had not allowed anyone to control the large amount of top-secret material stored there. But if it was found, it would be

Bill Parsons's violation, and not Moore's, as it was Bill's safe. On February 11, I instructed Bill to move Moore's material to another location outside the General Counsel's Office. Bill informed Moore, who strongly objected, fearing tampering with his files. It was moved to ACDA's fifth floor vault and then subsequently to the sixth floor vault—where the intelligence material was kept—there to stay in four boxes marked "JN Moore" until Moore and Bruce Tully could jointly inspect it (as part of the GAO search) on the mutually convenient date of February 19. Moore was assured that his material was now in ACDA's most secure storage area and would not be opened until he was present on February 19. Most reluctantly Moore agreed.

Meanwhile, on February 12, I made an unfortunate decision. The Office of General Counsel had many old files and I did not know if they were properly stored; many had not been looked at for years, and why run this risk with GAO. I asked Mel Christopher and Assistant General Counsel Walt Bauman on February 12 to box and ship off for destruction all pre-1976 files that were not in use or otherwise relevant to current work. So a number of burn bags were filled and placed on a cart to be taken off for destruction. Just as they were to be taken off, about three hours after I had given the order, from nowhere in pops Jerry Gideon, who accused me of shredding files just like Oliver North. It was only much later that we learned that he likely was quartered in Montgomery's office and, based on his assertions, may well have received his intelligence from Emory's office. He often used to say in early 1988 that I would never guess who was his principal sponsor in ACDA. Thinking back on my conversation of October 1987—and knowing of the disenchantment toward the director that existed in the deputy director's office—I thought I might know. But earlier we all thought he just came down from time to time from Dornan's office, not that he was quartered in ACDA.

Naturally, there was a story in the *Washington Times* claiming that ACDA was shredding documents related to the Strang case and naming me. The *Post*'s Jeff Smith reported it in a straightforward manner, but Michael Gordon wrote a long story in the *New York Times* about the incident and the charge, saying that it was just part of Senator Helms's and others' continuing efforts to discredit my views on ABM. He even included a quote from a Helms staffer who agreed with this assessment. This too all came to naught, but I sent no more files off for destruction for a long time.

But back to John Norton Moore. On February 16, Bill Parsons was informed by one of the sixth floor vault officers that Moore's files had been moved back to the fifth floor vault. I asked Bill to call Tully to find out what was going on. Tully replied the next day, February 17, and said that he had misunderstood the arrangement, it was too late to do anything about it but that Moore could still see his files on February 19.

On the morning of February 19, Bill called the office in charge of the fifth floor vault, which informed him that Moore's files had already been searched and that some documents had been destroyed. Bill raced over to the vault and found Moore's files about 90 percent destroyed. It was left to Bill and me to so inform John when he arrived later that day to review his files. To say that he was extremely angry would be to understate significantly the situation. I reported the destruction of Moore's files at a staff meeting later that afternoon. Bruce Tully responded, "This is the most amazing place; something completely unbelievable happens almost every day."

My understanding was that Moore eventually recovered most of his files from the computer and eventually completed his 4,000-page manuscript by the end of 1988. But since he was ACDA's consultant and had been paid to do this work, even without a contract, the entire manuscript—even the unclassified part—belonged to ACDA. Moore quickly petitioned for it to be released (and the classified part—most of the manuscript—declassified) so he could publish it. By this time Ron Lehman was director and Jim Baker was secretary of state. Ron checked with Baker, who let it be known that the last thing he wanted was some new study sponsored by the government on this subject. Ron so informed me and I instructed Fred Smith, our experienced and capable Freedom of Information Officer, to work on the declassification of the manuscript with "all deliberate speed." It has never been released.

This story is an example of why government policy disputes should be dealt with as such and not be dressed up as legal debates. Within the executive branch on all sides in this story, as is generally the case, it was not so much motives that were questionable but rather, upon occasion, it was judgment that was lacking. But in the fall of 1998, the missile defense issue remained alive and well. Shades of the past legal debates—several prominent Republican senators, including the majority leader of the Senate and the chairman of the Senate Foreign Relations Committee sent a letter to President Clinton asserting that the ABM Treaty had in effect disappeared because the Soviet Union had dissolved. In October 1998, the Council on Foreign Relations sponsored a debate on this subject, the legal status of the ABM Treaty. I debated a lawyer associated with the Heritage Foundation.

Whether the United States builds a nationwide ballistic missile defense system is a policy issue, not a legal issue. If the United States has money to spend on BMD after it has competed for dollars against funding international verification systems, strengthening our intelligence community, and providing for strong conventional forces, and if we believe it will strengthen our security—keeping in mind the importance of reducing the Russian arsenal of strategic nuclear forces and of cooperation with Russia, Europe, and China on this issue—we may decide to deploy it. And it may be the case that BMD will have a role to play in the all-important task of reducing nuclear weapons world-wide to the lowest level possible, as soon as possible—the essential task if we are to reduce the nuclear threat against the United States, not only by ballistic missile attack but also by other, far more likely means of delivery such as cruise missile, boat, aircraft, or truck by so-called "rogue states" or by sub-state actors such as terrorist organizations. But if we subscribe to the conclusion of the Commission to Assess the Ballistic Missile Threat to the United States (known as Rumsfeld Commission), it may be prudent to do something about defense against the ballistic missile potential of rogue states. Nonetheless, should the ABM Treaty be modified to accommodate such defenses, it is important that any such modifications be made cooperatively and that the viability of the treaty be preserved.

The senators argued in their letter to President Clinton that the ABM Treaty has gone away because of the collapse of the former Soviet Union, and that only the Soviet Union can carry out its terms as the treaty partner of the United States. This asserted disappearance of the treaty was alleged to have occurred without any involvement of the president and, in fact, contrary to his expressed policies. Again, the real issue was not the ABM Treaty but whether the United States should promptly build a nationwide BMD system and in that context either renegotiate the ABM Treaty or withdraw from it pursuant to its terms. This, in our system of government, is a presidential decision, just as would be declaring the United States no longer bound by the ABM Treaty because of fundamental change of circumstance and/or impossibility of performance as a result of the dissolution of the former Soviet Union. Congress has a role here through its power over the purse but it cannot on its own declare a treaty null and void or force the president to withdraw from a treaty. If any president and his administration are believed to be pursuing an unwise course on an issue such as this, there is a remedy—elections.

It is recognized in the Constitution, and has been recognized in our national life for over two hundred years, that Congress has the power to declare war but the president is the supreme national authority in foreign policy. Treaties are made by the president with the advice and consent of the Senate but the Senate's role generally ceases after its consent is given, as recognized by Professor Louis Henkin, our foremost authority on the Constitution and the treaty process. The sole power of the president to suspend or terminate international agreements for the United States has been recognized in the *Restatement of Foreign Relations Law of the United States* and elsewhere as being implied by his office. Likewise, it is part of the foreign policy power of the president to recognize successor states and governments, and to recognize successor states as treaty parties for the United States. Presidents have done this many, many times for both bilateral and multilateral treaties consistent with recognized principles of international law.

Determination of succession is part of the foreign policy power of the president. The Vienna Convention of the Law of Treaties does provide that a state may withdraw from a treaty on, among other grounds, fundamental change of circumstance or impossibility of performance, and the ABM Treaty has a withdrawal clause permitting a party to withdraw on six months notice if it judges its supreme interests to be threatened. But treaties just do not vanish or go away. A party must declare that it is withdrawing or that it regards itself as no longer bound for one of the above or some other legitimate reason. It is the head of a state or its government that makes this decision and declaration—in our case, the president.

There are numerous important multilateral and bilateral international arms control agreements to which Russia—and, as appropriate, other former Soviet republics—have succeeded in place of the former Soviet Union. To begin with, Russia replaced the former Soviet Union as party to the United Nations Charter with a permanent seat on the Security Council. The United States did not recognize the Baltic states as being incorporated into the former Soviet Union, so the United States regards the Soviet Union as being replaced by twelve new states referred to as the newly independent states (NIS).

In 1992, in the immediate wake of the collapse of the Soviet Union, the Bush administration scrambled to ensure, among other things, the continuity of existing arms control arrangements with the NIS. As recounted in chapter 6, in May the Lisbon Protocol to START I was agreed so as to multilateralize the treaty. In January, as a condition to recognition, the Bush administration insisted upon the continuance of arms control treaties already in force. Russia was recognized as the nuclear weapon state successor to the Soviet Union for the NPT, as the United States wanted to ensure there would only be one nuclear successor, and all the other NIS were urged to join the NPT as non-nuclear weapon states, which eventually all of them did. For the CFE Treaty, all of the NIS that have territory in the area of application were recognized as successors. All twelve NIS were recognized as successors to the INF Treaty, six active in continued INF Treaty implementation, because INF deployment bases had been sited on their territory, and six inactive, to ensure the prohibition on INF systems applied to the territory of all the NIS.

In January 1992, the United States and Russia confirmed that Russia would be a successor state to the Soviet Union for the ABM Treaty, thus providing for the treaty's continuance. It remained to be determined which of the other NIS would also be successor states for the ABM Treaty. In a subsequent conference at Bishkek, Kyrgyzstan, ten of the twelve NIS expressed a desire to do so. In the end, appropriately mimicking the Lisbon Protocol, Belarus and Ukraine were treated as successor states at the October 1993 ABM Treaty Review Conference, and Kazakhstan not long thereafter. The three states subsequently became regular SCC participants. Thus, only Ukraine, Belarus, and Kazakhstan—and no other NIS—joined Russia as agreed successor states to the ABM Treaty. This result was recorded (not agreed but recorded) in the 1997 Memorandum of Understanding on Succession (MOU), which has not been ratified by all the signatory states and is not in effect.

Thus, the ABM Treaty remains in force. Neither action or inaction by the U.S. Senate on the succession memorandum, which simply reflects the 1992–94 outcome and which was signed in New York in September 1997, nor a declaration by the Senate or the Congress that the ABM Treaty is null and void, will affect the legal standing of the treaty. Continued U.S. adherence to the ABM Treaty is a matter of national policy; absent a decision by the president to withdraw from the treaty, our obligation is to abide by its provisions.

Succession under international law is a question of fact and agreement. The United States and Russia—and in my judgment Ukraine, Belarus, and Kazakhstan as well—agreed that the latter four states are the duly constituted successors to the Soviet Union for the ABM Treaty. Signature of the MOU in September 1997 by the president's authorized representative reflected the fact that the succession had occurred for the ABM Treaty as a matter of law. For the United States, this is a presidential function which does not involve the Senate as it is not a question of a new treaty; rather it is a continuation of the old treaty.

President Clinton was obligated to submit the MOU to the Senate because of his agreement to do so, as reflected in the Senate Resolution of Advice and Consent for the CFE Treaty. The president should respect an expressed view of the Senate relating to the terms of succession, procedures, and the like, but Senate action on the MOU would have no direct effect on the fact of succession. Succession has already taken place and the ABM Treaty continues to be in force—as recognized by the president.

The following is worthy of note with respect to the initial decision on succession for the ABM Treaty. In Moscow on January 29, 1992, shortly after the dissolution of the former Soviet Union, President Yeltsin said, "Russia regards itself as the legal successor to the USSR in the field of responsibility for fulfilling international obligations. We confirm all obligations under bilateral and multilateral agreements in the field of arms limitation and disarmament which were signed by the Soviet Union and are in effect at present." In reply, U.S. Secretary of State James Baker indicated, "I made the point to the president that the United States remains committed to the ABM Treaty. . . . The fact of the matter is we've made the point that we expect the states of the Commonwealth to abide by all of the international treaties and obligations that were entered into by the former Soviet Union, including the ABM Treaty."

The succession arrangement agreed to by the United States for the ABM Treaty is appropriate. While it is true that the former Soviet Union posed a unique threat owing to its ideologically hostile totalitarian government, which Russia does not, its dissolution did not alter the potential for a strategic situation that it is the purpose of the treaty to avoid: strategic instability stemming from concern that a potential opponent with a massive nuclear arsenal might acquire a first-strike capability by building a nationwide ballistic missile defense system. At least as long as Russia has thousands of nuclear weapons and strategic delivery vehicles, it remains a unique partner in maintaining strategic stability. And it is appropriate that Ukraine, Belarus, and Kazakhstan are successor states for the ABM Treaty in addition to Russia, as it was on their territory that strategic offensive nuclear systems were located after the dissolution of the former Soviet Union. It is the mutual stability of the two superpower strategic arsenals—both of which still exist nearly a decade after the end of the Cold War—that was and is the object and purpose of the ABM Treaty and this remains an essential objective today. Thus, the dissolution of the former Soviet Union did not establish impossibility of performance of the ABM Treaty.

In 1999, as our relations with Russia and China dramatically worsened, one of the primary causes was the threat coming largely from Congress but to a degree accommodated by the Clinton administration, of unilateral abrogation of the ABM Treaty to build a national missile defense against "rogue" states. Our NATO allies were also strongly opposed. In February 1999, I did a seven-nation tour of Europe (Norway, Belgium, the Netherlands, Germany, France, Italy, and Spain) to discuss the proposed NATO Strategy Review and the related nuclear weapon use doctrine issue. Everywhere I found widespread dismay and anxiety concerning the prospect that the United States might unilaterally put aside the ABM Treaty. Rudy Hartmann, my old CFE colleague and then the German arms control commissioner, said if the United States did that it would be decoupling itself from Europe (the worst thing a NATO partner can do). French Ministry of Defense officials asserted that France would drastically increase the number of her deployed nuclear weapons should this happen. I also on this tour met with Sergei Kislyak, the Russian Ambassador to NATO, who said if the United States put aside the ABM Treaty it would "terminate the nuclear weapon reductions process with Russia." If anything, the opposition to a U.S. national missile defense system within NATO, Russia, and China intensified in 2000 but was somewhat alleviated by President Clinton's speech on September 1, 2000, in which he announced a decision to defer a NMD deployment decision to his successor. In early 2001, his successor, President George W. Bush reviewed U.S. policy on NMD. There were allegations made by some in the press, most notably Senator Jon Kyl of Arizona, that the new administration would proceed rapidly with NMD and in the process abrogate the ABM Treaty. By mid-2001, statements to this effect had been made several times by senior Defense Department officials, seemingly supported by the president.

The issues are whether or not there is a national missile defense system demonstrably capable of defeating real threats to the national security, how much deployment of this system would cost, and what is the likelihood that potential adversaries could circumvent such a system with decoys or by foregoing ballistic missile delivery in favor of alternative means of delivery. If after considering these issues and taking into account the effect on the strategic nuclear reductions process, as well as our relations with Russia, China, and Europe—and of any attempt at treaty amendment—deployment of a NMD system not compliant with the ABM Treaty still appears to be the correct course for U.S. security, withdrawal from the ABM Treaty would be the appropriate option. In the meantime, the object and purpose of the ABM Treaty remain valid. Treaty succession has been established as a matter of law. And all of this should be subordinated to the fundamental objective of reducing nuclear weapons to the lowest practical level in the shortest possible period of time, so as to safeguard the security of future generations.

On December 13, 2001, President Bush, carrying through on earlier administration statements, formally gave Russia notice of U.S. withdrawal from the ABM Treaty pursuant to Article XV of the Treaty. The preliminary response from Russia was critical but mild; the reaction from our allies and China was muted. Nevertheless, "the cornerstone of strategic stability" as recognized by the NPT parties in 2000 has been put on six months' notice of termination.

It should be noted that experts believe that there is a real question as to whether a BMD system can be relied upon in a military sense given that it can never be operationally tested in a realistic scenario. Also, experts believe that there is no technological need to withdraw from the treaty at this time. Necessary tests could go on for years without colliding with the treay's limits, and Russian President Putin has indicated flexibility toward modifying it. And there is no real threat at this time. North Korea has indicated a willingness to trade away its missile program, Iran is moving toward the West in the wake of September 11 and everyone agrees that Iraq must be taken care of some other way, without waiting for a missile shield.

Rather, ABM Treaty withdrawal could spark a nuclear arms race in Asia with China carrying through on its threat to more rapidly modernize and expand its strategic nuclear forces by, as stated, up to a factor of ten, and India—and then Pakistan and who knows who after that—following suit. Thus, ABM Treaty withdrawal could significantly increase the risk of nuclear proliferation. And Russia's reaction hopefully will remain mild for the time being, but a seriously negative response by Russia in the medium term cannot be ruled out given the political importance of the ABM Treaty to Russia.

Nevertheless, in the face of all this, the administration has apparently determined that deploying a NMD system not compliant with the ABM Treaty is the correct course for U.S. security. Let us hope that this assessment, in the context of other evolving world threats, proves to be sound.

CHAPTER EIGHT **CONVENTIONAL ARMED FORCES IN EUROPE TREATY**

In retrospect, the negotiations that led to the Conventional Armed Forces in Europe Treaty (CFE) moved incredibly quickly, despite taking place in the midst of breathtaking political change. I ran into Victor Smolin, my SALT II counterpart, in Moscow in the fall of 1988, and he said, "Our leadership is determined to get a conventional arms treaty in two years and we professionals have to tell them that's impossible." Well, it happened.

During the course of the CFE negotiations, which lasted about twenty months, five negotiating parties changed their names and one disappeared (the German Democratic Republic—the GDR or East Germany—merged into the Federal Republic of Germany on October 3, 1990). In fact, the last change to the CFE Treaty was on the morning when we were going to agree on the final text in Vienna. Ambassador James Woolsey got an anxious call from the Bulgarian ambassador who said, "You must change the name of Bulgaria from the People's Republic of Bulgaria to the Republic of Bulgaria. Our parliament acted yesterday." That was the last change, and it is representative of the process that went on in Vienna.

Previous negotiations on conventional arms involved a limited space (Central Europe), a limited number of parties in Europe, and a focus on manpower. CFE was different in all these respects. It covers all of Europe from the Atlantic to the Ural Mountains (the area of application). All twenty-two NATO and former Warsaw Pact countries (minus the GDR) were signatories to the treaty. After the dissolution of the Soviet Union, the eight successor states that have territory in the area of application of the treaty became parties and Czechoslovakia split in two. East Germany had disappeared during the negotiations. As a result of all this, today there are thirty parties to the CFE Treaty. Instead of personnel limits, it addresses equipment, in particular the five major categories of equipment that are viewed as necessary for a combined-arms surprise attack in Europe like the Nazi blitzkrieg at the beginning of World War II, or any similar major offensive action. The focus on equipment limitations was present from the beginning of CFE.

The CFE negotiations were designed to deal with the threat that the West faced from the beginning of the Cold War to its end—the huge Soviet conventional military superiority spearheaded by heavily armored forces pointed westward. That was a reality in Europe for forty-five years and it was what CFE focused on redressing. The Western objectives of establishing a secure and stable balance of conventional forces at lower levels, eliminating disparities prejudicial to stability and security, and eliminating the capability of launching a surprise attack were completely realized. When CFE is assessed and when various points are made about this provision and that provision, it is important to keep in mind that the West's three basic policy objectives were completely realized, and Europe was changed forever as a result, when the CFE Treaty entered into force. In fact, many assert it was the CFE Treaty itself that ended the Cold War.

The treaty is the basis of certainty and confidence in an era of change. It fixes strict, precise equipment limits on the size of forces in Europe on a permanent basis. It also fixes legally binding limits on the forces of all thirty parties, including originally sixteen, now nineteen, NATO parties and the remaining post–Cold War Eastern European countries, most of them successor states to the Soviet Union. This is the central accomplishment of the CFE Treaty. There are also very extensive, on-site verification and information exchange provisions which have added considerably to confidence building, openness, and transparency with respect to military policy and systems in Europe.

The CFE Treaty, when signed in 1990, established a limit of 20,000 battle tanks, 30,000 armored combat vehicles (ACVs)—with sublimits of 18,000 for armored infantry fighting vehicles and 1,500 for heavy armored combat vehicles—20,000 artillery pieces, 6,800 combat aircraft, and 2,000 attack helicopters for each of the two groups of countries, which were, when the treaty text was conceived, coterminous with NATO and the Warsaw Pact membership. In addition, the sufficiency rule in the treaty established that no one country can have more than approximately one-third of all such arms in Europe, from the Atlantic to the Urals. In 1988, the Soviets alone had 41,000 battle tanks, 57,000 armored combat vehicles, and 42,000 pieces of artillery in the area of application of the treaty. Under the sufficiency rule, the Soviets were permitted only 13,300 battle tanks, 20,000 ACVs, 13,700 artillery pieces, 5,150 combat aircraft, and 1,500 attack helicopters. Thus, the sufficiency rule itself imposed a very significant reduction in Soviet military power in Europe. After the demise of the USSR, these allocations were divided among the eight successor states party to the treaty, pursuant to the 1992 Treaty of Tashkent, although the figure for Kazakhstan was zero, as there were no forces on the ground there.

Further, under Article VII of the treaty, binding national limits were imposed on each of the thirty parties after each nation's total holdings were allocated within each group. For example, NATO divided up its 20,000 tanks among the then sixteen member countries. Those decisions are made within each group and then, pursuant to the terms of the treaty, all other parties are notified. When that notification takes place, obligations become legally binding and remain so until there is a further, subsequent allocation, and new legally binding limits or allocations are notified. In the East, given the state of the Warsaw Pact, it was necessary to negotiate a treaty (the 1991 Treaty of Budapest) among the six remaining countries (that is, the Warsaw Pact states in 1990 minus East Germany) to set these limits. That treaty then had to be ratified by the six countries. Under that treaty, the Soviets were allowed even a little bit less than the sufficiency rule would have permitted them in some categories. For example, they were allowed 150 fewer tanks than their sufficiency rule allocation, so in fact, the Soviets were limited, within the area of application, to 13,150 battle tanks, as opposed to the 41,000 they held two years prior.

In addition, there are active unit limits, which are about 10 to 15 percent lower than the total holdings in each category of weapons. The remainder is to be stored in designated permanent storage sites, which are open to inspection. The treaty also contains regional sublimits intended to prevent destabilizing concentrations of forces. The treaty established a Joint Consultative Group composed of all thirty parties. The treaty provided that the Joint Consultative Group could begin meeting provisionally even before the treaty had been ratified. By the end of 1990 it had already held some two-and-a-half weeks of meetings. The signatories initially discussed data, in particular Soviet data and other related issues.

From very early on it was clear to many that the Federal Republic of Germany and the German Democratic Republic, even before the Berlin Wall came down, already more or less considered themselves as one country. When we were working out our draft treaty text first in Washington and then in Brussels, it was, of course, circulated to all NATO members. It had a "Confidential" stamp on it and was considered a classified NATO document. Yet, the German delegation did not seem to have any hesitancy in passing it on to the East German delegation in Vienna, who passed it on to the Soviets. And it worked in reverse. We had the Soviet draft from early on. For someone who worked in the SALT, START, and INF treaty processes, that seemed incredible, but the Germans made it very clear that their objective was to get a treaty. In the end, the practice actually turned out to be helpful because by the time the treaties were on the table, each side knew what was in the other side's text. As a result, we were able to move faster in the negotiations.

Another interesting aspect of CFE was the origin of the concept of "groups of countries" as opposed to "alliances." Early in the negotiation, in September 1989, the Hungarians made it very clear to us that they did not intend to stay in the Warsaw Pact. We, in our original treaty draft, had mentioned the two alliances, NATO and the Warsaw Pact, and had it drafted that way. But if one country was going to leave an alliance, we had to develop a formula that would permit the treaty regime to continue even if one or more countries should do so. So we developed the idea of "groups of states parties," rather than basing the agreement on the then current alliance memberships. One group just happened to coincide with NATO and the other group just happened to coincide with the Warsaw Pact. But the treaty is unequivocally clear. Hungary could have withdrawn from the Warsaw Pact in 1990 when the treaty was signed and renounced everything associated with it, but it could not leave its group under the treaty without treaty amendment, and so it would remain a part of the treaty regime.

Also interesting was the Article VII national levels provision, which was conceived by the British and the French. The U.S. draft, which we took to Brussels for clearance by NATO as the NATO draft treaty, had in it simply group limits, collective limits. That is how the United States conceived of this negotiation from the beginning. But the British and the French said, "We can't just completely tie this treaty to existing alliances. There must be something else that imposes national limits on countries. We must have a means, a device under the treaty, whereby you can have group limits but you also have national limits because these alliances are not going to last in their current form forever." The United States strongly resisted this idea: bureaucracies are slow to change. But finally we were able to work out the text of a provision that was acceptable to everybody and that also fit in with the thinking of the non-Soviet Eastern countries.

Another example of this group-versus-national issue was that the West originally proposed inspections only of members of the other group. In other words, the United Kingdom could only inspect members of the Warsaw Pact and not the Netherlands, for example. The French were reluctant to support this for the same reason they supported the national levels article. They never liked the idea of a bloc-to-bloc negotiation, and they certainly believed that a new era had come. Nevertheless, they went along with this concept; but the Hungarians absolutely refused. For them it was a treaty-breaker. They had to have the right to inspect members of their own group. Finally, the Soviets conceded on this, after a long argument near the end of the negotiation. The treaty permitted each country to inspect any other member of its own group up to five times a year for each country.

Meanwhile, the Warsaw Pact caucus almost completely disintegrated. Whereas the lifting of the Iron Curtain and the taking down of the Wall were very positive from a political point of view, they made things more difficult in these negotiations because we were no longer dealing with a unified negotiating group. We were dealing with originally seven, and ultimately six, independent actors, and the Soviets became much more nervous and withdrawn given these events.

The total disintegration of the Eastern caucus became a very important factor late in the negotiations. By the end, it had almost become a negotiation between twenty-one and one (twenty-one countries and the Soviet Union), with subsidiary negotiations among varying parties on such questions as the flank limits. This latter was a five-sided negotiation with the United States acting as the midwife among Norway, Turkey, Greece, Bulgaria, and the Soviet Union. It is important to remember that this was not a bilateral negotiation. Every time the United States wanted to make a move with one country, it had to figure out what its effect would be on other countries. It was kind of like playing billiards—you bounce off one billiard ball to another.

A few more initial points about the process. In the closing days of the negotiation, because of the shortness of time, it was necessary for the United States, in effect, to negotiate directly with the Soviet Union on behalf of the NATO alliance. With regional issues and Turkish concerns over Soviet paramilitary forces being front and center, and a non-Soviet East as a kind of benefited third party, four or five members of the U.S. delegation led by Ambassador Jim Woolsey made a trip to Moscow about eleven or twelve days before the negotiations ended. We returned with a completed text that was sold in Vienna. The non-Soviet East accepted it *in toto*, but on our side a number of changes were made at the request of the Germans, British, and French. But the text was completed four days after our return from Moscow. Then, it went to capitals for a twenty-four-hour silence (or no objection) period for approval at noon on November 14, 1990. At 1:00 P.M. Vienna time on November 15, the silence period ended and Ambassador Jim Woolsey sent a cable to the bureaucratic world in Washington titled, over the strong objections of some State Department bureaucrats on the delegation, "The Fat Lady Sings in Vienna."

CFE was followed by a negotiation on personnel limits that ended in a political document that made broad commitments on personnel. These commitments were based on a German unilateral political statement at the close of the CFE negotiations that it would limit its military personnel to 370,000. At the time, this was important to the Soviets in the context of a united Germany.

Subsequent to the decision on NATO expansion, beginning in the wake of the 1996 CFE Review Conference, the parties began negotiating an adaptation of the treaty to reflect post–Cold War realities, which produced an agreement in principle on March 31, 1999, that was completed in the fall of 1999. The revision is based on national and territorial (including stationed forces) limits, rather than group limits and zones. The United States insisted on unlimited redeployment rights, even to the three new NATO countries, which the Russians, to put it mildly, opposed. This was finally resolved on the basis of the Russians conceding to the United States on the issue of redeployment rights in exchange for what they wanted on the flanks. This was converted into a complete treaty revision and signed at the November 1999 OSCE Summit. As I said, the CFE Treaty has been described as the treaty that formally ended the Cold War. But equally important, in my judgment, the regime established by the CFE Treaty is likely to be the basis for overall European and North American security, and, derivatively, world security, for many decades to come. It has no competitors.

One of the central issues of the early negotiations was how to deal with paramilitary units, whose equipment is not considered to be "in service." That equipment is nevertheless, in certain cases, counted against the treaty ceilings. Battle tanks, artillery, attack helicopters, and combat aircraft held by paramilitary units, even though they are not considered to be in service, are counted against all the totals in the various provisions. ACVs are not. However—and this was an issue that the Turks were particularly interested in—there is a provision that was worked out in Moscow in the last days of the negotiation that only 1,000 ACVs for each party are exempt from the totals. Any number above 1,000 for any single party must be counted toward the limits, and in addition, only 600 armored combat vehicles may be deployed by a party in the flank zone in paramilitary units within its country. In the case of the Soviet Union, that was a small part of its territory, but in the case of Bulgaria, that was its totality. So, only 600 ACVs in paramilitary units on the flanks, and only 1,000 overall, are exempt from ceilings.

After the dissolution of the Soviet Union, the flank limits became violently controversial for the Russians because of the wars in the Caucasus. This led to a new negotiation on the flank issue, which concluded at the 1996 Review Conference. However, there was still trouble afterwards until an understanding was reached between Russia and Turkey in 1999, in the context of the treaty adaptation process.

A brief description of how I became involved in CFE is useful here because, after all, most of my previous experience had been in the field of nuclear weapons and related technology. In the spring of 1989, by which time it was clear that I was going to stay as ACDA general counsel, I believed that I should involve myself in some new project. INF was in force, the ABM debate was over and the treaty review held, START was in the capable hands of Marshall Brown and did not appear to be moving forward rapidly in any case, and the CWC remained stalemated at the CD. However, in March 1989, as a result of direct personal intervention by President Bush, an agreement in principle was reached as to the broad outlines of the emerging CFE negotiations.

This all began with the conclusion of the Helsinki Final Act in 1975 and the termination in 1987 of the Mutual Balanced Force Reductions negotiations without any progress after fourteen years. It was decided by the Conference on Security and Cooperation in Europe (CSCE) parties that a new arms control negotiation would take place on the balance of forces in Europe. The CSCE was the institutionalization of the parties to the Helsinki Final Act and already the successful Stockholm negotiation on confidence-building measures relating to the military situation in Europe had been sponsored by the CSCE. A lively debate ensued as to whether the new negotiation on the military balance in Europe, which would derive from the CSCE, should involve all the then thirty-five CSCE parties, including neutral states such as Sweden, Austria, and Yugoslavia, or whether it should only involve the members of the two opposing alliances.

Over the objections of France, but pressed by the United States, United Kingdom, and others, the CSCE opted for the latter course. In January 1987, the Mandate talks began among the members of the two opposing alliances, with the talks to last until a date in January 1989. The U.S. side was led by Ambassador Stephen Ledogar, later U.S. ambassador to the CD, where with great skill he helped lead the CWC and CTBT negotiations. A superbly capable diplomat and effective negotiator, he is a large man with a somewhat gruff exterior, referred to by the Russians at CFE as the "American Bear."

The Mandate talks focused on the basic parameters of the negotiations to follow, including such matters as the area of application. These talks were difficult and had to be extended artificially for six days, in January 1989, while the Greeks and Turks fought over whether the Turkish port of Mersin, from which the invasion force for Cyprus was launched, was in the area of application or outside, in the Turkish zone of exclusion. The Turks were allowed to exclude from the application of the treaty restrictions a large area of their territory in eastern Turkey because of their need to deter neighbors such as Iraq. More on this Greek-Turkish dispute later.

It was agreed in the Mandate negotiations to focus on equipment limitations, precisely on those large weapon systems that form the basis of a combined arms assault. Unlike the ill-fated MBFR talks, personnel limitations, essentially unverifiable, would not be pursued. However, the Soviets wanted to include combat aircraft and attack helicopters along with battle tanks, artillery, and ACVs. The West did not wish to do this. But, in March of 1989, President Bush decided to concede on this point and the CFE negotiations finally began.

Steve Ledogar continued as the U.S. negotiator until November 1989, when he was replaced by Jim Woolsey. Jim had been close to Brent Scowcroft, returning as the Bush national security advisor, ever since he served as the legal advisor to the Scowcroft Commission, which addressed the question of the future of the U.S. ICBM force, in particular the MX, in 1983. I had thought Steve was excellent; Jim I found to be superb. As I mentioned above, I had encountered Victor Smolin at a meeting in Moscow in October 1988 where he said our leaders were speaking of a conventional arms treaty in two years—at that time the Mandate talks were drawing to a close. President Bush modified this to a declaration (in March of 1989) that he wanted it done in one year. Everyone believed that two years was pie-in-the-sky and that one year should not even be mentioned. In fact the CFE Treaty was signed twenty months after Bush's declaration. Compared to seven years for SALT II and ten years for START I, this was amazing. There were several reasons for this success: dedicated presidential commitment, Gorbachev and Shevardnadze's belief that this should be done, very talented negotiators in Vienna (to name a few: first Ledogar and then Woolsey for the United States, Hartmann of Germany, Alp of Turkey, Grinevsky of the Soviet Union), and a deadline agreed to by the French when they committed to a CSCE summit to sign CFE on November 19, 1990.

Contemplating this situation in April of 1989, it seemed to me that the delegation needed a lawyer and preparations for a draft treaty should be begun now that agreement in principle had been reached. Accordingly, Bill Parsons and I worked up a bare-bones draft CFE Treaty based on the Mandate Agreement. I called Ledogar and told him that he needed a lawyer and a treaty, that I was a lawyer, that I had a draft treaty, and that I was coming over to see him. He did not say no, so I was off to Vienna in June to persuade the U.S. CFE delegation that they in fact did need a lawyer and a treaty.

I spent a week in Vienna with the delegation. I circulated the draft text, which was only about ten pages long. The delegation had a number of comments, all of which I incorporated, and I think at least to a degree they were convinced that the time had come for a treaty text. Missy and Clover, both just short of their fourteenth birthdays, accompanied me on this trip. We stayed at the Ambassador Hotel and I tried to make it at least somewhat of a cultural experience for them. I was away all day every day with the delegation but every evening we did something together. We went to the Staatsoper, saw the Lipizzaner horses, went to the Vienna music hall, and on the weekend went to the Mozart Puppet Theater in Salzburg. I was taken in hand by the ACDA representative, who was finishing a two-year tour as a military detailee, and who had secured a beautiful apartment for ACDA.

When I returned to Washington I could say that I had a draft treaty text which had been approved by the delegation. All of this was made up from whole cloth. Of course, no one had asked for a draft treaty text; I was just saying we needed one and here it is. CFE was blessedly different from the SALT/START process, however. It was a negotiation everyone wanted and one that had been authorized and advocated by the president. Thus, there was not a high degree of bureaucratic infighting of the type that characterized those processes. I remember remarking what a pleasure it was working on a negotiation that everyone, in the U.S. government at least, wanted. As a result, no one objected to having my draft foisted upon them. It was just accepted. State, OSD, and JCS made comments. We circulated a new draft, and Heather Wilson, the new NSC official in charge of CFE, a former Air Force captain and later a member of Congress from New Mexico, held an interagency meeting at which the text was approved. It was somewhat longer now, perhaps twenty pages, and had only a very preliminary verification section. It took us about one month to get it through the U.S. government, and in August of 1989 it was sent to Brussels for review so that it could become a NATO draft treaty text.

About this time I persuaded Ron Lehman to send me to Vienna both as delegation legal advisor and as ACDA representative, since the latter job was now open. I arrived on Labor Day, 1989, and participated in the Brussels meetings called to review the treaty text from Vienna, traveling to Brussels several times to work on the text in September and October. When I returned to the delegation, Ledogar was still there, but it was clear that Woolsey would be coming soon. Ledogar was to go to Geneva as the CD representative as soon as the changeover took place. I remained in Vienna non-stop until New Year's Day. Christine took a leave of absence from her law firm and arrived two weeks after I did, and the children came over for Christmas. So I was working on the treaty text and participating in the negotiations, and Christine and I were taking weekend trips in the midst of the Soviet Empire collapsing around us, with practically a revolution a week. It was a rich experience.

One weekend in particular was a bit more memorable than the others. It was a weekend in early December, and Christine and I decided to make the three-hour drive from Vienna to Prague, where we arrived after a rather hostile inspection by Czech border guards and a near accident on the snowy AutoRoute. That night the "Velvet Revolution" came to the moment of truth and the Communist government resigned. A taxi driver told us what was happening and so we asked him to take us over to the castle where we waited outside to see the Communist premier leave. The next afternoon, as we were leaving to drive back to Vienna, we passed St. Wenceslaus Square where there was a huge crowd, it looked like 200,000–300,000 people. Vaclav Havel was speaking, announcing the fall of the Communist government and the advent of his new government, to take power in a few weeks. We parked the car on the roadway and went down into the square in order to soak up what was happening. To say it was inspiring does not do it justice. When we reached the border that night everything had changed. The guards were offering the motorists flowers and drinking champagne. What a difference a day makes.

Later in the month the children came to Vienna for the Christmas holidays. We went skiing over Christmas in St. Moritz and then drove across East Germany to Berlin. The Berlin Wall had been open for two months now; we passed through the new aperture by the Brandenburg Gate, only for Germans but I waved my diplomatic passport and somehow that persuaded the guard to let us through. This caused us to be held up on the way out, however, at Checkpoint Charlie, as they had no record of us going in (a little reminiscent of the ancien régime), and like so many others, we subsequently chopped off our own pieces of the Wall. We drove back toward Vienna through Dresden—still a dreary Communist place then—and arrived in Prague around lunch time, where once again St. Wenceslaus Square was filled with people. Havel was sworn in that day as president of Czechoslovakia.

We had a good afternoon touring around Prague, although Missy briefly disappeared into the crowd at the Square; she reappeared fifteen minutes later, having gone to a store to buy something for Christine. We arrived back in Vienna late that night.

The treaty text laboriously worked its way through NATO. As I said above, early on the British and the French insisted that while the group limits agreed to in the Mandate could be retained, they could not be the cause of violations by individual treaty parties. The U.K. representative put it this way: if NATO is at its limit of 20,000 battle tanks and Turkey, for example, acquires 500 tanks, this should not be a violation by the British government; there must be national limits. The French, who had always opposed bloc-to-bloc negotiations and therefore group limits, believing that a new era had come, strongly seconded the British view. The United States bureaucracy had believed for years that the British and French were opposed to national limits. Therefore, as I said, the United States argued against this idea because it could not believe that the British and French were not opposed to national limits. Eventually, the United States agreed and this idea became Article VII of the CFE Treaty, which provided that each group would agree on national limits within its group, and would announce these limits, which would be legally binding on each party until changed pursuant to subsequent group action.

The State Department European Bureau (EUR) had the backstopping lead in Washington and Jennifer Laurendieu, a most capable EUR official, had the pen for drafting the instructions to Brussels, Vienna, and our embassies in allied capitals when they were decided upon. She was a fierce partisan of doing what is right. Toward the end of the text negotiations in Brussels, the United Kingdom suddenly sprung a new text upon the representatives in the High Level Task Force (HLTF), the policy-making and treaty negotiation backstopping group for NATO. It appeared to undercut completely all the work that had been done. Jennifer's cable to our London Embassy on the subject of what embassy officers were to say to the British government would have curled your hair. Needless to say, the United Kingdom quickly dropped its alternative text and in early November NATO approved a text for tabling in Vienna.

Also, it should be mentioned that the draft article of greatest interest to the Europeans at Brussels was the one which would establish the Joint Consultative Group (JCG), the implementing body of the treaty. They saw this as a potential new security forum for the future. Fatefully included in the draft article was a provision permitting the treaty signatories to make, through the JCG (which would begin operations upon signature), certain provisions of the treaty operational even before entry into force on a provisional basis. The negotiators had in mind exchanges of baseline data and the like. This provision was used for an entirely different purpose in 1992, as I shall outline later.

The NATO draft text was in Vienna ready to be tabled by the NATO side by late October, having been approved by the HLTF. Jim Woolsey had replaced

Steve Ledogar as CFE negotiator by this time. Steve returned to Washington and was appointed U.S. ambassador to the CD, where he arrived in January. Information was flowing back and forth on the two German delegations' information highway, and we knew that the Warsaw Pact/Soviet Union was well on the way to completion of its text and tabling it in Vienna. Jim was anxious to put the NATO draft text on the table first, for whatever advantage that might give, as it was ready and had NATO's full approval. Normally, the caucus of the sixteen NATO ambassadors at the CFE negotiations met at the Canadian CFE Mission every Monday and Wednesday at 3:00 P.M. The ambassadors for the sixteen NATO countries sat around a long table with other delegation officers and staff seated in chairs right behind them. There was usually room for two from each country to sit at the table. It was at one of these meetings in early November that the ambassadors gathered to give formal approval to table the NATO draft. At this moment Greek/Turkish politics intervened once again.

During the Mandate discussions, the area of application of the treaty was agreed to in the Mandate text. It is described as stretching from the Atlantic to the Urals, with the exception of a 350-square-mile portion of southeastern Turkey. Turkey contended that threats from Syria and Iraq required that it maintain high levels of military equipment and personnel on the Turkish southeastern border. So a line extending southward from the southern end of the Urals had to be agreed and described to complete the definition of the area of application. It was set forth in the text that the line began at a point on the southern Black Sea coast and proceeded across Turkey from town to town until it reached a particular town near the Mediterranean (Gzne), from which it proceeded to the west of the port of Mersin, thereby putting Mersin in the exclusion zone for Turkey. This was agreed in early January 1989 shortly before the Mandate talks were to end.

The problem, as I said, was that Mersin had been the embarkation point of the Turkish army for the invasion of Cyprus in 1974. Just as the Mandate was about to be agreed and signed, and as the two-year period for the Mandate talks was about to expire, someone in Athens woke up to this. The Greek ambassador was directed to withhold his consent—like all multilateral arms control negotiations, the Mandate talks and the CFE negotiations themselves operated on the basis of consensus; thus, this action blocked progress to signature of the Mandate. The Greeks insisted that the line had to be drawn to the east of Mersin, thereby including the town in the area of application. The issue was primarily a political not a security one, as Cyprus in theory could be threatened from any of Turkey's other ports. The clock had to be stopped as the time for the Mandate discussion—two years—had ended, and it remained stopped for six days while the problem was addressed. German Foreign Minister Genscher and French Foreign Minister Dumas personally came to Vienna to search for a solution. The Mandate on its face says that it was signed on January 10, 1989 (the last agreed day for the talks), when in actual fact it was signed on January 16, 1989.

The dispute was resolved at the Mandate talks on January 15, 1989, in the following manner. The last few words of the descriptive paragraph setting forth the area of application of the treaty—the definition of the area of application—were changed to read, "from Gzne and thence to the sea." Thus the sentence took the line of demarcation to a town near the Mediterranean and from there "and thence to the sea." On the one hand, if in actually drawing this line one continued in the same direction as the described line, going "thence to the sea," one would have the line reaching the Mediterranean west of Mersin, which would place Mersin within Turkey's exclusion zone and outside the area of application of the treaty. If, on the other hand, one took the line over the shortest distance from Gzne to the coast, the line would be to the east of Mersin and this port city would be within the area of application, and all the relevant limitations of the treaty would apply to it. The Greek ambassador stated on the record that the latter was the correct interpretation and the Turkish ambassador stated on the record that the former was the correct interpretation. No other delegation made a comment, although all privately agreed with the Turks. This is known as "creative ambiguity." Much later, when the U.S. government prepared an official CFE map that showed the area of application, it placed the standard U.S. disclaimer on all such maps of U.S. non-recognition of the Baltic states' absorption by the USSR in the lower right-hand corner over the port of Mersin, so that the line to the sea could not be seen (the disclaimer was normally placed in the top right-hand corner). Since the treaty entered into force, there has not been a compliance problem involving Mersin.

Nevertheless, the NATO caucus had a real problem in November 1989. Naturally Brussels, in approving the text, had used the Mandate definition of the area. I think that it was in one of Bill's and my early U.S. interagency drafts. Athens woke up again as the text was about to be tabled and instructed their ambassador to have this provision rewritten to clarify the status of Mersin. No one wanted to do this as all knew that it was impossible. Six weeks of complete stalemate followed. The Mersin issue became a public political issue in Greece. Tempers grew shorter and shorter within the NATO caucus. Ambassadors were using epithets like "liar" in referring to their colleagues. (NATO has always seemed to me like a family, frequently squabbling, with national representatives saying unbelievable things to one another, but once an external threat arises, the representatives lock arms in solidarity like brothers and sisters.)

During this six-week period I had a meeting with a senior French official dealing with CFE at the Quai d'Orsay. Again, the French proposal had been to negotiate CFE at thirty-five—including all the neutrals, such as Sweden, Austria, Ireland, and the Vatican—rather than negotiating only among NATO and Warsaw Pact countries. In referring to the Greek-Turkish stalemate in Vienna, the French official said, "You see, we were right after all. NATO in Vienna cannot agree to table our text, but if the negotiation was at thirty-five, the Holy See could table it for us and say that it came from God."

Conventional Armed Forces in Europe Treaty

After intense politicking in Athens involving the U.S. ambassador and senior members of the Greek government, the logjam was finally broken and the Greeks agreed to stand down on the same basis that they had in January 1989. So the NATO draft treaty was tabled in mid-December 1989, just before the Christmas break and one week after the Warsaw Pact draft was tabled. Therefore, Jim Woolsey's hope that an early tabling by NATO would cause both sides to work from the NATO draft did not work out. On the positive side, however, the West Germans, during those six weeks, had fed so much of the supposedly still confidential NATO draft to the East Germans and thence on to the Soviets that the Warsaw Pact draft contained significant overlap with the NATO draft.

The NATO caucus was the source of a number of interesting dynamics and I shall relate a few here. Mersin excepted, the subject that was always the most hotly debated was when holidays were to begin and end. One day, after a very long wrangle about when the Christmas holiday should begin and end, given the different dates for Christmas in Eastern and Western Christianity—important in NATO to the Greeks and of course to the East—the Turkish ambassador, the most capable Ali Hikmet Alp, opined, "All of this is of little concern to us, as Christmas is not one of Turkey's most important holidays."

And language, the caucus was always arguing over language. Early in the fall of 1989, an instruction came from Brussels which used the phrases "treaty limited item" (TLI) and "treaty limited equipment" (TLE). A vigorous debate ensued in the caucus as to whether the former term in the instruction from Brussels could include limits on military personnel—largely excluded from CFE. In other words, was a soldier an item? Much back and forth followed. After a time French Ambassador Plaisant, later ambassador to China, intervened and lamented that it was unfortunate that the CFE negotiation was conducted in English "with all its ambiguities, because in French there are no ambiguities."

Another memorable event in the caucus took place in late September 1990, about three weeks before the German Democratic Republic was merged into the Federal Republic of Germany and the GDR ceased to be a negotiating party in CFE. The GDR delegation had done something particularly egregious and the NATO caucus was discussing this. Ambassador after ambassador expressed his outrage. Finally, the German ambassador, Rudy Hartmann, one of the great men of the negotiations, one of the finest representatives of his country that I have ever met, and quintessentially German, said in somewhat accented English: "Why do we worry about this delegation? This is a country that will soon be ours." You could see spines stiffen around the room as memories of World War II suddenly flashed before them. The next day I was having lunch with my German opposite number and friend, Hubertus Von Mohr, the German delegation legal advisor and former consul general in Houston. I expansively said, not focusing on anything in particular,

"Hubertus, one of the things that I find so interesting about this negotiation is that all the national stereotypes really prove to be accurate" (and they did). "Yes," Hubertus said with a smile, "it brings out your worst fears, doesn't it?"

In January of 1990, Mike Guhin came out to be the ACDA representative on the delegation. My family and I returned home on the first of January, after four months in Vienna. I reverted to legal advisor to the delegation with Bill Parsons, who was there almost full time, serving in my stead when I was not there. I was in Vienna for three weeks in late January and early February 1990, staying with Jim Woolsey. I visited Vienna for three weeks in the spring and returned there from early September to late November for the endgame and treaty signing on November 19, 1990, in Paris. As usual, we had my longtime secretary, Martha Kaulaity, there for the endgame, specially requested by State.

I admired and always enjoyed working with my good friend Jim Woolsey. He did a magnificent job as CFE negotiator. He was also the public member (like Harold Brown for SALT) on the START delegation in 1985 and 1986. When I was under heavy assault from the right on the ABM issue in 1987, I thought I needed a lawyer. I had come to know Jim on the START delegation, although we had first known each other during SALT I, when he was general counsel of the Senate Armed Services Committee. I went to see him and he offered his legal advice free of charge. He had a partner, Tony Lapham, who had been general counsel of the CIA, who usually sat in on our meetings. Every month or two I would go over to see Jim and catalogue the doings of Dornan and his crowd. Jim would just shake his head in dismay at all this and say, "Well, you haven't done anything wrong yet." It was most reassuring.

During the first half of 1990, the delegations focused primarily on working out system definitions, for example, the definition of "main battle tank," which was worked on by the generals (without lawyers, at their request). This included the increasingly elaborate Verification Protocol spearheaded by Lynn Hanson, the deputy U.S. negotiator at Stockholm and later brought to the CIA by Jim, for the United States and Yevgeny Yefstafiev, a KGB general and later a senior official with the Russian Security Service who later was in New York for the 1995 NPT Conference, for the USSR.

By September 1990, it was clear that the endgame had arrived. There was now broad agreement on many parts of the treaty text and the Verification Protocol, the Protocol on Existing Types (known as the POET, which listed the existing types of weapon systems subject to the obligations of the treaty— when new types were developed they would be added to the POET in the JCG), the protocol establishing the JCG and setting forth its mandate, and the Provisional Application Protocol. However, many of the important issues remained unresolved, in some cases involving treatment of specific weapon systems. There was a meeting on the margins of the United Nations General

Assembly (UNGA) between Baker and Shevardnadze at which progress was made, but it was also clear that the Soviet General Staff was growing increasingly restive with CFE. At about the same time, it was agreed that there would be a CSCE summit in Paris on November 19, so we had our deadline against which to work.

As part of the agreement that CFE would be a bloc-to-bloc negotiation, it was established that every six weeks or so the CFE delegations would make a report to all thirty-five CSCE ambassadors, often referred to as a report "at thirty-five" for the benefit of the neutral states. Pursuant to a rotation, one of the CFE ambassadors delivered the report and took questions from the ambassadors of neutral nations. These sessions were usually rather general in nature. The negotiations and discussions were all in the Hapsburg Palace in Vienna. The CFE negotiations held all their plenary sessions in a very comfortable room in the palace, the Ratshalle; the CSCE had a far more elegant room.

There were also ongoing negotiations on additional confidence-building measures. All of the CFE negotiating parties except the United States and Germany had the same ambassador for both negotiations, CFE and CSCE. This often caused scheduling problems but in my opinion it gave Germany and the United States an advantage in CFE as their representatives could apply their full effort to CFE. But the separate CSCE negotiation also meant that there would be another document to sign at the Paris Summit, which would go forward no matter what. This threatened to undercut the effectiveness of our deadline. On the other hand, CFE was the big-ticket item and the French would have been embarrassed if the negotiators had not been able to produce a CFE Treaty to sign at Paris. To some extent the United Kingdom, Germany (now united), and the United States were in the same position on substantive issues. (The German Democratic Republic was merged into the Federal Republic of Germany on October 3, 1990, pursuant to the Two Plus Four treaty. I remember having dinner that night in a cafe in Grinsing watching a group celebrating this event marching around the other room in the cafe to the tune of "Lili Marlene," the World War II song.)

The big problem was the Soviet military. The Soviet Union obviously was beginning to come apart. On my way to Vienna in mid-September I attended a conference in Moscow jointly sponsored by the American Bar Association and the Association of Soviet Lawyers. John and Jeanne Rhinelander attended, fresh from a tour of Central Asia, as did my friend and colleague of many years, Elizabeth Rindskopf, openly in her capacity as general counsel of the CIA, only the second agency official to do so. John and I gave addresses at one of the panels but we also visited a number of others. At a number of the panels, representatives from the legal profession in many of the Republics made it clear that in their view Republic law superseded Soviet law. Often these claims were made in strident tones; I remember a lawyer from Azerbaijan in particular in this regard. This seemed to me to go well beyond federation.

The Arbat shopping street in Moscow was very much in operation in those days and, although it was illegal to trade in U.S. dollars, many of the vendors did. One day while we were in Moscow I went shopping with Elizabeth and John and Jeanne. As Elizabeth was about to go into a shop, she pointed to a Matrushka doll being offered by a street vendor who was obviously trading in dollars and asked if I would buy it for her, as she did not dare risk it. She then escaped into the shop. I asked the man how much the doll cost and he said $25. I gave him the money, walked into the shop and handed the doll to Elizabeth. No sooner had I done so there was a tap on my shoulder and a plainclothes policeman flashed his credentials in front of me. He motioned for me to follow him outside. I did so and in the street he told me that it was illegal to buy goods with dollars. I replied that it was only a small purchase, hardly of any consequence. He said, "How much?" I said, "$25." He replied, "OK," and motioned for me to go. I guess it was best that I did what I did as it would not have been a positive thing for U.S.-Soviet relations for the general counsel of the CIA to be arrested in Moscow for illegal currency speculation. At the end of the conference Gorbachev hosted a black-tie dinner dance in the Kremlin. It was a glittering affair. Everybody at our table danced a bit, and I asked Elizabeth to do a few bars with me and we tried to dance as close to Gorbachev's table as we could. In retrospect I told myself that when I began at ACDA in 1970 never in my wildest dreams did I believe that I would ever be dancing with the general counsel of the Central Intelligence Agency at a black-tie dinner in the Kremlin hosted by the general secretary of the Communist Party of the Soviet Union. Times had indeed changed in several ways.

One issue that came up late in the negotiations in about the October time frame and to which I have already referred is worth further comment. Norway and Turkey were concerned that the final structure of the treaty, which aimed at thinning out the Central Zone where two world wars had begun, might push concentrations of forces out to the flanks. They therefore wanted some protection against this. There then ensued a largely quadripartite negotiation among Woolsey, Soviet Ambassador Oleg Grinevsky, Ambassador Alp, and Ambassador Yakin Bjorn of Norway, later their UN ambassador. The Greeks and Bulgarians were interested but they followed these negotiations from a distance. An arrangement was worked out, found in Article V of the treaty, which limited the flow of TLE to the flanks reasonably well. But at the outset achieving this arrangement to limit the flow of the TLE to the flanks appeared to be a difficult mountain to climb. In addition to Russian and other objections, it appeared as though the French might oppose it and that would likely block the deal. To avoid this, Jim Woolsey approached Norwegian Ambassador Bjorn and suggested a formula that he urged Bjorn to propose. Bjorn said it seemed fine to him, but he would have to check with Oslo. A few days later Oslo cautiously agreed. When Bjorn reported that he was ready to go ahead, Jim told him not to be surprised at anything that he, Woolsey, might say. Bjorn was a little puzzled, but duly proposed the concept at the next NATO Caucus. After Bjorn's presentation, Woolsey asked to be the first respondent. He said that he was shocked that Norway would propose such a thing without prior consultation with the United States and that Washington knew nothing about this and would likely be skeptical. This prospect prompted the French Ambassador, François Plaisant, to immediately say that he found the Norwegian proposal an excellent contribution and was confident that the Quai d'Orsay would approve.

However, this arrangement as ultimately negotiated came to be based on the eastern side upon military districts of the Soviet Union. After the close of the negotiation the Soviets supplied an official map to the depository, the Dutch government, depicting the Soviet military districts. It was never made part of the treaty package, however. (The Hague was sold to the Soviets as the depository on the basis that all agreed it should not be the United Nations and should be a treaty party. The Netherlands was seen by the Soviets as a slightly more neutral NATO member and not a big power. The United States argued that The Hague had a long history in international law and had the World Court located on its territory, and therefore was an appropriate choice.) Basing the arrangement on Soviet military districts worked acceptably when there was a Soviet Union, but when the Soviet Union fell apart, parts of their military districts became parts of independent countries, the Caucasus was aflame, and the flank limitations created a running sore for the treaty and unnecessary hostility between East and West.

Early in November there remained much that was not agreed and many brackets remained in the informal joint draft text being kept by the U.S. delegation. Woolsey proposed going to Moscow to deal directly with the Soviet military to try to come to a resolution on the remaining issues and thereby complete the treaty text. The delegation included Woolsey, Lynn Hanson to work verification issues with Yefstafiev, General St. John (our JCS representative) to help him with specific weapon issues, and me to work on the legal issues. We were joined by a group from Washington led by Reg Bartholomew, who headed the whole U.S. delegation in Moscow. We dealt directly with General Moiseyev, the chief of the Soviet General Staff—the last one before the collapse, I believe—and his staff.

After the opening statements both sides set to work with vigor, with the Soviet military being reasonably cooperative. In a few days, the United States, acting in effect for NATO, resolved the remaining issues with the Soviet Union, or more accurately with the Soviet military. This was then converted into a complete treaty text, given the substantial agreement that existed in Vienna. By the time we returned to Vienna, there was just one week remaining before the Summit. Bill Parsons and others worked vigorously to produce a complete text, which was achieved by Saturday night, then cabled off to Washington, and distributed to the other delegations. Initially, there was no response from Washington. On Monday morning we met with the non-Soviet East and they had no changes to propose to the text. Woolsey let the allies—most particularly the United Kingdom, France, and Germany—know that the text would have to be closed by Wednesday, November 14, at noon to allow a twenty-four-hour silence approval period for capitals and three days to do the translating work.

The Summit was set for Monday, November 19, and we would need those three days to convert the texts from English into Spanish, Italian, German, French, and Russian, the other official languages. This would begin as soon as the text was closed. The text could then be initialed by the negotiators on Saturday, taken to Paris on Sunday, and signed on Monday. The British, Germans, French, and others realized that they would have to take the text brought back from Moscow more or less as it was. They requested a number of changes, which were coordinated with the Soviets, but the text largely held in the form in which it returned from Moscow. Washington was a bit slow on the uptake and we did not hear from there until Tuesday, when a cable arrived demanding in a peremptory tone eleven changes to the text in order to have Washington's approval. Fortunately, the changes had already been made as some of them were simply errors in the text we had sent to Washington and others had been made at the request of the allies.

However, Washington had not finished. Early Wednesday morning another cable arrived, demanding seven more changes for Washington's approval, which was clearly impossible given that the negotiations were to end at mid-day. At our 8:00 A.M. staff meeting that morning, Woolsey held up a copy of the cable and asked if we had all seen it. We all nodded assent. He then said, "Here is how I want you to handle it," and he tore it in half. That is leadership. No one in Washington ever again mentioned the seven issues. Thus, the silence period began on Wednesday at noon and the next afternoon Jim sent his "Fat Lady" cable. A cable came back from Washington, from the White House, not the State Department, authorizing Jim to initial for the United States and close out the negotiations. The cable was signed by George Bush, the only time in my career I ever saw a cable with a president's name on it as the transmitting official.

So, after the Fat Lady had sung, two and a half days of around-the-clock negotiations—some of the toughest, most emotional that I have experienced—were required to convert the English text into equally authentic texts in the five other languages. Some delegations had several interpreters, while we had only one, an elegant, urbane man in his seventies known as Prince Obolensky, addressed simply as "the Prince." He had flawless English, Russian, French, German, and Italian (the Italian ambassador said that Obolensky spoke better Italian than he did), but it was said that his Spanish had perhaps one or two flaws. It was a very difficult negotiation. At one point a senior Spanish delegate in a dispute with a French delegate over the interpretation of a word threatened to quit the delegation, return to Madrid, and speak out against the treaty. But this job was finally accomplished to everyone's satisfaction and the text was ready for initialing.

On Saturday morning, November 17, the delegations gathered in a room at the Hofburg for the initial exchange of information. It was like a bazaar. Tables were set up around the room with each delegation handing out books containing the initial data exchange—the one to take place at the time of signature—with appropriate pictures of weapons systems, tanks, and the like. There were the Soviets, the French, the Germans, and all the rest, hawking their data presentations. Some of the delegations had slicker presentations than others but all were comprehensive. It was quite a scene.

The initialing of the text by each delegation in a formal ceremony was scheduled for later that day in the Ratshalle and then the approved text of the treaty was to be taken by a senior member of the Hofburg Secretariat to Paris for signature by the heads of government on Monday, November 19. The delegations would not see the official text again. There was, of course, a copy of the treaty text for each delegation in all six official languages—the product of our recent nearly three-day round-the-clock exercise. We were standing about, waiting for the ceremony to begin. Suddenly, the U.S. delegation huddled around Jim Woolsey. The CIA had analyzed the data and it was indisputable that the Soviets had substantially understated their TLE in the area of application. They claimed that a substantial number of TLE had been moved over the Ural Mountains and thus would be out of the treaty area, likely far more than actually had been accomplished by that date. Further, it was subsequently confirmed that the Soviets were asserting that the limitations of the CFE Treaty did not apply to TLE held by Soviet naval infantry (or marines) on the ground that they were subordinated to the Navy, not the Army—a preposterous notion. As a result, the Soviet TLE destruction obligation was substantially less than the United States had anticipated.

There was consternation among the U.S. delegation with the beginning of the initialing ceremony just minutes away. The entire six-language CFE text was in the middle of the room. The chairman of the negotiations, an assignment rotating among countries, sat at a table in front, flanked by two members of his delegation, and the delegations spread out in a horseshoe arrangement (the standard configuration) away from him. The interpreters were behind windows on the floor above the entrance—the room itself was two stories high. The United States delegation was the nearest on the chairman's right, the delegations sitting alphabetically according to the German language, in contrast to the United Nations, where French was used for this purpose. Woolsey's first reaction was to refuse to initial, given this substantial discrepancy. I urged him to initial anyway—let the Summit signing go forward—and we would get this straight later, since signature is not the same as ratification. In the end, that is what Woolsey did. He was the last of the ambassadors who walked into the center of the horseshoe and initialed the signature pages of the treaty. It was thought to be too long and arduous a task to initial every page of the text in all six languages—the usual practice. So the initialing took place in Vienna and two days later, on November 19, the treaty was signed in Paris.

The signing in Paris went smoothly. Woolsey took about ten of us with him to Paris for the signing, although only five people were actually able to sit in the space allotted for the U.S. delegation and thus see the ceremony, which was held in a quite small room. The signature pages, not the entire treaty, were simply passed around. For the United States, President Bush signed. He was accompanied by Secretary Baker, Brent Scowcroft, Woolsey, and Senator Pell. Some delegations had two or even three people sign. The Germans were very careful to have both Chancellor Kohl and Foreign Minister Genscher (his coalition partner and head of the Free Democrat Party) sign. After the ceremony we met with President Bush at the American ambassador's residence, where he generously posed for a picture first with the ten-person delegation and then individually with each one of us.

The data issue that surfaced in Vienna was the beginning of a lengthy conflict with the Soviet military, which was not resolved until June 1991—the last protest of the Soviet military against CFE. In fact, it really did not matter so much that the Soviets had not actually moved as much equipment as they claimed; eventually it did all leave Europe (as defined in the treaty), long before the entry into force of the treaty, and largely ended up rusting away in the harsh Siberian weather. Excluding TLE held by Soviet naval infantry was another matter, however—it was intolerable and an affront to the treaty regime. It had to be resolved. In the ensuing months after signature, Woolsey and Lynn Hansen, our verification expert, among others, made trips to Moscow to see what could be done on this issue and were met with a stone wall. It was clear that the CFE Treaty would not enter into force until this issue was resolved; every single other signatory to the treaty denounced Moscow on this point and it proved to be increasingly embarrassing to the Soviet leadership.

In May 1991, after months of confrontation over the data issue, General Moiseyev came to Washington to attempt to resolve the data issue, preceded of course by a number of diplomatic exchanges. His visit lasted two days, with the first day spent closeted in the State Department with the two delegations. Our side was led by Reg Bartholomew, with Woolsey present. I was there for most of the discussion as legal advisor. At the end of the day it seemed clear that an agreement in principle was possible; however, the State Department appeared to be willing to settle this issue on the basis of political commitments, rather than on legally binding obligations, which is what the treaty contained. This seemed unwise to Bill Parsons and me and likely to severely limit any prospect for U.S. Senate approval of the treaty. The next morning I spoke with Ron Lehman and Jim Woolsey and voiced my concern. I said that in my judgment this emerging agreement had to be legally binding, like the treaty itself. Later in the morning one or both must have spoken with Baker. The negotiation being over, Moiseyev spent the morning at the Pentagon with Secretary Cheney as his host and then had an early afternoon session with President Bush before his departure for Moscow that night. Baker must have spoken with Bush before Moiseyev's arrival, for reportedly as soon as he was ushered into the Oval Office and after the salutations were over, the first thing that the president said was, "It has to be legally binding." Moiseyev, a military man, not a lawyer, readily agreed. The speed with which this communication traveled to where it needed to go exemplified for me why Jim Baker was a great secretary of state. He ran the department with a small group but if you needed to communicate with him and had a good reason to do so, you always could, no matter who you were.

Shortly thereafter, Jim Woolsey was in Lisbon with Baker for the Angolan peace treaty meeting, where a side discussion with the Soviets reached agreement to formally conclude the data dispute with a written document to be developed at a meeting in Moscow the next week, the first week in June. I received word from Woolsey—while I was driving in my car with Eliza, Tommy, and Clover to Mercersburg Academy for Thomas's high school graduation—that I was to call him. I called Woolsey in Lisbon on my car telephone—it was Saturday morning—and he said that I had to be in Moscow by Monday to be ready for a Tuesday morning meeting. I called Bill Parsons and told him that he had to go as well. Saturday evening I went to Saint Paul's School in Concord, New Hampshire, for part of my godson Van Taylor's high school graduation, and left for Moscow Sunday night.

We met with the Soviets at one of the guesthouses owned by the Ministry of Foreign Affairs. It was a lovely old mansion located in the heart of Moscow. It had been owned by a wealthy businessman who supported Lenin and the Communists. Upon taking power Lenin had the businessman shot and appropriated his house for the state. We met with the Soviets for three days, concluding a legally binding change to part of the treaty regime that in effect included Soviet naval infantry as TLE. We had a long discussion which led to agreement on a Soviet political commitment to leave the equipment taken over the Urals in the open for our satellites to verify—and where it would more quickly deteriorate. After the meeting several of our group took the agreements, on naval infantry and the "beyond the Urals" political agreement, to Vienna for JCG approval, the former as a legally binding treaty change.

The CFE Treaty was sent to the United States Senate for advice and consent to ratification in the fall of 1991, and it was approved without great difficulty. The Senate, however, did not move swiftly and there were several encounters with Senate staff in which Jim Woolsey urged with some vehemence that the Senate not delay ratification of the treaty. After all, it was overwhelmingly in the interest of the United States that the military situation in Europe be stabilized, a military blueprint for Europe's future be established, and the Cold War ended, which was in effect what the CFE Treaty accomplished. The Senate was concerned that the collapse of the Warsaw Pact not allow any area in the East of any military significance within the area of application to escape the limitations of the treaty. Ultimately, an elaborate condition to ratification was developed that addressed this situation to the satisfaction of the Senate, and the treaty passed under the floor leadership of Senator Lugar. Not long afterwards, on Christmas Day 1991, the Soviet Union passed into history, with twelve successor states remaining in its wake. Already, the Baltic States had gained their independence and the JCG had by agreement decided to exclude the area of the Baltic States from the CFE area of application. Obviously, it was a different matter with respect to the remaining territory of the former Soviet Union west of the Urals and the vast amount of TLE that was located there. In retrospect, the Senate condition proved to be prudent.

There were eight successor states to the Soviet Union for the CFE Treaty, some or all of whose territory was located west of the Urals. All but one, Kazakhstan, had TLE located on its territory. The large Soviet TLE allotment would have to be subdivided among the seven successors who qualified for TLE: Russia, Ukraine, Belarus, Georgia, Armenia, Azerbaijan, and Moldova, with most of the TLE allotment logically to go to the first three. Secretary Baker made the trip mentioned above to Russia, Ukraine, Belarus, and Kazakhstan in early January, shortly after they became independent. This was followed by the interagency delegation trip headed by Reg Bartholomew, about a week later. One of the purposes of the Bartholomew delegation trip was to encourage the four states we visited, including Kazakhstan (even though no TLE was located or would be located on its territory within the area of application), to adhere to the CFE Treaty. To make the necessary, extraordinarily sensitive, TLE allotments appeared a Herculean task but miraculously, by means of the Treaty of Tashkent in February 1992, this was in fact accomplished. Gradually, the eight successor states began to join the treaty and, with United States ratification in place, Western and Eastern European governments were completing their ratifications.

At a special May meeting in Oslo the JCG formally approved an alteration of the treaty (by means of an Extraordinary Conference—which in those days became almost ordinary, e.g., the naval infantry adjustment, the exclusion of the Baltic States Area) to replace the Soviet Union with the eight successor states in a formal ceremony complete with a speech by the Norwegian foreign minister. Already, however, rumors were about that Czechoslovakia was likely to split into two states, the Czech Republic and Slovakia, which did in fact happen in January 1993. Since, with great effort, the JCG had dealt with the dissolution of the Soviet Union, and since there were now twenty-nine potential CFE parties, there was a desire to bring CFE into force before the JCG had to hold another Extraordinary Conference. The CSCE meeting in Helsinki in July was set as the time when CFE must be brought into force. But by June, Russia, Belarus, and Armenia still had not ratified the treaty. Nothing was possible without Russian ratification, and when that came in late June there was hope that the July target date could be met. However, the Belarussian Parliament was not in session and there was no chance that it would be brought into session by the prime minister soon, as it was the avowed intent of the majority to overthrow the government with a no-confidence vote at the first opportunity. Further, the Armenian Parliament, given the disastrous political and social conditions there at that time, could scarcely be found. By its terms the CFE Treaty could only be brought into force when all (now twenty-nine) signatories had ratified. There was no chance that Belarus and Armenia would ratify by the July meeting, and the separation of Czechoslovakia was ever more certain. The question was what to do.

I was staying at our house in Middleburg, Virginia, one weekend in late June when an idea came to me. The JCG, under its treaty mandate that was provisionally in force due to the Provisional Application Protocol, could make alterations of a minor technical or administrative nature to the text of the Provisional Application Protocol by a simple decision—no need to call an Extraordinary Conference. Why not amend the text of the Provisional Application Protocol simply to provide that on the specified date in July the entire treaty would actually be brought into force for the period of baseline inspection (four months) on a provisional basis and as a minor administrative change? This, I hoped, would give Armenia and Belarus time to ratify, the treaty would be in force, and we could face with equanimity the looming split of Czechoslovakia. The treaty text would not have to be adjusted again, as the treaty would formally be in force. The Czech Republic and Slovakia would simply be successor states. And the period of being provisionally in force could be extended if necessary.

On Sunday I called Jim Timbie and Ken Myers, Senator Lugar's key aide, and tried the idea out on them. Both cautiously supported it but Ken, after several telephone calls, made it clear that the leadership of the Senate Foreign Relations Committee would have to approve. As I have indicated earlier, in the 1980s, as a reaction to actual and alleged Soviet violations of arms control treaties (beginning with the INF treaty), implementing provisions such as data protocols and verification procedures were no longer allowed to be separate subsidiary agreements that could be adjusted as needed—for example, when a verification procedure is changed—by implementing bodies such as the SCC, but rather were required by the United States to be part of the treaty itself and therefore subject to Senate advice and consent to ratification. This, in the eyes of some, was more legally binding. Thus, there was a need for an adjusting mechanism so that minor technical or administrative changes would not have to be treated as treaty amendments calling for frequent advice and consent submissions. Such a mechanism for permitting the minor adjustments in the text could be argued to have flowed from the operation of the JCG protocol (which had a minor adjustment provision), which was built upon the JCG treaty article and was provisionally in force.

The Provisional Application Protocol had a different purpose. It was intended to bring certain data exchange provisions into force upon signature to facilitate the exchange of data. The minor adjustment provision concept was first set forth in the Threshold Test Ban Treaty in the context of the approval of the 1990 protocols, and in the course of ratification testimony the administration made a pledge that if in utilizing this procedure there was ever any question as to whether a particular change was or was not technical, the approval of the committee leadership (chairman and ranking member) must be obtained. I discussed with Ken the applicability of this procedure, as this would be the first, and to date the only, time it had been used. It was decided that Timbie and I would meet with Senators Lugar and Pell (who was in Rhode Island but would be represented at the meeting by his aide Dave Hafmeister). I discussed the concept with Ron Lehman on Monday and he approved it. That afternoon Timbie and I went off to meet with Lugar and Hafmeister. Ken Myers was at the meeting as well. I made the presentation as to why this was necessary, Ken made helpful comments, and Senator Lugar approved the course of action, but on the basis that this was an extraordinary step, necessitated by events, and should not necessarily establish a precedent. It was agreed that there would be an exchange of letters to this effect between Director Lehman on the one hand and Senators Pell and Lugar on the other. Ron would write asking for permission, setting forth the circumstances that necessitated this action and Pell and Lugar would reply giving their assent along with the aforementioned caveat that this was an extraordinary step required by events. This was accomplished the next day, and our delegation at the JCG was instructed immediately to propose this and lobby for support. Not surprisingly, there was resistance in Vienna because, to put it mildly, this was an unusual move. Nevertheless, Helsinki now was just a few days away and delegations increasingly came to support this procedure. Not without some anguish, however. The Italian ambassador told the U.S. representative that his government's international lawyers in Rome "had to swallow beach balls over this."

The JCG, with just a day to spare, approved this measure, but not all delegations were present. In the normal course of events, delegations from smaller countries—particularly those of the NIS—rarely attend JCG meetings. In this case, Georgia, Armenia, Azerbaijan, Moldova, and Kazakhstan were not present. But it was important that this decision be acted upon by all delegations. Accordingly, the U.S. representative to the Helsinki meeting was stationed at the airport to intercept representatives from these five countries as they arrived in Helsinki to gain their assent to bringing the CFE Treaty into force on a provisional basis for four months by making a "technical" change to the provisional application protocol. All of the assents were obtained and Timbie called me to tell me that the U.S. representative had been completely successful.

So the next morning, a sunny Saturday in July, Dave Webster, who succeeded Bill Parson and me as the CFE lawyer, called me as I was still lying in bed in Middleburg, to inform me that all had gone according to plan in Helsinki. The CFE Treaty was formally announced to have entered into force on July 16. Baseline inspections began one week later, Armenia ratified later in the summer, and Belarus ratified on November 9, one week before the expiration of the four-month period. As I said, Czechoslovakia did split in two in January but now the treaty was fully in force and the Czech Republic and Slovakia became successor states, bringing the number of CFE parties to thirty, which remains the number today.

The CFE Treaty ended the Cold War and is one of the central pillars of European security. Its tumultuous history continued with the flank dispute leading up to the 1996 Review Conference and treaty adaptation in the wake of NATO expansion. But the treaty overcame these problems as well, as it has no substitute. Simply in coming into being, it had to overcome the unification of Germany and the disappearance of one of the negotiating parties, the intense hostility of the Soviet military, the collapse of the Warsaw Pact and the independence of the Baltic states, the dissolution of the former Soviet Union, revolutions in Eastern Europe that changed the characters and even the names of a number of the negotiating parties, and the splitting up of Czechoslovakia. Truly, it is a treaty for all seasons.

After the conclusion of the naval infantry issue in 1991 and the entry into force of the treaty in 1992, the flank issue arose to threaten the treaty. In the wake of the breakup of the Soviet Union, the Caucasus region burst into flames. A long-simmering dispute between Armenia and Azerbaijan over the Nagorno-Karabakh area broke into open warfare. There were two civil wars in Georgia. Later, there was the revolt against Russia in Chechnya. Russia believed that it needed to reinforce its southern flank. However, as the CFE Treaty was reconstituted, Russia and Ukraine, alone among CFE parties, had territory in different CFE zones and therefore had internal reinforcement restrictions. Beginning in 1993, Russia sought relief from these restrictions, principally with respect to ACVs. The U.S. military and NATO allies were distinctly unsympathetic to the Russian request. Turkey was adamant against any change. Russia escalated the rhetoric and threatened to withdraw from the CFE Treaty but NATO was ready to call the bluff. NATO's position was that Russia had agreed to the current CFE arrangement and just wanted relief so that it could begin to reconstitute the Russian Empire. The NATO flank states (Turkey and Norway) were especially suspicious of

Russia for historical reasons. Beginning in 1995, Undersecretary of State Lynn Davis led an interagency team in negotiations with the Russians but progress was almost non existent.

After the 1995 NPT Conference, in the context of which I was serving as ambassador and special representative of the president for Arms Control, Non-Proliferation and Disarmament, I was casting about for something to do. Ralph Earle suggested that I become the roving NPT ambassador as Gerry Smith had done during the Carter administration. John Holum accepted Ralph's suggestion but soon reversed it when Larry Scheinman (then ACDA assistant director for non-proliferation) said he thought it would impinge upon his bureaucratic responsibilities. It was unfortunate, I guess, as I would have liked such an assignment and might have stayed in government indefinitely. John had also moved me back from isolation in the Columbia Plaza Annex in 1996 (where I had been sent in the fall of 1994, along with the U.S. SCC and JCIC representatives, in what was supposed to be a restructuring move—the quarters were so bad I sought to avoid holding diplomatic meetings there) because the building was going to be remodeled. In so doing, he gave me a good office. But now I needed to find work.

In the summer of 1995, Elizabeth Pryor, a former public affairs officer for CFE who had been working on OSCE (the successor to the CSCE) issues now for several years for U.S. Ambassador John Kornblum, came to see me. In the course of the conversation, she suggested that I try to head the U.S. delegation to the 1996 CFE Review Conference. John was no longer OSCE ambassador but had moved to be assistant secretary of state for EUR, and Elizabeth suggested that I go talk to him. If he was amenable, Elizabeth said, there wouldn't be a problem. I leapt at the chance and immediately sought an appointment with Kornblum. Asking and getting were two different things, however, as John was up to his ears in Bosnia. Elizabeth, whom I hoped would be on the delegation if I succeeded, was also unfortunately soon seconded to the Bosnia effort in Europe and was quickly lost from view. I finally did get in to see Kornblum. He remembered me from CFE when he was DCM at NATO and I had seen him at the Helsinki CSCE Conference in the spring of 1992 which I had attended, and he was supportive. I then spoke with John Holum, who was equally positive. After some time Holum sent a memorandum over to NSC recommending my selection. Kornblum regarded this as Holum's call, not his, but to be sure of his support I went to see him again. Finally, in due course, this was made official in the fall of 1995 and I had another assignment.

I began to assemble a delegation by asking Bill Parsons to come over from CIA (where he had gone after his year of temporary service with ACDA for the Senate Foreign Relations Committee), as he was the best on CFE. Next, following my 1993 practice with the ABM Treaty Review (see chapter 9), I asked Anne Witkowsky, who worked CFE for Bob Bell at the NSC, to join the delegation. She did so but could only make the last week of the three-week conference. I wanted to do consultations in capitals as I had with NPT (described in chapter 11), but could only do Bonn and Paris, in part because I was drawn into the Comprehensive Test Ban Treaty (CTBT) campaign and in part because Lynn wouldn't allow it, as she feared it would interfere with her flank negotiation. I attended three HLTF meetings on the subject, the first two in Brussels and the third at the invitation of the Norwegian government in Oslo. At the second meeting, it was decided to propose the second, third, and fourth weeks of May 1996 for the Review Conference. The dates chosen were a relief to me as I, as always, wanted to keep the first Saturday in May open for the Kentucky Derby.

In early April I went to Bonn for consultations with Germany and met with Ambassador Rudy Hartmann, the new disarmament commissioner succeeding Commissioner Hoëlich. (Hoëlich had come to the March 1995 meeting of the Agency for the Prohibition of Nuclear Weapons in Latin America and the Caribbean [OPANAL]—the implementing body for the Treaty of Tlatelolco—in Viña del Mar, Chile, and made an excellent speech on behalf of NPT indefinite extension.) I next went to Paris where I met with Michel Duclos, under-director for disarmament at the Quai d'Orsay. During lunch before more formal discussions he mentioned that in February, France had proposed five-power discussions on nuclear disarmament in a meeting with Lynn Davis but had received no response. He asked why this was so. (Yeltsin had made a speech at the UN in September 1995 to the same effect.) When I returned home, I tried to motivate ACDA to press for a positive response from State but did not succeed. I then went on to Oslo for a three-day meeting of the HLTF on the CFE Review Conference. As at Brussels, I was co-head of the U.S. delegation with Craig Dunkerly of State/EUR, who was the U.S. HLTF Representative. Also, I was working again with Jennifer Laurendieu of EUR and Jim Timbie back in Washington, which was great. NATO did much good preparatory work at the Oslo meeting.

The big issue was adaptation of the treaty to recognize that Europe was no longer divided into two hostile blocs, to provide for national limits, and to do away with group and zonal limits. This was an important Russian objective, but NATO was not about to agree to negotiate this without an agreement on the flank issue. The Russians had been in violation of the Article V flank limits as a result of deployments in the south for nearly a year.

At the Review Conference I had an excellent delegation. My deputy, with whom I stayed for the duration of the conference, was Brigadier General (ret.) Greg Govan, a former head of OSIA, who had been the ACDA and thus U.S. representative at the JCG for about a year. Lynn Davis came over in the first week and made a presentation on the flank issue to the Russians that appeared to fall on deaf ears. She returned home, and I wrote her a note at the end of the first week to urge her to stay in close touch, as I thought the Russians would deal by the end of the conference if we could give them a commitment on adaptation.

I made it a practice to meet privately with each delegation, including small ones like Georgia, Azerbaijan, Armenia, and Moldova. I had a difficult meeting with the Ukrainian delegation, headed up by Deputy Foreign Minister Konstantin Hryschenko, an old colleague. I had last encountered him in New York at the NPT Conference where he and Andrei Sanikov, then the deputy foreign minister of Belarus, were pressing for a nuclear-weapon-free-zone for Central Europe—to the horror of those in State/EUR for whom nothing should interfere with NATO expansion. Such a zone was not intended to interfere with NATO expansion, but rather was intended as a device for keeping Russian nuclear weapons out of their countries, something that the United States ought to want to support. I had first met Hryschenko and Sanikov at the 1993 ABM Treaty Review Conference, where they represented Ukraine and Belarus, respectively. After meeting with each CFE Review Conference delegation, I assigned a U.S. delegation officer to stay in touch with each of those countries. I convened a group consisting of members from the delegations of the United States, the United Kingdom, France, and Germany to work on language for a commitment on adaptation negotiations. We worked out a text in a few days.

There was an HLTF meeting every morning and conference committee meetings all day as we worked on a final document. It was an intense conference. One particular issue related to the flank negotiation was difficult for the Norwegians, so their ambassador came to see me and said he could not agree without specific authorization from his deputy foreign minister, who had been our host in Oslo. She had arranged for the meeting to be held at a beautiful hotel outside Oslo with a wonderful view of the Oslo fjord—which in April still had snow and ice on its shores. But now it was late May and it was Saturday, so the deputy foreign minister was likely to be on her boat on the Oslo fjord, he said. However, the ambassador had her cell phone number. So I called the deputy foreign minister on her boat on the Oslo fjord and gained her assent.

In the end, the Russians did deal on the flank issue. Lynn Davis and Craig Dunkerly came over for the last few days to work on this agreement. By this time a final document was far advanced, and it contained the commitment to adaptation negotiations that the Russians wanted. Michel Duclos and Rudy Hartmann also came for the last days. But I remember best a conversation that I had with a senior member of the British delegation in which he expressed the gravest misgivings about NATO expansion, saying that the only reason the Europeans supported it was because the United States wanted it. For him it was reminiscent of the British/French 1939 guarantee to Poland that immediately preceded World War II.

Russian Deputy Foreign Minister Mamedov, Lynn's opposite number, returned for the last days as well, and the Russians agreed to a deal whereby they would freeze their ACV deployment where they then were for three years and the map supplied to the CFE Depository in The Hague depicting the Soviet military district boundaries would be adjusted in the flank agreement to provide a smaller flank zone. The limitations would remain the same for this reduced flank zone and the Russians were to be in compliance with these limits in three years. Lynn, in the first meeting, agreed to 600 Russian ACVs in Pskov opposite Norway, thereby alarming the Norwegians, who were calmed down only with difficulty. All of this was incorporated in an agreement that was approved the last night in a full plenary session of the conference alternating as a JCG session (for the flank agreement).

There were some last minute heroics in which Lynn and I were talking with Kulebyakin, my old Russian colleague from Vienna CFE days, the head of the Russian Review Conference delegation, and the Russian JCG representative in Vienna. The Russians were balking on a particular point that we considered essential. Lynn threatened to call Warren Christopher to tell him the whole deal was off. I suggested a compromise based on an experience in the original CFE negotiation and she worked out the terms of it with Mamedov until around midnight. At the very end, around 10:00 A.M. the next morning, with the negotiations to close at noon, the Azeris threatened to bolt, but the Turks put the heat on them because they wanted the freeze in the south on ACVs, which was part of the agreement. The Azeris finally gave in and Lynn promised as part of the deal with the Azeris to lead a U.S. delegation to Baku for security talks, which were conducted several months later. The flank agreement and adaptation commitment were agreed just before the end, with all looking lost several times in the closing hours. As Lynn and I were walking out of the conference hall together after all was formally agreed, I passed by the French HLTF representative, who said to me, "If I hadn't seen it, I would not have believed it." Lynn wrote me a very nice note afterwards, so we closed our professional association in those years on a good note.

The map was not part of the CFE Treaty, so a change to it was not an amendment to the treaty. The map was provided voluntarily to the depository as the official Russian description of the boundaries of the Soviet military districts. Nevertheless, State/L, supported by NSC/Legal, but over the objections of ACDA/GC, decided the flank agreement had to go to the Senate for advice and consent. It was approved by a 100–0 vote, but one of the many conditions was the most unfortunate commitment of the administration to send to the Senate for approval the ABM Treaty Succession Agreement.

Sometime after the 1996 Review Conference the CFE Treaty Adaptation negotiations began, and they were concluded in 1999. However, as of the end of 2001, the adapted CFE Treaty was not in force nor had it been submitted to the U.S. Senate.

CHAPTER NINE **SURVIVAL OF THE ARMS CONTROL AND DISARMAMENT AGENCY**

In 1992, Secretary of State James Baker commissioned a panel to study the merits of integrating ACDA into the Department of State. The chairman of the panel was Ambassador Jim Goodby, an outstanding retired career officer with a distinguished background in arms control and my former colleague on the Rowny "hit list." Contemporaneous with this there was a brief Carnegie Endowment study, "Organizing Foreign Policy for the Twenty-First Century," chaired by Richard Holbrooke, later the architect of NATO enlargement as ambassador to Germany, assistant secretary of state for EUR in the first Clinton administration, author of the Dayton Accords, and later U.S. ambassador to the UN. The Carnegie study cursorily concluded that with the end of the Cold War there was no longer any justification for the independent existence of ACDA, the Agency for International Development (AID), and the United States Information Agency (USIA) and that these agencies should be folded into the State Department. It was sort of a manifesto of State Department bureaucratic irredentism.

The Goodby panel was far different. It did a thorough examination of the consolidation issue with respect to ACDA only. The panel interviewed former negotiators such as Max Kampelman, and nongovernmental organization leaders such as Michael Krepon, the president of the Henry L. Stimson Center. Max was in favor of consolidation, and Michael urged that ACDA either be revitalized or consolidated. Ron Lehman, a fierce supporter of ACDA independence, was quite worried about the panel and urged me to cooperate with it as fully as I possibly could.

The inspector general of State (and ACDA after 1988), Sherman Funk, contributed an important part of the final report. He strongly supported independence, and used the Pakistan case mentioned earlier as a justification. In brief, the Pressler Amendment (a substitute for more stringent legislation introduced by Senator Alan Cranston) provided for a complete cutoff of U.S. aid, both military and non-military, to

Pakistan, unless the president each year certified to the Congress that Pakistan did not possess a nuclear device, and that the provision of continued aid would make it less likely that Pakistan would acquire such a device. Each year after 1984 DOD, State, and ACDA submitted their views for the consideration of the president as to whether he could make such a certification. Beginning in 1986, when it became clear that Pakistan did in fact possess a de facto nuclear device, and there was no way to argue that continued aid would make it less likely that Pakistan would acquire a nuclear device, ACDA began to recommend against certification. State and DOD continued to recommend in favor of aid to Pakistan, with the Afghan War still going on, but both sides of the issue were in front of the president solely because of an independent ACDA. After the Soviet withdrawal from Afghanistan, President Bush and subsequently President Clinton declined to certify. As a result, U.S. aid to Pakistan was terminated and the transfer of a large number of F-16s, for which Pakistan had already paid, was blocked. Sherman Funk correctly made much of this example and later testified before the Congress to this effect.

The final report of the Goodby panel endorsed the Krepon concept of revitalizing ACDA, but if that could not be accomplished then ACDA should be consolidated with the State Department. It contained a list and description of revitalization suggestions such as housing all negotiations within ACDA and giving ACDA more authority with respect to the control of sensitive exports. The report contained a paragraph on the unique value of the office of general counsel and stated that the office was a special repository of the skill and knowledge needed to draft, negotiate, and implement arms control agreements. The report added that this was the case to an important degree because of the capabilities of the general counsel himself. This comment of course gratified me but it hurt Mary Lib and perhaps others. The authors, I am sure, were just being kind to me partly because of my long tenure and had no intention of slighting the contributions of anyone else. There were many outstanding individuals in the ACDA General Counsel's Office at that time, and Mary Lib was at the top of the list.

Bill Clinton won the election in 1992 and the State/ACDA transition team arrived a week or two later. Brian Atwood headed the State transition team. He had been Doug Bennett's deputy when Doug was assistant secretary for congressional relations in the early Carter years and became assistant secretary when Doug was selected to head AID. Brian was a friend and a most capable public servant. Later he was undersecretary for management for Secretary Warren Christopher until he went to head AID in late 1993, where he remained until 1999, well after the deal was made for State to absorb ACDA and USIA—but not AID—in 1997.

However, as head of the State transition team, Brian acted as though the Goodby report had never been written and as though the Carnegie report was the drum by which they should march. The ACDA transition team, sort of a subset of the State team, was headed by Rose Gottemoeller assisted by Laura Holgate, a young researcher from Harvard who had worked there for Ash Carter, the assistant secretary of defense designate. Bob Bell was on the ACDA team but he never overtly participated. Rose was from the Rand Corporation, where she had developed an outstanding reputation as an analyst. If it had not been for Rose, ACDA would have been destroyed in 1993. She gave me the chance to save it and she helped my efforts as a friend and a source of wise counsel from her subsequent NSC position responsible for arms control in the NIS. Rose was sympathetic about the future of ACDA, as were many who had experience working on arms control and national security issues. They knew that much of the arms control progress of the past thirty years simply would not have happened but for ACDA. Some months later I learned from a military officer detailed to ACDA, who had been primarily assigned to National Security Advisor Tony Lake during the inauguration, that he likely shared this view. Tony had said in effect, I was told, that the administration planned to do away with ACDA, that he did not believe this to be wise, but that there was little that he could do about it.

Early on it became clear that the Clinton administration was not going to make political appointments to fill the director, deputy director, and the four assistant director positions because, led by the State transition team, they planned to do away with ACDA and incorporate those ACDA functions that they wished to keep into Lynn Davis's office (she was the selection for undersecretary of state for international security). Years previously, in 1973, I remembered that Jim Malone had obtained an opinion from the Office of Legal Counsel in the Department of Justice that in the absence of incumbents in these six presidential appointee positions at ACDA, the general counsel, as the next senior official, could act as director. I discussed this with Mary Lib and she pointed out that most agencies had succession arrangements established that would cover this but ACDA did not. She offered to draft a document formally providing that the general counsel was next in line for succession after the six presidential appointee positions. She proceeded to prepare such a document in mid-December 1992. She then informally discussed it with Rose, who gave her assent. Subsequently, Ron Lehman, still director until January 20, 1993, was persuaded by her to sign the document, thereby putting the succession arrangement in place. Thus, now as a matter of law, I would become acting director, with all the powers of director, on January 20, 1993, if the six incumbents submitted their resignations, as was normal, if they were accepted by the president, as was usual, and if no one was designated as a nominee to fill any of those positions.

The inauguration was on a Wednesday and I spent the preceding weekend in Middleburg conferring by telephone regularly with Mary Lib and Barb Starr, the long-time ACDA executive secretary and a heroic figure. On Sunday morning, Barb called me and said there was some kind of a retrograde effort underway by the State transition team to hold over for a time Read

Hamner, the deputy director, and have him be acting director as a kind of figurehead. Supposedly, incoming White House Chief of Staff Mack McLarty had approved this. For the rest of the day, Barb tried to find out if this was in fact true and, if so, what it meant. Toward the end of the day, the rumor began to recede and by Sunday night, the story vanished as mysteriously as it had arrived. Thus, at 12:01 P.M. on Wednesday, January 20, I knew that I was the acting director of ACDA.

On the morning of January 22, I arrived at the office unsure exactly as to what I should do but knowing that it would take a Herculean effort to save ACDA. ACDA clearly was in the gun sight of the State transition team and there was no opposition anywhere to their plan. I would have to organize some kind of coalition to oppose State if ACDA were to have a chance. A third-hand report came to me that Spurgeon Keeny, director of the Arms Control Association (ACA), then the principal arms control non-governmental organization, had despaired of ACDA, saying that I was likely to "roll over" to State. I did not intend to do that.

The first week of my acting directorship, which in the end was to last from January 20 to November 22, 1993, I stayed in my GC office and ran the agency from there. But that was a bit unworkable so I moved into the director's office the next week, never to return to GC, after twenty-one of the past twenty-three years there. My GC office remained untouched, however, until early 1994 when John Holum, who had been sworn in as director, upon my urging appointed Mary Lib as general counsel. I was acting deputy at this point while awaiting appointment as ambassador. Mary Lib took over my former GC office and boxed up my 120 pictures for me. I took most of them to Middleburg until after I left government, although I kept a small number with me and hung them on the wall of the deputy director's office. Subsequently I took them to the small office that I was given across the street in Columbia Plaza after I was appointed ambassador in July 1994 (and left as acting deputy director upon the confirmation of Ralph Earle in late August 1994). I never brought any pictures to the director's office, however.

On January 23, before I moved over to the director's office, I received an important telephone call from Congressman Bob Carr, who, along with Tom Downey, had been such a strong congressional supporter of SALT II. He said that his and Tom's long-time employee and arms control expert, Bob Sherman, whom I knew well, was without a job. He had left the employ of the Congress in 1992 to work on the unsuccessful Senate campaign of Oregon Congressman Les AuCoin. Carr said that if Bob Sherman could be useful to ACDA, it would please him if I could hire him and he gave me his telephone number. Bob Carr was a friend and the chairman of our House Appropriations Subcommittee, and Bob Sherman could be useful at ACDA, especially with the survival campaign that lay ahead. I did not hesitate. I called Bob within the hour and offered him a job as my special assistant. Fortunately, while keeping ACDA in the deep freeze pending a decision on whether it would continue to exist, the State transition team had not put on a hiring freeze. I also asked Laura Holgate to stay as a special assistant while she was waiting for Ash Carter's confirmation as assistant secretary of defense. Both were of great help in the coming battle.

It seemed to me that I should try to galvanize the NGO community as much as I could, interest as many influential members of Congress who cared about arms control as I could, and try to tell the ACDA story to whomever in the media would listen. Also, to the extent that I could, I tried to find support in other agencies. Congressman Lee Hamilton had just taken over the chair of the House Foreign Affairs Committee upon the retirement of Dante Fascell. He naturally brought in his people to fill key positions, meaning that Ivo Spalatin, my long-time friend and colleague and arms control "maneuverer extraordinaire" in Congress, might be looking for a new job. His addition to the ACDA staff would make a huge difference.

I went to see Ivo early in February. We had lunch in the Longworth House Building cafeteria. I asked him if he might be willing to come to ACDA. I said that I wanted to try to save ACDA, and told him that no one knew the ACDA issues in the Congress as well as he did. He said that he was under no pressure to leave but clearly he would not have the influence under Hamilton that he had had under Fascell. He said that he would think it over and give me a reply after a short vacation in Florida that he and his wife were planning. About a week later, Ivo called me and said that he would like to come. This touched off a long struggle with the State transition team, which recognized the threat that Ivo posed. I had offered Ivo one of the agency's non-career senior executive service positions in order to give him a salary commensurate with his congressional salary. Since this was a political appointment of sorts I had to seek approval from White House personnel. The official responsible for national security appointments there was Margaret Carpenter, a former ACDA employee who had worked in the non-proliferation field. She was later a senior official at AID after Brian Atwood became director and she was working closely with the State transition team. Margaret refused to approve Ivo's position and this precipitated a meeting with her and Brian in which I was told that I was not authorized to make "political" appointments as there had been no decision about ACDA's future. I said that this was not a political appointment, and that ACDA needed help in congressional relations since the agency had to continue to operate, at least for now. They admitted that this was so, but it was the first week in April before Ivo was finally approved and by that time a lot of water had passed under the bridge. Ivo helped his case by applying continuous pressure from the Hill. Brian told me later that once he approved Ivo's appointment he knew that the battle for the survival of ACDA was over.

I formed a small group just to work on ACDA survival issues. The indefatigable Barb Starr was a member, as were Laura Holgate and Bob Sherman at the beginning. Ivo joined the group after he arrived, and Laura Holgate left in March to join Ash Carter at Defense. Mary Lib was also a regular member of the group. My original plan was to meet once a day to compare notes, but we met much more frequently than that, sometimes five or six times a day. We always had a meeting early in the morning before the agency staff meeting. I scheduled an agency-wide staff meeting at 8:30 every morning, as these were perilous times. As there had been no official appointments, the four bureau deputies (Norm Wulf, Don Mahley, O. J. Sheaks, and Lucas Fischer) acted as assistant directors; Mary Lib acted as ACDA general counsel. When ACDA was finally eliminated on April 1, 1999, all were still in place. Although I had reorganized and renamed the bureaus somewhat in September of 1993, they remained fundamentally the same. John Holum made no major organizational changes. Eric Kunsman, a career foreign service officer, had been brought to ACDA by Ron Lehman to work for his executive assistant. With the departure of Ron's executive assistant, I gave the job to Eric. Until he was assigned to Pakistan in June by State, he was a great help.

There was another personnel issue that emerged early on that did not have as happy a result. I had not long been functioning as acting director before I realized that I had the power to make appointments. The position of SCC commissioner was open—indeed, needed to be filled—as Bob Joseph, who had served with distinction in the position (with the accompanying ambassadorial appointment) under Ron Lehman, had resigned, and there would be another SCC session reasonably soon. The first incumbent, Sid Graybeal, had not had an ambassadorial appointment but was simply an executive branch selection. One of the first things that I did as general counsel in 1977 was to urge Paul Warnke to request from the White House ambassadorial rank for the SCC commissioner. It seemed to me, given the importance of the issues addressed by the commissioner, that the Senate should have a say in his taking the job. Paul agreed, and starting with Bob Buchheim, the Carter administration appointee, the commissioner had ambassadorial rank confirmed by the Senate. So I thought in early 1993 that it would be great if we could bring Sid Graybeal back to the SCC. It would be a good step for the country and the administration, and it would also help with ACDA survival to make so distinguished an appointment.

At NSC, Bob Bell had been given the arms control portfolio. Non-proliferation was kept separate and was retained by Dan Poneman, a most capable holdover from the Bush NSC and an important figure in mobilizing the entire U.S. government in the spring of 1995 behind the effort to secure indefinite extension of the NPT. Dan had similar responsibilities in the previous White House but with a lower rank.

I spoke to Bob about Sid Graybeal and he was very enthusiastic. I then offered Sid the job, noting that, with the ambassadorial rank, it was a presidential appointment. Sid wanted to think it over. He called me a few days later and said he would be happy to accept, but he would want a job on the scc delegation, or at least at ACDA, for his wife, Patricia McTate, with whom he had coauthored significant studies on the ABM Treaty and related issues and who was certainly qualified. I was anxious to have Sid at the scc and told him that, in principle, the idea was acceptable to me, but that the relevant ethics officials would have to approve. When I told Mary-Lib about the conversation afterwards, she was vehement in her opinion that I should not have agreed to that, even though I had made it clear that it had to be subject to ethics approval. I also discussed the issue with Bob Bell, who despite his negative reaction, said, "Let's try it with White House Counsel and see what they say."

Mary-Lib and Sid reviewed my memorandum to the NSC requesting an appointment for Sid and mentioning his request for a position for his wife. The White House counsel strongly disapproved, having recently endured the disastrous nominations of Zoe Baird and Kimba Wood for the post of attorney general. I told Sid that I still wanted to go ahead with his appointment, but that I could do nothing for Patricia, since ethics officials did not approve. Sid refused to accept this. He spoke with Bob Bell and wrote a strongly worded letter to the NSC. There was a lengthy discussion, but unfortunately Sid's condition could not be met. No offer was made to anyone. Subsequently, I asked Stan Riveles, who had succeeded Eric Kunsman as my executive secretary and who had expressed interest in the job, to go to the scc in an acting capacity. As a result of his fine work there, John Holum later appointed him commissioner, though without the ambassadorial rank, as ABM had become so controversial on Capital Hill that it was considered too risky to send such an appointment to the Senate.

I also approached Lint Brooks, the concluding START negotiator, about his heading the Joint Compliance and Inspection Commission (JCIC), the START I implementing body that was meeting on a provisional basis pending entry into force. I was interested in having Lint come on board for some of the same reasons that I had wanted Sid Graybeal, in particular, to add to ACDA's prestige. For the previous year, Steve Steiner, who since 1988 had been heading (with ambassadorial rank) the Standing Verification Commission, the INF implementing body, had been "double-hatting" as head of the JCIC. Lint seemed to think that my offer to him slighted Steve, which was certainly not my intention. I believed that there were two full-time jobs involved and that Lint, as Start negotiator, was ideally suited to head JCIC. To my regret, he declined the offer.

Another effort that I made to try to strengthen ACDA was to interest the press as much as I could in the ACDA survival story. Curiously, the only publication that I could interest on a consistent basis was *Defense News*, and they gave us a lot of coverage. I wondered if someone over in the Pentagon was helping us. Probably, the interest of *Defense News* was simply an example of the versatility of the publication. They did a long piece on me as acting director in their "One on One" feature, they covered other ACDA survival events, and they had a little piece on me when I was sent to the "woodshed," which I will describe later.

Further, I tried to engage the NGO community as much as I could. The Arms Control Association was by far the most helpful, although I received good advice and encouragement from many. Jack Mendelsohn, then deputy director at ACA, had good ties with *Defense News* and undoubtedly that helped. Meanwhile, Ivo was busily trying to stir up a hornet's nest on Capitol Hill. The only senator we could interest, with one most important exception that I shall discuss later, was Senator Dale Bumpers. The Congress in general seemed to have largely lost interest in ACDA, unlike in former years when they were very protective, but this was much better than the open hostility of the Republican Congress after 1994. In the House there was somewhat more support than in the Senate because of Ivo. We directly involved Congressman Martin Sabo, Chairman of the House Budget Committee, and Congressman Howard Berman, an influential member of the House Foreign Affairs Committee and chairman of the subcommittee with oversight over ACDA. Ivo also enticed the GAO into doing a cost study of State taking over ACDA, which rebutted one of Lynn Davis's key claims that a State takeover would save money.

Lynn, now an undersecretary of state, had taken over the point for State in the battle for ACDA, with the dissolution of the transition team and after Brian Atwood became immersed in a broad range of management issues as undersecretary for management. In February, I spoke with her several times about the advantages of an independent ACDA, but she had no intention of listening to such arguments. Also, I spoke with my friend Strobe Talbott, the new coordinator for policy toward Russia, with the rank of ambassador. Strobe was the architect of several important successes with Russia and the NIS, perhaps most significantly the return to Russia of strategic nuclear arms left on the territories of Ukraine, Belarus, and Kazakhstan after the dissolution of the former Soviet Union. He underlined the importance of the fate of ACDA and expressed neutrality on the subject for his part of the State Department. He urged that I get on as good terms as I could with Lynn. Hence, I tried to see her and talk with her on a number of substantive issues and sent her notes on various issues, but at the time I was never able to develop any kind of relationship with her—I guess our two positions were too polarized to permit that. However, with one notable exception, I did not have that problem with Brian—of course, we were former colleagues.

In late February, Brian Atwood called and said that the White House had decided to leave me in charge pending a decision on ACDA and thanked me for my helpful work. I tried to have as good a relationship with State as possible. I always went to Secretary Christopher's large staff meeting (about fifty people) on Wednesdays—the only one to which I was invited—and always spoke up, deliberately, with some kind of report on arms control. Several senior career people at State called me and said that ACDA had never been in better hands. That cheered me.

It was Christopher's practice to have topical reports made at these meetings. One Wednesday, Winston Lord, former Kissinger NSC and State Department aide, former ambassador to China, and new assistant secretary for East Asia and the Pacific, addressed the group on China policy. He opened his talk with a story about how, after several years as ambassador, he and his wife (the distinguished author, Bette Bao Lord) were granted the honor of being invited to one of the most famous monasteries in China. After a tour of the monastery led by the abbot, he politely asked if Win and his wife would each translate something from Chinese to English for the monastery. Taken aback by this singular honor, they both readily assented and, as Win put it, while the abbot went off to fetch the Chinese to be translated, he was busily practicing Kissingerian prose while his wife was doing Chinese couplets. The abbot shortly returned with two signs. One sign had "Men" in Chinese and the other "Women" written thereon.

Not long after my conversation with Brian, I decided to seek appointments with Bob Bell and Lieutenant General Barry McCaffrey of JCS to discuss the position that I was going to take on the CTBT as acting director. General McCaffrey—later the drug czar—was then the J-5 for JCS and responsible for arms control for the Chiefs, among other things. He had succeeded General Shalikashvili in that position. As J-5, Shali had been on the 1992 Bartholomew trip referred to in chapters 6 and 8. After we discussed CTBT, Barry told me that that a few weeks earlier "about ten guys in striped pants" (figuratively) had come over from the State Department to see him and asked him how he would view a State takeover of ACDA. He told me that he replied, in effect, "Gentlemen, please leave my office. What you are talking about is treason." I later paid a courtesy call on Shali after he became chairman in 1994. The principal subject he wanted to discuss was the CFE flank issue. He was an outstanding chairman and made a significant contribution to U.S. security.

There were other words of encouragement for ACDA. Tom Scoville, whom I later tried in vain to persuade to come back to ACDA after John Holum arrived and discussed with Tom a possible position, told me one day that Larry Smith (a long-time arms control figure now a special assistant to Secretary of Defense Aspin) had told him that OSD did not support those "shenanigans" at the State Department with respect to ACDA. The Department of Energy was also very much in our corner, and they made that clear.

The ACDA presentation before the House of Representatives for its appropriation request was scheduled for March 17, 1993, St. Patrick's Day. Bob Carr was the subcommittee chairman and we hoped for a good hearing. There still was no decision on the future of ACDA, but Bob Bell was preparing an interagency process to bring all agencies formally into the debate. Since there was no decision I had to make the best case I could for the ACDA appropriation. A statement was drafted for me, much like statements made in previous years, outlining the various ACDA programs and requesting appropriations to continue them. I decided two or three days before the hearing that, given the situation, I should send it to Brian Atwood and Lynn Davis so they could see what I was doing. Nothing was heard from State until the night before the hearing, when this draft was peremptorily returned with a paragraph inserted on the first page, along with a memorandum from Brian Atwood's office directing me to insert the paragraph. It said in effect that ACDA is requesting funding, but the agency may disappear in the near future. I was in a quandary as to what to do. Should I include it? Should I delete it and just go ahead since it was, after all, our appropriation? Eric Kunsman, Norm Wulf, and I talked about it until late into the evening. Norm suggested, "Why don't you keep the paragraph in the text, but note that it was included at the request of the State Department? That way, you clearly distance yourself and ACDA from the paragraph." This seemed the best of a set of bad options, so, reluctantly, that was what I did. I should note that Norm was a real stalwart. He was offered a job by Bob Galucci in the Bureau of Political-Military Affairs at State when the future of ACDA was still in doubt, but he declined and stayed with us. Norm was also the ACDA representative at the assistant secretary interagency level on CTBT. Norm did a superb job as he always did. I had been fortunate to have Norm as my deputy in GC in the 1983–85 period.

On the morning of March 17, I sent the statement to the subcommittee with the paragraph that State inserted on the first page, but with a lead-in saying that at the request of the Department of State, ACDA included the following in its statement. Also that morning, I decided that I would not simply give a summary of the statement and lay out ACDA's programs, as is normally done in these hearings. Rather, I would make an argument for ACDA independence from notes and close with a passage from John F. Kennedy's message to the Congress when he requested legislation to establish ACDA. And that is what I did. The small hearing room was filled to overflowing with about thirty people, among them no doubt watchdogs from State.

After my opening comments, Bob Carr asked me a few helpful questions, which led to answers about why ACDA mattered. Then he turned it over to Congressman Hal Rogers, the ranking Republican on the subcommittee, who obviously had read the statement. He said, "Mr. Graham, why did you include a paragraph because the State Department told you to do it? What right do they have to tell you, from another agency, what to put in your statement?" "Well sir, I was trying to accommodate them," I replied. "Who told you to do this?" "The Office of the Undersecretary for Management" (at this point I was thinking that it is a criminal offense to lie to the Congress). "What is the name of the undersecretary?" he asked. "Brian Atwood," I answered. And so it continued for about ten more minutes. After that I received some more helpful questions from a Democratic member who had worked for ACDA briefly in the 1960s. The hearing ended with some upbeat comments on the future of ACDA from Bob Carr, but I knew that there would be a firestorm waiting for me downtown, and I was not disappointed.

When I returned to ACDA I was informed that Brian and Lynn and others were meeting behind closed doors. I called both of them, but they would not take my call. I also sent a note to Lynn stating that I had not sought that line of questioning about the paragraph. I received no response. The next day I received a note from Deputy Secretary of State Wharton stating that I should meet him in his office two days hence, and that Lynn and Brian would be there. (After about a year as deputy, Wharton was made the fall guy for some difficulties with administration, so Strobe Talbott took his place. Wharton seemed a fair-minded man to me.) I informed Rose over in the White House about what was going on. She called Lynn, her former mentor at Rand, and tried to calm her down. Tony Lake called Wharton to try to keep the discussion in bounds. It somehow got around that I was being sent to the "woodshed" with Wharton, and this even found its way into *Defense News*.

The day came and I made my way to the deputy secretary's office. Wharton greeted me and invited me to sit on the couch in his outer reception area. He sat in a chair at one end of the couch and his special assistant, Bill Montgomery, later ambassador to Bulgaria, sat in a chair at the other end. There were two empty chairs directly opposite me. Then in came Brian and Lynn, their faces contorted with rage. They said very little at the inquisition. Rather, Wharton put questions to me in a sort of firm and rather authoritarian, but reasonably pleasant voice. He wanted to know why I was antagonistic to State. Several times I said that I was not, and that I had not solicited those questions. But, frankly, I did not know how to handle the paragraph, since it undercut our appropriations request. This went back and forth for about twenty minutes, and Wharton closed the meeting by saying, "Well, don't behave like that again." I assured him that I would not, and stood up and left without further words.

Later Barb Starr told me that she had spoken with Montgomery, who told her that Wharton said to him after the "woodshed" meeting, "He didn't sound so antagonistic to me." It was a painful experience and I wasn't sure what its impact would be. Barb Starr told me several times over the next few weeks that I should be proud of myself and that I would look back and regard this testimony as the turning point. I wasn't so sure, but she was right; it was the turning point in the ACDA survival battle.

A few weeks after this incident was over, I went to see Tony in his office to argue for the preservation of ACDA. He said that virtually every week when he had lunch with Secretaries Christopher and Aspin, "Chris" argued forcefully for the absorption of ACDA by State. What was he to respond? I made

Arms Control and Disarmament Agency

my standard argument, citing among others the Pakistan case. He asked me to put that on one sheet of paper and he would make sure that the president read it. I sent it to him the next morning. Also, I went to see Leon Fuerth, the vice president's national security assistant, a longtime colleague. He said, "What do corporations do when threatened with a hostile takeover? They manufacture a poison pill." He said that I should do the same with the Congress—good advice.

When I said above that because of a widespread loss of interest in ACDA in the Congress we could interest only Senator Bumpers—formerly Congress was very much the protector of ACDA, seeing it as its creature in a sense— there was one other senator whom we did not need to lobby and who always had been and remained passionately interested in ACDA, Chairman Claiborne Pell of the Senate Foreign Relations Committee (SFRC). He was the last of the founding fathers of ACDA left in the Congress and he really cared. He was a fellow Princeton alumnus, class of 1940. One day years before he had noticed me wearing my father's Princeton tie clasp that indicated the class of 1922. He asked me about it and I explained that it had been my father's. Ever afterwards he commented on my tie clasp, which I tried to remember to wear whenever I saw him.

Bill Parsons had been assigned by ACDA to the SFRC staff for one year, where he was working with Bill Ashworth on the ACDA situation. They tried to give the acting director and the agency as much exposure as they could. They asked me to be the lead witness for the ratification of the Open Skies Treaty in February and START II in May. Both hearings went forward without incident, but the May hearing had a special addition to it. Bill and I had discussed over the telephone the possibility of Senator Pell asking me a question as to whether the Clinton administration supported the broad interpretation of the ABM Treaty adopted during the Reagan administration (as explained in chapter 7), or whether the Clinton administration favored the traditional interpretation. I mentioned it to Bob Bell, who thought it a good idea, but my answer, which would repudiate the broad interpretation and declare the traditional interpretation correct, would have to be cleared interagency. Bob saw no serious problem with this. Therefore, in the hearing the chairman duly asked the question and requested an administration response for the record. I then drafted the response of only a few sentences, simply stating that it was the view of the administration that the traditional interpretation of the ABM Treaty is the correct interpretation. I then sent it out interagency and no one had any comment. I was therefore free to sign the letter to Senator Pell containing the response—by my signature I would be repudiating the broad interpretation and reestablishing the traditional interpretation of the ABM Treaty. All of GC was invited to stand behind me as I signed the letter—the picture hangs on my office wall. It was a long road from October 1985 to July 1993 and one that did not bring much credit to the executive branch of the United States government, until the end. I received a very happy letter from Gerry Smith and an even happier one from John Rhinelander, who said that he did not think that he would live to see the day when the broad interpretation would be repudiated. The *Washington Post* ran a story entitled "Clinton Administration Repudiates Broad Interpretation."

The struggle over ACDA continued. Lynn Davis, prior to testimony before the SFRC, told the staff that she had the votes in the Congress to merge ACDA into State. The GAO report now appeared indicating that merging ACDA into State would cost the government money, not save it. And in April, Brian Atwood finally relented on Ivo, and I brought him on board immediately in a non-career Senior Executive Service position. Ivo redoubled his efforts with the Hill, and by now the arms control subcommittee of the House International Relations Committee, chaired by Howard Berman, was showing definite partiality toward ACDA. Ivo took me to meet with Berman soon after he came on board and we had an excellent discussion. And the two Bills (Ashworth and Parsons) were keeping the fire burning with the legislation at the SFRC. Looking to the future, Bill Ashworth and I spoke about teaming up and asking Chairman Pell to urge Warren Christopher and the White House to appoint me as director and Bill Ashworth as deputy. Pell, as SFRC chairman, had great influence on selections such as this; it might have worked and I believe that Bill and I could have done the job effectively together. Bill was a virtual arms control institution in the Senate. Once John Holum was on the scene, Bill tried to make the same deal with him, but it did not work out, as I will later recount. Lastly, with respect to Senate support of ACDA, one of my major disappointments during this period was my inability to interest Senator Kennedy in saving the agency that his brother had founded.

In May, it turned out that Secretary Christopher was making a speaking trip to Minneapolis, so an attempt was made to have Hubert Humphrey's widow speak with him about the agency that her husband helped found and about which he had cared deeply. I was beginning to believe that we might win the ACDA battle, although I confess that somehow I never thought that we would lose. ACDA employees, however, did not all necessarily share this optimism, and except for those on the front line of the battle, morale was down a bit. Accordingly, I paid a visit to each bureau and office and I told people that I would do everything I could to save ACDA and that I believed that in the end we would win. These meetings did seem to help.

Congress, at least the two foreign affairs committees, were up in arms for ACDA now. The House committee was preparing its own legislation, which was pro-ACDA. Strong support was coming from the NGO community and I was able to do some more articles with the press. Stuart Taylor of *The American Lawyer* did a very positive piece on me as acting director. Bob Bell also had gone ahead with his interagency review of ACDA survival in lieu of a biased State study of the issue—a very positive development. The bottom line of this review—called Presidential Review Directive (PRD) 25, designed to lead to a presidential decision—was that three agencies, OSD, DOE, and ACDA, voted for an independent ACDA; two, JCS and CIA, took no position, but were perceived as leaning toward ACDA; and only one agency, the State Department, supported merger with State.

Several weeks after Christopher returned from Minneapolis, in early June, I was at home watching television when, around 9:00 P.M., the telephone rang. It was Wendy Sherman, Christopher's assistant secretary for congressional relations, later department counselor specializing on policy toward North Korea. She said that the secretary had decided to support an independent and revitalized ACDA, and that I should meet with Ted McNamara to discuss this and the ACDA-PM relationship. It was over! And ACDA had survived. I knew of course that we faced a long skirmish with State over where the border would be. But ACDA had survived.

The next day I did two things. First, I called Secretary Christopher and thanked him for his decision. He took my call right away, so he was probably expecting it. He said that Lynn had sent him many papers on the subject and her presentations had always been objective, setting forth both sides. But when he had gone to Minneapolis, he had learned, for the first time, how important ACDA had been to Hubert Humphrey and he would never want to do anything to derogate the legacy of Hubert Humphrey. Later, when John Holum came on board as director, at a staff meeting Christopher said that, with respect to ACDA independence, "It was not so much that I saw the light as I felt the heat, but now that John is here, I do not know how I ever got the idea of moving ACDA into State." Also, I called an all-hands meeting and announced that I had spoken with Secretary Christopher and he had said that he would support an independent, revitalized ACDA, so the conflict was over. There was long applause.

In July, after the ACDA battle was over and the agency vindicated, I testified before the SFRC on the ACDA authorization, accompanied by Ted McNamara, principal deputy assistant secretary of state for political military affairs, who was my opposite number in drafting the "peace treaty" as to how ACDA would in fact be revitalized. Bill Parsons and Bill Ashworth about this time began an effort to completely overhaul the ACDA Statute, including such things as abolishing the General Advisory Committee (GAC) and replacing it with a science-oriented committee, only the chairman of which would be confirmed (unlike the GAC, all fifteen of whose members had confirmable positions). The new committee never played any significant role, while the GAC had an important position in at least some previous administrations. I thought that the two Bills were going too far and that simple amendments would have been better, but I was far more interested in ACDA survival, and if that is what SFRC staff believed was desirable, then I could certainly accept it.

The discussions on revitalizing ACDA and determining where the line was between State and ACDA responsibilities lasted a long time and each point was sharply contested. Also, the reform legislation was wending its way through the Congress, pressed ahead by the SFRC. In the end, considerable improvements were agreed to and eventually enacted into law. But State dragged its feet on most and a permanent condition of border warfare prevailed between ACDA and State/PM during the remainder of ACDA's independent existence.

On July 2, 1993, after giving a speech in Chautauqua, New York, I received a call in my hotel room from John Holum, who told me that he had been selected by the president to be ACDA director, and that he wanted to work closely with me. We agreed to meet the next week in Washington. Meanwhile, Bill Ashworth had abandoned the idea of trying to persuade Senator Pell to call Christopher to propose the Graham/Ashworth combination, and he was now angling to become deputy under Holum. The White House, however, took the position that they wanted someone as deputy who had recognized executive branch experience in arms control-related work, because of John's lack of direct experience in the area. John and I met the next week and he was most gracious. He said that he felt inadequate replacing me. I told him to forget such a thought. He said he planned to lean on me heavily and that he wanted me to have whatever other position at ACDA I wanted. I thought about it overnight and concluded that trying to become deputy could be difficult, and I preferred to be an ambassador anyway. So the next day, when John and I met, I told him that I wanted to take the position of special representative of the president for arms control, nonproliferation, and disarmament with the rank of ambassador (Paul Nitze's old position), with special responsibility for NPT extension. He said the job was mine and that he would send my name to the White House after he was confirmed by the Senate and sworn in as director. In July this was still five and a half months away. During the remainder of my tenure as acting director, John concentrated on his confirmation and left the running of the agency to me.

One of the things that was long overdue in ACDA was a reorganization. Working with Barb Starr, Paula Scalingi, and others, I decided to enact one. I had long talks with the four acting assistant directors and came up with a plan that largely prevailed under John Holum to the end of ACDA. Lynn Davis attacked it as it was a perceptual improvement to ACDA, but when she complained to Holum, he said that he thought it was a good plan. Among the changes I made, the Bureau of Strategic Affairs became the Strategic and Eurasian Bureau (SEA) to match the current NSC structure. SEA was given a new Division of Defense Conversion because of Deputy Defense Secretary Bill Perry's committee on this subject and his personal interest in it. (This Division was effective for only a few years, as the committee slowly died on the vine after Bill became secretary.) CTBT was moved from the Non-Proliferation Bureau (NP) to the Multilateral Affairs Bureau (MA). Even though CTBT was preeminently a non-proliferation measure, as I had been saying during the CTBT debate, it was also an arms control measure and MA was going to be backstopping the negotiations in Geneva.

I worked long and hard on the Verification Bureau, which had been the focus of particular congressional interest since Richard Perle had called in 1977 and said the Senate was going to judge Paul Warnke's reliability by the fate of Fred Eimer, a deputy in the bureau, when Paul had abolished the bureau. The Pell Senate bill called for it to be an intelligence and verification organization. I decided to move Al Lieberman's separate, large, and efficient operations analysis shop, which did detailed computer modeling and the like, back into the bureau. I also tried to give the bureau an expanded intelligence role and to make it part of the Intelligence community (I went to speak to the new DCI, Jim Woolsey, about this, but the effort ultimately proved to be fruitless). I renamed it IVI, the Bureau of Information, Verification and Intelligence.

Later, on November 22, 1993, when John Holum was sworn in as director, I asked him for two things: that he appoint me acting deputy to serve until we had a confirmed deputy director, and that he select me as the delegation head of the second of the NPT Conference Preparatory Committee meetings (referred to as "prepcom") to be held in January 1994 in New York, since I was to be nominated as ambassador for the NPT. He promptly did both things on November 23, and he in turn asked me to help him recruit the other political appointees so that he could send all the names over to the White House in January. In the end all nominees but one, including myself, were sent to the White House in January: the deputy position took a little longer, as we had several false starts. As a result, I served as acting deputy until the end of August 1994 when Ralph Earle was sworn in, about a month past my swearing in as ambassador. I formally introduced John to ACDA at an all-hands meeting shortly after his swearing in. John was a close colleague for nearly four years and he did a superb job for the cause of arms control.

The White House was as insistent on diversity at ACDA as it was elsewhere. We had eight presidential appointment positions. It was decreed that two had to be filled by women and one by a person of Hispanic descent. The eight positions included the deputy, four assistant directors, two special representatives, with rank of ambassador (I was to get one), and the director (also already filled by a white male). The deputy position had to be someone of special qualifications, so it was implicitly decided that diversity would be the focus for selecting the remaining four assistant director positions and the one special representative position.

John quickly decided that he wanted Michael Nacht of the University of Maryland to head SEA. For MA he selected Katherine Kelleher and for NP he pondered for a long time between Larry Scheinman and Sandy Spector of the Carnegie Endowment. I did not know Larry, but I had known Sandy for a long time as one of the most preeminent experts in this field. He had written and frequently updated one of the best books on nuclear non-proliferation and annually hosted at the Carnegie Endowment the most prominent international conference in the field. I thought it would be a real feather in ACDA's cap to have Sandy come on board and, as a result, I supported him in the strongest possible terms. However, John and Sandy had an unfortunate interview in which John thought Sandy was telling him that he would not necessarily always follow his direction and in the end John selected Larry, whom others were strongly championing.

I worked hard on IVI, calling several qualified women, including Sally Ride, the astronaut, at the White House's suggestion, but she was not interested. Finally, John and I together decided on Amy Sands, a leading expert at Livermore Labs, who accepted. Meanwhile, John left it up to me to recruit the deputy. The first person I called was Stan Resor, who declined on the ground that he needed to spend more time at home. Next I called General Lee Butler, the retiring commander of the Strategic Command (STRATCOM). In retrospect, if he had been deputy, it would have been impossible for Senator Helms successfully to hold up the White House and force them to abolish, *inter alia*, ACDA in exchange for CWC. Lee said that he was intent on going into business. John then had several discussions with Janne Nolan, who had played a key foreign policy role during the campaign, but she declined, saying that she did not want a full-time position because she wanted to be home with her child. Finally, I spoke with Ralph Earle. John said that he knew him and liked him and believed he could work well with him. And he could not be challenged, since he was a distinguished former director. So I called Ralph and he said he would think it over for a few days. By this time I believed it most important that he accept because we really needed him. I saw his wife, Julie, at a party and she said not to worry. Finally, Ralph called back and accepted, but it was by this time too late for him to catch up with the other nominees.

One day in late January 1994, John came into my office and said, "You have to find me a woman for MA, and quickly, so we can send the nominees forward." Katherine Kelleher had just called and said that she could not accept because of her husband's illness. She had called a week earlier and said that she might have to withdraw. I thought and thought, "What woman do I know who would be good at that job?" After some time I thought of Lori Esposito, now Lori Esposito Murray, who had been a young staffer, fresh out of college, at ACDA during the Carter years. She had written her college thesis on the SALT I negotiations. Later, in the early 1980s, she worked for Spurgeon Keeny at the National Academy of Sciences and acquired a Ph.D. with a dissertation on Congress and SALT II. She had then worked for six years or so as the legislative assistant and arms control advisor to Senator Nancy Kassebaum. I had always been impressed by the quickness of her mind and her commitment to the subject. She was young, but perhaps she would be the right person, and, I thought to myself, she is Hispanic, so we would meet that requirement, and a Republican, which would be an added bonus.

I called Jim Timbie the next day and asked his opinion. He was enthusiastic, so I called Lori and told her what I had in mind. She replied that she had recently left Senator Kassebaum to take a less demanding job so that she could have more time with her children. An intense full-time job was not what she had in mind, but she suggested we meet and talk about it. We scheduled lunch at the State Department a day or two later. She arrived at my office on the scheduled day and won me over as we were walking down the hall toward the elevator to the eighth floor restaurant. She turned to me and said, "Tom, I was very young when I worked at ACDA before, so you probably still think of me as a young bimbo, but I am now a thirty-eight year-old mother of two." I replied, "Lori, you are on the mark, but I have to confess something to you. I am one of your great admirers and I believe you would be superb in this job, but I was also instructed to find a woman for this position."

At lunch we had a long discussion and Lori agreed to be considered for the job. I had mentioned her to John so after lunch I suggested that we stop by John's office to see if he was there and, if so, I could introduce her. He was there and we went right in. I introduced her to John, told him that she was highly qualified, and that he would never regret hiring Lori as assistant director. In a recklessly expansive mood I added, "John, with Lori, in addition to an outstanding, capable young woman, you have also an Hispanic Republican." Lori looked over at me with a sparkle (or a glint) in her eyes and said: "Tom, I am a registered Democrat and Esposito is an Italian name." So much for my ventures into diversity politics. I will say in retrospect, I believe the Clinton administration quota approach was positive as it forced me and no doubt many others to look where we otherwise might not have and we found capable, qualified people.

John did offer the job to Lori and she was confirmed after a long struggle. For whatever reason, Bill Ashworth appeared to try to block her in committee, claiming that she wasn't particularly effective when she worked for Senator Kassebaum. They were peers, and perhaps there had been a conflict in the past, but Lori stuck to her guns and, with the full backing of Senator Kassebaum, was passed out of the committee and confirmed. She did an excellent job as assistant director for a year and a half after which she left ACDA to work full-time on CWC ratification for the White House. And ACDA did meet its diversity goal by being lucky enough to hire for the second special representative position a leading member of the New Mexico Democratic Hispanic community who had the notably non-Hispanic-sounding name of James Sweeney. Jim had extensive engineering experience with the U.S. ICBM program and added much to ACDA in the scientific as well as diplomatic area for nearly four years. He helped me significantly on NPT with Latin America, being totally fluent in Spanish.

While I was acting director I tried to develop as good a tie to the military as I could. In a way, I thought of ACDA and JCS as natural allies. I had in mind the remark by a senior military officer complaining about Fred Ikle's moving ACDA too far to the right, to the effect that "State and OSD should be in the center slightly to the left and right respectively and ACDA should be on State's left and JCS should be on OSD's right, then let's fight out the issues, and that is how you get the best policy." This was somewhat consistent with what Harold Brown had told me in 1975 on a weekend trip from Geneva to Burgundy with him, his wife, Mike May, and Mike's wife. He said that he had upbraided Henry Kissinger for the downgrading of ACDA, saying, "Henry, you are going to be a lot more vulnerable at State without ACDA on your left." I proposed to STRATCOM that I bring a group of ACDA senior officials out to Omaha for a day of briefing. The commander-in-chief (CINC), General Lee Butler, graciously agreed, and I led eight senior ACDA officials to STRATCOM headquarters one day in August 1993. I spent the night before the discussion at Butler's house where I had a superb dinner and conversation with Lee and his wonderful wife, Doreen.

Needless to say, the next day was a most interesting experience, being briefed by the generals and admirals of STRATCOM, which now has the entire strategic triad under its command: the ICBM force, the strategic bombers, and the SSBNs. The highlight of the day was a full hour-long presentation by the CINC himself, in which he briefed us as to how nuclear weapons really could be, safely and effectively, drastically reduced and eventually prohibited someday in the future under appropriate verification and enforcement arrangements. And the enforcer could be STRATCOM, North Korea could be a type of test case, and we were fortunate that the first breach of the non-proliferation regime was by a country as reprehensible as North Korea. It was a brilliant presentation and it confirmed my long-held view that some of the most sensible and enlightened views on arms control come from the top ranks of the military.

As acting director I was the logical choice as head of delegation for the ABM Treaty Review Conference scheduled for late September in Geneva. I began assembling the delegation in the summer and I asked Bob Bell to be my deputy. He accepted, and at the first interagency meeting on the review, I introduced Bob as the deputy. He said, "Without objection, so ordered," the way they do it on the Hill, after I announced him. I had a large and capable delegation, including Stan Riveles from ACDA, who was to be the SCC commissioner. We were uncertain which newly independent states would actually show up, although earlier in the year at Bishkek, Kyrgyzstan, ten of the twelve had signed a declaration that said that they were ABM Treaty successor states (all except Armenia and Georgia). Russia of course was there, led by Ambassador Grigory Berdennikov. A Latvian representative appeared, asserting that he was there as an observer because of the Skrunda ABM radar located in his country. Belarus was represented by Andrei Sanikov, who later represented Belarus at the 1995 NPT Review and Extension Conference after he had become deputy foreign minister. Ukraine was represented by Konstantine Hryschenko, later also deputy foreign minister and at the NPT conference. Kazakhstan did not appear, although later they were active participants in the SCC and became one of the four ABM Treaty successor states. It was also reported that an Armenian general was seen in Geneva, but nothing came of that. That was it for participation. The two subjects discussed at the review were how formally to provide for succession and what to do about theater missile defense and the ABM Treaty, or what the United States referred to as "demarcation" (drawing a technical legal line between unregulated theater missile defense and regulated strategic missile defense).

The United States made clear that, as far as it was concerned, the two issues were linked, and while work could proceed on the two subjects separately, one subject could not be concluded alone; the two subjects must be resolved together. I delivered the U.S. plenary statement, and the table was set up with the United States on one side, Russia in the center on the other side, with Ukraine and Belarus on either side, and Latvia sitting by itself down at one end. Bob Bell and I did most of the negotiating and we met with each delegation separately, and in the case of the Russians, several times. Both Sanikov and Hryschenko expressed considerable objection to the United States' unwillingness to agree to the so-called Sullivan Plan (after the Australian ambassador) for expansion of CD membership from forty-eight to sixty-six countries. The U.S. delegation had carefully worked this issue since early in the year in Geneva, keeping Washington informed by cable. However, at the very last moment, Frank Wisner at OSD and Secretary Christopher learned that Iraq was among the potential new members (Israel and Iran had signed off on membership for Iraq). Their view was that a country under Chapter VII UN sanctions could not be a member of the CD. I went to see Lynn to try to stave off Christopher's decision, but to no avail. Tony Lake decided that the United States had to break consensus at the CD on the plan at the last moment when all others expected it to be approved.

This created a lot of bitterness, especially, of course, among those nations that had been expecting to become CD members, some of which had been observers in Geneva for years. It was this anger that Sanikov and Hryschenko were expressing to Bob and me at the ABM Treaty review. This stalemate lasted for years, until a compromise was formally worked out to permit Iraq to join—which could probably have been worked out in 1993 if there had been enough time. ACDA came in for criticism, but its reporting record was impeccable; it was just that the top-level people were not reading their mail—or, more accurately, were not being briefed as well as they should have been. The Iraq issue had been in the reporting for months.

Bob and I were able to negotiate a brief final document for the review that referred to the two issues, stated that the SCC would take them up, and protected the United States' position, which was that they could be worked separately but must be concluded together. And, in fact, with many ups and downs, that is what did happen in the SCC, with both issues being concluded and signed as agreements in September 1997. The Agreement on Succession was worked out relatively quickly and declared that Russia, Belarus, Ukraine, and Kazakhstan were the ABM Treaty successor states. The Memorandum of Understanding on Demarcation, by contrast, was very difficult. The line between prohibited and permitted systems was set at five kilometers per second RV reentry speed for the target vehicle against which the defensive missile could be tested, whereas in 1972 it was understood to be a little over two. Later, at the SCC, it was informally agreed in the 1970s that the demarcation was 3.2 kilometers per second. This was the reentry speed of the SS-N-6 RV, the slowest of the modern strategic ballistic missiles. Thus, the memorandum was unquestionably an amendment to the ABM Treaty requiring Senate advice and consent. On the other hand, succession occurs as a matter of law, and there was no requirement to submit the succession agreement to the Senate. However, in the Resolution of Advice and Consent to the CFE Flank Agreement worked out at the 1996 CFE Treaty Review, as I have mentioned, the administration unwisely agreed to submit the Succession Agreement to the Senate. This created the potential for a political attack on the ABM Treaty dressed up as a legal matter.

Nevertheless, in October 1993, everything looked rosy for the ABM Treaty, with the broad interpretation reversed in June and succession on track in October. But a serious threat lay just around the corner. There is nothing wrong with strategic defenses. In fact, they could be a good thing, and there may be an important role for them in a nuclear-weapon deep-cuts regime. They are good as long as they work, are cost effective at the margin (to use Paul Nitze's phrase)—or at least close, and as long as they do not make the strategic situation more dangerous than before. That any of these propositions is in fact the case remains to be proven today, much less in 1993. But there is so much money involved in these programs for defense contractors, and the issue of strategic defense can so easily be made into a religion, that it therefore becomes a political issue that is difficult for administrations to resist, despite the negative potential for national security.

With the termination of the SDI program in 1993, missile defense was searching for a new way to surface. It found the answer in part of the SDI program: the Theater High Altitude Air Defense system or THAAD. THAAD is, on the basis of capability, a strategic system, but it was labeled a "theater" defense system that could be argued to be necessary to counter Saddam Hussein's SCUD missiles and their successors. I attended two principals meetings on THAAD for ACDA, one in November while still acting director and one in January 1994, subbing for John, at which Defense vigorously

Arms Control and Disarmament Agency

made the argument that whatever was worked out on ABM demarcation in the SCC (or in some other forum) had to permit THAAD. OSD presented the case at the first meeting, arguing that THAAD would be deployed in such a way that its "footprint," the area covered by each deployment, would not be such as to threaten the effectiveness of Russia's strategic force. That it opened the barn door to subvert what the ABM Treaty was designed to do was without question. It was THAAD, therefore, that led to the insistence that the demarcation line had to be five kilometers per second. ACDA and State (Lynn Davis) strongly opposed this, but we lost.

In the end Russia agreed to this concept, hedged somewhat by constraints on even more advanced systems, and it appeared as though the treaty regime might be able to absorb this change and remain viable. However, the press for national missile defense in 1999–2000 brought into question whether the strategic stability associated with the ABM Treaty can last much longer. Perhaps it can if the national missile defense against the potential missile threat from so-called rogue states—the stated issue—remains limited. It seemed essential that any changes to the ABM Treaty to permit such a defense be minimal and that the ABM Treaty remain viable. Also, this issue must be addressed by the United States cooperatively with Russia, Europe, and China.

Another most important issue that should not go unmentioned here is the crisis with North Korea in 1993 and the negotiation of the Framework Agreement by the Clinton administration. North Korea had been suspected of diverting plutonium usable for nuclear weapons to a possible nuclear weapon program during a reactor shutdown in 1989. The United States persuaded the IAEA to ask for on-site inspection of two waste storage sites to check on this in 1992. In response, North Korea gave the required three months' notice of its intent to withdraw from the NPT pursuant to the terms of the treaty in early 1993. On the last day before withdrawal became effective, threatened with sanctions by the UN Security Council, North Korea agreed to negotiate. Ambassador Bob Galucci brilliantly worked out in the next eighteen months the Framework Agreement by which North Korea agreed to give up its existing nuclear program and agreed to eventual inspection of the two sites in exchange primarily for two 1,000-kilowatt, western-style nuclear reactors to be built on its territory by South Korea and financed by South Korea and Japan. It was a great achievement. As acting director and acting deputy, I sat in on many of the related principals meetings and it was my opinion that if the agreement had not been worked out and North Korea had proceeded to reprocess the spent fuel that it had abruptly withdrawn—over protest from the United States—from its operating reactor (enough plutonium for perhaps five bombs), we might well have attacked the reprocessing plant, which could have led to a catastrophic war. North Korea had spoken of turning Seoul into a "sea of fire." The stakes were high on this one.

Shortly after I was appointed acting deputy in December 1993, I asked

Norm Wulf and Susan Burk to come to my office. I told them that I was to be nominated special representative and ambassador to lead U.S. government efforts to extend the NPT. This began one of my best professional associations, with Susan Burk as we pursued indefinite extension around the world. Norm suggested I conduct some bilaterals in New York with the UN ambassadors of several key countries and volunteered Juliet Swiecicki (now Giese) who worked for Susan, to go with me. While riding up to New York on the shuttle with Juliet in mid-December, I told her that I thought I should not limit myself to UN ambassadors and representatives in New York and Geneva, but rather should go to the capitals of relevant countries. So we prepared a list on the plane. This was the inception of the worldwide campaign as described in chapter 11.

Jim Leonard, a long-time leading activist and thinker in non-proliferation and a former ACDA assistant director, called me in early January 1994 and said I should go to Geneva and make my pitch for indefinite extension to the UN Secretary-General Advisory Committee, which would meet there in mid-January. He arranged for me to be invited to the dinner given by the committee, where it was understood I would speak. This was my first serious presentation on behalf of indefinite extension and the beginning of the active campaign.

Beginning in mid-January 1994, I commenced the campaign for indefinite extension as acting deputy director, and after July as ambassador. While still acting deputy I did my best to help John between commitments made to the NPT campaign. After I left as acting deputy and Ralph was sworn in, I was sent to the office complex in the Columbia Plaza annex to the department, which I have mentioned. Once I moved from the central ACDA offices and concentrated on NPT extension, I usually was not included in front-office deliberations on wider agency policy. On the plus side, from 1993 to early 1995, NPT extension received relatively little attention. Thus, I could write my own instructions and proceed to get the job done, which is what I did.

Arms Control and Disarmament Agency

CHAPTER TEN **COMPREHENSIVE NUCLEAR TEST BAN TREATY**

The Comprehensive Nuclear Test Ban Treaty (CTBT) issue began to take center stage during my tenure as acting director. Perhaps the very first disarmament issue of the nuclear era was the effort to halt nuclear explosive testing. It began in 1955, just a year after the *Lucky Dragon* incident in which a thermonuclear test produced a much larger than expected yield and, as a result, Japanese fisherman aboard the *Lucky Dragon* were struck by fallout outside the area of the central Pacific cordoned off by the U.S. government. Fallout from a Soviet test fell on Japan the same year and concerns began to be expressed about the byproducts of nuclear explosions entering the food chain—particularly strontium-90 in milk. During the 1956 campaign presidential candidate Adlai Stevenson suggested a moratorium on nuclear testing, for which he was denounced, but in 1958 President Eisenhower announced a U.S. testing moratorium and the Soviet Union followed suit. However, in 1960 France conducted its first nuclear test in the Sahara desert and in 1961 the Soviet Union broke the moratorium with the largest nuclear explosion of all time (58.6 megatons). The United States responded with a vigorous test series.

Thereafter, there was renewed effort to move the test ban negotiations forward. The negotiations had been going on for several years, with verification and inspection issues remaining the principal stumbling block. The United States wanted on-site inspections and unmanned seismic stations on Soviet territory. The Soviets accepted both in principle, but the two sides could not get together on the numbers: the United States wanted the right to seven inspections per year, but the Soviets would only agree to three. The same was true for remote sensors—the principle was agreed, the numbers were not.

In order to bypass this stalemate and at the same time address the environmental issues associated with nuclear testing, President Kennedy, in a June 1963 commencement address at American University, proposed a treaty banning nuclear tests in the atmosphere, underwater and in outer space. The Limited Test Ban Treaty (LTBT), which was negotiated in ten days in July 1963 and entered into force in October 1963, resolved the most prominent environmental issues, but—except for the Threshold Test Ban Treaty and the Peaceful Nuclear Explosion Treaty—it led to more than twenty-five years of inaction on a comprehensive test ban. Also, with tests now underground for the United States and Soviet Union, it actually resulted in a considerable increase in the number of tests.

However, if the United States and the Soviet Union were inactive on the test ban, the rest of the world was not. In the late 1960s, the NPT was negotiated based on a central bargain of no further proliferation of nuclear weapons by the non-nuclear weapon states in exchange for eventual nuclear disarmament by the nuclear weapon states. By the time of the signature of the NPT in 1968, the non-nuclear weapon states had made it clear that they considered the negotiation of a comprehensive test ban as the litmus test of the commitment of the nuclear weapon states—principally the United States and the Soviet Union—to upholding their end of the bargain. For twenty years after NPT entry into force in 1970, most of the NPT review conferences essentially failed over the issue of U.S. and Soviet commitment to completing a CTBT.

But then there began to be movement. In 1990 President Gorbachev announced a Soviet nuclear test moratorium, which was continued by Russia after the collapse of the Soviet Union. President Mitterrand of France—apparently to the surprise of his military—announced a French moratorium, and in fall 1992 the Hatfield-Mitchell-Exon legislation, which called upon the United States to pursue a CTBT and provide for immediate commencement of a nine-month testing moratorium, passed the Congress. According to the legislation, after the expiration of the moratorium, if the government so chose, it could conduct five tests per year for three years (a total of fifteen) for strictly limited purposes. Three tests per year were to be for the testing of new safety devices for nuclear weapons, one test per year could be for reliability and the other for Britain (which had for years been conducting its nuclear testing program at the Nevada Test Site). After that, in 1996, a moratorium should be observed until a CTBT was signed unless "another nation" tested, at which point the moratorium would end. In earlier drafts of the legislation, the language read "Russia" instead of the phrase "another nation," but the co-sponsors agreed to broaden the escape hatch as a concession to the White House, which opposed the legislation and which hoped that China would bail the United States out after the fifteen authorized tests were completed. President Bush reluctantly signed the legislation because it was attached to the Department of Energy appropriations bill, which included money for the supercollider to be built in Texas and which was important in the context of the presidential elections (incidentally, the supercollider was never built). The Hatfield-Mitchell-Exon legislation had the effect of forcing the Clinton administration to make some key decisions in the spring of 1993. Bob Bell called me in February and said he had to hire a small staff to help him deal with this issue among others. He said that he was thinking of taking on Steve Andreason, who had worked for Paul Nitze, and asked if I knew him. I said I did not, but that I had heard good things about him.

I might note here that for many years at the State Department there had been circulating an apocryphal story about the LTBT negotiations. It was probably legend, but it is one of those stories that one wants to believe. As the story went, W. Averell Harriman, the United States negotiator at the LTBT negotiations in Moscow, about halfway through the negotiations which lasted approximately ten days, became convinced that if he could just make one key concession he could conclude the negotiations. He was negotiating with Lord Douglas-Hume, soon to be prime minister, for the United Kingdom and with Khrushchev himself for the Soviet Union. Since he did not have authority to make the concession, Harriman cabled Washington by secret cable to request permission. The answer came back the next morning—"permission denied." But Harriman, being Harriman, went ahead and made the concession anyway in the morning meeting with Douglas-Hume and Khrushchev. Khrushchev looked at Harriman and said, "You have exceeded your instructions."

Another of my favorite CTBT war stories involved Paul Warnke and President Carter's abortive attempt to achieve a CTBT during his term. Unfortunately, unlike 1993, his effort was never supported by the JCS or the nuclear weapons establishment, and therefore came to nothing. The Cold War was going on at full force at that time. Nevertheless, there were negotiations with the United Kingdom and the Soviet Union, initially led for the United States by ACDA Director Paul Warnke, later by Ambassador Herbert York, another distinguished former head of Livermore National Laboratory. Warnke was an effective advocate for the United States position based on years of success as a practicing lawyer. At one point early on, the Soviet Union unexpectedly introduced a novel and indeed absurd proposal for CTBT entry into force. The Soviet proposal, abruptly introduced at a plenary meeting in 1978, called for the CTBT to be signed and ratified by the United States, the United Kingdom, and the Soviet Union. It would then lie dormant for a period of eighteen months and if during that period the French and Chinese joined, it would enter into force. If not, the treaty would just go away. Warnke responded immediately at the table. He said he found the Soviet proposal "romantic." The treaty would just lie there like Sleeping Beauty waiting for the French and Chinese princes to come along and kiss it to give it life. The Soviets never again mentioned the proposal.

In February 1993, Bob Bell was circulating the idea that NSC would support a CTBT with a one-kiloton threshold, which was argued to be needed for verification reasons. OSD had similar ideas. And no one was supporting continuation of the nuclear weapon test moratorium imposed by the Hatfield-Mitchell-Exon legislation after the expiration of the nine-month period in

June 1993. Rather, all supported conducting the five tests per year for three years allowed by the law, after which a CTBT was to be signed unless another nation tested. At the time both Russia and France were observing nuclear weapon test moratoria, and the United Kingdom was bound by what the United States did because they used the Nevada Test Site. Only China was conducting tests. Through Timbie I sent Lynn Davis a note saying that it seemed to me that a threshold was a bad idea. After a few days, I received a vague response. With Mary Lib's strong backing and encouragement, I decided as acting director to have ACDA formally take the position of opposing any threshold, and extending the moratorium past June for the foreseeable future in the expectation of a CTBT. I decided that if I were going to go significantly against the emerging interagency consensus on the threshold issue, and totally against it on the moratorium issue, I had better seek counsel at least with NSC and JCS in advance. I had already tried with State, but to no avail.

As noted, the annual five tests allowed by the law were divided into three permitted to test new nuclear weapon safety devices, one for reliability, and one for the British. The problem was that the military had no interest in purchasing the safety devices that would be tested. Such devices would have cost around $6 billion, and one of the safety devices was a fire resistant "pit" (or core of a nuclear weapon) for weapons allocated to bombers that were no longer on alert. Reliability testing is not something that had been done very often historically. And a test program driven entirely for British testing would not have been acceptable to the three nuclear weapon laboratories or the Congress. There was no demonstrable purpose in doing the testing except simply to have nuclear tests (of course, other measurements could conceivably be piggybacked onto the tests). This did not seem to me to be sustainable. Further, and more important, in about two years we were going to seek to extend the NPT, we hoped, indefinitely. Negotiations being what they are, it seemed to be highly unlikely that we would have a CTBT in place by April 1995, a CTBT being the sine qua non objective of the non-nuclear weapon states. To add to the lack of a CTBT, a U.S. and U.K. test program, and probably the resumption of testing by Russia and France in response, would most likely eliminate any possibility for a permanent NPT. The threshold issue was also important in that a CTBT proposed by the nuclear weapon states with a one-kiloton threshold would be viewed as no CTBT at all, and simply as a cynical attempt to keep testing programs, albeit at a low level.

I called Bob Bell and told him what I planned to do. He told me that I should, of course, advocate what I thought was right. And when I met with General McCaffrey, he told me that my responsibility was to defend the NPT and that I should take whatever position would best accomplish this. In March, some of the CTBT issues began to sort themselves out. Since I was the acting director and had no acting deputy, I represented ACDA at both the deputies level and the principals level for CTBT as well as other issues. In these meetings, I opposed the one-kiloton threshold (embraced by all other agencies except State, which had a vague threshold proposal) on the ground that it would be viewed as no CTBT at all. I urged the continuance of the moratorium on the grounds that the fifteen tests were not necessary, since DOD had no interest in purchasing the safety devices, and that at the NPT Review and Extension Conference in 1995—with no CTBT in hand, which was likely—an active U.S. (and likely British, French, and Russian) test program would probably eliminate our chances for a permanent NPT. Further, how were we going to persuade Ukraine to give up the nuclear weapons on its territory if we were emphasizing the usefulness of nuclear weapons with a test program? Even so, all agencies came in strongly against the moratorium, including DOE.

At the deputies meeting I sat next to John Deutsch, who was then DOD undersecretary for policy. He vigorously opposed the moratorium and we had a bit of a back and forth. But he is a gentleman with whom debating serious issues is always a pleasure. In March, OSD began to move away from the idea of the one-kiloton threshold and the idea began to emerge that perhaps we could say we had a zero threshold, but argue to exempt experiments that did not produce more than four pounds of explosive yield (which is about what the United States had done during the 1958–61 nuclear test moratorium). Also, JCS put out a proposal to have a special withdrawal clause ten years into a CTBT if there was concern about the safety and reliability of the stockpile, so that tests could be conducted to address any concerns. I decided not to fight this one and was inclined to accept the four pounds idea, but I wanted to continue strong advocacy of the moratorium. The interagency battle carried on into the spring. Mary Lib had a series of talks with White House Science Advisor John Gibbons, and he was coming around to support the continuation of the moratorium.

Later in the spring, Bob Bell called a meeting in his office with Lynn, Frank Wisner (a long-time leader at State who had been inter alia ambassador to Egypt and undersecretary of state, who was now at Defense as undersecretary and would later be ambassador to India), and myself. Bob said that, now that all agencies had conceded on the one-kiloton threshold, we all should support the fifteen nuclear tests permitted by the legislation. Lynn and Frank, of course, said they would. Much to the consternation of all, I said that I could not, and that I would continue to support extension of the moratorium. The meeting broke up on a bit of a bad note.

In May the issue finally reached the principals or cabinet level. Present at the meeting were Tony Lake, his deputy Sandy Berger, Bob Bell, and Steve Andreason; DOE Secretary Hazel O'Leary and several aides; CIA Director Jim Woolsey; the White House Science Advisor John Gibbons; JCS Chairman General Colin Powell, Secretary of State Christopher, and Defense Secretary Les Aspin, each with several aides; and myself. There were three issues on the agenda: the threshold, the ten-year withdrawal clause, and the moratorium. I had gone to talk with DOE on the moratorium issue prior to the meeting and Mary Lib had again talked with the science advisor. I had not been able to see Hazel, but I spoke with her deputy, and he said that it was their view there that there is a time for an end to everything, and that nothing should just continue on forever with no rationale. I was cheered by these words. At the meeting, Bob Bell gave an opening presentation as to where the agencies were on the various issues. We spent a long time on the first issue, finally agreeing on no threshold and on the four-pound experimental exception. We also agreed on the ten-year escape clause for our opening position in the negotiations—this seemed minor at that time and I wanted to concentrate on the moratorium with the threshold issue largely won.

Finally, with about fifteen minutes to go in the one-hour meeting, Tony said, "Who will speak for the moratorium?" I raised my hand and gave the speech that I had used in the deputies meeting, stressing NPT extension and also Ukraine. I argued that if the United States resumed testing (and having the British tests in Nevada), Russia and China likely would discontinue their moratoria. Indefinite extension of the NPT in 1995 against a backdrop of all five nuclear weapon states testing likely would prove impossible. I further argued that the tests were not necessary and should not jeopardize NPT extension if they were not. Moreover, what credibility would we have with a Ukraine that wants to keep Soviet nuclear weapons left on its territory if we have an active test program.

General Powell said that our nuclear weapons were our "crown jewels," so we had to be careful in our decision. Secretaries Christopher and Aspin said that the political deal in the fall of 1992 was fifteen tests, so we should conduct fifteen tests. White House Science Advisor John Gibbons said he agreed with me. Hazel, however, to the annoyance of Tony, stopped the show. She said she was a new kid on the block and that she had not really had time to study the issue and consult her experts. She wanted to put off any discussion of this issue for two weeks so that she would have time to study and understand it. This created something of a furor, but she stuck to her guns. When asked about the position of DOE at lower levels that opposed the moratorium, she noted that she was the secretary. Grumpily, Tony announced that there would be no decision, no outcome to send to the president, and that the principals would meet again on this issue in two weeks' time. I reported back to ACDA that there had been no decision, but that DOE might change its position. I think everyone except Mary Lib (who always said whenever I went off to a CTBT meeting, "Now don't you give an inch") was a little surprised we had gotten this far with the moratorium issue.

A few days before the next principals meeting, I had an appointment with Hazel O'Leary to discuss the moratorium issue. Present, among several senior DOE aides, was Vic Reis, the overseer of the nuclear weapons program. Ivo went with me. It was an inspirational meeting. Hazel said that she was with us and that stopping testing was the right way to go. Of course, it would require a lot of laboratory support to maintain the weapons without testing. Vic made no dissent and seemed happy.

The second principals meeting on CTBT duly assembled in late May. This meeting largely focused on the moratorium issue, which was the remaining unresolved interagency issue. Hazel brought with her, among others, two senior lab experts to give a briefing on the status of the nuclear weapon stockpile. They explained how, for at least ten years, even if we were to do nothing, there was no problem with the safety and reliability of the stockpile. After that period of time they could not be so certain, but they were confident that any problems could be addressed successfully through means other than testing. After a lengthy discussion on this Tony went around the room on the moratorium issue. First, Tony turned to General Powell, who said that it is the responsibility of the secretary of energy to ensure the safety and reliability of the nuclear weapon stockpile. "My responsibility," he said, "is to the military. If the secretary of energy tells me that I need to test, then I want to test; if she tells me that I do not need to test, then I don't want to test." Secretaries Christopher and Aspin, who spoke next, reiterated their position at the first meeting—that there was a political deal for the fifteen tests, and that we should do the tests. Tony then asked, "Who will speak for the other side?" I raised my hand and gave again my by now standard speech, concluding that the moratorium should be extended until we have a CTBT, assuming no other nation conducts a test. Hazel then said, "I agree," and Jack Gibbons said, "I agree." Tony thanked everyone and, with that, the meeting ended. Since there was a split decision, the president would have to decide. I understand that Tony, in the next weeks, consulted senior members of Congress, such as Senators Nunn and Exon, and was assured that there would be congressional support for a continuation of the moratorium. Accordingly, on July 3, the president announced that, looking toward a CTBT, he was continuing the moratorium as long as no other nation tests, until September 1994 (renewable each year thereafter until a CTBT is achieved).

France and Russia had been observing a test moratorium for some time. Thus, it was up to China, and nobody was really sure what it would do. Hopefully, I thought, they would not want to isolate themselves. The summer passed in uncertainty, but then in late August intelligence reports came in that the Chinese were likely to test. By the time a principals meeting was scheduled in early September to address this, the likelihood had grown to certainty. Many feared the moratorium decision would be reversed. However, by contrast with the meeting in May—the same principals were present except that Jane Wales was substituting for Jack Gibbons—when Tony opened the meeting for discussion, Les Aspin said, "Our policy should not be determined by what some people in Beijing do." He was strongly seconded by Christopher, and it was quickly apparent that this was the unanimous view in the room.

So what some had feared might be a divisive debate and a threat to the moratorium turned out to be unanimous support for the moratorium policy. Thus was the moratorium issue institutionalized for the United States. The moratorium was continued each year from September to September until the signing of the CTBT in September 1996.

The First Committee of the United Nations, which deals with disarmament, meets from about mid-October to Thanksgiving. It has been traditional for the ACDA director to give the principal U.S. speech, and I did so as acting director in 1993. Ambassador Rick Inderfurth, Madeleine Albright's number three at the U.S. UN Mission (later assistant secretary of state for South Asia), sat with me. I had known Rick since 1977 when he was on the NSC and subsequently when he was chief of staff of the Senate Foreign Relations Committee in 1979 and 1980. Between 1980 and 1992 he was a prominent television journalist with ABC News.

In my speech, which was rather long and which I had to abbreviate somewhat because of time constraints, I announced that the United States, for the first time, would vote for the annual CTBT resolution at the United Nations. Afterwards, the Russian Ambassador Grigory Berdennikov congratulated me on a good speech, and Mexican Ambassador Miguel Marin-Bosch—long a thorn in the United States' side on CTBT—asserted that I had stolen his talking points.

After my speech, U.S. CD Ambassador Steve Ledogar gave a luncheon for me on the margins of the United Nations and many of the CD ambassadors were there. Steve introduced me as the man who had single-handedly brought about the moratorium, standing alone against the entire U.S. government. Sir Michael Weston, the distinguished United Kingdom CD ambassador, referred to being shut out of the Nevada Test Site for the one British test per year and complained about being treated like colonials.

I had expressed a brief interest in becoming the CTBT negotiator during the summer to Bob Bell, as I thought for a while that it was going to be an independent negotiation based in Washington. Phil Schrag, my deputy during the Carter years, was campaigning for the job, as he had an abiding interest in arms control. Ultimately, bowing to a degree to the wishes of our allies, the administration agreed to have the negotiations in Geneva, and Steve Ledogar, who negotiated the CWC, became the negotiator. Steve did a superb job as he always did, but the location of CTBT at the CD later demonstrated the complete obsolescence of that institution, in my judgment.

Since 1976, the CD has negotiated only two treaties, CWC and CTBT, both highly important to be sure, but both forced out of the CD rather than negotiated by it. CWC was forced through the CD—without the required consensus—by a strong-willed German ambassador who gave the CD his own draft treaty and a deadline, after which he would accept no changes. Of course, there had been groundbreaking work by Australia, and he had the strong support of the United States, the United Kingdom, and France. The CTBT was forced through the CD by the United States with great pressure because of our commitment to the Statement of Principles and Objectives of Non-Proliferation and Disarmament linked to the 1995 NPT extension, which called for a CTBT by 1996. In the end, the United States had to lead, along with Australia, an effort to bypass the Indian veto and take the treaty draft to the UN in New York for approval. The United States was indeed assisted enormously by Australia, which, in the end, carried the ball here as it had so many times in the past in the disarmament field. Australia asked New Zealand and Mexico, which traditionally along with Australia co-sponsored the annual CTBT resolution at the United Nations, but both countries declined, so Australia, to its very great credit, courageously agreed to go it alone and introduce a resolution in the United Nations in early September calling for UN endorsement of the CD draft of the CTBT.

During the NPT extension effort from 1994 to 1995, there were four preparatory committee meetings, and all were very important. The three held in New York were constructive, and important decisions were made. The one held in Geneva was nearly a disaster. To a degree, the CD has over time come under the influence of a clique responsible to no government, only to themselves. This makes serious negotiations very difficult. A case in point: In February 1996 I met Egyptian Foreign Minister Amre Moussa in Cairo and asked him not to support the various Indian positions in the negotiations, which were designed to block the CTBT, but rather to support the United States in our effort to push the CTBT through. I reminded him that the CTBT was a long-sought goal of Egypt. He said that Egypt very much supports the CTBT, the implication being that Egypt would not support the Indian positions. This seemed to have no effect on the actions of the Egyptian ambassador in Geneva, however, who continued to support the Indians.

Later on, in July 1996, when we were down to just a few issues in Geneva (most importantly the Indian objection to Article 14, the entry into force provision), Egypt was still supporting India at the CD. Moussa came to Washington late that month and Pierce Corden (in charge of backstopping in Washington for CTBT) and I met with him. I reminded him of his February statement and he reiterated support for the CTBT. That afternoon, I received a call from Kathy Crittenberger in Geneva saying that the Egyptian ambassador had just made a strong speech supporting the Indian position. She asked me if I could do something quickly. I called Nabil Fahmy, special assistant to Moussa, with whom I had worked closely during NPT and who was traveling with him. I recounted the situation to him. He said that he would take care of it immediately. The next day Kathy called me and said that you never saw anyone backpedal so fast. The CD should be kept as a useful debating forum, but any major multilateral negotiations should be held elsewhere, preferably in New York, where the UN permanent representatives are broader gauged and care about their countries' relationship with the United States—as do their political leaders in their capitals.

The CTBT proved to be as important to the achievement of the NPT indefinite extension in 1995 as I had argued in the interagency debate in 1993. Indeed, the commitment of the nuclear weapon states to conclude a CTBT by 1996, in the accompanying Statement of Principles and Objectives on Nuclear Non-proliferation and Disarmament, was the single most important step toward success at the NPT Review and Extension Conference. This will be discussed in chapter 11. The Hatfield-Mitchell-Exon legislation called on the United States to negotiate a CTBT. This was decided upon by the administration in 1993 and, as described, there was an ensuing interagency debate about the parameters of that decision.

The negotiations began in Geneva in 1994. There was no way negotiations for a multilateral CTBT beginning at that time could be concluded by April 1995, in time for the NPT conference, so the moratorium was crucial to indefinite extension. But also important was the absence of any testing threshold in the outcome of the negotiations envisioned by the delegates to the NPT conference. The United States still maintained its two- to four-pound mini-threshold in Geneva, but, by the spring of 1995, it was clear that this position was not going to prevail, and, just prior to the NPT conference in January, Washington had dropped its ten-year out clause. Thus, to keep faith with the NPT conference decision on indefinite extension and the accompanying commitments set forth in the Statement of Principles and Objectives, it was important to maintain this vision. But by the time I attended a NPT conference in Tokyo in June 1995, shortly after the conclusion of the NPT Review and Extension Conference, there were developments that threatened both the emerging CTBT and the NPT itself, specifically the announcement by France of its plans to resume testing and an effort to reopen the threshold issue in a major way in the United States.

Not long after my return from Japan rumors began to surface from OSD that they wanted to revisit the CTBT threshold issue. Secretary Perry was reported in the local California press as having made a statement at Livermore Laboratory that there should be a threshold of 500 tons. Other unnamed alleged Pentagon voices quoted in the press suggested 300 tons. At the same time, President Chirac of France, elected in May 1995, announced that France would no longer observe the Mitterrand moratorium. The moratorium had come too soon; France needed some further tests, and would conduct eight tests at its South Pacific test range, he said. This provoked a huge protest in Australia, New Zealand, and Japan. In New Zealand, French restaurants changed their names; Australia cancelled some major defense contracts (and a national union of prostitutes announced that one could no longer speak of the French kiss). Japan threatened to cut off all trade. Chirac was quoted in the press as complaining to an aide, "Why didn't someone tell me that this was the 50th anniversary of Hiroshima?" (1945–95). It appeared as though the indefinite extension decision might just unravel with this trampling on the associated Statement of Principles and Objectives.

I telephoned Jack Mendelsohn at ACA and called the Perry Statement to his attention. He began vigorously working the press. He created a small firestorm on the theme that if this idea of a threshold for CTBT was actually pursued by the United States, it would be a serious breach of faith with the commitments we had made at the NPT conference just two months before in achieving indefinite extension. John Holum commissioned me to lobby the State Department bureaus. It was obvious where ACDA was going to be on this issue, but it was important to prevent a State Department position in support of OSD, which Lynn Davis might try to organize. I then set out to lobby each of the bureaus in turn. The African bureau, the Near East bureau, and the East Asia and Pacific bureau were all adamant on the issue. They had clients who would believe that they had been betrayed if the United States should adopt the OSD position. The Latin America and South Asia bureaus were sympathetic as well. PM, influenced by Lynn, wanted to support OSD, and I spoke with Dick Holbrooke at EUR, who ended up siding with Lynn. In the end, five bureaus on June 20 wrote an extremely strong memo to Secretary Christopher, based on the recommendations I had made, that the United States must not adopt the OSD position as this would be a serious breach of trust. The five bureaus asserted that a test ban had long been regarded by the international community as the litmus test of the seriousness with which the nuclear weapon states take their NPT Article VI commitment. A U.S. decision to permit the nuclear weapon states to continue testing under a CTBT within a threshold would be regarded as inconsistent with the deal struck on NPT indefinite extension at the NPT Review and Extension Conference just one month before. The United States could be seen as acting intentionally in bad faith and this would be viewed as one more example of the double standard applied by the nuclear weapon states. The PM/EUR memo was somewhat unfocused and ineffective. As a result, State took a neutral (but leaning against) position on the OSD proposal on the threshold issue.

In the end, Tony Lake, with his usual brilliance, worked out a compromise with OSD. Washington announced on August 9, 1995, that it would support a zero-yield CTBT, the only negotiable option: the United States had advocated a two- to four-pound threshold; the Russians said that this was too low for them, that they needed ten tons if there was to be any threshold; the French said 300 tons; and the Non-Aligned Movement (NAM) said zero. In return for OSD and lab support of the zero-yield, the president made a statement in support of a strong stockpile stewardship program (to maintain the United States' nuclear stockpile in the absence of testing with computer simulations, etc.), initially budgeted at $4 billion per year. Under this program, each year the secretary of energy and the secretary of defense would have to certify jointly that the stockpile is safe and reliable—any failure to certify and the president is committed to consider a withdrawal from the CTBT under the supreme national interests provision and to resume nuclear testing so as to make whatever corrections are necessary. Many NGO supporters of CTBT in one and the same breath attack the Stockpile Stewardship Program, the laboratories' now established $5.3 billion-plus per year program to maintain the U.S. nuclear stockpile without explosive testing. But this is like biting the hand that feeds you. Without this program, there is no U.S. government commitment to a zero-yield nuclear test ban or to the CTBT in its current form. It is the equivalent of a vote against CTBT and reminiscent of the attacks by arms control supporters on SALT II as not enough arms control. The very next day, August 10, 1995, France announced its support of a zero-yield CTBT. Paris had been under tremendous pressure, having cut their tests from eight to six and announcing they would cease testing by the following spring and close their South Pacific test site.

The French had indeed unleashed a worldwide storm of protest. In addition to the enormously negative reaction in Japan, Australia, and New Zealand, they were being denounced around the world. Chile held a one-day nationwide work stoppage in protest. Ecuador blamed its recent series of earthquakes on the French tests, 10,000 miles away. Greenpeace sailed its ship near the test site and a young woman staffer broadcast to the world over the radio the sounds of the French military crudely storming the ship. In retrospect, the French tests were one of the best things that happened in the CTBT negotiation. As a result of this experience, the French really got religion. They closed their test site, they supported zero-yield CTBT, and they became one of the strongest supporters of CTBT, having been one of the most recalcitrant. The CTBT now seemed assured, but a new threat was to arise in January, in the form of the government of India.

In January 1996 an interagency CTBT White House strategy session was held with Bob Bell in the chair. The discussion focused on, among other things, the actual and anticipated CTBT tactics of the Indians in Geneva. India was creating procedural problems that were preventing the continuation of the CTBT negotiations at the CD by, for example, opposing the reestablishment of the ad hoc committee negotiating the CTBT at the CD. They were linking their efforts to a demand for a "time-bound" commitment to nuclear disarmament. This idea sounds good, but everyone knew it was a non-negotiable proposal, the idea being to have the nuclear weapon states agree to eliminate their nuclear weapons in specific stages and entirely by a specific date. No one can predict in advance the course of nuclear disarmament negotiations; there can be a commitment eventually to eliminate nuclear weapons, but not by a specific date—we do not yet live in a world where elimination is possible, given the worldwide intrusive verification and enforcement mechanisms that would be required. It was an impossible, even cynical, proposition advanced only for political purposes and everyone knew it.

I said in the meeting that I believed that we should accept the fact that the Indian government had decided to try to block the CTBT negotiations and that we should lobby their natural allies. Someone suggested that maybe I should assume this task. Earlier, I had spoken with Jayantha Dhanapala (see chapter 11) about it and he said that the key Non-Aligned Movement (NAM) countries to lobby were Egypt, Indonesia, and Malaysia, and that at all costs we should try to prevent Pakistan from making common cause with India, as this would impress many NAM countries since the two can agree on so little else. A few days later I agreed with John Holum and Lori Murray that I would try to lobby these countries. We decided to add two countries: Israel, to urge it to stay with CTBT, and Singapore, because a stop there would be convenient and it has influence.

A plan was drawn up in which I would visit those countries in early February 1996. However, Embassy Pakistan cabled back and said a visit in February would not be timely, as someone else was going to be there then (it was Sandy Berger)—I should come later. All other posts gave me clearance to come. I decided to go ahead, but postponed the trip to Pakistan until March. Also, since I had to make a six-hour stop in Tokyo between planes, I asked my assistant, Doug Shaw, to contact the *Asahi Shimbun* newspaper to see if they wanted to interview me. They had several times interviewed me in Washington since the June 1995 conference in Tokyo.

I was joined by Alex Liebowitc from Lori's MA staff, who caught up with me in Israel. In Israel, Foreign Ministry and Atomic Energy Commission officials told me that Israel planned to stay with and sign the CTBT if its verification concerns could be met. The Palestine area is one of considerable seismic activity. Already Israel had been accused of an underground nuclear weapon test by Libya, a charge supported by Egypt as a result of an earthquake on the floor of the Red Sea. Israel wanted protection from this type of false charge. If it could have this protection, then it would support the CTBT.

In Egypt, Foreign Minister Moussa told me that, while Egypt had a certain sympathy with the Indian arguments, CTBT was too important. He implied that Egypt would support the United States' effort to conclude a CTBT in 1996. Next, we went to Singapore, Kuala Lumpur, and Jakarta. We had good talks in Singapore and in Kuala Lumpur. Deputy Foreign Minister Karin said that Malaysia would not support the Indian position on CTBT and indeed he would speak to the Indian foreign minister about what they were doing.

In Indonesia, we met with Foreign Minister Alatas, a longtime leader in NAM circles and an advocate of the CTBT. He for years had worked closely with Parliamentarians for Global Action, an NGO that supported nuclear disarmament measures that helped Indonesia successfully advocate and ultimately chair the 1991 LTBT Amendment Conference, an effort to try to force a CTBT by amending the LTBT to extend its ban to underground tests. Parliamentarians for Global Action had a very resourceful staff man named Aaron Tovish, who was the liaison with Alatas. I had met Alatas twice before, both times when I was acting director, once in Washington and once at the UN. During 1993, I even called from my office in Washington to his cell phone in Jakarta to lobby his support on some CD issue. I began this meeting in 1996—Alatas was truly a central figure in the quest for a CTBT—with a speech emphasizing how long the world community had been pursuing a CTBT and that Indonesia had long been in the vanguard of this effort. Now we almost have a CTBT in our hands and we must not let Indian political objectives prevent us from achieving this long-sought goal. Alatas said that he agreed with me and Indonesia would not support the Indian position. Indeed, the very next week in Geneva, Indonesia withdrew its support for a particular Indian proposal at the CD. As a result of my discussion with Foreign Minister Alatas I could tell the *Jakarta Post* that "the Indonesian government enthusiastically supports the conclusion of a CTBT this spring."

On the way home we stopped in Tokyo for about six hours to change planes, arriving from Jakarta on the red-eye. I had heard nothing from Doug, so I had forgotten all about *Asahi Shimbun*. At Tokyo I was surprised to be met by an *Asahi* reporter shortly after I disembarked. He invited us to have lunch with him at the *Asahi Shimbun* offices in downtown Tokyo, with an interview to follow. I had not received a reply from *Asahi Shimbun* before I left on the trip and, assuming there would be no interview, I did not clear the interview with the United States Embassy in Tokyo. And I did not think to call from the airport. I was on the tail end of an 11–day trip around the world, having just stepped off the red-eye from Jakarta and perhaps was not at my sharpest. Of course, I should have called the Embassy. In any case, we had a good lunch and interview and I left for Washington. The next day the newspaper published the interview, and someone at the Japanese Foreign Ministry saw the interview and called the Embassy asking to see me. The Embassy had to admit that they did not know that I was in Tokyo. The day after I returned home a stinging rebuke arrived by cable from Ambassador Mondale. He said I was not to return to Tokyo without clearing it with him first. And, for whatever reason, the Embassy decided to leak the cable to the press. The resulting brief story, which appeared in the *Washington Post*, looked ridiculous, referring to Ambassador Mondale as an "American Shogun." I wrote an apology to Ambassador Mondale explaining the circumstances and cabled it to Tokyo. John Holum said in an ACDA staff meeting that he thought I had received bad treatment by the Embassy and he called Mondale. Mondale told him that he guessed that "he overreacted." I never received a reply to my letter, however. In June 1998 when I visited Tokyo for the Lawyers Alliance for World Security (LAWS), I had a good discussion with Ambassador Foley, and when I was there in September 1997, I met with the DCM and several Embassy officers. There seemed to be no lasting effect.

In March 1996, I scheduled a trip to Pakistan. In addition to discussions with the government in Islamabad, it was considered important that I meet with Ambassador Munir Akram, the Pakistani ambassador to the CD and an architect of their policy toward CTBT. Also, while I had been in Egypt the previous month, Nabil Fahmy had renewed an invitation to address the Diplomatic Academy in Cairo, which I had accepted. Further, the CFE Review Conference was now only two and a half months away, so I had work to do for that, as I wanted to make at least some capital visits as I had with NPT and I needed to go to the relevant HLTF meetings. Accordingly, I accompanied Craig Dunkerly to Brussels for two days for a meeting of the HLTF on the CFE Review Conference. I then went from Brussels to London to Liverpool, where the plane filled up with 500 Pakistanis, seemingly half of them young children in severe pain because of earaches, and then on to Islamabad. I had to keep the earphones for the airplane music at nearly full blast for most of the trip. After my discussions in Islamabad, I went from there to Abu Dhabi—the airport there is an interesting one; it has the only duty-free shopping area that I have ever seen that sells luxury automobiles—where I caught a plane to Cairo. Three days in Cairo, then on to Vienna for a stop-over at the JCG where I could have bilaterals with Kulybyakin, the Russian CFE representative who would also be their representative at the Review Conference, as well as other JCG representatives who were expected to represent their countries at the Review Conference. Then I went on to Geneva, where I had breakfast with Munir Akram, Bob Einhorn from Washington, and Steve Ledogar.

In Islamabad I stayed with Tom Simons, our ambassador. We had a long working lunch at the Foreign Ministry, which Tom and several Embassy officers attended with me. In my presentation I urged the importance of CTBT to the United States and world community and that Pakistan not obstruct its completion in Geneva. There was an interesting and civilized discussion, and the Pakistanis were sympathetic, but noncommittal. Afterwards, we had a meeting with the foreign secretary (the number two in the ministry), more or less to the same effect. He was perhaps slightly less sympathetic and urged me to discuss this with Munir Akram in Geneva.

This was my second trip to Pakistan in two years. While still acting director, I had decided to try to revive the practice of arms control bilaterals with key countries, conducted by ACDA. State/PM was initially hostile to this, but after several conversations with Ted McNamara, he finally agreed on the condition that the discussions be ACDA only, with no one from other agencies invited. The inspiration for the idea came from the military attaché at the Pakistani Embassy who, in the summer of 1993, invited me to bring an ACDA delegation to Islamabad. Because of scheduling concerns in Islamabad, I could not schedule this before February 1994. (While I was acting director we conducted one other ACDA bilateral in Mexico in October 1993. In this bilateral, the outgoing deputy foreign minister of the Salinas government said that if progress is made toward a CTBT by December 1994, Mexico would support indefinite NPT extension.)

In the February 1994 discussions in Islamabad, Munir (he was then probably the equivalent of a deputy secretary, later Pakistan's CD ambassador) headed up a broad interagency team for the bilateral arms control discussion and I brought Norm Wulf, Lucas Fischer, and others. We had a useful, free-ranging discussion of all major arms control subjects in the two days of talks. I had come to Pakistan via Colombo, Sri Lanka, where my discussion with the Foreign Ministry had been aborted (I had hoped to see Jayantha Dhanapala, who would serve as president of the 1995 NPT Review and Extension Conference, for the first time in connection with the NPT extension, but he had left the country the day before) as our plane broke down in Abu Dhabi for eight hours on the way there. Susan Burk accompanied me on this trip as far as Katmandu, where we attended an annual UN-sponsored arms control conference. I made a presentation there, and we had a discussion on the NPT extension with the Nepalese Foreign Ministry. They were quite wary of India and at this stage were non-committal. It was on to Pakistan from there, overnighting in Karachi, then up to Islamabad. While we were in Islamabad, the *Pakistani Times* had a front-page story on our visit and there was a cartoon that depicted paratroopers with "ACDA" on their helmets landing on the farm of an astonished Pakistani. One of the paratroopers was pointing a gun at the farmer and the caption read, "OK, hand over all your nukes, and do you have any chewing gum?"

Thus, when there in 1996, I had some background with Pakistan. I did a radio talk show in which I praised the Pakistani ambassador to the CD. There was also an interview with *The International News* published on March 8. I noted that in Geneva the world community had an opportunity to achieve a goal that it had sought for forty years, ending nuclear testing. I said that the CTBT being negotiated would represent "the best, and perhaps only, chance the world will ever have to achieve this long-sought goal." I reiterated what I had previously said on the radio: that the United States was asking countries not to create any linkages with the CTBT (as India was with time-bound disarmament). I was also asked a question about reports of Indian plans for a second nuclear test (the 1974 PNE being the first), to which I replied, "the United States has had a number of discussions on the topic with India. Indian officials have stated publicly that India does not plan to conduct a nuclear test and we take what they say at face value."

Tom took me to a meeting with the commander in chief of the Pakistani armed forces. He was also sympathetic, but noncommittal. I visited the house of Munir Khan, long a leading Pakistani nuclear weapons expert. He advocated some delinking of Pakistani nuclear weapon policy from Indian policy. And, most interestingly, the last night I was there Tom invited approximately thirty leading Pakistani thinkers on nuclear weapons (with diplomatic, military, technical, and journalistic backgrounds) for dinner. I was allowed to put forth the proposition that Pakistan should sign, not ratify, but sign, the CTBT, even if India did not. A lively three-hour debate ensued, the bottom line of which was that it was in Pakistan's national interest to do this, but that domestic politics would not permit it.

In Cairo, I spoke to the Diplomatic Academy, supporting indefinite NPT extension, and had an interesting discussion in the auditorium and later over the lunch that followed. The Egyptian diplomatic community remained hung-up over Israel in considering NPT policy, even after the 1995 NPT conference. Ambassador Ned Walker also arranged for me to speak at the Nasser Military Academy. After Walker, I was only the second American to do so, I was told. I was given a grand red-carpet reception and I gave a general non-proliferation speech to about 400 attentive senior officers. In the question period, they seemed much softer on the Israel/NPT issue than their diplomatic counterparts. I found all their questions, and there were a considerable number of them, to be informed ones. While in Cairo I had an interview with *Al Ahram*. The interviewer asked: "This is your second visit to Egypt within a month. What's going on?" I replied, "I came as part of U.S. efforts to urge the key non-aligned countries—Egypt being one of the founding members— to approve the Comprehensive Nuclear Test Ban Treaty in Geneva no later than the end of June."

I traveled on to Vienna and then to Geneva. In Geneva, I had another sympathetic but noncommittal discussion with Munir Akram, and in the end Pakistan did not join India in attempting to block the CTBT in Geneva. Bob Einhorn pressed Munir on commencing the Fissile Material Cutoff Treaty (FMCT) negotiations, one of the points in the 1995 NPT Statement of Principles and Objectives, a subject on which Pakistan had been particularly recalcitrant. Back in 1994, Munir had said at the bilateral discussion that India had significantly more nuclear weapons than Pakistan and the capability to produce much more fissile material.

In July 1996 came the great confrontation with India over Article XIV of the CTBT. Essentially, China and Russia, supported by the United Kingdom, took the position that the three threshold states, particularly India, had to be necessary parties for the CTBT to enter into force. Most notably, China made it very clear that they would not undertake a legal commitment to stop testing unless India did the same. Accordingly, in the final draft text of the treaty, Ambassador Raamaker of the Netherlands, the 1996 chair of the ad hoc committee, to avoid singularizing India, Pakistan, and Israel, fashioned an entry-into-force article that made all states (some forty-four, including North Korea) with nuclear facilities on their territory necessary parties to entry into force (EIF) of the CTBT. In addition, there would be an EIF conference three years after the opening of the treaty for signature and, as necessary, every year thereafter, to discuss ways of bringing the treaty into force. This essentially is Article XIV of the CTBT. At Chinese insistence, this conference was to have no power to bring CTBT into force, just to discuss how to do it, but of course sovereign states are sovereign states.

The Indians went ballistic and announced that they would break consensus and block the treaty from being sent to New York to be opened for signature, as was the CD practice. And after several procedural steps, India did just that: it blocked the ad hoc committee from submitting its report to the plenary, and it blocked the plenary from considering forwarding the completed draft treaty to New York without the report.

Immediately before the Indian action, there had been a lively debate within the State Department as to whether to concede to the Indians, drop Article XIV, and require a simple number of states to ratify in order to achieve EIF, as with the CWC. This was the traditional approach. India argued that Article XIV forced them to join the CTBT and was thus contrary to international law—both assertions untrue. However, this became a huge domestic political issue in India, with the government's stand being wildly popular. State favored concession. At a meeting in John Holum's office in mid-July 1996, attended by State Department Director of Policy Planning Jim Steinberg and a number of other State officers, as well as ACDA officials and Bob Bell, I argued strongly, supported by Bob, that we might be able to turn around the United Kingdom, but not Russia and China. They both had made it clear that they would not join a CTBT without India. And several months earlier, we had tried to placate India on this, but China and Russia had nearly scuttled the negotiations. We had no choice—without Russia and China there was no CTBT. John subsequently made that argument at a meeting in Strobe's office and we won the day.

But, what to do? Clearly, we had to bypass the CD and introduce the CTBT in the UN General Assembly (UNGA) in New York. As I noted earlier, we approached the traditional troika group (Mexico, New Zealand, and Australia) that each year for some time had been the introducers of the CTBT resolution in the UNGA in the fall. Mexico and New Zealand refused to cooperate, but Australia did take up the challenge. In early September, Australia introduced a resolution that called for the UNGA to approve the opening for signature of the attached draft CTBT (the CD draft). After floor debate, the vote was held and the resolution passed by a vote of 158–3 (India, Bhutan, and Iraq voting no). This was a stinging defeat for India. India was mortified that it was linked with Iraq. The foreign policy of Bhutan is controlled by India, thus in reality it was India and Iraq voting no. I was on the floor for the vote with Kathy Crittenberger, among others. After the vote, she tried to arrange a bridge game for that night, and she had lined up Michael Weston and me. She approached Munir Akram, a world-class player, and offered him a game, the stake of which would be Pakistani CTBT signature. Munir begged off.

So the treaty was opened for signature on September 24, 1996. The United States was the first to sign and eventually some 165 nations followed suit.

As of December 2001, there are 89 ratifications, including the United Kingdom, France, Russia, and Japan, but only 31 of the required 44. Many were waiting for the United States. However, the prime minister of India did say on August 16, 1999, that the government was attempting to build a national consensus on joining the CTBT. This commitment likely was overtaken by events in the wake of the subsequent and extremely ill-advised U.S. Senate rejection of the CTBT. The CTBT has indeed been the litmus test in the eyes of many of the NPT non-nuclear weapon state parties as to the bona fides of the nuclear weapon state parties' commitment to their NPT disarmament obligations. And a CTBT by 1996 was an important part of the price for indefinite NPT extension in 1995. On September 24, 1996, the United States (along with the other nuclear weapon states) paid the debt by check, but the U.S. Senate bounced the check in October 1999, with CTBT not even receiving a majority vote, much less the required two-thirds..

A few descriptive points about the CTBT are worth making here. Article I of the treaty sets forth the basic obligations. Pursuant to its terms, a party is not to carry out any nuclear test explosion or any other nuclear explosion, is to prohibit any such explosion at any place under its jurisdiction and control, and is to refrain from causing or participating in the carrying out of any other nuclear explosions. This language is based on the LTBT, but does not specify the four environments (i.e., atmosphere, outer space, underwater, and underground) set forth therein. To avoid any arguments about possible loopholes, the ban on nuclear explosions is universal. The phrase "any other nuclear explosion" is included to make it clear that the ban extends to so-called peaceful nuclear explosions, advocated by China during the negotiations, similar to the position advocated by the Soviet Union during the TTBT negotiations of the 1970s. There is a concession to China in paragraph one of Article VIII (review conferences), which provides that the first Treaty Review Conference (ten years after EIF, but with no special withdrawal right, as advocated by the United States until January 1995) may consider whether to approve by consensus peaceful nuclear explosions which must be conducted under approved procedures pursuant to a treaty amendment designed to preclude any military benefits (which is impossible).

It is important to understand that the treaty prohibits only nuclear explosions, not all activities related to a nuclear weapons program, for example, subcritical experiments. The negotiating parties were well aware of President Clinton's announcement on August 9, 1995, of the United States' acceptance of the goal of a zero-yield CTBT, but at the same time announcing the establishment of the Stockpile Stewardship Program with its attendant safeguards referred to above. Thus, the program was in effect tacitly approved by the CTBT negotiating parties and is contemplated by treaty language. But opponents of the CTBT should understand that the cost of the Stockpile Stewardship and Management Program (to use its original name) is only politically supportable if the United States does not conduct any nuclear explosive tests. And, from the standpoint of U.S. national security, it does not make sense over the long term to continue the voluntary moratorium on nuclear testing without the elaborate verification provisions of the treaty, which can only become fully operational upon entry into force of the treaty. In my judgment, anyone who opposes the CTBT inadvertently opposes a strengthening of U.S. national security, especially in view of the vast lead in nuclear weapon explosive technology that the United States currently enjoys and that will be dissipated if other countries conduct further nuclear weapon test explosions. One hopes that the Versailles-like action of the U.S. Senate can be remedied in the not too distant future. It is greatly in the interest of the United States and world security that this happen.

CHAPTER ELEVEN **NUCLEAR NON-PROLIFERATION TREATY**

The Nuclear Non-Proliferation Treaty (NPT) is the centerpiece of international efforts to control the spread of nuclear weapons. The treaty was signed in 1968, a time when the tool of multilateral nuclear arms control was relatively new and widespread nuclear proliferation was considered a likely development. Indeed, there were predictions during the Kennedy administration that by the late 1970s there would be twenty-five to thirty declared nuclear weapon states with nuclear weapons integrated into their arsenals. The NPT stopped this trend and formed the foundation for further successes in international arms control. There are still only five nuclear weapon states (the United States, Russia, United Kingdom, France, and China) recognized by the NPT, the same as in 1968. There are three nuclear capable states or threshold states (India, Pakistan, and Israel—with India and Pakistan, to the detriment of the world community, having conducted tests in 1998 and declaring themselves to be nuclear weapon states) that are not recognized by the NPT.

The multilateral arms control forum in Geneva where the NPT was negotiated—as well as the BWC (1971), CWC (1993), the Seabed Arms Control Treaty (1972), the Environmental Modification Convention (1976), and the CTBT (1996)—originally was called the Ten Nation Disarmament Committee and was designed to bring the East and West together in a common forum. Later, as explained earlier herein, as it expanded to ultimately sixty-six nations, it was called the Eighteen Nation Disarmament Committee (this was its composition at the time of the NPT negotiation), the Conference of the Committee on Disarmament, and finally simply the Committee on Disarmament (CD). It gradually lost its East-West character and became instead a smaller version of the United Nations First Committee.

During the NPT negotiations, most of the seventeen negotiating parties at the CD in Geneva (France didn't take its seat for many years) wanted an NPT of unlimited duration, as is the case with all other arms control agreements, but three countries (Germany, Italy, and Sweden) would not agree to a treaty of indefinite duration. They were unwilling to permanently give up the nuclear option. The Cold War was at its peak, no one knew how effective the NPT would be and whether many countries would join, and there was concern over whether the verification provisions—administered by the International Atomic Energy Agency (IAEA) and called "safeguards"—might put countries at a commercial disadvantage. This difference of view gave rise to the compromise language of Article X.2 in the treaty, which provided that twenty-five years after the entry into force of the treaty a conference would be convened to decide by majority vote whether the treaty should continue in force indefinitely, or be extended for an additional fixed period or periods. In other words, the NPT would be in force for twenty-five years and then the parties would decide by majority vote whether or not it should be made permanent.

This decision was delegated by Article X.2 to the conference, where it could be taken without reference to national legislatures (which would make extension a practical impossibility given the large number of states parties). Since the treaty authorized only one extension decision pursuant to this delegation to the conference, any further NPT extension after the one agreed to in 1995 could only have been done by amendment, which would of course require approval by legislatures. Further, because of the treaty's provisions on amendment, it is virtually unamendable. The conference thus provided a one-time opportunity to give the NPT the same permanence all other international arms control treaties enjoy.

Article X.2 provided for a decision by a majority of the parties, not just those present and voting; thus the location of the 1995 conference would be an important decision. The location would determine how many would attend, and, because of this voting provision, it was important to achieve as broad an attendance as possible. The treaty also provided for periodic five-year review conferences to review the operation of the treaty. The 1995 conference was to both review the treaty's operation and consider its extension. Soon after the 1990 NPT Review Conference, ACDA began analyzing the option of holding the 1995 conference at United Nations headquarters in New York, rather than in Geneva, where all the previous NPT review conferences had been held. New York would encourage broader participation, since many countries had a diplomatic presence there, but not in Geneva. It was decided by the states parties at the May 1993 preparatory committee meeting to hold the conference in New York. ACDA's analytic effort grew into an ACDA White Paper on the implementation of the NPT and strategy for the 1995 conference, referred to officially as the NPT Review and Extension Conference. (It was important for the NAM that "Review" be in the title of the conference, indicating that nuclear weapon state performance would be reviewed and that the review would come before any decision on extension.) This paper made a strong case for the indefinite extension of the treaty without conditions, and shaped the United States' position to actively promote this outcome. Indefinite extension was always favored within the U.S. government, but initially there was some internal consideration of a fallback position.

In 1991 ACDA began to identify opportunities for promoting indefinite extension without conditions. ACDA officials began to meet bilaterally with NPT parties to promote support for indefinite extension. In addition, U.S. representatives to several meetings of international organizations were armed with talking points in support of indefinite extension. In this fashion, first NATO, then the Group of Seven industrialized nations, and then the CSCE (now OSCE) were persuaded to endorse group statements in support of indefinite extension of the NPT without conditions as the most desirable outcome for the 1995 conference. The United States undertook these multilateral diplomatic efforts in close consultation with allies, including the two other depository states, Russia and the United Kingdom.

The other two nuclear weapon states, France and China, became NPT parties in 1991 and 1992, respectively. France was an early and consistent supporter of indefinite extension and made a significant contribution to the outcome in discussions in both the European Union and the Western Group, as well as through bilateral efforts with francophone states in Africa. China, however, remained an enigma throughout the process, publicly stating only that China wanted a "smooth" extension. At a dinner in Geneva in June 1994 French Ambassador Errera asked Chinese Ambassador Ho whether China favored indefinite NPT extension. Ho's answer was, "Indefinite? That is a good word, but we do not have that word in the Chinese language." It was my understanding during this process that China preferred indefinite extension, but they never said so publicly.

By 1993 a large number of supporters had been rallied behind indefinite extension, but a majority remained uncertain. NATO and OSCE comprised only about fifty of the then 160 NPT parties in 1993. In 1993 the South Pacific Forum (which included the membership of the Raratonga Treaty—the South Pacific Nuclear-Weapon-Free Zone Treaty) declared as a body for indefinite extension, thus adding ten more for a total of sixty. (Not all of the South Pacific Forum members were NPT parties in 1993. Three, Micronesia, the Marshall Islands, and Palau, joined the NPT before the conference in 1995, and supported indefinite extension. Two of these, Micronesia and the Marshall Islands had not yet joined the Raratonga Treaty in 1993.) However, support for indefinite extension among these sixty states was far from monolithic. The Soviet Union passed into history on December 25, 1991, and its twelve successor states spent much of 1992 trying to create foreign policies, including policies on NPT extension. Switzerland was reluctant to support indefinite extension, stating that it feared that a narrow majority might prove divisive. (I always suspected that their reluctance was not unrelated to the fact that the conference was to take place in New York, not Geneva.) This left approximately 100 states (almost all of them members of the NAM) uncommitted in 1993. Clearly, the NAM, which constituted a majority of the parties, would play an important role. No option could prevail against coordinated NAM opposition.

Indefinite extension appeared in 1992 and 1993 to be a long shot. NAM countries had a long history of attempting to use the NPT as leverage against the nuclear weapon states to extract arms control progress. The 1980 and 1990 NPT review conferences failed because of lack of progress toward a CTBT, and the 1975 and 1985 review conferences essentially papered over the differences. It appeared unlikely that the NAM leadership—such states as Indonesia, Mexico, Egypt, and Malaysia—would be willing to give up this leverage even for the security that a permanent NPT would bring. As a result, there was substantial skepticism within the Western Group that indefinite NPT extension was possible. Many viewed indefinite extension as a bargaining position from which a compromise such as rolling twenty-five-year extensions could be obtained. Rolling periods meant, for example, that at the end of each twenty-five-year period there would be another Review and Extension Conference and a majority vote would be required to go to the next twenty-five-year period. In addition to placing the NPT at risk every twenty-five years, I always believed that this was of questionable legality— Article X.2 contained no authority for further delegations of authority without reference to national legislatures. Of course, a series of fixed periods could have been agreed to—X.2 authorized that—with automatic transition from one to the next absent a majority vote not to do this. This would have been little more than specified group withdrawal—unsettling to the NPT regime, but legal under X.2. Until near the end of the process Conference President Ambassador Jayantha Dhanapala viewed successive twenty-five-year periods with automatic transition from one period to the next as the best possible outcome for the NPT, but he was not sure even this could be achieved. Indonesia, influenced by Greenpeace, was flirting with five-year rolling periods dependent on specific arms control progress at the end of each period to get to the next.

Only the United States never wavered in its pursuit of indefinite extension, although France and Australia remained generally positive throughout. However, given the number of NAM parties and the hard-line position of its leadership, it was clear that for the United States and others to prevail they would have to bypass the NAM leadership and appeal directly to the security interests of the individual NAM countries. When I took over the leadership of the U.S. effort to extend the NPT in December 1993 I made up my mind that I would give indefinite extension my best effort. Although few agreed, I believed that it was achievable if we remained optimistic, were creative, and never wavered. I also resolved to appeal to countries directly in their capitals, rather than deal with their disarmament representatives at the

CD or the UN. These representatives tended to form their own groups and many wrote their own instructions.

When John Holum was selected as director in July of 1993, he told me that he wanted me to have the position that I wanted. I decided not to ask for deputy director, since it seemed to me likely to be complicated, and I preferred a negotiating position in any case. So I said I would like the special representative position with the rank of ambassador and to have the NPT extension assignment as a first task. It was understood at that time that ACDA would select someone to head U.S. government efforts to achieve NPT extension. Therefore, the day after he was sworn in on November 23, 1993, he signed two memos, one assigning the NPT leadership to me and the other appointing me acting deputy director. It was understood that my name would be sent to the White House for the position of special representative of the president for arms control, non-proliferation, and disarmament with the rank of ambassador early in 1994 along with the other ACDA presidential appointees. Also, as part of this, I was designated the head of the U.S. delegation to the second, third, and fourth NPT prepcoms.

The first prepcom, held in New York in May of 1993, was chaired by the Netherlands, a Western Group country. The program of work for the conference was adopted, the date and location of the Review and Extension Conference (April 17–May 12, 1995, in New York) and the dates of the three additional prepcom meetings were decided, and the chairs of the second and third (but not the fourth) prepcom meetings were selected. Decisions were also taken on working languages and summary records. The NAM proposed Ambassador Jayantha Dhanapala of Sri Lanka for conference president, and the Eastern Group proposed Poland for the presidency. Controversy over the Federal Republic of Yugoslavia, including its status as a party to the NPT, led some delegations to seek its ouster from the prepcom; finally, it was decided to let the Yugoslavia nameplate remain in place so long as no one occupied the chair. This agreement held throughout the prepcom process and the conference, although there were periodic alarms. The U.K. chaired the Western Group at the first prepcom and remained in the chair throughout the NPT extension process. Russia was to a degree the leader of the Eastern Group, but it met only to discuss procedural issues. Indonesia as NAM chair was the non-aligned leader.

As I have described, in July of 1993, the United States fortunately took a major step toward the achievement of indefinite NPT extension when President Clinton announced that the United States was prepared to negotiate a CTBT and would continue the existing nuclear testing moratorium. The CTBT had been the main NPT-related objective of non-nuclear weapon states parties since the entry into force of the NPT. This decision put the United States squarely on the right side of this issue looking forward to the 1995 conference. Given the centrality of this issue, it clearly was important to make as much progress as possible toward a CTBT before the conference so as to convince NAM countries that a CTBT would in fact happen.

In October 1993 ACDA increased its efforts to promote indefinite extension. As acting director, I created a separate division dedicated to NPT extension (headed by Susan Burk) in the ACDA Nonproliferation Bureau and in December 1993, as indicated, John Holum selected me as special representative for NPT extension. I was later confirmed by the Senate as special representative and ambassador in July 1994. This made the United States the only country to have a dedicated NPT extension ambassador. I began the campaign for indefinite extension with an increased number of bilateral consultations commencing in December 1993.

The basic argument that I made to other countries was that because the Article X.2 procedure is built into the treaty, it was approved by parliaments in the course of ratifying the treaty, and thus on a one-time basis the delegates at the 1995 conference have the authority to extend the treaty. Any further extension would have to be approved by all the 160-plus parliaments—an impossibility in today's world. Thus, the 1995 conference would be the only opportunity to make this treaty, which is the cornerstone of international peace and stability and the base on which all other arms control and nonproliferation agreements are built, permanent like all other arms control treaties. Indefinite NPT extension is the best foundation for further progress in nuclear arms control as the nuclear weapon states doing the disarming need the security of a permanent NPT. And a permanent NPT is the best basis for peaceful nuclear cooperation. For example, a nuclear power reactor requires ten years to build and thirty years to operate, and the spent fuel has to be safeguarded forever. For the appropriate economic decisions to be made there must be assurance that the IAEA safeguards which flow from the NPT will not expire.

I conducted an intense schedule of bilateral (as well as multilateral) meetings in New York, Geneva, Vienna, and many capitals throughout the NPT extension process. During 1994 and 1995 I visited more than forty capitals in North and South America, Europe, Africa, Asia, and the Pacific. The idea behind these visits was to try to avoid discussing NPT extension with the NAM as a bloc, but rather to attempt to address this question with individual countries—to go to capitals to listen to the concerns of governments, and to the extent possible respond to them. It was important to avoid, if possible, a NAM-bloc position against indefinite extension. Many countries stressed the importance of a CTBT and some also emphasized the need for updated and legally binding negative security assurances—pledges by the nuclear weapon states not to attack non-nuclear weapon states with nuclear weapons (most of the NAM wanted this)—and positive security assurances— pledges by the nuclear weapon states to come to the aid of non-nuclear weapon states threatened or attacked with nuclear weapons (Egypt wanted this). Some countries, primarily in the Middle East, underscored the problem of Israel not being an NPT party. All countries urged more technical cooperation pursuant to Article IV.

However, the tone was usually different in NAM capitals than the positions taken by NAM representatives in New York and Geneva. Officials in capitals appeared to be more interested in a dialogue on the issue with the United States while representatives in New York and particularly Geneva appeared to be more influenced by NAM-bloc politics. But the most important thing was for the United States to make the effort to go to capitals and listen to individual country's concerns. Also, by means of these visits to capitals, I developed many professional relationships with diplomats and other officials in NAM countries that proved decisively valuable at the conference. Other ACDA and State officials visited additional capitals. In addition, U.S. ambassadors and other embassy officials around the world continuously and effectively made the case for indefinite NPT extension. The NPT Extension Division at ACDA played a vital role within the U.S. government effort by coordinating the global campaign of demarches and consultations in support of indefinite extension.

John Holum made many presentations on NPT extension at various fora during the process, as did I and others. ACDA Deputy Director Ralph Earle chaired the U.S. interagency effort in the endgame and was deputy U.S. representative at the conference itself, thereby freeing me from the administrative management of the now very large U.S. delegation so that I could continue to work with the delegates. It all worked out well. Secretary of State Warren Christopher (who made the welcoming speech to the conference and who, along with Holum and Undersecretary Lynn Davis, made a presentation to the Washington ambassadorial corps shortly before the conference) and the relevant assistant secretaries of state (the regional bureaus as well as PM) supported the effort and, when possible, made the case for indefinite extension personally to their foreign counterparts. During the conference itself Assistant Secretaries Pelletreau (Middle East), Raphel (South Asia), Watson (Latin America), and Moose (Africa), and East Asia and Pacific Office Director Huddle from Assistant Secretary Lord's bureau, came to New York to talk directly with the representatives from their regions.

In the fall of 1994 I prepared an interagency paper setting forth what I believed was needed to achieve indefinite extension. It focused on the need to get as close to completion of the CTBT negotiations as possible so as to make it appear to be a near-term certainty by the time of the conference (if the negotiations could not be completed before the conference); the need for updated positive and negative security assurances, and the strong preference among NAM states that they be legally binding; and the need to adhere as a protocol party to the South Pacific Nuclear-Weapon-Free Zone Treaty soon, and to be prepared to similarly adhere to the protocols of the emerging African Nuclear-Weapon-Free Zone Treaty when it was completed. It also discussed the threat posed to the process by the conflict between Egypt and Israel over the Israeli nuclear program, and the conflict between the Egyptian insistence that Israel take a "concrete step" before the conference in the direction of eventual NPT membership and the inability of Israel to take such a step at that time. The ACDA paper led to the development of an interagency paper on a game plan for achieving indefinite extension.

These papers caused increasing U.S. government-wide attention to the effort to achieve the goal of indefinite NPT extension. This process culminated in a deputies meeting held during the fourth prepcom (in late January 1995) at which an all-out U.S. government effort to achieve indefinite NPT extension was agreed. It should be noted that the deputies meeting was scheduled only after Barbara Crossette's major piece appeared in the *New York Times* in January 1995, during the fourth prepcom, describing how the U.S. government was unprepared for the soon-to-begin NPT Review and Extension Conference. Up to this time there was only marginal White House interest, and with Susan's help I wrote my own instructions.

The increased effort began in late January, after the deputies meeting, and continued through the end of the conference. By February of 1995, the entire U.S. government was visibly committed at the highest levels to achieving indefinite extension as a first priority. The Department of Defense and the National Security Council staff joined in with vigor. At my urging Hazel O'Leary made a highly influential personal appearance at the conference itself at a meeting of approximately 100 representatives sponsored by the Campaign for the Non-Proliferation Treaty—an alliance of prominent NGOs headed by Joseph Cirincione, a most effective supporter throughout the process. One of the NAM ambassadors told me, after her presentation, that it was the most persuasive speech that he had ever heard. I had negotiated with DOE and Joe for some time for Hazel to come and make this speech, particularly after she had made a useful speech on the margins of the fourth prepcom that had been praised by many delegates. And finally, the president and the vice president made clear their personal commitment: President Clinton mentioned it in his January 1995 State of the Union address, and Vice President Gore headed the U.S. delegation and made the all-important U.S. national statement at the opening of the conference.

All along, the position of the United States was for indefinite NPT extension without conditions. "Without conditions" meant simply that the extension of the treaty could not be voided and that the NPT would not expire if, for example, in the future certain disarmament goals were not met. In a July speech at Livermore, California, John Holum argued that one should not "gamble with something that you cannot afford to lose." I reiterated this in many of my speeches. Japan and some other parties initially had difficulty with the "without conditions" part of the formula because of their interest in ensuring that progress toward disarmament continued. However, this phrase was never meant to exclude a commitment to continued efforts

Nuclear Non-Proliferation Treaty

to meet disarmament obligations under the NPT. "Unconditionality" was simply intended to exclude legal threats to the continued life of the treaty, which would have in effect negated an indefinite extension decision, threatening a "worst of both worlds" outcome if a CTBT, for example, were not achieved. Japan and other states came to accept this and to support indefinite extension without conditions.

Most NGOs in the United States, while supporting indefinite extension, thought it impossible to achieve because of NAM opposition. However, they were stalwart in their support, through the campaign organization, primarily with the idea that by remaining firm the United States could get the longest possible extension at the conference, which they hoped would be some variation of twenty-five-year periods succeeding one another automatically, a series of fixed periods. They often urged the U.S. government to keep open the door for fallback positions, but I kept the door firmly closed. As mentioned above, many of the Western Group were of the same view, and Russia was as well. They were willing to fight hard for indefinite extension, but believed a fallback was inevitable in the end. I found myself often giving pep talks to the Western Group in 1994 and early 1995 to the effect that indefinite extension could and would be achieved. In this I was consistently supported only by France and Australia.

Among the many important members of the NAM in the NPT extension process, I identified five as particularly influential: Indonesia (as chair of the NAM), Egypt and Mexico (long-time leaders in non-proliferation and disarmament), South Africa (enjoying both President Mandela's global leadership role and being the only country to have destroyed its nuclear weapons and joined the treaty as a non-nuclear weapon state party), and Colombia (the next NAM Chair). Special attention was paid to these countries in addition to the efforts undertaken to appeal to the NAM membership as a whole. Most NAM members, above all, wanted to see a CTBT concluded. The United States, thus, put as much pressure on the CTBT negotiating process as it could and strongly defended the testing moratorium. For his part, President Clinton called for a CTBT "at the earliest possible date." The United States also well understood during the extension process the basic bargain of the NPT—no additional states would acquire nuclear weapons and those that had them would engage in disarmament negotiations aimed at their reduction and ultimate abolition. The United States worked hard to bring START I (succeeding on December 5, 1994) and START II into force, and I stated the U.S. commitment to the basic bargain of the NPT on a number of occasions.

It was also important for the United States to reiterate its continued commitment to the NPT-mandated goal of the ultimate abolition of nuclear weapons. Vice President Gore included this in his national speech to the 1995 conference. It was also included in the communiqué from the meeting in early 1994 between President Clinton and Prime Minister Rao of India, in which the two leaders stressed their commitment to the ultimate abolition of all weapons of mass destruction. I made much use of this document in speeches and bilateral consultations.

Virtually all NAM countries wanted to see more peaceful cooperation in the nuclear energy field under Article IV of the treaty and I did my best to listen closely and do what I could to lay the basis for increased cooperation. Australia and Japan were also quite active in bilateral NPT diplomacy supporting indefinite extension, and later on France, Russia, Germany and a number of others participated in a significant way.

SOUTH AFRICA

In August of 1994 Susan Burk and I, in the course of visiting several African countries to advocate indefinite extension, stopped in South Africa for two days of meetings. South African government officials emphasized South Africa's commitment to the NPT regime and they explained their new domestic legislation that buttressed the NPT regime. While dedicated to the NPT regime, in August of 1994 South Africa had not yet made a decision on NPT extension. They wanted a long extension, but also did not want a divisive result. I argued that indefinite extension would be the result most likely to establish the basis for further arms control progress and increased peaceful nuclear cooperation. Also, a permanent NPT would be a distinct security benefit to South Africa.

Part of the visit included a tour of its low enriched uranium (LEU) enrichment plant, the shut down highly enriched uranium (HEU) plant at Pelindaba, and the nuclear weapon fabrication facility at Wallendaba. Extensive briefings accompanied the tours. We were informed by our South African hosts that we were the first Americans to see the HEU plant and the nuclear weapon fabrication facility, except for two Americans on the IAEA inspection team. The South Africans explained that the entire nuclear weapon program produced six nuclear weapons (with a yield of approximately twenty kilotons each), involved a total of only 150 people, was very low budget, involved relatively simple "gun barrel" technology that did not need to be tested, and was completely hidden from view. They took us into the room at ARMSCOR where the weapons were assembled. They said, "Look around you, nothing has changed." There was nothing there that you would not find in a high school machine shop. They showed us the cases they used to move the weapons around, so we had an idea of their size: they would have easily fit in the back of a panel truck. They said that they were showing all this to us to make the point that a large infrastructure, such as the one Iraq had developed prior to the Gulf War, is not necessary to acquire nuclear weapons. Many countries, indeed, even sub-state organizations, could do what South Africa had done if they could acquire the fissile material.

Vice President Gore had several communications with First Deputy President Mbeki and I persuaded General Colin Powell to write to President Mandela. Both urged South Africa to think positively about supporting indefinite extension of the NPT. When I called General Powell to ask him to write the letter, saying it could be important to NPT extension, I told him that the South African desk had told me that he was one of two Americans to whom President Mandela might listen, and that was why I was calling. He replied, "who is the other one?" "Henry Kissinger," I said. "I've made the big time at last," he said.

I wrote the letter in draft while riding on a train to New York with Christine one weekend. I showed it to her and asked her if she thought it would work. She said she thought that it would be OK with a few editorial changes. I made the changes she suggested and then sent it to Powell, who made only a few changes himself. I had cleared the idea, but not the text, with Tony Lake and Strobe Talbott. NSC subsequently wanted to clear the text interagency, but no one would challenge a text that was now in the former chairman's language.

Early in 1995 South Africa began to speak of an NPT that was extended "in perpetuity." At the Nuclear Suppliers Group (NSG) meeting in March 1995 (South Africa being a new member), South Africa agreed to a communiqué that supported "perpetual" (changed at South Africa's request from "indefinite") extension of the NPT. South Africa had decided that it wanted to be a bridge between the Western and Eastern Groups and the NAM with respect to NPT extension. Its preference was for a permanent NPT, but whether the least divisive outcome was that or a rolling twenty-five-year extension had not yet been decided in Pretoria. Also in March, the South African government formally responded to the same effect in Pretoria in response to a U.S. demarche.

In early April 1995, the South African government told the U.S. embassy in Pretoria that it would support indefinite extension, but in a way that would bring the two sides together. The United States subsequently learned that this decision had been made personally by First Deputy President Mbeki after a long internal debate about whether South Africa's national interest lay in supporting indefinite extension or the NAM position for something less, with members of the ruling African National Congress on both sides of the debate. This decision was confirmed in Washington in early April in a discussion among the South African ambassador to the United States, ACDA Director Holum, and myself. The ambassador said that South Africa wanted a permanent NPT, but also wanted the NAM parties to be content with the outcome. After our NPT discussion in John's office, the ambassador reminisced a bit about President Mandela. He was a long-time colleague of the president's. He said that we might have noticed that the president never makes religious references in his speeches, even though he is a profoundly religious man. In South Africa, during the apartheid period, the Bible was used to justify the system, said the ambassador. So the president does not refer to the Bible in his speeches, he simply tries to ascertain what it is that Jesus would have him do—and does it. Impressive words, I thought.

It was apparent by this time that virtually all of southern Africa, as well as other states in Africa, would follow South Africa's lead. In August 1994 I had visited Namibia shortly before my stop in South Africa. At that time Namibia was strongly supportive of indefinite extension. However, by March 1995 Namibia had moved in line with the other members of the Southern African Development Commission in following South Africa's lead on the NPT. Foreign Minister Nzo—speaking on the third day of the conference, the same day as Vice President Gore—stated that South Africa would support indefinite NPT extension, but in the context of a statement of non-proliferation principles and objectives that would be the "yardstick by which all states parties can measure their non-proliferation and disarmament achievements and a strengthened review process."

Initially, the government in Pretoria was attacked in the local press for having sold out African interests and the NAM in response to U.S. pressure. By the end of the conference, however, the criticism had turned to widespread praise of the government as South Africa emerged as the key broker of the decision in New York.

EGYPT AND THE MIDDLE EAST

Egypt presented a special problem. During my April 1994 visit to Cairo with Susan Burk, Foreign Minister Moussa made it clear in no uncertain terms that Egypt, although devoted to the NPT, would not support indefinite extension or even a long extension unless, prior to the conference, Israel took a "concrete step" in the direction of eventual NPT membership. Moussa expressed his views in this meeting in the strongest of terms. Our voices were rather loud during this first meeting. Before we went in to see Moussa, Nabil Fahmy, his special assistant and a most influential official (he is the son of a former foreign minister and, beginning in 1999, Egyptian ambassador to the United States), spoke with Susan and me. He said, "Why Susan, by urging indefinite extension you are suggesting Catholic marriage (to a Muslim) for the NPT." "And what is wrong with Catholic marriage," bristled Susan, a devout Roman Catholic.

Afterwards, Nabil assured me that despite the harsh rhetoric, the meeting had been a success. I wasn't so sure. In my various discussions in Cairo on this trip, Egyptian officials noted that a large number of nuclear weapons with the capability of destroying all Arab nations in a few minutes existed right next door to Egypt. What guarantee did they have that some day— Egypt had no problem with the present Israeli government—some crazy extremist might not come to power in Israel? Like the man who had recently shot to death twenty-nine Palestinians at prayer in a mosque? No state could assure that such a thing could not happen.

The discussion with Egypt continued in Washington, New York, and again in Cairo. Foreign Minster Moussa's continual argument was that Egypt could not live forever with a huge, unconstrained nuclear arsenal on its border. What assurance could Egypt have that the Israeli government would always be in stable hands? I would reply that a short extension could destroy the NPT and did Egypt really want to risk the possibility of many states in the region and elsewhere acquiring nuclear arms? Egyptian officials would respond that perhaps a short extension would terminate the NPT, but that even so they did not think widespread proliferation would threaten Egypt more than it was threatened then. The Egyptians were never entirely clear as to what the desired "concrete step" by Israel would be, but mentioned things like agreement to negotiate a nuclear-weapon-free zone in the Middle East Arms Control and Regional Security Forum (ACRS), and something with respect to the nuclear reactor at Dimona in Israel. I made a second trip to Cairo to speak with Foreign Minister Moussa in December 1994, and went on to make public and private presentations in Israel and Jordan. During the second meeting, Moussa agreed to keep an open mind on NPT extension, but the Egyptian position never changed appreciably in spite of a number of direct discussions with the Israelis and meetings between President Mubarak, President Clinton, Foreign Minister Moussa, and Secretary of State Christopher. U.S. Ambassador Ned Walker believed by the end of 1994 that the Egyptians had made the NPT issue too public and thus could not move from their position. However, Egypt was never able to persuade the Arab League to back their position.

In my first visit to Egypt I did visit Arab League headquarters and had a useful, but quite general, discussion with the deputy secretary general, a Syrian. Jordan was skeptical of the Egyptian position. In Amman, Abdullah Toucan, the key figure in the Jordanian government for these subjects—as well as other senior officials—told me that they thought the Egyptian position was misguided, that Israel would eventually join the NPT, not as a result of confrontation but only after a long evolutionary period in which Israel's security could be assured. My first meeting in Jordan was a tumultuous public presentation in which the response to my plea for support from Jordan for indefinite extension drew strong denunciations of the Israeli nuclear program. Thus, I anticipated that my private, official meetings with the Jordanians would be difficult as well, perhaps like the meetings with Moussa. At the initial meeting one of the first things that one of the senior Jordanians said was how much he enjoyed his summer home on Cape Cod. I then thought that perhaps everything would be alright.

An Arab League meeting in March of 1995 held in part to address the subject came to no decision on NPT extension. In 1994, after visiting Cairo, Susan and I went to Riyadh and had useful discussions with Saudi officials, but received no commitment at that time. We also met with representatives of the Gulf Cooperation Council (the organization of Persian Gulf states). Their chairman said that the Israeli nuclear program did create political problems, but he did not speak in the strident tones of Foreign Minister Moussa. He said it would help if occasionally the United States would denounce the Israeli program "even if you don't mean it."

Also, in the spring of 1994 on our way to Cairo, Susan and I visited Morocco to solicit support from its government for indefinite extension. We stopped in Paris on the way and met with two of the leaders of the indefinite extension effort in Paris, Thérèse Delpeche of the Atomic Energy Ministry, an influential official and close advisor of Ambassador Gerard Ererra, French CD Ambassador and the leader of their NPT effort, as well as Daniel Parfait, a key official in the Ministry of Foreign Affairs. We also met with U.S. DCM Avis Bohlen at the embassy. Avis, one of the major figures in the U.S. Foreign Service in the arms control field, gave us good insights into French NPT policy. She was always someone you could rely on.

In Morocco, Susan and I were successful in obtaining a commitment from the government to support indefinite extension, although they waffled a bit later when all that trouble concerning Egypt surfaced. While Susan was laboriously typing up our reporting cable, I somewhat callously played hooky in the form of a round of golf on the Royal Salaam Golf Course—a great course. Late that night, after a good Moroccan dinner, we were driven to Casablanca and took the red-eye to Cairo.

My discussions in Israel in December 1994 were comprehensive. Israeli officials regarded the NPT as important. They said they would be willing to again consider taking some kind of step to address Egyptian concerns, but even though many meetings between the foreign ministers of the two countries were held during the run up to the conference, Israel never concluded that it was in a position to do anything. Before I went to Israel, State Department officials indicated that I would be given a very difficult time by the Israelis, perhaps the most difficult that I had ever experienced. Thus, my visit had to be carefully prepared. Nothing could have been further from the truth. I gave a speech on the importance of the NPT at the Jaffe Center at Tel Aviv University and the questions were all polite and constructive. Both Defense and Foreign Ministry officials understood the importance of the NPT. Several officials said that when Israel could be assured that Iran and Iraq were not threats to acquire nuclear weapons they would consider the NPT, but not before. In any case, they did not do anything specific to respond to Egypt.

Many discussions were held by the United States and other NPT parties with both Egypt and Israel. A considerable number of the discussions involving the United States were conducted directly by Secretary Christopher and Assistant Secretary Pelletreau. Foreign Minister Moussa made several trips to Washington and President Mubarak came to Washington just before the conference. Secretary Christopher discussed the NPT in Cairo several times. Nabil Fahmy also sought several additional meetings with me in Geneva, New York, and Washington to press the Egyptian case. This issue was never fully resolved, although an attempt was made to be responsive to Egypt and some of the Arabs by negotiating a resolution on the Middle East at the conference. It was only partially successful. Egypt and its Arab allies did sit still for indefinite extension, but reluctantly.

Interestingly, in early March 1995, the Senate Governmental Affairs Committee held a hearing on the NPT Review and Extension Conference—the only Congressional hearing on the issue. I testified, backed up by Susan, along with Jim Schlesinger (who held up for me to see a copy of *Arms Control Today*, which had reprinted my February 18, 1995, speech at an ACA luncheon, providing a comprehensive defense of the U.S. position) and Ken Adelman. Chairman William Roth presided and five other senators, including Glenn and McCain, attended. At one point Senator McCain asked me how Mexico and Egypt could justify opposing the United States on indefinite NPT extension, which is so important to the United States, given all the financial and other support that they get from us. I replied that I could not explain the Mexican position, but it had to be recognized that Egypt was located in a dangerous and difficult neighborhood. In March, when Moussa was in Washington preparing for Mubarak's visit, Nabil Fahmy came to see me. He said that the foreign minister had read my testimony and had sent Fahmy to express his personal gratitude.

At the conference, Egypt and other Arab states, in the absence of action by Israel, wanted a conference statement or resolution on the subject. Moussa was in New York and I had the opportunity, arranged by Bob Pelletreau, to speak with him early in the conference and urge Egyptian support for indefinite extension. Nevertheless, the night before indefinite extension was approved two days before the end of the conference, the Middle East situation was completely unresolved. Thus, around 4:00 P.M. a marathon session began with Dhanapala in the chair, the Egyptians and the Syrians primarily representing the Arabs (the Saudis, who had been out front, had faded from view somewhat), negotiating with the United States, represented by Ambassador Albright, Bob Einhorn, and me. This was the last piece of the four-part conference decision to be made the next day: the Indefinite Extension Resolution, the Statement of Principles and Objectives, the Statement on Enhanced Review, and the Middle East Resolution. At issue was an appeal in the Middle East Resolution that Israel join the NPT along with the three other states in the Middle East region that had not joined (Oman, the United Arab Emirates, and Djibouti). Israel objected to being mentioned by name and the Israeli mission was called every half-hour from our negotiating room by Bob Einhorn. After several hours of stalemate, representatives of the three states appeared and said that they did not want to be explicitly mentioned either. There was no solution other than a general exhortation for all non-

NPT parties in the Middle East to join. Egypt and Syria were so disgusted they refused to co-sponsor the text. Dhanapala firmly declined also and turned to me to ask if the depositaries would agree to co-sponsor—even though we did not yet have a written text. I replied in the affirmative for the United States, but said I would have to check with the United Kingdom and Russia. I told Dhanapala that I would let him know early the next morning.

I knew where the United Kingdom and Russian ambassadors were; they were at a dinner where I was supposed to be as well. So I walked over to the wall telephone and called the restaurant. Michael Weston, the U.K. ambassador, came to the telephone first and promptly agreed. Sergei Kislyak, the Russian ambassador said that he would have to check with Moscow. I then proceeded to join them along with the others from what we privately called "the Board of Directors" (the United States, United Kingdom, France, Russia, and Germany). This group of five states had agreed to meet together daily during the conference to coordinate efforts to achieve our common objective. Our meetings were essentially kept quiet and they proved to be most useful. The next morning at 7:30 A.M. Sergei called me in my hotel room and said that Moscow had informed him that he could co-sponsor. There was one condition, however. "What is that," I asked. "Moscow says I have to read it first," Sergei replied.

I then called Dhanapala and told him that the depositaries would co-sponsor (presumably Sergei would get his chance to read the text—which had only been printed that morning). This was duly done after the first three documents (the Indefinite Extension Resolution, the Statement of Principles, and the Enhanced Review) were approved. It did sound a bit odd: the Resolution on the Middle East was offered by the United States, the United Kingdom, and Russia after the first three were offered by the conference president. The resolution was held up on the floor for about two hours by the Iranian representative because of a positive reference to the peace process. A huge huddle developed around the Iranian representative, but this too was resolved and the last piece of the indefinite extension package was gaveled through about noon.

INDONESIA

Indonesia, as NAM chairman, regarded itself as the leader of the opposition to indefinite extension and remained so until near the end of the process. Many discussions were held with UN Permanent Representative Ambassador Wisnumurti in New York to no avail. Indeed, as late as the end of the week before the conference, Ambassador Wisnumurti, along with Ambassador Ibrahim from Jakarta, the head of the Indonesian NPT delegation until Foreign Minister Alatas arrived during the last week, invited me to their mission to discuss alternatives to indefinite extension. When I said that the United

States would not concede on indefinite extension, but would be prepared to discuss related issues, they broke off the discussion. During a mid-February 1995 trip to Jakarta, I found the Indonesian Ministry of Foreign Affairs to be immovable. Ambassador Ibrahim, the MFA director of political affairs, and Ambassador Sutresma, who was in charge of NAM relations, listened politely as I argued that a permanent NPT would be best for world stability, arms control progress, and technical cooperation, but they said essentially that if the United States would not compromise, it would be a difficult conference. A day or so previously, Ambassador Ibrahim had said at a hearing before the Indonesian House of Representatives that the reason Indonesia was reluctant to support indefinite NPT extension was the absence of a compulsory NPT deadline requiring the nuclear weapon states to eliminate their stockpiles. I was carrying a letter from President Clinton to President Suharto on NPT extension which also said that the United States would look "positively" on a Southeast Asian nuclear-weapon-free zone—long desired by Indonesia—if longstanding U.S. criteria for such zones were met. The letter was to be delivered personally by me to President Suharto, but I was denied admittance. The Chief of Indonesia's nuclear agency (BATAN), Dr. Djali Ahimsa, along with his staff, with whom I had a lengthy session in his office in Djakarta, favored indefinite extension—being concerned about nuclear trade—but had little influence on the MFA. My meeting with Ambassadors Ibrahim and Sutresma was reported in the February 17, 1995, *Jakarta Post* and I was accurately quoted as saying, "I wouldn't say that there had been great progress, I didn't expect that when I came here."

At the very end of the conference Indonesian Foreign Minister Alatas, observing the overwhelming support for indefinite extension, came to New York and made a proposal that cleared the way for agreement on indefinite NPT extension without a vote or, in effect, by consensus. This proposal was to link the agreed Statement of Principles and Objectives on Non-proliferation and Disarmament with the agreed Statement on an Enhanced Treaty Review, so that it was clear that the strengthened review process would consider observance by the states parties of the NPT Principles and Objectives. I wavered for a time because I was unsure how OSD would view this, but I had to decide on the spot. The Indonesian ambassador to the IAEA came up to me and said, "Oh come on, Tom, give us a crumb." I finally decided to take the chance. Unanimity was important, and no one ever complained. Upon acceptance of this, Ambassador Dhanapala's formulation on indefinite extension was agreed by consensus.

COLOMBIA

Colombia, after long deliberation, agreed to support indefinite extension. I visited Bogota in January 1995 for NPT extension consultations, arguing that a permanent NPT would be the best possible basis for further progress in arms control, that the nuclear weapon states doing the nuclear disarmament needed the security of an NPT extended indefinitely. The foreign minister and the vice foreign minister spoke positively about the benefits of indefinite extension and also of the need for arms control progress, particularly a CTBT. However, the foreign minister said that Colombia had to keep in mind its traditional positions. Traveling around Bogota with U.S. Ambassador Frechette was an experience—a cavalcade of armored vans, and sixteen body-guards armed with automatic weapons.

An exchange of letters took place between President Clinton and President Samper in February 1995. When I had visited Bogota in January 1995, Colombia was on the fence. The president's letter coming the next month appeared to turn the tide and gradually Colombia, the next NAM chairman, came around to support indefinite extension.

MEXICO

Mexico also supported indefinite extension, but in its own proposal (containing certain conditions) that was separate from the Canadian-sponsored proposal for indefinite extension without conditions submitted by 105 parties (eventually 111) at the end of the third week of the conference. Ralph Earle and I met virtually daily at the conference with Mexican Deputy Foreign Minister Gonzalez-Galvez, who attended Michigan State University for a year on a football scholarship and, after failing to make the team, spent his last three years at Georgetown University. These discussions were always constructive and they did help to move Mexico along the road to support of indefinite extension, but they did little to calm the anxiety in Washington. Mexico never sought support for, or co-sponsorship of, its proposal, but Mexico was the subject of many demarches during the extension process from President Clinton and Secretary Christopher on down. Indeed, its separate proposal was referred to in one of our intragovernmental discussions in the heated atmosphere of the final days of the conference as a "clear and present danger" to the national security of the United States. It was feared by some that supporters of the Canadian resolution might depart and support the Mexican resolution, which implied conditionality. Mexico did not seek this, nor was there any risk of it happening.

I had visited Mexico City in October 1993, and at that time was informed that Mexico would make its decision on NPT extension at the end of 1994. If the nuclear test moratorium was still holding among the four nuclear weapons states (U.S., U.K., France, and Russia) that were then observing a test moratorium and there was "significant progress" toward a CTBT, Mexico would support indefinite extension. In July 1994 the Mexican government assured Secretary of State Christopher that Mexico could support the

United States at the end. In January 1995 I visited Mexico and met with Vice Minister Rebolledo (Gonzalez-Galvez, the new deputy, was in Tokyo with Guerria, the new foreign minister) and asked that the new Mexican government reaffirm the position of the old. The response was equivocal. In February, Ted McNamara visited Mexico City carrying a letter from President Clinton to President Zedillo urging support for indefinite extension, but, like my experience in Djakarta, he was not permitted to deliver it personally. In McNamara's discussions with Deputy Foreign Minister Gonzalez-Galvez and Foreign Minister Guerria, he was asked by the Mexicans for special bilaterals with the United States on NPT extension prior to the conference. After several weeks, this was agreed.

Two special bilaterals were held between the United States and Mexico in the weeks before the conference. Prior to their commencement, in March 1995, I met with Deputy Foreign Minister Gonzalez-Galvez on the margins of the OPANAL general conference, held every other year in Vina del Mar, Chile. In the first special bilateral, held in Washington, Gonzalez-Galvez, accompanied by Ambassador Marin-Bosch, had several meetings with John Holum, Ted McNamara, and myself, as well as with Lynn Davis and Strobe Talbott. The second bilateral was in New York on the eve of the conference. Gonzalez-Galvez met alone with Ralph, Lynn, and me. Little was accomplished at these meetings.

For twenty-five years, Mexico had been a thorn in the U.S. side at disarmament conferences. In part it was a result of the strong Mexican desire to eliminate nuclear weapons, and in part it was the result of the overall testy U.S.-Mexico relationship. Also, following the Cuban Missile Crisis, Mexico was determined that it never be caught up again in such a crisis. This had been the motivation for the Treaty of Tlatelolco, the Latin American nuclear-weapon-free zone treaty. And from time to time Mexican diplomats would bring up the Mexican-American War and the loss of half of Mexico's territory. I was never sure whether they were really still consumed by this or whether it was a ploy. Mexico's rallying cry for a long time was to press for a CTBT against U.S. resistance. It was led for many years by Ambassador Garcia Robles, who received the Nobel Peace Prize for his efforts. He was succeeded by his able lieutenant, Miguel Marin-Bosch, who also pressed the United States for years and single-handedly wrecked the 1990 NPT Review Conference over the CTBT issue.

Marin-Bosch was seen by many as our great antagonist, and was still Mexican CD ambassador in 1995. He was from Brooklyn, went to Yale and Columbia Law School, and carried a big chip on his shoulder about the United States. He was brilliant, witty, and charming. The newspapers somehow picked up the idea that he and I were *mano a mano* over NPT extension. The *Washington Post* ran a six-part series on the extension issue right before the conference and in the last part had our pictures on the front page with the headline: "A Hard Sell for Treaty Renewal." The next day, the opening day, I walked up to the Mexican delegation on the floor of the UN General Assembly and asked if they had seen the *Post* story. "Oh, we have all read it," said Foreign Minister Guerria with a wink. Miguel suggested that he and I stage a fistfight on the floor for the benefit of the press. Marin-Bosch and the Mexican government were not, nor did they intend to be, a serious threat to indefinite extension by the time of the conference.

LATIN AMERICA

An Argentine delegation came to Washington for arms control bilaterals in the fall of 1993 and I hosted them as ACDA acting director. The delegation leader, a senior official from the Ministry of Defense, said in an emotional speech at dinner that Argentina had kept open the nuclear option, thinking it would add to their security, but it only served to cut them off from the countries with which they wished to be associated. So with the fall of the military dictatorship, they were free to end their nuclear program and join the NPT. Undersecretary Pfirter, later ambassador to the United Kingdom, and Assistant Secretary Enrique de la Torre were key figures in overcoming the military influence on this policy. In April 1994 I attended a conference in Bariloche, Argentina, on the peaceful uses of nuclear energy. At this conference Argentina made it clear it would join the NPT before the Review and Extension Conference, which it did in February of 1995, and support indefinite extension. I met with the Argentine ambassador to Washington in the summer of 1994 and he said in response to my inquiry as to whether Argentina remained committed to indefinite NPT extension, "We will be with you all the way." Argentina was a real inspiration and I often said so in speeches. At Bariloche I made the luncheon speech the first day. I spoke on behalf of indefinite extension, but I also used the platform to indirectly castigate Brazil, the largest country in Latin America, for not joining the NPT.

A Peruvian representative in Bariloche made an eloquent speech announcing support for indefinite extension and Peru remained a stalwart supporter to the end of the extension process. Peru was the last country I visited immediately prior to the conference, on my way home from the OPANAL meeting in Chile in March 1995. I wanted to thank them for their support. Bolivia had stated privately at the Bariloche conference that it would support indefinite extension, as did Ecuador when I visited there later in 1994. The members of CARICOM (the association of English-speaking Caribbean states) in New York, by means of a concluding statement by the chair (Grenada), indicated support for indefinite NPT extension at a meeting with me in June 1994 (nine of the thirteen members being present). Although there was debate, at the end of the discussion the chairman said, "Well, I guess we all support indefinite extension." No one refuted him and all these countries did support it. In January of 1995 at the United Nations, Honduras declared the support of the six Central American countries for indefinite extension.

An OPANAL seminar in January 1995 (a joint OPANAL/ACDA project) and the OPANAL biennial general conference in Chile in March 1995 were important meetings for rallying support in Latin America, leading ultimately to unanimous support from Latin American NPT parties for indefinite extension (having in mind the special position of Mexico). The January seminar, held in Cancun, Mexico, was attended by thirty-three Latin American states, including Cuba, and important progress was made there. This seminar, which was funded by ACDA and organized by OPANAL, was carefully worked out and proved to be a useful and constructive step along the way. Shortly before the OPANAL general conference I also made a presentation in support of indefinite NPT extension to the Organization of American States in Washington, which was well attended by member states.

ACDA and OPANAL (led by the most capable secretary general, Ambassador Roman-Moray, a distinguished career diplomat from Peru) worked closely together in 1994 and 1995. Ambassador Roman-Moray was a significant factor in the widespread support in Latin America for indefinite NPT extension. After the general conference in Chile, he was my host for the encouraging stop in Peru. Deborah Bozik, an ACDA expert on peaceful uses of nuclear technology, accompanied me to Chile and Peru (as well as Kenya and Ghana earlier). The 1995 OPANAL general conference was attended by representatives of all the other nuclear weapon states, as well as Ambassador Höelich of Germany, who made a persuasive presentation in behalf of indefinite NPT extension. I made a speech there as did the ambassadors from the United Kingdom, Russia, France, and China. At a bilateral discussion in Santiago shortly after the general conference, Chile indicated that it would join the NPT soon and that it favored indefinite extension. (Chile became an NPT party in late May 1995.) El Salvador, speaking at the conference on behalf of the six Central American states, reiterated their support for indefinite NPT extension. Argentina and Peru also made strong statements in support. Following up on Ralph Earle's meeting with the Prime Minister of Belize (CARICOM chairman for 1995) in Washington the previous week, I met on the margins of the general conference with Ambassador Martinez, the representative for Belize (and also ambassador to Mexico and former national chairman of the prime minister's party, who said that he spoke with the prime minister two or three times a week). He stated that there was no question that Belize would support indefinite NPT extension. We also had a useful discussion of Article IV (peaceful uses of nuclear energy) issues and he was surprised to learn that Belize could acquire nuclear medical equipment from the IAEA. This, combined with the previous meetings, suggested that CARICOM's thirteen votes would be for indefinite extension. (Four or five CARICOM states had at this time declared for indefinite extension in bilateral exchanges with the United States—most notably and firmly the Bahamas.)

OTHER IMPORTANT NPT PARTIES

Ethiopia indicated privately in the spring of 1994 that it could support indefinite extension. Ghana also declared its support for indefinite extension during my January 1995 visit. While in Accra I spoke with the foreign minister and First Lady Nana Konadu, an important political figure—my visit with her produced rather broad press coverage. I stressed peaceful nuclear cooperation. Later in the year, she came to Brookhaven National Laboratory in Chicago to attend the signing of a U.S.-Ghana laboratory-to-laboratory exchange agreement. I visited Kenya after South Africa and paid a visit to the Jomo Kenyatta Hospital to view the IAEA-provided nuclear medical equipment. (Apparently I was one of only a few official visitors to visit the hospital, judging from the press interest—there was a front-page story with a picture in *The Daily Nation* on August 27 quoting me as saying, "We want a peaceful and cooperative world civilization and this includes the peaceful use of the atom.") Kenya declared its support in 1994.

The UN ambassador from Senegal told me in 1994 that Senegal did and would continue to support indefinite extension as long as there was no official NAM position to the contrary (since they could never go against the NAM—that was the principal risk). Ivory Coast, Togo, and a number of others in conversations with U.S. diplomats or in diplomatic notes in 1994 and early 1995 stated that they would support indefinite extension.

In a dramatic presidential statement in early February 1995 the Philippines declared for indefinite NPT extension. When I arrived at Foreign Minister Romulo's office in Manila later in the month, the minister said, "We have announced our position. What else can we do for the cause?" This was important, as the Philippines was the chair of the Group of 77 at the United Nations, the non-aligned organization. In my press conference in Manila on February 14, I expressed the gratitude of the United States for President Ramos's decision to support indefinite extension. I was questioned about China by the press and replied that in the end China would probably support indefinite extension—as eventually it did.

Thus, by mid-February 1995 a majority appeared to be in hand for indefinite extension, and this number continued to rise to over 100 by the opening of the conference. In the April 9 article in the *Washington Post* mentioned earlier, the *Post* estimated that as of that date there were 79 NPT parties in favor of indefinite extension, 37 leaning toward it, 17 against, 23 leaning against, and 19 undecided. However, as support for indefinite extension grew, the goalposts moved somewhat. Article X.2 provided for a decision to be taken by a majority of the parties to the treaty. Countries began to join the NPT more rapidly as the conference approached, and, thus, the 160 NPT parties in 1993 became 177 parties at the conference (187 today with the accession, for example, of Comoros, Oman, Vanuatu, and, at long last, Brazil in July of 1997), raising a simple majority from 81 to 89.

The small number of countries opposed to indefinite extension never really coalesced around a single position until the waning days of the conference. In May 1994 Ambassador Taylhardat of Venezuela advanced a proposal at a Programme for the Promotion of Nuclear Non-Proliferation meeting in Caracas that attracted some interest. It called for a twenty-five-year extension and then another extension conference with the same powers as the one provided for in Article X.2 for 1995. Under Article X.2, the 1995 conference delegates had the power on a one-time basis to bind their governments to an extension without reference to national parliaments—any further extension could only be by treaty amendment, a practical impossibility. Since the original treaty text ratified by national parliaments provided for only one extension conference, this power was delegated by parliaments in Article X.2 when they approved ratification of the NPT, but on a one-time-only basis. Thus, as a legal matter, there could be no second conference with the power to bind parties to an extension decision without amending the treaty. The Venezuelan proposal would have required an amendment. This was persuasively pointed out by the French representative, Thérèse Delpeche, at the meeting in Caracas. I also made a strong statement along these lines at the Caracas meeting and in a June 1994 speech to the American Bar Association. This argument was reiterated by the European Union in a legal opinion submitted to the third prepcom meeting, and by Mary Lib Hoinkes, now formally ACDA general counsel, in a July 1994 article in the *Virginia Law Quarterly*. Mary Lib engaged thereafter, at my urging, in a spirited six-month battle with Bill Epstein, formerly of the United Nations legal staff, in a series of contending articles in that publication. One of his articles bore the simple title "Hoinkes Is Wrong." After these events there was a gradual loss of interest in the Venezuelan proposal.

The second prepcom in New York in January of 1994, chaired by the Eastern Group (Hungary), worked in a relatively constructive fashion. A number of prepcom procedural decisions, such as opening the meeting to non-party observers on the floor and NGO observers in the galleries, were agreed and Ambassador Jayantha Dhanapala was approved as the conference presidential nominee. The third prepcom in Geneva in September 1994, chaired by the NAM (Nigeria), initially worked effectively—draft rules of procedure and the conference agenda were almost agreed—but it broke down on the last day amidst a disagreement between the NAM, the Western Group, and the Eastern Group over the chairmanship of the fourth prepcom and the allocation of conference leadership posts. This dispute was not resolved until shortly before the fourth prepcom and for a time threatened both the orderly continuation of the extension process and the confirmation of Finland as the chair of the fourth prepcom.

Acting on behalf of the NAM, Indonesia submitted a document to the third prepcom that identified six areas in which "substantive progress" by the nuclear weapon states would "contribute to the successful outcome" of the conference. Mexican CD Ambassador Marin-Bosch played a prominent role in this effort, as he did during the entire NPT extension process. Briefly, these six objectives of the non-aligned states were:

1. agreement on a time-bound framework for the total elimination of all nuclear weapons;

2. adherence by the nuclear-weapon states to nuclear-weapon-free zone agreements, especially in the Middle East and Africa;

3. completion of a CTBT;

4. conclusion of a treaty providing legally binding positive and negative security assurances to non-nuclear weapon states parties to the NPT;

5. conclusion of a treaty banning the production and stockpiling of fissile material for nuclear weapons that is non-discriminatory, effectively verifiable, and universally applicable; and

6. guaranteeing free and unimpeded access to nuclear technology for developing non-nuclear weapon states.

The United States responded in February 1995, in a speech that I made before the annual meeting of the Arms Control Association with answers to each of the NAM objectives, demonstrating substantive progress in five of the six areas, while observing that the sixth was a non-issue. The real agenda for the sixth objective was nuclear assistance for Iran.

The first of the NAM objectives addressed the core obligations undertaken by the nuclear weapon states in Article VI to end the arms race and seek nuclear disarmament; I argued in my speech that it was perhaps here that the record of the nuclear weapon states was most demonstrably strong. In recent years the United States and the former Soviet Union had eliminated over 2,500 intermediate-range missiles and taken an entire class of weapons out of commission, decided unilaterally to withdraw and dismantle thousands more tactical arms, and in START I and START II, agreed to take more than 17,000 nuclear weapons off missiles and bombers. START I entered into force upon Ukraine's accession to the NPT on December 5, 1994, Kazakhstan and Belarus having joined earlier.

Further, I argued that the NPT's call for an end to the nuclear arms race had been met. Now, the race was on to bring nuclear force levels down as quickly and securely as possible. Since 1988, I said, the United States has reduced its total active stockpile by 59 percent; its strategic warheads by 47 percent; and its non-strategic nuclear force warheads by 90 percent. The United States is dismantling up to 2,000 nuclear weapons a year, the highest rate that technical limitations will permit, I said.

Second, I argued that the negotiation of an African Nuclear-Weapon-Free Zone Treaty (now the Treaty of Pelindaba) was nearing completion in January 1995. The United States had declared that it hoped to become a protocol party to this treaty and that it had the question of becoming a protocol party to the Treaty of Raratonga (South Pacific) under serious study. And, as noted above, in February 1995 President Clinton, in a letter to President Suharto of Indonesia, stated that the United States would look positively on the development of a Southeast Asian nuclear-weapon-free zone, assuming that long-standing U.S. criteria for such zones were met.

Third, the negotiation of a CTBT was actively being pursued in Geneva and considerable progress had already been made. The testing moratorium was being observed by four of the five nuclear weapon states.

Fourth, active negotiations on a new UN Security Council resolution updating positive and negative security assurances for NPT non-nuclear weapon states parties were well under way.

Fifth, in 1994 and early 1995, active efforts were underway to secure a mandate so as to commence the negotiations on a fissile material cut-off agreement in Geneva. A mandate to establish an ad hoc committee and commence negotiations was agreed in early 1995 (this later fell apart because of obstructionism by Pakistan).

Sixth, I argued that the reference in the NAM document to unimpeded access to nuclear technology was simply a front for Iran. No NPT party fully committed to its NPT obligations has ever been denied access to nuclear technology under safeguards. The reason that technology has been denied to Iran is because of concern over its commitment to its NPT obligations.

In order to make the Article IV case convincingly, ACDA and the Department of Energy compiled a database detailing instances of U.S.-supported technical cooperation with each NPT party. Having specific examples of past technical cooperation on hand, coupled with a ready willingness to discuss opportunities for future technical cooperation, allowed U.S. officials to quickly and effectively counter the argument, heard from many non-aligned states, that the United States is unresponsive to its Article IV technical cooperation commitments. Effective communication, backed by thorough preparation, turned discussion of U.S. compliance with Article IV from a potential negative into a strong positive in support of indefinite extension with many developing countries. Many countries thought Article IV assistance meant only power reactors, which a large number could not afford. They were unaware that it also meant assistance with things such as nuclear aid to agriculture and nuclear medical equipment. Ambassador Martinez of Belize in our discussion in Vina del Mar was surprised by this and said cancer patients in Belize had to go to Mexico for radiation treatment. I urged him to suggest that the government of Belize seek IAEA help in acquiring nuclear medical technology.

The fourth prepcom in New York in January 1995, chaired again by the Western Group (Finland), was constructive throughout. Under Mary Lib's leadership, the draft rules of procedure were agreed, except for the rule on voting, which was not agreed until immediately before the vote at the conference (some in the NAM were arguing for a secret ballot). The conference agenda, all conference leadership posts, and the financing formula for the conference were also agreed.

It should be noted that even then most parties believed that the United States would eventually back off indefinite extension and agree to something else. At a joint press conference with Egyptian United Nations Ambassador El Araby, sponsored by the Campaign for the NPT, I was asked about a proposal by George Bunn (the first ACDA general counsel from 1961 to 1969 and then a distinguished Stanford University professor and NPT expert) for automatic rolling twenty-five-year extensions. I replied that the United States did not support it, but rather supported indefinite extension. However, unlike the Taylhardat proposal, it was at least legally consistent with the Treaty. This was interpreted by a Reuters reporter unfamiliar with the issue as the United States falling off indefinite extension. The resulting inaccurate story was picked up by numerous papers, including the *Boston Globe*. The story was also reproduced and widely distributed to delegates and others at the conference by Greenpeace, even after I disavowed it publicly in a subsequent press conference called for this purpose in which I said that the United States had no intention of ever backing away from indefinite extension. Indeed, the story received front-page headlines in *Al Ahram*, Egypt's influential newspaper. The United States could be outvoted, I said at the press conference, but would itself vote for no other option. Ambassador Ned Walker in Cairo had to personally reaffirm this to Foreign Minister Moussa as a result of the *Al Ahram* article.

The role of Ambassador Ayewah of Nigeria should also be mentioned. He had been chairman of the third prepcom and chaired Main Committee I (on disarmament) at the conference. Several times in 1994 he publicly stated that the NPT should be extended only for two or five years and expressed Nigerian interest in nuclear weapons. While somewhat more moderate in private bilaterals, he continued this public stance. On the margins of the fourth prepcom, at another meeting sponsored by the campaign for the NPT this time for African ambassadors, a spokesperson for Ambassador Ayewah sharing the podium with me stated that "the only reason that Nigeria does not have nuclear weapons is that we cannot afford them now" (with the "now" emphasized). This attitude helped the cause of indefinite NPT extension among West African states. Indeed, after the speeches at this meeting about ten African ambassadors in the audience rushed up to me and asked how they could sign up right now for indefinite extension. In the chair of Main Committee I at the conference, Ambassador Ayewah seemed to regard the committee as a court to try the nuclear weapon states' observance of the Article VI obligations and as a result he was ineffective.

In January 1995, on the margins of the prepcom, the United States had suggested the formation of a small group of states interested in actively supporting indefinite extension to manage preparations for the conference. There were three useful meetings of this group in February and March in Geneva (on the margins of the CD) and early April in New York. Discussions in this group led to the idea that supporters of indefinite extension should try to submit a proposal to the conference with a majority of parties supporting it, if possible. Canada was suggested as the coordinator and this was later endorsed by the Western and Eastern Groups in Geneva in March. Canada did submit this proposal with 105 co-sponsors at the end of the third week of the conference, demonstrating conclusively that indefinite extension had the legally required majority support.

Negotiations on a new UN Security Council resolution updating positive and negative security assurances for NPT non-nuclear weapon states parties, referred to in the list of NAM demands at the third prepcom, had been under way in Geneva among the nuclear weapon states parties throughout 1994. Originally I had been asked by Assistant Secretary of State for PM Bob Gallucci to do this, but Steve Ledogar took it over in Geneva and did a fine job. Positive security assurances were especially important to Egypt because of the Israeli issue. There were also P-5 negotiations held on the subject of security assurances on the margins of the second, third, and fourth prepcoms and, in June 1994, in Vienna. This was a priority objective for Egypt as well as other NAM parties.

Egypt made a strong demarche to me on the margins of the second prepcom on the subject of security assurances. Ambassador El Araby said that it was important that positive and negative security assurances be updated and expanded beyond the existing 1968/1978 versions (1968 was the signing of the NPT, and in 1978 assurances were given by the United States, Soviet Union, and United Kingdom at the UN Special Session on Disarmament), and that they be made legally binding. Egypt was most interested in expanding the commitments of the positive assurances to increase the likelihood of international support should they ever be threatened by the Israeli nuclear program.

Most other NAM states were primarily interested in legally binding negative assurances as one of their quid pro quos for renouncing nuclear weapons. In 1994, twelve NAM states introduced a draft treaty on positive and negative security assurances in the CD. However, France—because of the importance of ambiguity in their nuclear doctrine—and Russia were strongly against explicitly making the negative assurances legally binding. Under the Treaty of Tlatelolco, the Latin American Nuclear-Weapon-Free Zone Treaty, parties enjoy a legally binding negative security assurance from all five nuclear weapon states as a result of signature and ratification of Protocol II of the Treaty by all five. The same is now true for parties to the Treaty of Rarotonga, the South Pacific Nuclear-Weapon-Free Zone Treaty, as well as parties to the Treaty of Pelindaba—the African Nuclear-Weapon-Free Zone Treaty—since all five nuclear weapon states signed the protocols of the three treaties after the conference in order to fulfill one of their commitments in the Statement of Principles and Objectives to support existing and future nuclear-weapon-free zones. The United States unfortunately is the only nuclear weapon state that has not ratified the South Pacific and African Protocols.

Security assurance negotiations were completed in Geneva in March 1995 and the draft resolution was forwarded to New York. The Security Council adopted it unanimously in early April, but only after vigorous debate. It expanded somewhat on the 1968 positive security assurances, and France and China were added to the three who made the assurances in 1978. The negative security assurances in the resolution followed those made by the three in 1978 (using the U.K. version, which, as explained below, has a narrower exception), adding France and associating China, albeit with a statement of its own based on its "no first-use policy." Neither the positive nor the negative security assurances were made legally binding and the negative assurances were outside the body of the resolution in the form of national statements. Several of the NAM parties, most notably Egypt and Indonesia, expressed considerable disappointment concerning the form of the assurances. Even though not legally binding—arguably—this commitment was very important to non-nuclear weapon states. After all, if they were permanently to forswear nuclear weapons, the least the nuclear weapon states could do was to promise never to use nuclear weapons against them. There was no qualification to this commitment (such as for an attack with chemical or biological weapons), with the one exception of an attack by a non-nuclear weapon state party in alliance with a nuclear weapon state (that is, the attack itself is made in alliance with a nuclear-weapon state—a narrow exception indeed), a holdover from Cold War days. These assurances were made most solemnly in association with a resolution of the Security Council and indefinite NPT extension depended upon them. The next year, 1996, the World Court indicated that these assurances should be considered legally binding as was already the case with respect to the protocols to the nuclear-weapon-free zone treaties. The French and the British have always regarded these commitments to be of special seriousness because of their form and the circumstances under which they were given.

Another important part of NPT extension diplomacy was persuading Belarus, Kazakhstan, and Ukraine, which had nuclear weapons left on their territories by the former Soviet Union, to join the NPT as non-nuclear weapon states and to support indefinite extension. Belarus joined the NPT in 1993 and its UN ambassador informed me in New York in June 1994 that Belarus would support indefinite extension; Kazakhstan joined the NPT in early 1994 and its Washington ambassador came to my office and informed me that his country would support indefinite extension in August 1994. In doing so, he mentioned that some 500,000 people in his country were suffering from radiation-related sicknesses as a result of the Soviet tests at Semipalatinsk. This focused all attention on Ukraine. As explained in chapter 6, I appeared before the Rada in October 1994 advocating NPT membership. The Ukrainian Rada finally approved the NPT in October 1994, having ratified START I in March, which opened the door for START I entry into force at the OSCE summit conference in December 1994. At the 1995 NPT conference, Ukraine was a firm supporter of indefinite NPT extension. Very important to persuading Ukraine to join the NPT was the negotiation and ultimate agreement by four of the five nuclear weapon states (absent China) to provide Ukraine country-specific negative security assurances. What was ultimately agreed to was the language of the 1978 U.K. declaration, which—as I indicated—had a narrower exception than the 1978 U.S. declaration and was the basis for the 1995 NPT assurances in that the actual participation of the nuclear weapon state in the attack creating the exception was required—not just a paper alliance. The assurance language was made Ukraine-specific and updated to include France, with the Helsinki Final Act language about borders being changed only by peaceful means added. The security assurance signed by the United States, the United Kingdom, Russia, and France was not made legally binding, although, as I said, in its 1996 decision on nuclear weapons, the World Court strongly implied that all these commitments are legally binding.

Ambassador Jayantha Dhanapala proved to be the best possible conference president. He was at the same time a committed non-aligned diplomat and dedicated to the strongest possible outcome for the NPT regime. On the margins of the second prepcom, in a bilateral meeting with Susan Burk and me, Jayantha expressed the view that rolling twenty-five-year periods, one succeeding the other automatically unless a majority of the parties voted "no," would be the best possible outcome. This was his preferred position throughout most of the process. In June of 1994, in a bilateral in Washington, I informed him that the United States had no intention of ever supporting an extension option other than indefinite. It was pointed out that the United States would be directly affected by proliferation should it occur anywhere in the world and as a result this was too important for United States' security to support a second-best option. The United States recognized that the decision was to be by majority vote and that it might be outvoted, but the United States would not support another option.

As the support for indefinite extension grew in the run-up to the conference, Ambassador Dhanapala changed his position. All along he had said that he wanted to see a consensus or near consensus result. Many in the NAM argued for this as a way of blocking indefinite extension. This contrasted with the stated United States and Western Group view that the treaty calls for a majority decision (because consensus could not be achieved in 1968), and a small majority for indefinite extension would be sufficient. But Jayantha believed a consensus outcome was important for the future health of the NPT regime. By the time of the conference, he had apparently concluded that perhaps he, as president, could find that there was a consensus that a majority favored indefinite extension and thus could gavel through indefinite extension without a vote on a no objection basis—a "parliamentary consensus," in his words. Thereafter, throughout the conference, his efforts were largely in this direction. Ralph Earle and I had many bilaterals with Ambassador Dhanapala during the conference to work toward this result.

In his 1995 State of the Union Address, which took place during the fourth prepcom meeting, President Clinton pledged that the United States would "lead the charge" for the indefinite extension of the NPT. Further, declaring 1995 a year of decision for arms control and non-proliferation, National Security Advisor Tony Lake had announced in a speech on January 31 that the United States would withdraw its proposed ten-year withdrawal clause from its CTBT proposal. This was an important step not only for the effort to conclude a CTBT, but also for the effort to achieve indefinite NPT extension, because it committed the United States to a permanent CTBT while it was arguing for a permanent NPT. NAM members had frequently attacked the inconsistency between a permanent NPT and a CTBT that could disappear (because of the ten-year clause).

On March 1, President Clinton reiterated his personal support for a permanent NPT, saying "nothing is more important to prevent the spread of nuclear weapons than extending the [Nuclear Non-Proliferation] Treaty indefinitely and unconditionally." He reaffirmed the commitment of the U.S. government to the central goals of the treaty: non-proliferation, the peaceful use of nuclear technology, and the pursuit of nuclear arms control and disarmament.

The president went further in a speech celebrating the 25th anniversary of the entry-into-force of the NPT. He reemphasized the importance of nuclear disarmament negotiations and made an additional U.S. commitment to the goals of the treaty by ordering 200 tons of fissile material—enough for thousands of nuclear weapons—to be permanently withdrawn from the U.S. nuclear stockpile. None of that material will be used to build a nuclear weapon ever again. The president decided that this bold disarmament gesture was an appropriate way to emphasize the commitment of the United States both to Article VI and to the NPT in general.

On the eve of the conference, the United States remained committed to building the largest possible majority in support of indefinite extension, but many officials in the U.S. government and other governments as well as most NGOs were not overly optimistic about the prospects for consensus. The public position of the United States regarding the predicted outcome was that the "only vote that counts is the one in May, but if the vote were held today, we believe a majority of the parties support indefinite extension." However, efforts were underway to increase support.

As stated, the conference opened without agreement on the procedure by which the vote (or votes, if the first failed to establish a majority) on extension options would be taken. With the decision procedures undecided, the effort to gather a majority of co-sponsors for a proposal for indefinite extension under Canadian leadership took on added importance. This effort was conducted in a low-key way so that questions about whether or not a majority had been achieved would be minimized. The objective was to try to accumulate the largest possible number of co-sponsors, a majority if possible, before submission. As stated, Canada was designated as the coordinator and as such was given custodianship of the original list, and representatives of other countries sought signatures on duplicate copies. Canadian Disarmament Ambassador Chris Wesdahl, the successor to Ambassador Peggy Mason, who was most effective in supporting indefinite extension in 1993 and 1994, did a superb job in leading the resolution effort. Many of us will long remember his introduction of the Canadian resolution for indefinite extension on the floor of the General Assembly in the third week of the conference, in which he solemnly intoned the names of the 105 co-sponsors. The die was indeed cast at that point.

Vice President Gore, in making the opening U.S. national statement at the conference, as U.S. delegation head, reaffirmed (consistent with the joint communiqué signed by President Clinton and Prime Minister Rao of India in 1994, which, as I said, I had hawked around the world) that complete nuclear disarmament remains the ultimate goal of the United States:

> [T]he treaty did not create a permanent class of nuclear weapon states. What the treaty did create was a requirement that those who already possessed nuclear weapons did not help others to acquire them, coupled with a binding legal obligation in Article VI to pursue good faith negotiations on nuclear arms control and disarmament. By extending the NPT indefinitely, non-nuclear weapons states will ensure that this obligation remains permanently binding and create the conditions for its ultimate achievement.

The vice president also made clear the U.S. commitment to achieve a CTBT at the earliest possible date. Vice President Gore's speech, coming early in the conference, provided a major boost to efforts to achieve indefinite extension.

South African Foreign Minister Nzo played an indispensable role in bridging the gap between the developed and the developing world by providing the basis for the development of principles and objectives on nuclear non-proliferation and disarmament, and for beneficial enhancements to the NPT review process. After Nzo's speech, in bilateral consultations with the foreign minister, and with the senior leadership of the two NPT conference delegations also present, Vice President Gore seized the opportunity presented by the South African proposal and committed the United States' delegation to work very closely with South Africa. He stated very firmly to both delegations, "I want all of you to work closely together," and he left no doubt who would be in charge. For, in taking its decision to support indefinite extension, the new government of South Africa demonstrated its ability to think beyond Cold War categories. It recognized that the treaty was too important to South Africa to be placed in jeopardy. This decision was a courageous one because the government faced criticism from within the NAM for being too closely linked with Europe and the United States. South Africa's unique status as a *former* nuclear weapon state, a developing nation that is a member of the NAM and the Nuclear Suppliers Group, and President Mandela's own great personal moral authority made the country a central player in brokering indefinite extension. Through able diplomacy, Foreign Minister Nzo helped to deliver the long-sought "significant majority" into the camp of supporters of indefinite extension without conditions.

In the past, NAM decisions were often made by a vocal few riding roughshod over a silent majority. Accepting the mantle of this type of "leadership" usually fell to states who took radical positions in opposition to one or both of the superpowers during the Cold War, attempting to maximize the developing world's leverage in the global zero-sum competition between the United States and the Soviet Union. Although this process had become an anachronism with the end of the Cold War, it was observable during the NPT prepcoms and the conference itself as some states tried to maintain their leadership role based on reflexive antagonism directed toward the nuclear weapon states and the West in general, and the United States in particular. In contrast to UN practice, meetings were often called early in the morning and dominated by well-rested and prepared members of larger delegations from states with an animus against the developed world (such as Malaysia, Nigeria, and Indonesia). They sought to promote narrow national interests unrelated and often at odds with the broader interests of the developing world. Indeed, one day during the fourth prepcom I was seated right behind the ambassador of Venezuela. The NAM had just made an ill-advised proposal clearly contrary to the national interests of Venezuela among others. I tapped the ambassador on the shoulder and asked, "How can you support that as a member of NAM? It is contrary to your interests." He replied, "But you have to understand NAM. The meetings are called at 9:00 A.M. and of the 110 delegations only about fifteen are present. Only one or two speak, there is no dissent and silence is taken as consent. Thus, all are bound." It did not seem very democratic to me. A large number of non-aligned countries were represented at the conference only by their UN permanent representatives, who had less time and resources to devote to the NPT process than larger delegations from capitals. These meetings often produced "consensus" positions, from which member states were quick to disassociate themselves in bilateral consultations with the United States. Much of the success of the NPT extension is owed to the United States' strategy of sidestepping the NAM "leadership" and appealing to individual non-aligned states in capitals on the basis of their own security interests.

During the week of April 24, the second week of the conference, the foreign ministers of NAM states met in Bandung, Indonesia, the site of the movement's founding, to observe its 40th anniversary. Many ambassadors left the conference in New York for several days to attend this meeting. When the Indonesian chairman of the Bandung meeting called for consensus support from the NAM for a proposal for a limited NPT extension, Ambassador Mongbe, the permanent representative of Benin in New York, stood up and objected. He clearly stated his country's support for indefinite extension. This was followed by a number of others, including South Africa, and thus no position on NPT extension was agreed to at Bandung. Ambassador Mongbe was referred to afterwards at the NPT conference as the "hero of Bandung." It took courage to do what he did.

During the May 5 plenary at the conference, Canadian Ambassador Wesdahl presented the proposal for indefinite extension without conditions co-sponsored by 105 states parties to the NPT, easily a majority. This number quickly grew to 111. (This co-sponsorship list did not include South Africa or a number of states closely aligned with it. With their support the number of NPT parties supporting indefinite extension exceeded 150.)

After the Bandung meeting, Indonesia introduced (also on May 5) a proposal of its own calling for a rolling twenty-five-year extension, which was sponsored by eleven countries. However, in the final week of the conference, as I said above, Indonesian Foreign Minister Alatas proposed a linkage between the emerging Statement of Principles and Objectives on Non-Proliferation and Disarmament and the Statement on an Enhanced Review Process, thus making possible consensus agreement on the conference president's three-part package of indefinite extension, non-proliferation principles and objectives, and an enhanced review process. These documents had been developed as such in a twenty-five-state President's Committee. The Committee had been established and was chaired by Ambassador Dhanapala. It was inspired by the South African proposal to establish principles to measure disarmament progress related to the NPT and a strengthened review process. Thus, Foreign Minister Nzo's speech was arguably the most important of the conference. The proposal of Foreign Minister Alatas made near the end of the conference was accepted and became part of the package.

This final settlement (not anticipating the last-minute Indonesian addition) was foreshadowed and essentially worked out at a dinner for about a dozen representatives on May 8 hosted by Australian Ambassador Richard Butler (later head of the UN Special Commission on Iraq) and attended by, among others, Ambassador Dhanapala, myself, U.K. Ambassador Weston, Ambassador of France Ererra, Russian delegation head Kisliak, German Ambassador Hoffmann, Chinese Ambassador Sha Zukang, South African delegation head Minty, and Indonesian Ambassador Wisnumurti. (Mexican Deputy Foreign Minister Gonzalez-Galvez was invited, but had to decline at the last minute because of an urgent call from Mexico City.) As Ambassador Dhanapala later observed, "This resulted in three parallel decisions being presented to the conference with built-in linkages, although it was acknowledged that while the extension decision was legally binding the two other decisions were politically binding." This development brought consensus on the president's package of decisions within the grasp of the conference.

At the plenary scheduled for 10:00 A.M. on May 11, the president put forward his package of decisions for consideration. The package included the extension decision itself, the Statement of Principles and Objectives on Nuclear Non-Proliferation and Disarmament, and the strengthened review process decision. The president's intent was for the three decisions to be adopted together without a vote, followed by the adoption of the depositaries resolution on the Middle East. However, a late objection by Iran to the text of the Middle East resolution precipitated two hours of fevered negotiations. The plenary resumed at noon with the positive references to the Middle East peace process in the depositaries resolution sufficiently watered down to be acceptable to Iran. First the president's package (with a healthy fast gavel), followed by the Middle East resolution, were adopted without a vote. After the decisions were taken, eleven countries spoke in favor of indefinite extension, while eleven others voiced opposition (all having a firm grasp of the boundaries that their dissatisfaction should not cross).

A conference final document could not be achieved in the final day and a half, largely because of disagreements in Main Committee I (chaired by Nigeria), which were too great for first the Drafting Committee (chaired by Poland), and then the President's Committee on May 11 and 12, to bridge. This result was quite disappointing to President Dhanapala, and many in the NAM blamed this outcome largely on the unwillingness of the United Kingdom and France to make any further concrete disarmament commitments.

However, support for increased peaceful cooperation and for the International Atomic Energy Agency's "93 +2" Program to improve safeguards was expressed by the conference in the largely complete reports of Main Committee II (peaceful uses, chaired by Hungary) and Main Committee III (safeguards, chaired by the Netherlands), among broader areas of agreement.

The enhanced review process established the virtually annual prepcom meetings leading to the five-year review conferences and provides that disarmament progress is a valid subject of this process. The Indonesian proposal explicitly links the commitments of the Statement of Principles and Objectives to this enhanced review so progress in meeting those obligations is to be an integral part of the review process. All of this is part of the indefinite extension package and it is important to understand that a failure to meet the obligations of the Statement of Principles and Objectives—especially reductions in nuclear weapons—will endanger the permanent status of the NPT or even the NPT regime itself. Several important NAM ambassadors made this point to me privately at the conclusion of the conference in emphasizing that the NPT created two classes of member states, and they were only willing to remain second-class states under the NPT temporarily as negotiated disarmament proceeded. They were not willing to be second-class states on a permanent basis.

The agreed Statement of Principles and Objectives on Nuclear Non-Proliferation and Disarmament inspired by South Africa and adopted by the President's Committee committed the nuclear weapon states, and indeed all NPT parties, to nuclear disarmament progress in support of the NPT. In general, the statement called for, among other things, a CTBT in 1996 (explicitly approved by the five nuclear weapon states in the President's Committee); continued commitment to negotiated reductions in nuclear weapons (a most important obligation); NPT universality of membership (read Israel, but much progress was made after the conference, so that by 1998 there were only four states outside the NPT—India, Pakistan, Israel, and Cuba); support of existing and future nuclear-weapon-free zones particularly in the Middle East and Africa (the Raratonga and Pelindaba Treaties are important here); and improved NPT verification (the 93 + 2 Protocol adopted by the IAEA in June of 1997 is an important advance as it adds a number of verification improvements, such as environmental sampling, and it needs to be widely ratified).

One of the most important characteristics of the indefinite extension of the NPT is that it was a collaborative and inclusive success. It was a victory of all the states parties to the NPT, not against each other, but against a common problem threatening their survival and prosperity: the proliferation of nuclear weapons. The extension decision that was taken was a much stronger one for the health of the treaty regime than many had even hoped for on the eve of the conference. It was taken without a vote, or by consensus as the term is used in parliamentary procedure. The NPT will continue in force indefinitely and without conditions. Review conferences will continue to be held every five years, with the first prepcom meeting held in 1997, three years before the review conference. Unfortunately, largely because of nuclear weapon state intransigence, the 1997 and 1998 prepcoms ended in disarray, with the 1998 prepcom, because of U.S. resistance, unable even to reaffirm the text of the 1995 depositaries' Resolution on the Middle East. Oman, the Arab Emirates, and Djibouti had since joined the NPT, so a call for all states in the Middle East region to join could only mean Israel. The 1999 prepcom result was marginally better. The prepcoms after 1995 were charged with addressing substantive as well as procedural and organizational issues. The review process will use the Statement of Principles and Objectives to evaluate and guide future progress, but the agreement to extend the NPT indefinitely and to have an enhanced review process will not be limited to measures in the principles and objectives document.

The 2000 Review Conference—in the wake of the rejection of the CTBT by the U.S. Senate in 1999, nuclear tests in India and Pakistan in 1998, continuing pressure on the ABM Treaty by the U.S. NMD program, continued adherence to first-use options by the United States, United Kingdom, France, and Russia (as well as NATO), and a lack of negotiated disarmament progress—nevertheless reached a quite positive result, indicating the continued commitment of most of the world community to the principles of the NPT. This was due to the important contribution of the New Agenda Coalition, seven states (Mexico, South Africa, Brazil, Ireland, Sweden, New Zealand, and Egypt) which have banded together to press for disarmament progress, and gives the world community an important respite, but only a respite which should be understood as such, in the effort to save the NPT for the long term. The 2000 Review Conference, among other things, agreed to the preservation of the ABM Treaty, a nuclear test moratorium until the CTBT enters into force—making these NPT-related commitments—a fissile material cutoff treaty by 2005, a report on security assurances for the 2005 Review Conference, and an "unequivocal undertaking" by the nuclear weapon states to proceed to nuclear disarmament.

In sum, the 1995 NPT conference agreement to extend the NPT indefinitely and without conditions amounted to the achievement of one of the United States' highest foreign policy objectives. The president had the support of the Congress for indefinite NPT extension throughout the process. In February 1995, after the above-mentioned hearing on the forthcoming conference, Chairman Roth and Senator Glenn (the ranking Democratic member) of the Senate Committee on Government Affairs co-sponsored a strong resolution supporting indefinite NPT extension. It passed the Senate unanimously. After the conference result, I received a congratulatory telephone message from Senator Nancy Kassebaum, among others. Senator Roth made a floor statement on May 11 in which he kindly mentioned me along with Ambassador Dhanapala and set the right tone in saying, "We have achieved a critical victory in making the post–Cold War period safer and more secure. This is a victory for all the world's people." It was also important that the U.S. NGO community was active in support of indefinite NPT extension.

This achievement is representative of the kind of foreign policy victory the United States should favor: collaborative success. In a press briefing in Washington on May 16 with John Holum, I said, "The United States recognizes that in effect, through this enhanced review process and statement of principles, it . . . and other nuclear weapon states—have given an IOU to the rest of the world for the future." As Conference President Dhanapala, who demonstrated at this conference that he is a leading world statesman, noted in his closing conference remarks, the success of the NPT Review and

Extension Conference rests on "enlarging areas of agreement." (Ambassador Dhanapala is now UN undersecretary-general for disarmament.) The objective of the United States was to move this debate away from narrow bloc politics by engaging individual states in the spirit of sovereign equality, and appealing to them to address their own security concerns themselves rather than follow bloc leadership. In doing so, we collaborated with our partners around the world to reveal and pursue a common interest, which is something we will be called upon to do many times in the post–Cold War world.

CHAPTER TWELVE NPT AFTERMATH AND THE END OF ACDA

After the successful conclusion of the NPT Review and Extension Conference, I thought that a possible subject that I might work on was the development and extension of nuclear-weapon-free zones. It is one of the commitments in the Statement of Principles and Objectives document, and I had written a memorandum to John Holum before the end of the conference emphasizing its importance. In one of the many letters I received after the conference, Fiji's ambassador to the United Nations reminded me of our commitment to the South Pacific Forum and that he hoped "your government will be able to adhere as a protocol party to the Raratonga Treaty soon."

At the conference, I had been impressed by private statements of several prominent NAM ambassadors who said that they were content with a permanent NPT, but in agreeing to an NPT of indefinite duration, they were not agreeing to the indefinite possession of nuclear weapon privileges by five states. Either substantial progress toward fulfilling the commitments of the Statement of Principles and Objectives, most importantly significant reductions in the number of nuclear weapons, needed to be made or at some point they would consider reviewing their commitment to the NPT. If nuclear weapons were going to remain a criterion of distinction between states that have special influence and those that do not, then they did not intend to remain second-class citizens forever. Thus, nuclear weapons must become less important politically for nuclear non-proliferation to succeed for the long-term.

There was an effort to conclude a conference final document based on the work of Committee I of the conference. That committee, chaired by Ambassador Ayewah of Nigeria, as I said, had been run like a court trying nuclear weapon states for the crime of the possession of nuclear weapons. Not surprisingly, the committee made little progress, whereas the other two committees on peaceful uses and safeguards were close to agreement on language. In the last two days of the conference, the proceedings to conclude a final document had been taken over by the conference president, Ambassador Dhanapala. Nigeria and Egypt were very difficult in these meetings, and Britain and France drew a line in the sand against strong language about the importance of nuclear disarmament and of achieving the abolition of nuclear weapons.

Ralph Earle and I went to see Dhanapala around mid-day on the last day of the conference. He was very upset. He said that if Britain and France were going to continue this kind of behavior for the next five years (which they most definitely did not; they were the nuclear weapon states who had delivered on the Statement of Principles and Objectives by the year 2000), this could lead to a movement of states to withdraw from the NPT. Dhanapala is a great man to whom the world community owes much. He is devoted to the NPT regime, but he very much shares the NAM view of the political significance of nuclear weapons and the importance of nuclear disarmament. I reported the situation not long after to a full meeting of the Western Group, referring to nuclear weapon states rather than to Britain and France. I described the president as being very upset with the final document proceedings to the forty or so ambassadors and their aides. It was decided to send our capable group chairman, Ambassador Sir Michael Weston of the United Kingdom, to go and talk with Dhanapala. The Western Group meeting then concluded and I called a quick huddle of the United States delegation. I emphasized that Dhanapala was *not* talking about the United States. (Christine visited me for the last days of the conference and she was present at that meeting. Undoubtedly, she thought it was all a bit crazy—and it was.) Shortly after, Michael Weston walked by on his way to see Dhanapala. I was standing next to French Ambassador Errera, who expressed misgivings as to whether this would work out well. Errera was always a keen observer of representatives of other states. He once said that we must not suggest something to the Russian delegates, as this would only strengthen for the particular issue the "nihilist" tendency that all Russians share. The conference ended that night with no final document. But Michael Weston, an outstanding ambassador who had most effectively led the Western Group throughout the extension process, in my impression, did in fact make progress in addressing the quite legitimate concerns of Ambassador Dhanapala.

Early in 1996 I decided that it would be useful to make a disarmament progress report to the NAM caucus as the Dhanapala concerns are widespread among the NAM states. When I proposed this to the U.S. mission to the United Nations it was as though I had suggested entering a free-fire zone in Bosnia. I guess few if any U.S. representatives had ever done such a thing. But they reluctantly agreed and I developed a cleared statement in Washington. Contrary to expressed concerns, I was politely received and the delegates (about forty-five countries were there) were attentive. Only the Indian ambassador walked out. Most of the questions were routine except for one: "How are you going to persuade India and Pakistan to join the NPT?" I replied that someday when very substantial reductions in nuclear weapons had occurred it might become possible. Afterwards, Munir Akhram, who was there for Pakistan, came up to me and said that he would like to see my game plan for carrying this out. It was a positive experience that should be repeated by U.S. diplomats.

In June 1995, I went to Japan to attend a public non-proliferation conference sponsored by *Asahi Shimbun*, one of Japan's most prestigious newspapers. I was on a panel speaking to a crowd of about 500 interested Japanese. On the panel was the Indian nuclear expert Subramanian, who gave a typically hard-line Indian speech on the evils of the NPT, referring to NPT indefinite extension as "the saddest event . . . a defeat for all mankind." In my speech, I strongly defended the NPT and the importance of the conference decision on extension, saying by contrast that indefinite extension was a "common victory that established a permanent landmark on the arms control horizon that we will be blessed to have for years to come." *Asahi Shimbun*'s lead article on the conference the next day was entitled, "Extension Tension." One of the questions from the large audience was why hadn't President Clinton apologized for Hiroshima and Nagasaki. (This was at the time of the flap over the exhibit at the Smithsonian Museum on the atomic attack on Japan. The exhibit was cancelled after a considerable outcry.) I replied that the atomic bombing of Hiroshima and Nagasaki was a terrible human disaster, but even more so was World War II, which the United States did not start. It was best to put all this behind us and promise ourselves that it will never happen again. The next day, at a more private seminar-like discussion, I listened to a representative of the Japanese Self Defense Force say in a presentation that Japan would never have a missile defense system, as it could never be agreed which service would have it, and those cities not covered would claim discrimination. Interesting, I thought, reminds me of 1972 and the ABM Treaty national capital area defense provision. I spent a day and a half after the conference in the Republic of Korea where I made a presentation at the Korean Institute for Defense Analysis (KIDA). I met with the director of KIDA for forty-five minutes before my presentation. All he wanted to discuss was North Korea. He said, "You Americans must understand this issue, and to understand the problems of the Peninsula you must remember that the Koreans are the Irishmen of Asia." I said that I understood when it was put that way.

In October 1995, I went to Ecuador to visit Eliza for a week. She was teaching English there for a year under the aegis of World Teach of Cambridge, Massachusetts. In March 1994, I had gone to visit her at Carleton College shortly before her graduation. At dinner while I was there she said, "Dad, do you know what I would really like as a graduation present?" "No, Eliza," I responded. "Take me on a trip to the Galapagos Islands." I had always thought of the Galapagos as the end of the earth, but I did take Eliza there in October and it was fascinating. (In fairness, I should say that Eliza denies being so direct, but that is the way I heard it—and I am glad that I did.) On the way back we stopped in Quito where I did my NPT consultations with the government, which as I have recounted were very positive. The U.S. ambassador was very helpful, as was always the case in my experience, and we stayed at the residence. His wife, a former practicing lawyer, interested Eliza in returning to Ecuador to work, which is how she came to do so later.

One night while visiting her in Ecuador in 1995, I received an urgent telephone call from Washington in my room at the Oro Verde Hotel. I was asked if I could lead a delegation to Jakarta, Indonesia, to talk to the Association of South East Asian Nations (ASEAN), who were negotiating a nuclear-weapon-free zone treaty for the ASEAN area (later called the Treaty of Bangkok, where it was signed). They were refusing to listen to U.S. concerns at all—or to those of any of the other nuclear weapon states—contrary to the request from President Clinton in a letter that I delivered to Indonesia earlier that year. A colloquy between the nuclear weapon states and ASEAN had been arranged for a date in November. I replied that I would be happy to do so—at last I was getting *some* work on nuclear-weapon-free zones.

For the South Pacific Nuclear-Weapon-Free Zone, the United States had signed the protocols to the Treaty of Raratonga in the summer of 1995, as promised to the South Pacific Forum countries at the NPT conference. I had held a lunch for South Pacific Forum members during the NPT Review and Extension Conference to firm up their support for indefinite extension. We had persuaded several members of the forum to join the NPT in time for the vote. One of their members, Palau, an NPT member but not a UN member, needed money to fly a representative to the conference to deliver a vote for indefinite extension. The money was found at DOE and he arrived in time for the vote. Pursuant to instructions, at this lunch I had stated that U.S. signature of the Raratonga Treaty protocols was under active consideration and I had emphasized this firmly. These states did vote in a bloc for indefinite extension, thus the United States had an obligation to them. The protocols provide that the United States will not deploy nuclear weapons in the zone and will put its territory in the treaty area under the treaty obligations; will not test nuclear weapons there; and will not use or threaten to use nuclear weapons against parties to the treaty—a legally binding negative security assurance as in the Tlatelolco Treaty. By the time the United States signed it was nine years after the signing of the treaty by the South Pacific parties, but the treaty was one more deliverable to the NPT Statement of Principles and Objectives. The Russians and Chinese had long been parties to the three protocols; the United Kingdom and France (after its tests) quickly signed and ratified. As of late 2001, however, the United States still had not ratified the protocols or even sent them to the Senate. The United States also indicated to South Africa in 1995 that it would sign the comparable protocols to the emerging African Nuclear-Weapon-Free Zone Treaty (ultimately designated the Treaty of Pelindaba, after the South African nuclear center). This was a key desideratum for South Africa, which had sent a red-hot demarche to Washington—as the father of the Statement of Principles and Objectives—during the debate over the CTBT threshold.

Working with ASEAN would be some hands-on experience with the nuclear-weapon-free zone issue. There were four of us on the delegation. In addition to myself, there was Dave Fite from ACDA, a representative from State/EAP, and a naval officer who was an expert on the law-of-the-sea issues in the region. The format of the consultation was that the United States would have the first day, China and Russia would split the second day, and the United Kingdom and France the third. We, of course, had sent several written communications to the Indonesian chair of the ASEAN working group, but this did not seem to affect the successive drafts of the emerging Southeast Asian Nuclear-Weapon-Free Zone Treaty and the protocol for the nuclear weapon states. Among other things, the United States strongly objected to the extension of the obligations of the treaty zone to the high seas within the Exclusive Economic Zone (EEZ, the 200-mile limit) and the waters above the continental shelf. The Treaties of Tlatelolco and Raratonga, and later the Treaty of Pelindaba, applied the treaty obligations only to the land areas within the treaty zone. The United States regarded the draft treaty proposal as an infringement of the right of passage on the high seas and also, in signing the protocol, which contained a negative security assurance, it would mean the United States would be giving such an assurance, inter alia, to Russia and Chinese ships on the high seas within the zone. Also, there was no clear right of transit through the zone for vessels carrying nuclear weapons, which were carefully preserved in the other three nuclear-weapon-free zone treaty regimes.

We arranged to arrive the day before the United States' presentation and meet with the Chinese delegation and perhaps with sympathetic delegations such as Singapore. These high seas issues were very important to the United States Navy and we planned a comprehensive presentation. We were to fly to Tokyo non-stop from Detroit and then on to Singapore, arriving late at night. Our meeting with the Chinese was set for 3:00 P.M. the following day. We caught a plane to Detroit and I assured the others that Detroit was on Central Time so we had several hours to strategize between planes in one of the airport coffee shops. Of course I was wrong. Detroit is in the Eastern time zone, and we arrived at the gate thinking we were an hour early only to see our plane pulling away from the gate, too late for us to board. Frantically, we asked the Northwest Airline representative at the gate if there was a later plane. He said no, but he was a thoughtful and resourceful man. He said, "We will send you around the other way at no additional charge and you will arrive at noon on the following day" (three hours before the meeting with the Chinese). So that is what we did. We traveled on KLM, Northwest's partner, to Amsterdam and went to the National Art Museum and Anne Frank's house during our eight-hour layover there. The flights were on time and we arrived at Jakarta at noon, showered at our hotel, and met with the Chinese at 3:00 P.M. They agreed with all our concerns. They believed the EEZ issue was aimed at them because of the dispute over the Spratley Islands in the South China Sea. They wanted to be sure that this treaty did not affect their territorial claims.

There was another issue of some importance. The protocol as drafted was open to any state, not just the nuclear weapon states, again unlike the other three treaties. The Indonesians said this was to permit India to join. We were opposed to that as we did not want India recognized as a nuclear weapon state. Also, Japan was concerned that they might be forced to join the protocol and that this might compromise their position under the United States nuclear umbrella. We met with the Japanese Embassy staff in Jakarta to reassure them. We took a strong position, and on this issue ASEAN did listen to us and changed the text of the protocol to be open only to the five nuclear weapon states. We also had a discussion at the Australian Embassy. The potential Southeast Asian nuclear-weapon-free zone was of interest to Australia, both because they were neighbors and because the Raratonga Treaty was its brainchild.

When I had been in Jakarta in February 1995 having a difficult discussion on NPT, I had stayed with Bob Barry, the United States ambassador and a former colleague. By now, November 1995, he had departed, but the new ambassador, Stapleton Roy, had not yet arrived. Nor had he when I came in February 1996 to discuss CTBT with Foreign Minister Alatas. When I was in Jakarta in December 1996, attending a track II ASEAN meeting on nonproliferation, Stape had finally arrived and gave a very nice dinner for me. I had previously met him in Beijing when I was there in October 1994 for NPT consultations where I also joined John Holum, who was in Beijing at the same time for broader issues. At that time Roy was our ambassador to China. A few weeks earlier in 1994, the Russians and Chinese had signed a no-first-use agreement that said, in effect, that each party would not use nuclear weapons against the other first, unless it changes its mind. John decided to propose to the Chinese that Washington might consider such a formulation as well. This was within his instructions to do so. That of course would unlock many closed doors with the Chinese. No first use had been their policy since 1964—the time of their first test. There was an Asian Pacific Summit coming up, and the United States wanted a detargeting agreement with China, like it had with Russia, for the president to sign at the meeting to be held in Manila. But the Chinese consistently refused detargeting without no first use. I asked Sha Zukang (the soon-to-be Chinese ambassador to the CD, who was replacing Ambassador Ho, and who was later chief of the newly formed Disarmament Division of the Chinese Foreign Ministry; he also played a most important role in Geneva in the CTBT negotiations) on the margins of the meeting, why no first use was so important to China, since it was only words. He responded, "Because it was Mao's policy." John said he would forward the idea to Washington and we did so under the joint recommendation of John, Stape, and myself. When John and I arrived in Washington, it was more like we had sent a tactical nuclear weapon instead of a telegram. Apparently, General Shalikashvili had called up Ralph Earle personally to complain and Bob Bell directed that a cable be sent to Roy, instructing him to tell the Chinese nothing doing. I had told Sha that Washington probably would not approve, even though, based on the agreement with Russia, it would be the loosest of commitments. China eventually did agree to detargeting without no first use during Clinton's visit there in 1998.

In Jakarta in November 1995, after our meeting with the Chinese, we had a meeting with the Singapore delegation in the evening. They said that they agreed with all our points and that the Indonesians did as well. The problem was that ASEAN could not arrive at a consensus—Malaysia was the principal holdout. As an aside during a break, I asked a member of the Singapore delegation, a woman of about thirty-five, why Chinese diplomats are so difficult. They often would not even tell you China's position. (One example of this was at the NPT dinner in Geneva in June 1994, when Errera asked Ambassador Ho whether or not China supported indefinite extension.) The member of the Singapore delegation said the Chinese were somewhat more open with them, considering them as sharing Chinese civilization, but essentially there were two reasons. It had been traditional Chinese diplomatic practice during the Chinese Empire to give representatives in the field little authority and to force foreigners to come to Beijing. Also, China was very suspicious of the West, and, since the United States was the leader of the West, the Chinese were the most suspicious of us. This was not going to change, so we might as well get used to it. I said, "You mean because of Taiwan?" "Oh no," she said, "because of the Opium Wars and the Boxer Rebellion." In a later, similar discussion with Sha at the annual arms control conference at Sandia Laboratory in Albuquerque, New Mexico, in April 1997, he blamed it on the Cultural Revolution. He was in London during the Cultural Revolution and thus was unaffected by it. He said, "There is a great difference in the younger Chinese in this regard. People too young to be scarred by the Cultural Revolution, tend to be as frank as anyone else." My experience would tend to confirm this.

I opened the next day with a very long statement. I reminded the seven ASEAN delegations seated around the horseshoe table in front of me that their nuclear-weapon-free-zone treaty could not be truly operational unless the nuclear weapon states signed on. Speaking for the United States, we wanted to sign the protocol, but could not unless these points were cleared up. I then went through each issue at some length: the EEZ, transit rights, accession rights to the protocol, right of protocol parties to be notified of changes in the treaty, and the right to attend implementing body deliberations. My presentation lasted nearly an hour, we took two hours of questions, and then broke for lunch followed by informal discussions. On all of the points there were positive noises, on the last three points there were corrections in the next treaty draft, on transit rights there was some movement, but on EEZ and continental shelf there was never any change. (The treaty was signed in December 1995 in Bangkok, and, as I mentioned, is known as the Treaty of Bangkok. The protocol was left in draft so the necessary corrections remained possible through changes in the protocol. Malaysia took the chair of the working group in mid-1996 and the Philippines took over in 1997, but the central issues were never corrected and were made slightly worse by Malaysia during its period of holding the chair. By December 2001, none of the nuclear weapon states had signed the protocol. And, without changes in the protocol, it would seem unlikely that they will.)

The next day we met with the DCM at the Russian Embassy. He said Moscow was not sending anyone, but instead sent a letter for him to present. It was only mildly helpful. We also met with the British and the French before their presentations. Michel Duclos, who had come from Paris, gave a dinner at the French Embassy the last night of the discussions. The British representative was Bruce Kleghorn, former number two on the British CFE delegation. We had a good discussion on CTBT and NPT at the table. Also, while in Jakarta, we met with the undersecretary of the foreign ministry, Ambassador Ibrahim, who had been my top interlocutor during my February 1995 NPT consultation in Jakarta. In that meeting, the Indonesians had been completely unmovable, saying simply that if the United States was going to insist on indefinite extension, "it would be a difficult conference." They were not even very friendly, and I did not see Foreign Minister Alatas. This time it was different. Undersecretary Ibrahim was all smiles and said that he was coming to New York in January 1996 and perhaps we could resolve our differences then. He did meet with our delegation in New York in January. I made a shorter version of the same pitch I had made to the ASEAN working group. He made some positive noises, but nothing ever came of it.

In February of 1996, as recounted in chapter 10, I made a CTBT consultation trip to several countries, including Indonesia and Malaysia and in those countries took the opportunity to raise Treaty of Bangkok issues. I met with Foreign Minister Alatas in Jakarta and made another strong pitch on EEZ, even though the Treaty of Bangkok had been signed. It was not yet in force, however. Alatas said that he had not followed the issue, but would look closely into it. In Kuala Lumpur I met with Malaysian Deputy Foreign Minister Karim, then acting foreign minister. On the Treaty of Bangkok point, he said that the Malaysian position on EEZ was inspired by concern about China in the South China Sea and that I should report this to Washington. The United States ambassador there was an old colleague who put me into the hands of a capable political officer. The officer told me about the Royal Golf Club in the center of town where the senior members of the government often played and much business was conducted. Foreign ambassadors were invited to join, but it was necessary to pass a golf etiquette test. A recent U.S. ambassador had flunked this test and was never able to join the club. Diplomacy puts strange demands on you.

Whenever I visited Jakarta, Manila, and Kuala Lumpur in those years the Embassy always arranged for me to do TV and radio shows, give press conferences, and do press interviews. I came away with a positive view of the professionalism of the press corps in Southeast Asia, a view I had had of the Japanese press corps for some time. I visited Southeast Asia twice more in those years pursuing a settlement on the Treaty of Bangkok. In December 1996, at the specific invitation of Indonesia, I attended a track II ASEAN-sponsored discussion on NPT. Track II meetings are supposed to be informal with a mix of government and NGOs. The NGOs are to make the presentations with the government people joining in the discussions. It was clear that the Chinese were having none of this unstructured stuff, as they coordinated every move with Beijing. This time, the Russians sent a superbly talented expert on Asia, a Mr. Vassiliev, and I wished that he had been there the year before for the consultations. The high note of the meeting was a denunciation of the Indian position on CTBT (which had been signed in September at the UN after the Indians had blocked conclusion of the Treaty in Geneva) by the Indian delegate at the Jakarta meeting, a university professor. The Indian Embassy had to rush in a representative the next day to deny everything he had said. Also in June 1996 I had been invited to speak at the Asian Round Table, an annual event in Kuala Lumpur hosted by the premier defense research organization in Malaysia. I was to be on a panel with former Australian Foreign Minister Gareth Evans—the government had just changed—and I arrived about an hour before I was to appear, coming up from Singapore. I rushed from the airport and arrived at the speaking hall fifteen minutes before going on. Gareth Evans walked by where I was sitting working on my text and asked the Malaysian host, "Where is Tom Graham?" I was able to reply, "Right here." Although side efforts on the subject were made both times, at neither of these meetings was any progress made on the nuclear-weapon-free zone question.

In the spring of 1997, it was decided to make one more go at ASEAN on the Treaty of Bangkok. Malaysia was recognized as important to the solution of the problem and they were leaving the chair of the working group in July. They had recently made positive noises. A U.S.-Malaysia bilateral, with other ASEAN states in attendance, was proposed for early June. The other nuclear weapon states were informed, and all participated. Susan Burk, my old colleague, was working with me to prepare our presentation. Ted Hirsch of the ACDA general counsel's office, a capable international lawyer, went with us. The experience was similar to Jakarta, except that the five nuclear weapon states made their presentations on the same day. My presentation was only about twenty minutes long this time, and I stressed how much the United States wanted to sign on to the zone if only it could. At dinner that night, I was seated next to the Malaysian chairperson and the French and Russian ambassadors were also at the table. During dinner we worked out the concept of a possible compromise on EEZ. Ted Hirsch brilliantly put it in writing and the next morning I telephoned the chair and she said that she would try out the compromise at the working group the next week. We dropped off a text at the office of the Malaysian chair and, when back in Washington, achieved grudging interagency approval of the compromise language. To my knowledge, we never heard anything on this proposal from Malaysia or the ASEAN working group, however. I did a long interview with the *Malaysian Straits Times* on June 10, 1997, which was published on June 24. In that interview I laid out all the U.S. objections to the Treaty of Bangkok in its current form that I had presented in Jakarta in 1995 and just reiterated in Kuala Lumpur. I also reemphasized the desire of the United States to sign the protocol, but said we simply could not until the problems were corrected. Also, I spoke extensively about the NPT and disarmament progress, saying, "I really do think that the world is coming together. There is an understanding everywhere that the threat to all of us is the spread of weapons of mass destruction into the hands of unstable countries, terrorist organizations, criminal conspiracies and subnational regimes." I hope the coming together that occurred in the aftermath of the terrible September 11, 2001, attacks will continue this trend.

I had one other nuclear-weapon-free-zone diplomatic experience in 1997 before leaving government. I was asked to represent the United States at the 30th anniversary celebration of the Treaty of Tlatelolco in February 1997. Dave Fite went with me. At the formal lunch I sat next to Ambassador Icaza, the Mexican CD representative, and found him to be an interesting interlocutor—disarmament is not his special interest, however. Michael Weston was also at our table. At the formal substantive session, Ambassador Enrique Roman-Moray, our colleague from OPANAL, was on the dais and made a speech along with President Zedillo and IAEA Director General Hans Blix. At a subsequent session, not quite as prestigious, I gave a speech and delivered a statement of congratulations from President Clinton.

A word about the Treaty of Pelindaba. U.S. signature is something that we owed South Africa: it was their baby, U.S. advisors had participated throughout the treaty drafting process, and it was scheduled for signature, including the protocols, in Cairo in April 1996. In some quarters there was concern that Libya would be in the zone and therefore reluctance to forswear legally the possibility of using nuclear weapons against their chemical weapon facilities. The supreme interest withdrawal provision in the treaty and protocols required twelve months' notice. In the interagency it was decided to enter a reservation shortening this period to three months for the United States. Normally, reservations are in the form of a counteroffer and have to be agreed to by the other parties. However, in this arrangement, the negative security assurance obligation in the protocols did not truly create treaty relations with the treaty parties, and certainly not with the other protocol parties. Thus, a unilateral reservation could be effective and this is what the United Kingdom did, shortening the notice to three months. However, at the last moment, the United States government decided against a reservation because of the legal murkiness associated therewith. The United States went ahead and signed in Cairo, with Ned Walker, ambassador to Egypt for a number of years and a leader in the government on Middle East issues, signing for the United States.

While a reservation was not made at that time, this issue was not settled internally. Of course, we were free to do so at the time of Senate transmission, but it was feared that this might be regarded by South Africa as bad faith. DOD was not happy, however. The compromise was for Bob Bell in a press conference on Pelindaba to enunciate the doctrine of belligerent reprisal, an old international law rule. It holds that if attacked in violation of international law (which would be the case with chemical or biological weapons, as the first use in war of both is outlawed by the Geneva Protocol, which has been recognized as customary international law), all bets are off with respect to weapons used in response (including nuclear weapons), no matter what the international legal commitments might be (although it could be argued that the "never under any circumstances" language in the CWC and the BWC might in effect prohibit a response with chemical weapons or biological weapons as parties to these treaties are obligated not to possess such weapons). However, the response must be *proportionate* and *necessary* to stop the attack, which nuclear weapons almost never would be (except perhaps in the case of a massive, almost unimaginable BW attack). The NGO community did not like this much, but I thought that it was a fine outcome. It is noteworthy, however, that neither Raratonga nor Pelindaba had been submitted to the Senate for advice and consent to ratification as of late 2001.

In January 1996, during the presidential election, President Clinton made a campaign stop in Louisville and while there visited my old high school. On the morning of January 24, Mary Lib called me and said, "Do you know where the president is going to be today?" "No," I said. "Louisville Male High School." She said I should pass on to the White House somehow that that was my high school. So I called John Holum's very talented speech writer, Terry Basyluk, and told him. He asked me if there was anything recognizable about me in the school and I told him that I was a member of the school's Hall of Fame (for alumni) and as such my picture was in the hallway. "Great," he said, "I'll pass this on." He called back about an hour later saying he had spoken with the person preparing the president's remarks. He was very pleased, saying that the president "loves this sort of stuff." So, in his remarks, which of course were televised, the president said, "Since I am in this high school, too, I could not leave without acknowledging a graduate of this high school who is making a contribution of singular importance to the United States. Thomas Graham Jr. is serving today as my special advisor for arms

NPT Aftermath and the End of ACDA

control, nonproliferation and disarmament. His picture hangs in the school Hall of Fame here and I just want you to know that he's in my hall of fame too. He's doing a great job for the United States of America." I must have received forty telephone calls that night from Louisville friends—just goes to show that it's good to have a lawyer watching out for you.

In December 1996 I headed a U.S. delegation to London for political/ military talks with the British. Eric Newsome, the principal deputy in State/ PM (later the assistant secretary), was the delegation deputy. Susan Burk and Lucas Fischer were on the delegation among others. We had particularly interesting discussions on NPT, implementation of the 1995 commitments and the prospects for CTBT entry into force. As I later testified before the Defense Committee of the House of Commons in March 2000, the British really delivered on their 1995 NPT commitments, as did the French.

That December I suffered a small reverse at ACDA. Based on my 1995 NPT experience, I had become convinced that it was important to begin five-power discussions on nuclear disarmament. The START process, while important and useful, is too uncertain and slow to effectively ward off future attacks on the NPT regime. The commencement of five-power discussions might do so. I do not favor any kind of negotiation on nuclear weapons involving the CD, because the details of nuclear disarmament are properly the business of the nuclear weapon states and not the NAM, no matter what some countries might assert. But the nuclear weapon states could report regularly to the CD or the UN First Committee, as was done in 1989–90 with CFE and CSCE, as certainly there is a political obligation to do. The NAM, indeed the entire world community, has an important stake in the success of nuclear disarmament. Clearly, for some years all the five nations would be able to do would be to discuss subjects such as transparency and verification. But this would be useful and the mere existence of such a forum might take the sting out of potential attacks on the NPT. The Russians publicly advocated this, and the French and British (later in 1999) indicated their support privately to me. China likely would come along if the United States proposed it. This process could be located at the CD with periodic reports by the five to the full CD, but, given my experience with the CD during NPT and the CTBT, I thought then and I believe now that the best place for this would be New York because of the broader political interests of UN permanent representatives. In a sense it is probably only the United States that is truly holding back on such a process, much against our interests.

I discussed this with John Holum in early December 1996 and he encouraged me to write a paper that could be the subject of a meeting. I promptly wrote a short five-page paper making the above points. The four ACDA bureaus commented on the paper and all opposed the idea, Strategic Affairs most vigorously. This idea, it was argued, would disrupt the START process, and that was where we should concentrate our efforts. This culminated in a mid-January meeting attended by John, the four bureau heads, Mary Lib, and a number of other ACDA officials, totaling about forty people. There was virtually no support for even studying the subject, and everyone was concerned only with their bureaucratic turf. Only Pierce Corden and Mary Lib favored further consideration of the proposal. John was of course neutral, and as we were leaving the room he said that this had been a useful discussion, and perhaps we could do it again, but of course we never did. The idea that an organization calling itself the Arms Control and Disarmament Agency would not even consider such an idea was unfortunate. And a number of months later in May—long after I had announced my July 1, 1997 retirement—Steve Ledogar, at a large meeting in John's office (at which the possibility was mentioned as something that conceivably could happen at the CD as a counter to the NAM call for an ad hoc committee on nuclear disarmament) noted lightly that I had proposed something earlier, but that I had wanted it to be in New York, where I could control it. That was not what I had in mind in December and certainly not in May. I had ceased to think of the possibility of ACDA supporting such a development. Ironically, after the ACDA discussion in February, I was going through my files and I found a memorandum that Paul Nitze had written to Secretary Shultz in 1986. It proposed a five-power nuclear weapon reduction process, given the problems that British and French weapons were causing in the United States-Soviet INF negotiations. It also, of course, was summarily rejected by Secretary Shultz's staff.

After the Republican takeover of Congress in 1994, Jesse Helms, the new chairman of the Senate Foreign Relations Committee, raised again the 1992/1993 reorganization issues and made a run at merging ACDA, as well as AID and USIA, into State. This proposition was effectively fended off by John Holum, with the support of the president and vice president. Also, Secretary Christopher did not seem to be under any compulsion to "get along" with the chairman, so that even though the intensive border war between State/PM and ACDA continued, there was no new pressure from State to eliminate ACDA. Thus, relative calm and progress prevailed for ACDA in 1995 and 1996.

In the summer of 1996, Rolf Ekeus, who was about to leave after five distinguished years as chairman of the United Nations Special Commission on Iraq (UNSCOM) to become Swedish ambassador to the United States, and Brian Urquhart, former undersecretary general, came to visit John. I sat in on the meeting. They were there to discuss Secretary-General Kofi Annan's plans to revitalize the disarmament function at the UN, and to concentrate especially on joint world community efforts to maintain existing disarmament regimes. In addition, they mentioned Annan's desire to put Jayantha Dhanapala at the head of the revitalized function, something Jayantha wanted, but only at the undersecretary general level, not assistant secretary general.

This was eventually worked out after many difficulties, with the last push coming from Jonathan Granoff, a LAWS board member and post-retirement colleague, and myself. Such a position for Jayantha had eventually become acceptable to the Bureau of International Organizations at the State Department, but in December of 1997, unbeknownst to anyone else in the government, an arm of USUN was blocking the undersecretary-general level for Jayantha at the last moment for administrative and organizational reasons. Jonathan found out from whom the opposition was coming, even though State and the NSC could not, and with John Holum's help I spoke with the responsible official and he graciously agreed to step aside on Jayantha. It was a typical U.S. government situation. Former U.S. Supreme Court Justice Jackson was right when he said many years ago that the United States government is a hydra-headed monster. But there was something that Rolf said during the discussion in June 1996 that I remembered. He said, in justifying the concept that he and Urquhart had proposed to the secretary general, that the day of traditional arms control and disarmament negotiation is over now, and it is the implementation of what we have, e.g. NPT, etc., that is most important. I had heard this for years, as an excuse for eliminating ACDA, but coming from Rolf one had to take it seriously.

In the summer of 1996 CWC was laboriously struggling toward Senate approval as more countries were ratifying and getting ever closer to the number of sixty-five that would bring it into force. The administration effort continued, largely leaderless in the sense that no senior figure was spending full time managing the ratification process. This had not been the case in the past with arms control and disarmament treaties. Not surprisingly, the effort was languishing. Finally, it passed out of committee and a floor date of September 12 was secured. But then came the Dole letter I described in chapter 2, which unfortunately created consternation among the Senate CWC supporters as well as the administration and the secretary of state. Secretary Christopher called Senator Lugar to postpone CWC to the next year. It would have been catastrophic for the United States not to ratify the CWC, undermining our non-proliferation efforts everywhere. So attention turned to an early date in 1997, but we had to go back through the committee, and Senator Helms vowed to oppose the CWC. It looked like a dicey situation, even though the Chemical Manufacturers' Association strongly supported CWC and the Dole letter turned out to be simply someone getting to the wrong staffer. Then Helms made clear his price in exchange for supporting CWC: the elimination of ACDA, USIA, and AID and their absorption by the State Department.

In December 1996 John Holum called Ralph Earle, Barb Starr, and me into his office. He said that Sandy Berger, the incoming national security advisor, had told him that the White House position was that the ACDA "independent box" had to disappear and that Strobe had told him that the political situation would no longer support an independent ACDA. John also had been advised by several long-time congressional supporters of ACDA that there was no longer significant congressional support for ACDA. The NGO community was largely indifferent. John's question was, should we negotiate or fight? Having in mind Rolf Ekeus's remark, the constant, unremitting border warfare with State/PM and the disappearance of White House as well as other support, I said to negotiate. Barb said the same thing, and Ralph went along with this decision. Perhaps I could fashion a position for us in which we could at least hold our own and perhaps improve the situation from the standpoint of the independence of the arms control process, I said. I thought that I might try to prepare something based on the 1961 Senate bill for the establishment of ACDA, which had ACDA in the State Department headed by an undersecretary (now deputy secretary). So I reviewed the 1961 legislative record and studied the 1961 Senate bill. I then wrote a memorandum to John, describing what an ACDA with an independent arms control process, located in the State Department, could look like, based on the 1961 Senate bill authored by Senators Humphrey and Pell, among others.

LAWS had now been pursuing me since October of 1995, well over a year, and I decided in January to accept their offer and retire on July 1. I did not see any significant work that lay ahead for me—at least in the foreseeable future. I was back in a nice office, but many days I had little to do. I did go to Mexico City in February and Kuala Lumpur in June, as I have related, and I gave speeches in Ottawa, Albuquerque, Livermore, and Charleston in March and April, but this was not full-time work. I went to see John and told him, but said I would continue to work on our merger negotiations. I also went to see Strobe and he said he was sorry, but happy that I was not going far. The discussion then turned to ACDA. He said that, much to his regret, an independent ACDA was not politically possible. And he said if ACDA did not disappear, the State Department would see to it that ACDA was cut out of everything. This of course would probably have happened anyway, as all four ACDA assistant directors had left or were soon leaving, with no prospect of getting replacements past the chairman of the Senate Foreign Relations Committee. Thus, the normal operation of the interagency process under these conditions would have been to chop ACDA to pieces. I replied to Strobe that I was working on a plan for John, based on the 1961 Senate bill, and that he would hear more from John soon.

John, Ralph, Barb, and I worked out a negotiating position based on my Senate bill memo and what we thought that ACDA needed to have. A central concern was that the undersecretary/director had to have the right, formally approved, to go to all NSC meetings related to arms control, disarmament, and non-proliferation. Furthermore, he or she had to have a vote, separate from that of the secretary, just as the independent ACDA director now did. This meant that his or her vote alone could cause an issue to be sent to the president for decision, since the NSC operates on the basis of consensus.

Further, he or she had to have the right to communicate directly with the president. We did a little research and discovered that the chairman of the JCS has the right to communicate directly with the president, through the secretary of defense. As we understood it, he sends his memorandum to the president, through the secretary, who cannot stop or change the memo, but can comment on it. We based our ACDA position on this issue on that practice. We also said that the undersecretary should have the chair of the interagency non-proliferation process as well as the interagency arms control process and that these should be brought back from the NSC. All negotiators should report to him, and he should have some special hiring authority, outside normal civil service rules as ACDA did in order to be able to secure technical experts. Most important, all other arms control functions in the Department of State should be brought under the undersecretary. Particularly, CFE should be moved from State/EUR. Also, he should have his own independent intelligence and verification function and his own Office of General Counsel. And the undersecretary's title should be undersecretary of state for arms control and international security/senior advisor to the president and secretary of state for arms control, non-proliferation and disarmament. This is probably the longest title in government, but one which would imply direct access to the president, just as the ACDA director then had.

Barb Starr was designated as our negotiator, with Bill Burns her opposite number at State. Burns, the son of the former director, was executive secretary at State (and subsequently assistant secretary of state for the Middle East) and had a good relationship with Barb. John, Ralph, and I were sort of the principals for whom she was negotiating. The only ones regularly involved on the State side in addition to Bill were Secretary Albright, State Department spokesman James Rubin, and Strobe. Barb did the negotiating, John and I occasionally spoke with Strobe (I, once by telephone from Ottawa, tried at some length to persuade him that what we were asking for was consistent with the 1961 Senate bill), and Rubin. John intervened from time to time on key issues with Albright and with Sandy Berger.

The negotiations lasted from February to April and went through many twists and turns. We achieved almost all our demands. The question of the undersecretary's right to communicate directly with the president was a tough one. Although in the end we did prevail, no State Department official other than the secretary has this right. However, it is essential to the independence of the arms control process and implicit in the full title of the undersecretary we had designed. We could not win on the independent legal office, much to my chagrin, but we did get some special rights for an associate legal advisor assigned to disarmament. This is a serious loss if one thinks back to the ABM Treaty broad interpretation debate. However, agreement on a separate Verification and Compliance Office was achieved. Originally this was to be a separate office attached to the undersecretary, but eventually with congressional pressure it became one of the four bureaus subordinate to the undersecretary. This preserved the integrity of the ACDA verification and compliance staff, which had resided in a separate ACDA bureau for the past sixteen years. Preservation of the independent ACDA take on verification and compliance issues was significant.

With Albright's strong support we acquired non-proliferation from the NSC, but Sandy drew a line in the sand on arms control. Bob Bell would quit if that happened, he told Madeleine, so we compromised on the chair staying at NSC, but both NSC and the undersecretary had the right to raise an arms control subject in the interagency. With respect to other arms control functions in State coming under the undersecretary, State/EUR fought for a long time for CFE, but we held to our position and eventually prevailed on that issue. However, both the decision on transferring the non-proliferation chair from the NSC and moving CFE to the undersecretary took a long time to implement, as there was much continuing resistance from NSC and State/EUR respectively, but Barb and John finally succeeded in 1998. John had overall leadership on CFE in any case, and the CFE bureaucratic structure was to move in 1999 after the then ongoing NATO expansion process, with which CFE was linked, was completed.

The deal was struck in April and jointly announced to an all-hands ACDA meeting by John, Ralph, and me. I said that there was an opportunity here for the arms control process to be even stronger and the ACDA independent advocacy role to be more effectively institutionalized. It all went down very badly. The recriminations were many. Holum established a daily meeting process chaired by Ralph. Barb Starr as the senior agency representative began her long, detailed negotiating process with Bill Burns and others to make the agreement in principle operational. Several times I argued in these meetings that we had to work together to maximize our opportunities. In particular, we had an opportunity to get CFE and we must not jeopardize it. These arguments were to no avail; no one was interested. Perhaps understandably at this difficult time, people were only interested in their own positions. Other agency officers also negotiated to a degree with their contact points in State/PM. There were several private, serious personal attacks on Barb and on John, along with the open recriminations. Ultimately, Barb and others worked out the details, but the necessary legislation was stalled in Congress for a long time because an abortion rider was attached to the bill. Finally, at the end of 1998, the legislation passed and ACDA disappeared, appropriately, on April 1, 1999. The State Department Reorganization Plan, which implemented the law authorizing the ACDA merger and which itself cannot be modified without further legislation, provided that the new undersecretary will have a "unique" role reflecting authorities transferred from ACDA and the new structure will "ensure that unique arms control and non-proliferation perspectives will continue to be available at the highest levels of the U.S. government, including the president." These are the correct objectives, but the story will be in the telling.

So, were we correct in December 1996 when we decided to negotiate? Should we have fought instead? Brian Atwood fought for AID and was largely successful. Certainly an independent ACDA would have been better, even if only partly viable. I was influenced to some degree by Rolf Ekeus's comment and to a degree by what Strobe had said. But beyond that, I could not see where our allies would be found. Congress was the traditional supporter for ACDA, but Congress had gone from mild indifference in 1993 to active hostility following the Republican takeover in 1994. Our supporters Bill Perry and Hazel O'Leary had left the Cabinet, and Tony Lake was no longer at NSC.

Thus, ACDA decided early on to negotiate the best deal that it could. And a good deal was negotiated. At least on paper it was good enough to have the potential to make the arms control process in the U.S. government stronger rather than weaker. However, and this is a large caveat, it is heavily dependent upon the people involved and relationships within the department. For this to work, the undersecretary's authorities have to be respected by others and exercised by him or her in future administrations, not an easy task given for whom the undersecretary works. Time will tell. Independence would have been better, but under the circumstances this seemed like the best deal possible. So, in my judgment, ACDA came out reasonably well. USIA never got into the process, and as a result, did not do well. AID, after a long struggle, did succeed in preserving its independence.

We had neither the Congress nor the White House with us, nor any of the other government agencies. As I have mentioned, in 1993 Bob Bell had run an interagency exercise on whether ACDA should remain independent or be acquired by State. This process resulted in benevolent neutrality from NSC, CIA, and JCS, and support for the independence and strengthening of ACDA from OSD, DOE, and ACDA. Only State supported State acquiring ACDA. This positive situation for ACDA no longer existed in 1997. The limited support we received from the NGO community in 1993 had dwindled to practically nothing by 1997. The only way we could have made any headway as a small, controversial agency with no allies left would have been a no-holds-barred press campaign. It might have succeeded if John Holum had been prepared to divert from their substantive assignments all the best officers of the agency into a six- to twelve-month public campaign. And even if we had prevailed and maintained the independence of ACDA in 1997—an unlikely proposition—ACDA probably would have been destroyed anyway in the interagency process. At the time I thought we were definitely doing not only the right thing, but the best thing, perhaps the only thing, for the arms control process. Now, after several years, I am not as confident. Maybe it would have been better to abandon substantive work and do everything we could to preserve the shell of ACDA for future presidents. But perhaps the new structure will work as advertised and the independence of the arms control process will be preserved. I wrote an article on this subject that was published in September 1999 in the *Foreign Service Journal* expressing some optimism. I hope that it proves justified. The fact that John Holum's confirmation as the new undersecretary was blocked in the Senate until the end of the Clinton administration was not a good sign for the future.

In sum, if the undersecretary's authorities are respected and exercised, the new structure can work and the independence of the arms control process can be preserved—the central issue. The real test will come in the years ahead. I hope the new structure will succeed, but if it does not, it will be the future duty of a Congress and a president to reenact the ACDA Act and reestablish ACDA.

EPILOGUE

As I indicated, the Lawyers Alliance for World Security (LAWS) had been pursuing me for some time. A number of times I had met with LAWS Board members Mark Schlefer and John Rhinelander, as well as Louise Walker, beginning in September 1995. At that time, I told them I was interested, but that I could do nothing until after the CFE Review Conference in May 1996. Mark raised the salary offer to an attractive level and by the end of 1996, as I said, I did not see many prospects for full-time projects in the government. Accordingly, in January 1997, I told Mark that I would come aboard as LAWS president on July 1, and would retire from the government on that date. I had kept John and Ralph informed and I told John of my decision in January. So I retired from the government on July 1, 1997, and an hour later I was installed as president of LAWS. Jeff Smith, the dean of arms control reporting, wrote a very nice piece on me in the *Washington Post*. He emphasized my role in the ABM debate and quoted me as saying that the ABM Treaty interpretation question was an important issue because the United States is a country that stands for the "rule of law and sanctity of contract." The title of the piece was "Retired from Government But Not from the Cause," which I hope is true, and the picture with the piece showed Barb Starr giving me a farewell hug. Christine and several of the kids are in the background. It is a great memory.

Contemporaneous with my retirement from government, the United States National Academy of Sciences published a report of a study group chaired by General Bill Burns entitled "The Future of U.S. Nuclear Weapons Policy." The central theme of the report was that the United States should pursue deep cuts in nuclear weapons, down to the low hundreds for the United States and Russia, fewer for the other three nuclear powers, with some account taken of India, Pakistan, and Israel. The report also recommended that the United States should limit the role of its nuclear weapons to the "core deterrence" function, simply deterring their use by others or, in other words, that the United States should adopt a policy of no first use of nuclear weapons. Upon assuming the presidency of LAWS, I adopted these objectives as the central message of LAWS because I believed them to be sound and correct—and do all the more today in late 2001.

Initially, we began with trips to Japan and Germany in 1997. It had long been an argument against adoption of a U.S. no-first-use policy that the United States could never do this, otherwise, Japan and Germany would lose faith in the United States nuclear umbrella and build nuclear weapons themselves. Of course nothing could be further from the truth, and officials in the two countries made that clear. In Germany we met with Gerhard Verheugen and Rudolph Scharping, the foreign policy spokesman and the parliamentary floor leader of the Social Democratic Party (SPD), respectively, and they both said they strongly supported a no-first-use policy for NATO. Verheugen said that he would find a colleague from the Christian Democratic Party and do an op-ed article for the *International Herald Tribune* and Scharping said he would raise this issue with Secretary Cohen when he saw him the next month (October 1997) in Washington. I came to the conclusion that if the German government changed in the 1998 election, and I thought it might, there was a good prospect for a change in the German government position on the issue of NATO nuclear weapon use doctrine. And this is in fact what happened, led by Chancellor Schroeder, Foreign Minister Fischer, and Defense Minister Rudolph Scharping.

Officials in both Germany and Japan were also committed to the concept of deep cuts in nuclear weapons. In Japan I was impressed with the powerful desire of the Japanese public to see nuclear weapons totally gone forever on the one hand and the caution of the government on the other. Ambassador Imai, one of the leading figures in Japan both in nuclear disarmament and in nuclear power, in one of our discussions spoke of the growing gulf between the Japanese public and its government on nuclear issues, both disarmament and nuclear power.

NATO conducted a strategic review during the run-up to its fiftieth anniversary summit. As part of this process, Germany and Canada called for a review of NATO nuclear strategy, including the NATO first-use option. This appeal by Germany and Canada was strongly rebuffed by the United States—in spite of several key realities: that the rationale for the first-use option, the conventional superiority of the Warsaw Pact, had long since passed into history; that nuclear weapon proliferation is the principal threat to NATO security; and that the NATO first-use option is potentially inconsistent with the 1995 negative security assurances undertaken by three of NATO's members (the United States, the United Kingdom, and France) which are central underpinnings of the NPT regime. And there were calls in the United States for overt deterrence of chemical and biological weapons by nuclear weapons— potentially even more inconsistent with the assurances in that it would inevitably involve implying the use of nuclear weapons against non-nuclear weapon state parties to the NPT.

The basic problem is that the prestige value of nuclear weapons, made high during the Cold War, remains very high. The five permanent members of the Security Council are the five nuclear weapon states—an historical accident, but nevertheless a fact. If the prestige value of nuclear weapons is not lowered, if states are going to continue to perceive that there is a link between status and possession of nuclear weapons, then these weapons will simply be too attractive, and the 1945 technology on which they are based too simple, for states to continue to forswear them and for the NPT regime to survive. How can the political value of nuclear weapons be reduced? By making deep cuts in their numbers and restricting their role to core deterrence, which is the LAWS program inspired by the National Academy report. This is the program I have consistently advocated since July 1, 1997.

The 1998 Indian and Pakistani nuclear tests created in my opinion the most dangerous situation since the dawn of the nuclear age, with the exception of the Cuban Missile Crisis. On the one hand, the breaking of the thirty-year norm based on the NPT regime against the creation of new nuclear weapon states raised the specter of nuclear weapons gradually spreading over the entire globe, thereby establishing the nightmare situation that the NPT sought to avoid: a world filled with nuclear weapon states, where every crisis threatens to go nuclear and the survival of civilization truly is in question from day to day. On the other hand, the tests established a condition in which a significant risk of nuclear war between India and Pakistan now existed, with an attendant tens of millions of deaths resulting—a singular catastrophe far greater than has ever occurred before in the history of the world. It was unpersuasive for India to offer that it had done this because of national security needs, asserting that it had in mind that the United States and the Soviet Union had managed their nuclear confrontation with maturity and stability for fifty years. Now, instead of a situation of massive conventional superiority, every Indian city was at risk from Pakistani nuclear-tipped missiles. The United States and the Soviet Union had only with luck managed to avoid nuclear Armageddon; there were many near misses. The Indian tests, in my judgment, were entirely motivated by a desire by India for great-power status, given the continued political significance of nuclear weapons. Indeed, the Indian prime minister asserted, in May 1998, in effect, that India is a big country now that it has the bomb.

In mid-September 1998, I traveled to India and participated in a conference organized by Professor M. Sondhi of Jawaharlal Nehru University, who without warning appeared in my office in June 1998 and invited me to come to India. He is now a senior official in the Hindu nationalist BJP Party–led Indian government. The conference was on the subject of South Asia and nuclear weapons. Most of the participants were hard-line members of India's nuclear weapon establishment. To some extent, I was a voice crying in the wilderness. In my speech I pointed out that India was now less safe than before the tests, and that the prestige value of nuclear weapons simply had to be reduced if widespread proliferation endangering us all was to be avoided. Deep cuts and restricting the role of nuclear weapons to core deterrence is the road to follow. I said that the five nuclear weapon states should adopt policies of not being the first to use nuclear weapons in future conflicts. Of course, China has had a no-first-use policy for thirty years and one of the first things that India did after its tests—at the urging of the United States—was to adopt a no-first-use policy. I recommended a START process that would have the United States following the Russian Federation to lower levels as the latter had to reduce for economic reasons. First, the two parties should negotiate a level of 1000 strategic weapons, then with a commitment first to a limitation on tactical nuclear weapons of perhaps 500, adopt a limitation of 1000 total weapons.

I continued in my presentation to the conference that the stage would then be set for a five-power negotiation to deep cuts with account taken of weapons held by India, Pakistan, and Israel. An appropriate end point, until the world has changed sufficiently for the prohibition of nuclear weapons to be considered a serious objective (worldwide intensive verification and effective enforcement—nowhere in sight in 2001—would be a *sine qua non*) could be reductions to perhaps 300 weapons each for the United States and Russia, fifty each for the United Kingdom, France, and China, and zero for India, Pakistan, and Israel, but with the fissile material stored on their territories under IAEA safeguards (as South Africa did) as a hedge against breakdown of the agreement. India, Pakistan, and Israel would join the NPT as non-nuclear weapon state parties. And all non-nuclear weapon state parties to the NPT would pledge again their non-nuclear status and joint action (perhaps military) against any violator. In this way, the growing nuclear danger might be averted.

The speech went over reasonably well. There were no violent objections. Ambassador Ghose, the Indian ambassador to the CD during the CTBT affair and as tough as they come, said she wished that I was making U.S. policy. While in Delhi I had a meeting with Jaswant Singh, then head of planning and a close confidant of the prime minister (he would became external affairs minister a few months later) in his office. He said, "Now that India has done the tests, for better or for worse, it simply has to move back into the mainstream of the international disarmament and non-proliferation process." My impression was that the Indian government did want to do what Dr. Singh suggested. It had demonstrated, at great cost to the NPT regime, its national security bona fides and now it wanted to come back into the world community. We should be tough, but we should try to help it do so.

Before a parliamentary no-confidence vote dissolved the Indian government, India had committed itself (and Pakistan could have followed) to sign CTBT in May 1999, which had raised a real possibility of CTBT entry into force. So my thinking about India evolved after this to believing that the United States can and should try to work with the BJP government. After the testing of a newer longer-range Agni missile and the response by Pakistan of two missile tests of its own, renewed fighting over Kashmir, and serious border tension in December 2001, the future of the Subcontinent is very much in doubt. The BJP government of India had privately committed itself to the United States to sign and ratify the CTBT if it was returned to power in the fall elections, which it was. Pakistan likely would have followed suit after Indian signature, but this commitment vanished after the disastrous U.S. Senate rejection of the CTBT.

The NPT is in trouble. The Statement of Principles and Objectives called for continued commitment by the nuclear weapon states to reduce significantly their number of nuclear weapons, as well as to achieve a CTBT in 1996. In April 1995 the nuclear weapon states formally pledged, pursuant to UN Security Council Resolution 984, essentially never to use nuclear weapons against non-nuclear weapon state parties to the NPT (the negative security assurances). This number includes 182 states, that is, all of the world except the five NPT nuclear weapon states, the three threshold states, and Cuba. The only exception to the negative security assurances was that if one of the non-nuclear weapon states attacked a nuclear weapon state in alliance with another nuclear weapon state, holdover language from the Cold War—referring to a satellite of the former Soviet Union—then the assurance would not apply. There is no exception for chemical or biological weapons, and the World Court implied that this NPT-related commitment is legally binding in its 1996 decision. At the very least the nuclear weapon states can agree not to attack with such weapons countries that permanently forswear nuclear weapons.

I refined my views on the issues of deep cuts in nuclear weapons and restricting the role of nuclear weapons to core deterrence, as part of the central task of reducing the political value of nuclear weapons so that the NPT regime would survive and prosper, in presentations in Washington before the Center for Strategic and International Studies on December 4, 1998, and at the annual Carnegie International Non-Proliferation Conference on January 12, 1999. At the same time, the beginning of the NATO strategic review at the December NATO Ministerial, looking forward to the April fiftieth anniversary summit, and the new SPD/Green German government's public espousal of a NATO no-first-use policy, brought this issue into still sharper focus. I had been in Germany in November, shortly before the German announcement on NATO nuclear doctrine by the foreign minister and also at a government-sponsored conference in Victoria, British Columbia, in December where it was clear that the Canadian government was under heavy U.S. pressure to back away from pressing for a revision of NATO doctrine so as to restrict the role of nuclear weapons to core deterrence. In December, I also held consultations with British government officials on this issue. Subsequently, in February 1999, I visited the capitals of Norway, the Netherlands, Belgium, Germany, France, Italy, and Spain to discuss the NATO review and NATO use policy, accompanied to the first four countries by General Lee Butler.

Unfortunately, while there is wide sympathy for a NATO no-first-use policy in all these countries, even France, there is also a concern about offending the United States. NATO, led by the United States, has been the most successful military alliance in history and, rightly, no one wants to do anything to disrupt the Alliance. At the same time, virtually all these countries believe that NATO would be more secure with a revised nuclear doctrine in today's world, if only the United States could be persuaded to go along. The French, of course, said their nuclear weapon policy is separate from NATO and they have not made up their minds on this issue. The Germans said that they have not changed their minds on their policy and they intend to pursue core deterrence for NATO vigorously for as long as it takes. The British said that they agreed, but they have this long-standing policy position "at the top." Italy (at least before the election of the Berlesconi government in early 2001) supported a change in NATO nuclear doctrine away from the first use option.

In March 1999, LAWS Board member and former Secretary of Defense Bob McNamara, Lee Butler, and I appeared before a joint session of the Canadian Parliamentary Committee on Foreign Affairs and International Trade and the Canadian Senate Foreign Relations Committee testifying on behalf of a Parliamentary Committee Report on the future of Canadian policy toward nuclear weapons. It was appropriately titled "Reducing the Political Value of Nuclear Weapons for the Twenty-First Century." Among other things the report called for a review by NATO of its nuclear weapon policies. We also had separate private meetings with the prime minister, the foreign minister, and the defense minister. During those meetings, which were arranged by my friend and colleague Canadian Senator Douglas Roche, who chairs the Middle Power Initiative (MPI), we urged them, above all, to try to get a commitment to a review in the Summit Communiqué. They were not optimistic, but they said they would try. They succeeded in this, in Article 32 of the NATO Summit Communiqué, publicly pointed to with pride by Foreign Minister Axworthy on the day it was released. I might say that this is but an example of the effectiveness of MPI's efforts to energize the governments of key non-nuclear weapons states to encourage steps that would promote implementation by the nuclear weapons states of NPT Article VI.

In the fall Bob McNamara and I, along with Jack Mendelsohn, returned to Europe to discuss NATO nuclear weapon use doctrine. We had consultations in Prague and Rome, and testified before the Arms Control Subcommittee of the Bundestag in Berlin. In December, pursuant to the Summit Communiqué at the ministerial, a formal NATO review was established. It seemed to us that it was important for the NPT regime that nuclear weapon use doctrine be on the agenda of the review. Paragraph 44 of the NATO Ministerial Communiqué in December 1999 formally established the review and provided that it would be completed in December 2000. The language simply repeated that of the April summit which, at least in the view of the Canadian foreign minister, included a review of nuclear weapon use doctrine. December 2000 and the NATO Ministerial came and went, however, without any effect on NATO nuclear weapon use doctrine.

Additionally, all of the countries we talked with in February 1999 were deeply concerned about possible unilateral U.S. abrogation of the ABM Treaty and the attendant construction of national missile defenses. The French said that if we touched the ABM Treaty, they would significantly increase their number of nuclear weapons, which had been trending downward, and we could expect the British to do the same. The Germans (Rudi Hartmann was still the disarmament commissioner for a few more months) said, in strong words, that an action by the United States to unilaterally put aside the ABM Treaty would "decouple" the United States from Europe, and the Russian ambassador to NATO, Sergei Kislyak, my NPT colleague, with whom I also met, said such an action would "permanently" end the nuclear weapon reduction process. There was increasing political pressure in the United States to develop missile defenses to counter the alleged missile threat by so-called "rogue states," now referred to as "states of proliferation concern." There were discussions with Russia on this and on START III levels in the last years of the Clinton administration, but they did not go well. It was judged important for U.S. and world security that any modifications to the ABM Treaty to accommodate such defenses be the minimum necessary and carefully preserve the viability of the treaty. Development of such defenses should be cooperative with Russia, Europe, and China if irreparable harm to the international security system is to be avoided. Because of these concerns and the lack of success in NMD tests, President Clinton wisely deferred all decisions on NMD to the next president in a speech on September 1, 2000.

In late March 2000, Bob McNamara and I testified before the Defense Committee of the British House of Commons on the NATO review and NMD. We urged that NATO nuclear weapon use policy be reviewed in the ongoing NATO review and that consideration be given to NATO adopting a policy of not being the first to introduce nuclear weapons into future conflicts. After our opening statements, a lively question period of an hour and a half ensued, but no one disagreed with our basic arguments. I included in my statement a comment that the United Kingdom had delivered on its 1995 commitments as a result of its review of nuclear policy, which led to a significant reduction in the number of deployed British warheads and the removal of those that remained from high alert. For this I received a nice thank-you note from Prime Minister Blair.

We also made the same arguments in Paris to senior members of the National Assembly and the Senate as well as before a meeting of the French Institute on Foreign Relations. Our impression was that the French are relaxed about the prospect of a NATO core deterrence policy and they certainly oppose NMD. It is my firm conclusion after all these meetings over a year and a half with NATO government officials, parliamentarians, academics, NGOs and media representatives that virtually all NATO members would be comfortable with a change in the NATO nuclear weapon use doctrine and that many would actively support it if only the United States would cease its opposition. And further, that a U.S. unilateral NMD policy, if combined with abrogation of the ABM Treaty, could seriously jeopardize the viability of the NATO

Alliance. In the late spring of 2000, I participated in two debates on the legal status of the treaty, which I discussed in chapter 7. Also, I participated in a straight-out debate on NMD policy with Steve Hadley before the Council on Foreign Relations in New York in June. We should all be mindful of the warning of Ambassador Gerard Errerra in Washington in March 2000 that if the United States should abrogate the ABM Treaty—coupled with the Senate's rejection of the CTBT—we should over time expect other countries, not necessarily our friends, to question their commitment to multilateral arms control obligations, beginning with the NPT.

The administration of President George W. Bush took office in January 2001. Consistent with a speech then-candidate Bush made during the campaign, increasingly there were rumors that the new administration was contemplating the unilateral reduction of nuclear weapons to a significantly lower level, but allegedly as part of a policy of "flexibility," implying that these cuts would not be intended to be permanent. If reported correctly, the effect of such a policy could be to destroy the START process of negotiated reductions and the rest of the international arms control regime. This would lead to an era of strategic uncertainty and development of worse-case scenarios, which it is the purpose of the arms control process to avoid and would be a long stride in the wrong direction. Also in 2001, there was a strong push in the administration for NMD (newspaper reports in March suggest that Secretary of Defense Donald Rumsfeld had already personally reviewed seventeen NMD deployment plans) and a possibility that the ABM Treaty might be abrogated. Such an action, combined with the continued U.S. rejection of the CTBT and in the context of this unilateral approach to nuclear force levels, would put the NPT at great risk and would be an even longer stride down that wrong road. At the 2000 NPT Review Conference all of the parties to the NPT, including the United States, agreed in the conference's Final Document—a politically binding part of the NPT regime—to endorse the preservation of the ABM Treaty as a "cornerstone of strategic stability." This is language from the U.S.-Russian agreement in Helsinki from 1997 and, while it may mean different things to different NPT parties, it unites all NPT parties behind the preservation of the ABM Treaty. Thus, a move against the ABM Treaty would be a move against the NPT regime. We simply must as a nation and as a world community return to the path of strengthening international constraints on weapons of mass destruction and building peace for the twenty-first century.

On May 1, President Bush in a speech at the National Defense University said that "we must move beyond the constraints of the thirty-year-old ABM Treaty" and that "a new framework that allows us to build missile defenses" is needed. The president added that the new framework should encourage "further cuts in nuclear weapons"—even though nuclear weapons "still have a vital role to play in our security and that of our allies"—and it should be based on a "new cooperative relationship" with Russia. From this position, the president could have moved in almost any direction; let us hope that eventually it is toward worldwide cooperation, strengthening the international arms control and nonproliferation regime, and enhancing peace and stability for the twenty-first century. An NMD program that is cooperative with Russia, China, and our NATO allies is far different from a program which is not. By August of 2001, Pentagon spokesmen were implying that the United States would abrogate the ABM Treaty "in a matter of months" and President Bush for his part was to a degree going along with such rhetoric. U.S. abrogation of the ABM Treaty and a unilateral NMD program could cause Russia to keep its weapons on hair-trigger alert, create a nuclear arms race with China, damage NATO, and seriously undermine the NPT regime. This would be a dangerous path for U.S. and world security.

On September 11, 2001, the real enemy of world civilization revealed itself in the horrific terrorist attacks in New York and Washington. But as terrible as these attacks were, they would have been orders of magnitude worse if nuclear weapons or fissile materials had been involved. And no missile defense would have stopped them. As Prime Minister Blair, President Chirac, and Chancellor Schroeder stated in their *New York Times* editorial (October 1999) urging favorable action by the U.S. Senate on the CTBT, "nuclear proliferation will remain the principal threat to world safety" in the twenty-first century. The more states that have nuclear weapons and the more fissile material there is, the more difficult it will be to prevent terrorist organizations, rogue states, violent sub-national groups, and the like from acquiring nuclear weapons. Our principal defense against this is a strong NPT regime and the web of associated international agreements that have kept the peace for thirty years, including the START treaties, the agreements to control fissile material, the CTBT, the nuclear-weapon-free zone arrangements, the ABM Treaty, the negative security commitments, and the commitment to further significant reductions in nuclear weapons. Therefore, at the center of anti-terrorism policy—in addition to efforts to suppress terrorism and efforts to deal with its underlying causes in the Middle East—must be a commitment to strengthen the NPT regime as much as possible as well as the international cooperation upon which the regime is based.

To date, the Bush administration has done a superb job in rapidly constructing a broad anti-terrorism coalition. The coalition—which includes Russia and China—will, I hope, endure so as to continue to build and strengthen the international treaty regime and the international rule of law. Following from the 2000 NPT review conference, the world community recognizes that the ABM Treaty is the "cornerstone of strategic stability" and thus any missile defense plans should be consistent with the existing—or mutually amended or superseded—ABM Treaty, with account taken of the views of China. One of the lessons of September 11th is not, as some have suggested, that missile defense is more important than ever, but rather that the international treaty regime and international cooperation are essential to a peaceful, stable world.

In early October 2001, Bob McNamara and I, accompanied by LAWS

Communications and Programs director, Damien LaVera, conducted a series of discussions with senior government officials and lawmakers in London, Copenhagen, and Moscow. It became clear to me in the course of those meetings that, as a result of the September 11th attacks, the international community—hopefully including the United States—understands anew this need for international cooperation. So, too, does it understand that the world has finally moved beyond the post–Cold War transition period. As Mikhail Gorbachev told us in Moscow, the fact that the United States and Russia have "come to the point of a new relationship based on a new agenda" and that attitudes toward the attacks have "drawn a straight line between the United States, Russia, China, India, Pakistan, and Cuba" indicates that we have reached a crucial time in world history. If this spirit of cooperation is to persist, and as a result international anti-terrorism efforts are to succeed, the United States must be careful to act in a manner that de-emphasizes unilateralist steps taken at the expense of the interests of our coalition partners. This is a lesson that—for the sake of international peace and security—I hope will not soon be forgotten and international security will guide America's relationship with nuclear issues for the foreseeable future.

The United States gave notice of withdrawal from the ABM Treaty in December 2001 to take effect pursuant to Article XV of the Treaty on June 13, 2002. By that time it will probably be known whether the historic effort by President Bush to bring Russia into NATO as a de facto member will in fact happen. The outcome of this effort will make a difference in the geopolitical effect of ABM Treaty termination. The administration has proposed reductions in strategic nuclear weapons by the United States and Russia to approximate the level agreed to in Helsinki in 1997, but not in a legally binding forum. Russia wants a binding agreement. The outcome of this as well will be important for the future of the NPT. This is a time of great promise as well as great danger. If the world community, led by the United States, can move in the direction of strengthening the global security system by enhancing the international treaty system and relying on international law and cooperation rather than force, in the first instance, to deal with the real security threats that exist, this time of promise can be fully realized.

For me personally, it continues to be a rewarding experience to work on these issues. In addition to having the privilege of working on important and intellectually challenging issues, there has been the pleasure of association with all the dedicated people who work and have worked in the field of arms control, disarmament, and non-proliferation. There are good people on all points of the spectrum and, as the JCS representative told me in the mid-1970s, the best policy emerges from the clash of disparate views. And to paraphrase the great sportswriter Grantland Rice, "When the One Great Scorer comes to mark against your name, it is not whether you won or lost [or were right or wrong, liberal or conservative], but how you played the game." It has been and continues to be quite a game.

CONCLUSIONS

In reviewing the history of arms control, non-proliferation, and disarmament events over the last thirty years, perhaps it would be useful to attempt to draw some conclusions, or at least some lessons. Of particular interest are the issues related to what the role of disarmament policy should be, and the maintenance of arsenals of weapons of mass destruction by democratic states. Ultimately, can democratic states effectively deal with the imperative to drastically reduce nuclear weapons and restrict their role, pursuant to NPT obligations, given the extensive internal political pressures that surround such subjects? In 2001 this remains to be demonstrated. The political pressures are many and, once having acquired nuclear weapons, it is difficult for democratic states to cut back the levels they have attained.

Again, disarmament should not be thought of as an end in itself. Rather it should be considered a part of national security policy or, in the international sense, another means by which security can be achieved. A nation state has a multiplicity of tools available to maintain its security. It has its armed forces, its diplomatic capability, its intelligence apparatus, and its economic strength. Disarmament is a subset of national security policy. It is the achievement of security through control of arms rather than, for example, through the threat of the use of armed force, or economic pressure. Sometimes the pursuit of the solution to a national security problem through the adoption of a certain disarmament policy or certain disarmament negotiations is appropriate. Sometimes it is not. It simply is one of the options that national security policymakers should consider when addressing a particular problem. It should not be thought of as a morally superior policy. Rather, policymakers should use those tools that are most likely to enhance national security and to bring peace and stability—that is the objective. And, in my judgment, this is as true on the international level as it is on the national level. Both the nation state and the world community should pursue policies that work; policies, whether they be peacekeeping, disarmament, economic sanctions or whatever, that are most likely to achieve international peace and security.

Disarmament, as we have seen, is not a new issue. As far back as 1139 the Second Lateran Council, convoked by Pope Innocent II, outlawed the crossbow, declaring it to be "hateful to God and unfit for Christians." However, at the battle of Agincourt in 1415, the English longbow, in decimating the French knights, proved to be superior to the crossbow in killing capability because of its more rapid rate of fire. And both the crossbow and the longbow were not long afterwards eclipsed by the destructive firepower of the cannon. The Church also proscribed the rifle when it appeared on the scene, but this effort was quickly overtaken by events. Military technology continued to develop at a faster and faster pace over the centuries. As the controlled and limited warfare of the eighteenth century gave way to the *levée en masse* under Napoleon, armaments became increasingly sophisticated. The appearance of long-range artillery, and then the machine gun, led to a period of defense dominance which lasted until World War II and also significantly increased the level of violence in warfare.

It was with these developments as a backdrop that Czar Nicholas urged the convening of the first Hague Peace Conference in 1899. That conference was followed by a second in 1907. The measures adopted were largely ineffective. Dum-dum, or expanding, bullets were effectively proscribed, but the prohibitions on poison gas warfare and aerial bombardment were ignored in World War I. Recently, the 100th anniversary of the 1899 Hague Declaration was observed. It is difficult to argue that the world is more secure now than it was in 1899. Future world wars now seem unlikely, but military technology still threatens humanity. Then, as now, the relevance of arms limitation measures is often under pressure from advances in military technology. Thus, there are three questions that pertain to any particular disarmament measure: Is it effective? Is it verifiable? Is it likely to remain relevant as technology develops?

It could be said that the modern age of arms limitation began after World War I. Horrified by the spectacle of poison gas warfare in the trenches, the international community moved to outlaw this military technology in the 1920s. The Washington Naval Treaty of 1922, which never came into force because of French objections to the submarine limitations, contained a proscription on poison gas warfare. The world community tried again in 1925 when in Geneva, on the margins of a conference on the international arms trade, a protocol outlawing the use in war of poison gas—or chemical weapons—was agreed to by the states present. At the last minute, at the suggestion of the Polish delegate, bacteriological weapons of war (an old means of warfare, e.g. dead horses catapulted into walled cities under siege, but not a problem in World War I) were included in the ban. This agreement has been known ever afterwards as the Geneva Protocol. It is a rule of warfare, but at the same time, the first modern disarmament agreement.

As nation states ratified the Geneva protocol, many took reservations freeing themselves from its obligations if either of the outlawed weapons were used against them, thus, in effect, converting the protocol into a ban on the first use in warfare of the proscribed weapons among protocol parties. Although chemical weapons were used by Italy in Ethiopia in 1936, by Egypt in Yemen in 1967, and by Iran and Iraq in their war against one another in the 1980s, the agreement did hold during World War II and largely thereafter. Thus, the protocol does meet the three tests mentioned above: it is effective, it has been largely observed and this observance is verifiable, and it remains at least as relevant today as it was in 1925.

The naval limitation agreements of the inter-war period failed, as did other attempts at limiting the destructiveness of war (except for the Geneva Protocol) in the face of the rising military power and aggressive intention of the Axis powers—Germany, Italy, and Japan. Their collision with the rest of the world community led to World War II, the most destructive of all wars, in which approximately 60 million people died. World War II was accompanied by huge advances in military technology, creating what appears to be a permanent state of offensive dominance. Strategic bombers, flame throwers, rockets, and missiles such as the V-1 and V-2 greatly increased the destructiveness of war. And at the end of World War II, the atomic bomb appeared. This enormously destructive military technology forever changed the world. For the first time mankind had created the ability to destroy itself. The atomic bomb made world war little more than mass suicide, and it is to Hiroshima in 1945 that the establishment of the modern era of disarmament negotiations is correctly dated. Now it was no longer a question only of limiting the destructiveness of war, but of ensuring the survival of humanity and preserving world civilization.

Man's inhumanity to man predates the beginning of civilization. In ancient times humans in organized groups killed one another for territory and empire. Only in relatively recent times have organized groups, later kingdoms and now nation states, as well as sub-national groups, made war on one another for the worst of motives—to advance the cause of a religion or ideology. To make war to further a religious or ideological cause is to escalate the commitment of those involved. To believe that one is fighting either God's or history's war is to make compromise and peace even more elusive. It could be said that, as military technology has grown in capability since the time of the Vikings, the motives for war have to a degree evolved from a simple attempt at territorial acquisition or empire to a reliance on revolution, ideology, or religion as the motivating force. Thus war has become more violent and solutions to conflict more intractable. The intolerance of political movements on the left and the right is well understood, but organized religion is not blameless. Too often priests, ministers, rabbis, and mullahs encourage the more violent in our world community. All religions tend to move away from the idealism of their founders as they become more organized and their leaders more worldly. Truly, it can be said of the world's major religions what I recall as being attributed to Bernard Shaw with respect to Christianity: "The only trouble with it is that no one has ever tried it." In the modern world there is no holy war, only war. And as the proliferation of weapons of mass destruction becomes an ever greater threat to the security of the world community, religious extremists and cults—along with violent sub-national ethnic groups, terrorist organizations, and criminal conspiracies—are at the core of the problem.

After the Reykjavik meeting in October 1986, where Presidents Reagan and Gorbachev came close to discussing the elimination of strategic offensive arms (only to be staved off by Reagan's advisors impressing upon him between sessions with Gorbachev the importance of not limiting SDI to the laboratory), Prime Minister Margaret Thatcher flew to Washington for a heart to heart talk with her friend Ronald Reagan. As she boarded the plane in London she was heard to remark, in effect, that "nuclear weapons have kept the peace in Europe for forty years and I am not about to give them up." To a large degree that may have been true. Churchill spoke in the 1950s of the "balance of terror." Certainly the existence of large numbers of nuclear weapons on hair-trigger alert on both sides of the East-West divide induced caution in Moscow and Washington. The United States and the Soviet Union, while engaging in all sorts of provocative acts such as spy-plane overflights and aircraft incursions to test military reactions, were very careful to avoid direct military action against one another. Thus, the Cold War remained cold and there was no worldwide military conflagration involving the United States and the Soviet Union or NATO and the Warsaw Pact.

But at what a risk! For more then forty years the world remained on the brink of total destruction, with thousands of enormously destructive nuclear weapons poised on high alert to be delivered at intercontinental range on long-range ballistic missiles in thirty minutes. And we are lucky that this did not happen, as subsequent analysis of the Cuban Missile Crisis has demonstrated. There were many false alarms and near misses that could have developed into a thermonuclear war. So did nuclear weapons in fact keep the peace for forty years? Who can say with certainty? On one hand, huge armies did face each other across the inter-German border for decades without clashing despite the aggressive totalitarian ideology of the Soviet Union, which called for world conflict. On the other hand, Russia has a military tradition of fighting extremely well in defense of Mother Russia, but less well in wars of conquest abroad. In general, the few attempts by the Soviet Union to advance communism by foreign military intervention ultimately ended in failure, e.g., in Greece and Afghanistan. It was of course quite another thing when the Red Army was already in place in post-war Eastern Europe.

However, as a result of the spread of nuclear weapons from one nation to five between 1945 and 1964, and the increasing accessibility of the technology, there were predictions in the Kennedy administration that by the end of the 1970s there would be 25–30 avowed nuclear weapon states with these weapons fully integrated into their military arsenals. Such a development could likely have led to 50–60 nuclear weapon states today, creating an intolerable national and international security situation. The IAEA estimates that at the present time some 70 nations have the capability to build nuclear weapons. If such proliferation had occurred, every confrontation, no matter how small, would raise the specter of nuclear war. And it would be impossible to keep these weapons out of the hands of terrorists, religious cults, and criminal organizations. There would be day-to-day uncertainty as to whether civilization as we know it would survive. The reason that this nightmarish scenario did not occur was the signing of the Treaty on the Non-Proliferation of Nuclear Weapons in 1968 and its entry into force in 1970. There are today still only five recognized nuclear weapon states, the same five as in 1968. There are three so-called nuclear-capable states—Israel, India, and Pakistan—that had until recently undeclared nuclear arsenals. Much to the detriment of their own security, the security of the world community, and the viability of the NPT, both India and Pakistan conducted a series of nuclear weapon tests in the spring of 1998 and declared themselves to be nuclear weapon states. It is important that no one else so regard them. It was gratifying that at the 2000 NPT Review Conference, the now 187 NPT states parties made clear that India and Pakistan, despite the May 1998 nuclear tests, will never be recognized as NPT nuclear weapon states and should join the NPT as non-nuclear weapon states.

In more positive developments, Argentina and Brazil after ridding themselves of military rule and restoring democracy, as well as South Africa as the end of apartheid neared, gave up their nuclear weapon programs. Argentina and Brazil joined both the Treaty of Tlatelolco, which established the Latin American nuclear-weapon-free zone, and the NPT. South Africa organized the negotiation of the Treaty of Pelindaba, the African nuclear-weapon-free zone treaty, signed in Cairo in 1996, and some years earlier destroyed the six nuclear weapons it built and joined the NPT. Now, 182 nations have joined the NPT as non-nuclear weapons states, and undertaken never to acquire nuclear weapons. Only Israel, India, Pakistan, and Cuba stand outside the NPT.

The NPT seeks to convert what had been an act of national pride, the acquisition of nuclear weapons (witness the rejoicing in Paris when news arrived of the first successful French nuclear test in the Sahara), into an act of international outlawry. The Indians, when they conducted their nuclear weapon test in 1974, did it figuratively in the middle of the night and referred to it as a "peaceful" nuclear explosion. Even so, there was a vast international outcry. India in 1998 again challenged this norm of international behavior based on the NPT, which had stood for thirty years. Its prime minister claimed that it is a "big" country now that it has exploded atomic bombs, unfortunately underlining the high prestige value given to nuclear weapons.

The NPT is at the very center of the existing system of international security. It is the basis on which all subsequent disarmament regimes are built and it is the fundamental document of international security after the United Nations Charter. But one must remember that the NPT contains a bargain between the nuclear weapon states and the non-nuclear weapon states. The latter undertook never to acquire nuclear weapons, and the former undertook to share the benefits of peaceful nuclear technology and to engage in disarmament negotiations aimed at the ultimate elimination of nuclear weapons. The NPT is at one and the same time a cornerstone of international security and a treaty aimed at the eventual prohibition of nuclear weapons.

And it should be noted here that the nuclear arms race wrecked the economy of the Soviet Union and likely was the real cause of its downfall. During a significant portion of the Cold War, in an attempt to keep pace, the Soviet Union was spending in the range of 40 percent of its GNP on the military. By contrast, with its larger economy the United States was spending less than 10 percent of its GNP, but nevertheless consumed approximately $5.5 trillion in developing and maintaining its nuclear weapons complex, an amount approximately equivalent to the national debt of the United States in the mid-1990s. And the psychology of the nuclear arms race during the Cold War greatly expanded the secret state within the state. Vast nuclear bureaucracies shrouded in secrecy emerged on both sides. On the United States side, it was never really subject to democratic control or even the knowledge of most people's representatives in the Congress, much less the people themselves. On the Soviet side little of this information was known outside the membership of the Politburo. And did all of this make much of a strategic difference? Perhaps not. In the case of the Soviet Union, the Red Army would still have been present in Eastern Europe and Moscow might have been an even more intractable and implacable foe with a smaller, relatively cheap city-busting nuclear deterrent and its economy unweakened by the huge nuclear weapon expenditures of the Cold War. The United States, as a democracy subject to popular pressures, since Hiroshima and Nagasaki has never been able to utilize its large nuclear stockpile for militarily or politically useful strategic purposes, e.g., Korea and Vietnam. The arsenal's only real utility was to deter Soviet nuclear weapons.

It is essential for the peace and security of the world community that the NPT regime—the treaty and all the associated arrangements such as the IAEA safeguards regime and the Nuclear Suppliers Group—succeed in the long run. If the horrifying predictions of the 1960s ever come to pass and the NPT regime fails—the threat to the regime presented by India and Pakistan in 1998 is real and serious—the result would be even more catastrophic because of the increasing availability of 1945-era nuclear technology and the expansion of the number of dangerous sub-state groups: e.g., terrorists, religious cults, violent sub-national organizations, and criminal groups.

In order for the twenty-first century to be one of peace and progress, unlike the greatly destructive twentieth century, the NPT regime must succeed and for this, the basic 1968 NPT bargain described above and reaffirmed at the time of the indefinite extension of the treaty in 1995, must be kept. The nuclear weapon states—the United States, the United Kingdom, France, Russia, and China—should negotiate the reduction of their nuclear weapon stockpiles in the near to medium term to the lowest level possible—down to the few hundreds, perhaps in the range of around 300 for the United States and Russia, and in the range of around fifty weapons each for the United Kingdom, France, and China. In this context, India and Pakistan should roll back their weapon programs and join the NPT as non-nuclear weapon states, as did South Africa. Israel should do the same, and, as part of this commitment, these three states could keep their fissile material on their territory under IAEA safeguards in the event of the failure of the disarmament regime. All the NPT non-nuclear weapon states would be required to pledge again their non-nuclear status as part of this arrangement, and all NPT parties would agree to joint action, military if necessary, against any violator of the treaty regime. If the number of nuclear weapon states cannot be held at five, the line is unlikely to be established at any other number. Thus, for the NPT to survive, the number of accepted nuclear weapon states probably cannot exceed five. Stopping things where they were in 1968 and providing for their reversal is what the NPT is all about. Since in 2001 the nuclear weapons states do not appear ready to do what they should and negotiate a deep-cuts regime, perhaps there is a temporary measure that could be pursued to address the dangers posed by the nuclear programs of India and Pakistan. Conceivably there could be some kind of separate agreement of NPT association for India, Pakistan, and Israel to keep things from becoming worse and to impose some obligations on those three states. But it must be seen as only a temporary measure designed to hold the line until the political situation will permit a solution along the lines outlined above.

In the long run, likely there are only two real alternatives: gradual nuclear weapon proliferation all over the world, or commitment by all the nuclear weapon states to a process leading to deep cuts in nuclear weapons until the world situation changes sufficiently to permit the eventual negotiation of an international agreement prohibiting nuclear weapons. Such reductions in nuclear weapons to the lowest levels consistent with safety and security for the five nuclear weapon states would be the residual level until complete prohibition, the ultimate objective of the NPT, can be achieved. Until there is a worldwide intrusive verification system in place that could detect in a timely fashion any violation, and until there is an international enforcement regime in place, supported by the world community, that would be capable of quick resolution and elimination of any violation, by force if necessary, prohibition does not appear to be achievable.

During the Cold War the Warsaw Pact maintained a huge conventional arms preponderance over NATO. NATO was created in 1949 to stop the gradual advance of the Red Army in Europe, which looked like a terrible threat at the time, with the advent of the Korean War, in the aftermath of the 1948 coup in Czechoslovakia and the weakness of the war-torn economies in Western Europe—which ultimately were restored by the Marshall Plan and the vigor of the peoples of Western Europe. After the founding of NATO moderated the immediate danger, the division of Europe gradually hardened along the inter-German border in a manner similar to the front in World War I, but without the hot war and the incredible casualties. But the Western democracies, even after recovery, were never willing to spend the money required to offset the conventional military superiority of the Warsaw Pact and instead opted for smaller forces and the right to use nuclear weapons first. In other words, Western Europe, and most importantly West Germany, was placed under a U.S./NATO nuclear umbrella. In this context, West Germany by international agreement forswore the nuclear weapon option in the Brussels Treaty of 1948, joined NATO in 1954, and ultimately joined the NPT even though, of course, it easily and quickly could have built nuclear weapons with its long and distinguished history in nuclear physics. And one should remember in contemplating the contribution of the NPT that in the first decades after the end of World War II Sweden had a rather advanced nuclear weapon program and Switzerland twice by national referendum voted to acquire nuclear weapons. As late as 1968 in the negotiation of the NPT, West Germany, Sweden and Italy were unwilling to permanently renounce nuclear weapons.

A similar situation arose in East Asia, with the large North Korean army to an extent offset by the presence of U.S. nuclear weapons in South Korea as well as on ships near Japan, which has forsworn nuclear weapons in its basic law. Undoubtedly, the provision of the United States nuclear umbrella did make it easier for Germany and Japan to give up the nuclear weapon option, and it certainly made it easier for these two countries to join the NPT. But in the aftermath of World War II, nuclear weapons were probably never a realistic option for Germany and Japan. U.S. nuclear weapons are now withdrawn from South Korea, Germany supports a policy of no first use of nuclear weapons and studies of this concept are currently underway in Japan. With the Cold War over, the nuclear umbrella, with little to deter, has blended into the international background.

In the short term the most important imperative is to reduce the prestige value of nuclear weapons. As long as the possession of nuclear weapons appears to distinguish states with worldwide influence from states without it, the NPT regime will remain imperiled, as the Indian tests have demonstrated. The perceived value of nuclear weapons was very high during the Cold War and it remains high. With the end of the Cold War, this condition should change. In November 1997, a Conservative Party spokesman on the floor of the House of Commons stated that the United Kingdom cannot reduce its Trident nuclear weapon system further, otherwise the United Kingdom would no longer be a respectable nuclear weapon state, and therefore would lose its permanent seat on the United Nations Security Council. This is not the kind of psychology that should be encouraged.

Recently some commentators have been urging the use of nuclear weapons to deter, for example, Iraq's biological weapons program. If the United States needs nuclear weapons for this purpose, why doesn't Iran or indeed any other state in the Middle East need them as well? During the Cold War, the huge conventional weapon superiority of the Warsaw Pact in Europe indeed was offset in part by the United States and NATO reserving the right to use nuclear weapons first to stop an overwhelming conventional blitzkrieg by the Warsaw Pact in Western Europe. This situation no longer exists, and the Cold War and the conventional military confrontation in Central Europe have passed into history. It is NATO that has the conventional superiority now. There is simply no excuse—if they desire the ultimate success of the NPT regime—for the nuclear weapon states overtly to retain the option to use nuclear weapons first.

China has long maintained—for its own historical and political reasons—a policy of no first use of nuclear weapons applicable to all states, not just NPT non-nuclear weapon states. China and Russia in 1994 signed an agreement in which they apply no-first-use nuclear weapons policies to one another. The United States, the United Kingdom, and France should adopt policies of committing themselves not to introduce nuclear weapons into future conflicts. Given the weakened state of its conventional forces, such a declaratory policy may be difficult for Russia. Russia may need help to do this—perhaps an even closer association with NATO. An essential element of peace in the future is to reduce the prestige value of nuclear weapons, to reduce their role to that of "core deterrence," that is, simply deterring the use of other nuclear weapons. This would then permit the pursuit of the very low levels of nuclear weapons needed to buttress the NPT regime.

Many terrible weapons exist. The proliferation of weapons of mass destruction, particularly nuclear weapons, was the principal threat to national and world security in the late twentieth century, and this is likely to remain the case in the twenty-first century. The regimes to control these weapons and protect the world community—the NPT, the CWC, and the BWC—must be supported and strengthened. It should be noted that the CWC and the BWC ban the weapons that they regulate, but not the NPT. Thus, the NPT does not directly address the question of the legitimacy or, put another way, the perceived political value of nuclear weapons—another reason why a policy of not introducing nuclear weapons into future conflicts should be considered by the nuclear weapon states. There have been some promising signs. South Africa in the 1990s and Ukraine in 1994 came to believe that NPT non-nuclear weapon state status was a prerequisite for good standing in the world community. But this promising trend has now turned in the other direction with such developments as the South Asian tests, the new Russian nuclear doctrine (emphasizing the potential first use of nuclear weapons), and the United States Senate rejection of the CTBT.

Missile technology and advanced conventional weapons need to be brought under more stringent control as well. Many states are threatened from without or within by the proliferation and increasing capability of sophisticated major conventional weapon systems. Also, the international flood of deadly small arms, such as the AK-47, which are spreading over the globe, enhances the power of criminals and threatens regimes everywhere. For major conventional weapon systems, perhaps the concept of the CFE Treaty can be used elsewhere.

But nuclear weapons are a thing apart. Only they can threaten the ultimate survival of humanity. A firebreak must be maintained between them and other weapons of mass destruction. They deserve special attention. We live in a dangerous world—perhaps in a day by day practical sense more dangerous than during the Cold War. If peace and progress are to be preserved, the means of violence—most importantly nuclear weapons—must be brought under increasing control by the world community. This is an urgent task for all states and all peoples, working together, in everyone's self-interest, and in the interest of our world community.

An important part of all this are current international efforts to help Russia better safeguard and reduce the vast amount of fissile material for nuclear weapons left over from the Cold War. The Nunn-Lugar Threat Reduction Program cosponsored by the two senators in June 1991 has made an important contribution to this. The procedural shortcomings have been many, but gradually progress has been made in bringing nuclear weapons and fissile material under tighter control in Russia. The 45,000 nuclear weapons and fissile material for 90,000 more referred to by former Russian Minister of Atomic Energy Mikhailov in 1996 as having been created during the Soviet period are a threat to Russia as well as everyone else just as nuclear weapons, wherever they exist, are a threat to everyone including their owners. It is important to eliminate as much of this detritus of the Cold War as possible. The HEU Purchase Agreement whereby 500 tons of weapons grade material will be converted into power reactor fuel is a significant effort. Some way needs to be found to effectively reduce the large plutonium stocks that exist as well. The 1997 Plutonium Disposition Agreement can be a start.

The military role of nuclear weapons, at least for the United States, United Kingdom and France, has disappeared in the twenty-first century and their political role is largely eliminated. General Colin Powell in his autobiography, *An American Journey*, states that Secretary of Defense Cheney asked him to do a study of the possible battlefield use of nuclear weapons with the Persian Gulf War looming. General Powell commissioned the study, reviewed its findings, showed it to Cheney, and destroyed it. He said that if he had ever had any doubts about the use of nuclear weapons on the field of battle, that report removed all doubts. Others in the United States, however, continue to argue that a policy of calculated ambiguity—attempting to leave uncertainty in the mind of a potential foe as to whether or not there might be a nuclear response—deterred the use of chemical weapons by Iraq during the Persian Gulf War and is appropriate to deter threats of the use of chemical and biological weapons by states such as Iraq in the future. Secretary of Defense Cohen made such an assertion in late 1998 in rejecting German Foreign Minister Fischer's call for NATO to consider a revision of its nuclear doctrine and give up the first use option.

Who can say if Saddam Hussein was so deterred? Of the three items on Secretary Baker's ultimatum in 1991 to which he threatened an unspecified very destructive response—no use of weapons of mass destruction, no continuance of worldwide terrorism and no torching of the Kuwaiti oil fields—the Iraqis clearly did not observe the third, with no response from the United States. But whatever was the case in 1991, such a policy appears to be of little use now. The principal U.S. figures in the war—President Bush, General Scowcroft, Secretary Baker, and General Powell—have made clear in their memoirs that the United States never had, under any circumstances, any intention of using nuclear weapons, even in response to the Iraqi use of chemical or biological weapons. So the world now knows that the stated 1991 policy—whatever its effect may have been then—was a bluff, a bluff that could be called in the future and cause the United States to consider an overt nuclear threat, the last thing anyone should want.

The possibility that the United States—after the attacks on Hiroshima and Nagasaki in the heat of World War II—would ever initiate the use of nuclear weapons is out of the question. The use of such weapons in 1945 as part of a terribly savage and enormously destructive world war and with the prediction of nearly a million casualties as a result of an invasion of Japan's home islands and the rapid Soviet sweep in Manchuria was one thing, but the initiation of the use of such weapons by the United States or any other Western democracy after fifty years of a precedent of non-use, and the resultant destruction of the NPT, is quite another. And in connection with the indefinite extension of the NPT in 1995 the nuclear weapon states in effect pledged never to use nuclear weapons against NPT non-nuclear weapon states, 182 nations or most of the world. This commitment was essential to the extension of the NPT and is central to its ongoing viability. Thus, the initial use of nuclear weapons against a NPT non-nuclear weapon state would destroy the NPT and to use them first against a nuclear weapon state—in other words, to start a nuclear war—would be a disaster. Indeed, President Truman hinted at the use of nuclear weapons to force the Soviets out of Iran in 1946, possibly spurring their determination to acquire such weapons. President Eisenhower less than ten years later refused to make a similar threat to help the French in Indochina, despite recommendations by his secretary of state and chairman of the Joint Chiefs to do so.

With Russia and China today it is somewhat different. The precipitous decline in the Russian conventional forces and the very real threats that Russia faces along its southern border, make its shift to a policy similar to that of NATO regarding the first use of nuclear weapons regrettable, but somewhat understandable. And the temptation to use these weapons in a possibly increasingly desperate situation could grow. If there is to be hope of retaining a viable NPT, hope of preventing nuclear weapons from spreading all over the world, such use must at all costs be prevented. Russia increasingly should in the long-term be given the protection of NATO.

China has, at present, no similar need to contemplate the use of nuclear weapons. It views its minimal strategic nuclear deterrent as protecting it from nuclear blackmail by the United States, but sees its deterrent as potentially threatened by the United States national missile defense program. If such a program should go forward over the objections of Beijing, China is likely to go well beyond its current program of strategic force modernization and expand those forces into the several hundreds. Were China to do this, it probably would cause a reaction in India to conduct further nuclear tests and solidify its commitment to further nuclear weapon expansion. This in turn would have an effect on Pakistan, which ultimately could affect Afghanistan and states in the Middle East as well as Israel.

So the world community today may be approaching a fork in the road. The September 11, 2001, attacks dramatized the overwhelming importance of ensuring the non-proliferation of weapons of mass destruction, particularly nuclear weapons. The 2000 NPT Review Conference underlined the commitment of the world community to the viability of the NPT. The parties recommitted themselves to the 1995 Statement of Principles and Objectives—and pledged themselves "unequivocally" to the elimination of nuclear weapons (without the qualifier of this being an "ultimate" goal). The 2000 Review Conference Final Document also records the agreement of all NPT parties to preserve the ABM Treaty and to continue to observe a moratorium on nuclear explosions pending entry into force of the CTBT. However, U.S. officials were quick to assert that there was no change in U.S. policy—business as usual. But, if current policies toward nuclear weapons are continued by the nuclear weapon states, such as the U.S. failure to ratify the CTBT and U.S. withdrawal from the ABM Treaty to emphasize commitment to NMD, U.S. and NATO retention of the first-use option, and Russia's increasing reliance on nuclear weapons, the world community could gradually proceed down the road of the dissolution of the NPT regime and the widespread proliferation of nuclear weapons. This would nullify the current overwhelming U.S./NATO military superiority based on conventional forces. Eventually, the world could become filled with nuclear weapon states. The world community would simply have to try to manage such a situation. Alternatively, with the end of the Cold War and the permanent extension of the NPT, the opportunity exists to reduce significantly the political significance of nuclear weapons, to delegitimize them, to narrowly restrict their role, and to drastically reduce their numbers, so that they gradually fade almost entirely from the arsenal of states. The result would be a far safer and more secure and stable world in the twenty-first century.

As has been the case for many years, the key to accomplishing this is the United States of America, the greatest nation on earth. Whether the United States government, as led by this and future U.S. administrations, will avoid being mired in the detritus of the Cold War and be prepared to meet creatively and address effectively this difficult challenge of central importance remains to be seen. I ardently hope that it will be.

GLOSSARY

ABM: Anti-ballistic missile

ABM Treaty: Antiballistic Missile Treaty. Signed in 1972 at the conclusion of the first Strategic Arms Limitation Talks (SALT I), the ABM Treaty prohibited the deployment of national missile defenses by either the United States or the Soviet Union (now Russia) and, pursuant to a 1974 protocol, limited each side to one ABM deployment site. The treaty was intended to stabilize nuclear deterrence between the superpowers, thereby allowing arms limitations and reductions. The United States gave notice of withdrawal to Russia under Article XV (six-month withdrawal clause) on December 13, 2001.

ACDA: Arms Control and Disarmament Agency

ACV: Armored combat vehicle

Agent Orange: A defoliation chemical widely used in Vietnam, later determined to cause genetic damage in human beings

ALCM: Air-launched cruise missile

Alternat: If a bilateral treaty is prepared in two languages, e.g., English and Russian, the United States is listed first in the English version and Russia first in the Russian version. The Russian *alternat*, for example, would be the direct translation of the English version into Russian and in this text the United States would be listed first. It would be one of the two copies retained by the United States. The opposite of this would be the case for Russia. All four copies are signed.

ASBM: Air-to-surface ballistic missile

ASEAN: Association of Southeast Asian Nations; includes Brunei, Cambodia, Indonesia, Laos, Malaysia, Myanmar, Philippines, Singapore, Thailand, and Vietnam

Australia Group: Founded in 1984, the Australia Group is a group of 30 countries that have agreed to enact common export control standards on materials related to the proliferation of chemical and biological weapons. Its members are Argentina, Australia, Austria, Belgium, Canada, the Czech Republic, Denmark, Finland, France, Germany, Greece, Hungary, Iceland, Ireland, Italy, Japan, Luxembourg, the Netherlands, New Zealand, Norway, Poland, Portugal, Romania, Slovakia, South Korea, Spain, Sweden, Switzerland, the United Kingdom, and the United States.

AWACS (E3): Airborne Warning and Control System. This distinctive aircraft is essentially a Boeing 707 jet with a rotating radar mounted on top.

Backfire Bomber (TU-22 M): The NATO designation for a Soviet (Russian) medium range bomber asserted by U.S. arms control conservatives to be actually a heavy bomber and thus a strategic weapon covered by SALT II, a problem for years during the SALT II negotiations

BMD: Ballistic missile defense

BW: Biological warfare

BWC: The Biological Weapons Convention, which opened for signature in April 1972, requires parties not to develop, produce, stockpile, or acquire biological agents or toxins "of types and in quantities that have no justification for prophylactic, protective, and other peaceful purposes," as well as weapons and means of delivery.

CARICOM: The Caribbean Community. The association of English-speaking nations in the Caribbean now includes Antigua and Barbuda, the Bahamas, Barbados, Belize, Dominica, Grenada, Guyana, Haiti, Jamaica, Montserrat, St. Kitts and Nevis, St. Lucia, Suriname, St. Vincent and the Grenadines, and Trinidad and Tobago.

CD (ENDC, CCD): Conference on Disarmament in Geneva. Originally the Ten-Nation Disarmament Committee, then the Eighteen-Nation Disarmament Committee, then the Conference of the Committee on Disarmament, and finally the Conference on Disarmament as the number of members grew from 10 to 66. The CD currently consists of 66 member nations and operates by consensus. The CTBT and the CWC were negotiated in the CD.

CFE Treaty: Conventional Armed Forces in Europe Treaty. Signed in 1990 and entered into force in 1992, this treaty set limits on the number of major units of combined arms including battle tanks, armored combat vehicles, artillery pieces, combat aircraft and attack helicopters that the states parties may deploy in Europe as defined in the treaty (i.e., between the Atlantic and the Ural Mountains).

chemical herbicides: Defoliating agents, of which Agent Orange is one

CIA: Central Intelligence Agency

CS: A tear gas

CSCE (OSCE): Commission on Security and Cooperation in Europe, now the Organization for Security and Cooperation in Europe

CTBT: Comprehensive Nuclear Test Ban Treaty. Signed in 1996, the CTBT bans all nuclear explosions and establishes an extensive International Monitoring System to verify compliance with its provisions. As of December 2001, it has been signed by 165 nations and ratified by 89, but it cannot enter into force until 44 specified states (those CD members that have nuclear facilities in their territory) have ratified. As of the same date, 41 of these have signed and 31 have ratified.

customary international law: International law rules which have existed sufficiently long and which have been recognized by a large enough number of states to be considered to have passed into an international common law binding on all nations. An example is the Geneva Protocol deemed now to bind all nations whether parties or not.

CW: Chemical warfare

CWC: The Chemical Weapons Convention, which entered into force on April 29, 1997, bans the development, production, acquisition, stockpiling, retention and direct or indirect transfer of chemical weapons. It also prohibits the use or preparation for use of cw and the assistance, encouragement, or inducement of anyone else to engage in activities prohibited by the cwc. As of December 2001, there are 145 parties and 165 signatories to the cwc.

DCI: Director of Central Intelligence

DCM: Deputy Chief of Mission, the second-most senior official in an embassy

Delta: NATO designation for the Soviet (Russian) ballistic missile submarine class of the 1980s

DOD: Department of Defense

DOE: Department of Energy

double zero: The agreement by the United States and the Soviet Union during the INF Treaty negotiations to eliminate intermediate-range and shorter-range nuclear missiles

EEZ: Exclusive Economic Zone, recognized by international law to extend 200 miles off a state's coast

EIF: Entry into force

ENDC: Eighteen Nation Disarmament Committee

FMCT: Fissile material cutoff treaty

FRG: Federal Republic of Germany, or West Germany

Galosh: NATO designation for the Soviet (Russian) antiballistic-missile defense system deployed around Moscow

GC: Office of General Counsel at ACDA

G-class submarine: Soviet conventionally powered submarine developed in the 1950s

GDR: German Democratic Republic, or East Germany

Geneva Protocol: Formally known as Protocol for the Prohibition of the Use in War of Asphyxiating, Poisonous or Other Gases, and of Bacteriological Methods of Warfare, the Geneva Protocol opened for signature on June 17, 1925 and entered into force on February 8, 1928. It bans the use in war, but not the production or possession, of chemical and biological weapons. With reservations taken by many parties, it is considered to be in fact a ban on the first use in war of chemical and biological weapons. The U.S. Senate approved the protocol on December 16, 1974, and it entered into force for the United States on April 10, 1975.

Glassboro Summit: In June 1967, President Lyndon Johnson, Soviet Prime Minister Aleksei Kosygin, and their diplomatic and military advisors met at Glassboro, New Jersey, to discuss the Arab-Israeli tensions in the Middle East following the Six Day War of June 1967, U.S.-Soviet arms limitations, and an agreement to prevent the proliferation of nuclear weapons to other nations.

GLCM: Ground-launched cruise missile

H-Class submarine: The first Soviet nuclear-powered ballistic missile submarine, developed in the 1960s

heavy bombers: a SALT II Treaty term meaning those bombers considered strategic weapons and therefore covered by the Treaty

Hercules Corporation: A U.S. company in Magna, Utah, that fabricated rocket engines for the Pershing II missile

HEU: Highly enriched uranium. Uranium 238 (U238, widely found in nature) enriched by its unstable isotope, U 235, to constitute fissile material suitable for a nuclear explosive device—usually about 90 percent. Along with plutonium (Pu239), the principal fissile material used in nuclear weapons.

HLTF: High-level task force, an important NATO policy committee

HUMINT: Human intelligence

IAEA: International Atomic Energy Agency

ICBM: Intercontinental ballistic missile (defined in the SALT II treaty as having a range in excess of 5,500 km

INF Treaty: Intermediate-Range Nuclear Forces Treaty. Signed by the Soviet Union and the United States on December 8, 1987, the INF Treaty is the only treaty to eliminate an entire class of nuclear weapon delivery vehicles (ground-launched ballistic and cruise missiles with ranges of between 500 and 5,500 kilometers).

ISP: International security policy (DOD)

JCG: Joint Consultative Group, the implementing body established by the CFE Treaty

JCIC: Joint Compliance and Inspection Commission, the implementing body established by the START I Treaty

JCS: Joint Chiefs of Staff. The Chairman of the Joint Chief of Staff is the principal military advisor to the President of the United States.

Krasnoyarsk: The site of a Soviet ballistic missile early warning radar station built in Central Siberia during the 1980s in violation of the ABM Treaty

launch-weight: The launch-weight of an ICBM is the weight of the fully loaded missile at the time of launch

LAWS: Lawyers Alliance for World Security

LEU: Low-enriched uranium, reactor-grade uranium enriched in U235 to less than 20 percent (usually around 3 or 4 percent)

Lisbon Protocol: Signed in 1992, it multilteralized the START I Treaty by adding Belarus, Kazakhstan, Russia, and Ukraine as parties in place of the Soviet Union.

LPARS: Large Phased Array Radars. In 1972, at the time of the signing of the ABM Treaty, large phased array radars were used for ballistic missile warning, space tracking and national technical means of verification, as well as for missile defense. Those used for ballistic missile early warning pursuant to the Treaty were supposed to be located on the periphery of the state and oriented outward.

LTBT: Limited Test Ban Treaty of 1963. Signed and entered into force in 1963, the LTBT bans nuclear explosions underwater, in the atmosphere and in outer space, but not underground.

MAD: Mutually assured destruction (originally, assured destruction). Cold War nuclear deterrence relationship based on the threat of overwhelming retaliation in the event of an attack. MAD depended upon the ability of each nation to reply to a first strike with a massive nuclear response. This meant that both sides had to have so many strategic nuclear weapon delivery vehicles that enough would survive the enemy's initial attack to be able to retaliate in a manner that would incapacitate the enemy. Its purpose was to establish crisis stability—to remove any incentive to launch a first strike against the other side—and arms race stability—to remove any incentive for one side to believe it must build more nuclear weapons to overcome defenses being built by the other side. It is the basis on which reductions in strategic nuclear forces became possible and it was codified in the ABM Treaty, which obligated that strategic defenses be kept at a very low level.

managed access: On-site inspection provisions that permit a nation to shield sensitive items from inspectors or otherwise limit inspectors' access to facilities, used in the CWC

MBFR: Mutual Balanced Force Reduction negotiations in the 1980s. While they produced no formal agreement, the MBFR talks were an important precursor to the CFE negotiations.

MFA: Ministry of foreign affairs

Minuteman I, II, III missiles: The principal U.S. ICBM, initially built in the 1960s, the total deployment being 1,000 in fixed silo launchers

MIRV: Multiple independently targetable reentry vehicle. A MIRVed ICBM is an ICBM with several warheads, each capable of being independently delivered to a separate target.

M-X (Peacekeeper) Missile: A more modern and highly accurate ICBM, the subject of much controversy resulting in the deployment in the 1980s of only 50 in silo launchers

mycotoxins ("yellow rain"): Refers to an illegal (under the BWC) toxin allegedly used by the Soviets in Vietnam

NATO: North Atlantic Treaty Organization

NGO: Non-governmental organization

NIS: Newly independent states formed after the collapse of the Soviet Union, i.e., Russia, Ukraine, Belarus, Kazakhstan, Georgia, Armenia, Azerbaijan, Kyrgistan, Tajikistan, Uzbekistan, Turkmenistan and Moldova

NMD: National missile defense

NPT: Nuclear Non-Proliferation Treaty. In exchange for a commitment from the non-nuclear weapon states parties (today numbering 182 nations) never to develop or otherwise to acquire nuclear weapons and to submit to international safeguards intended to verify compliance with this commitment, the nuclear weapon states—the United States, the Soviet Union (now Russia), United Kingdom, France, and China—promised unfettered access to peaceful nuclear technologies and pledged (in NPT Article VI) to engage in disarmament negotiations aimed at the ultimate elimination of their nuclear arsenals.

NSA: National Security Agency

NSC: National Security Council

NSG: Nuclear Suppliers Group, a group of 39 nations which have agreed to limit the export of dual-use goods related to the development of nuclear weapons. Its members include Argentina, Australia, Austria, Belarus, Belgium, Brazil, Bulgaria, Canada, Cyprus, the Czech Republic, Denmark, Finland, France, Germany, Greece, Hungary, Ireland, Italy, Japan, Latvia, Luxembourg, Netherlands, New Zealand, Norway, Poland, Portugal, Republic of Korea, Romania, Russian Federation, Slovak Republic, Slovenia, South Africa, Spain, Sweden, Switzerland, Turkey, Ukraine, United Kingdom, and United States.

NST: Nuclear and Space Arms Talks. The U.S.-Soviet strategic arms negotiations of the 1980s, which led to the INF and START treaties

NMT: National technical means of verification, primarily referring to photographic and data collecting satellites used to verify arms control agreement commitments

OJCS: Office of the Joint Chiefs of Staff

OMB: Office of Management and Budget

OPANAL: Agency for the Prohibition of Nuclear Weapons in Latin America and the Caribbean; the implementing agency for the Treaty of Tlatelolco

OSD: Office of the Secretary of Defense

OSI: On-site inspection

OSIA: On-Site Inspection Agency located in the Department of Defense

P-5: The permanent members of the UN Security Council: China, France, Russia, the United Kingdom, and the United States—also the five nuclear weapon states recognized by the NPT

Pershing I, II: U.S. solid fuel medium-range ballistic missiles deployed in Europe. The Pershing II, a highly accurate replacement for Pershing I, was deployed as part of the NATO Dual Track decision of 1979 which led to the INF Treaty in 1987.

PNET: Peaceful Nuclear Explosion Treaty. Signed in 1976, PNET was the companion treaty to the 1974 TTBT. PNET banned all underground peaceful nuclear explosions with yield above 150 kt.

Polaris: The first U.S. nuclear-powered ballistic missile submarine, it carried the single-warhead A-1 and A-2 SLBMs as well as the three-warhead (but not independently targetable) A-3 SLBM. The Polaris was phased out of service many years ago.

Poseidon: The second and more modern U.S. nuclear-powered ballistic missile submarine, which carried the C-3 and C-4 MIRVed SLBMS

PREPCOM: NPT Conference Preparatory Committee meetings

Pressler Amendment: U.S. legislation that required a cut-off of U.S. military and economic assistance to Pakistan if the President was unable to certify that Pakistan did not possess a nuclear device.

RCA: Riot control agent or tear gas

SA-12: The U.S. designation for a Soviet (Russian) highly capable air defense missile

SALT: Strategic Arms Limitation Talks (or negotiations); the first, sometimes referred to as SALT I, took place in 1969-72, and the second, sometimes called SALT II, took place in 1972-79

SALT I: The 1972 Interim Agreement on the Limitation of Strategic Offensive Arms. It placed limits on the number of strategic offence nuclear delivery missile systems the Soviet Union and the United States could deploy. It essentially froze the parties where they were and had a five year term.

SALT II: The second Strategic Arms Limitation Treaty, signed in June 1979, would have placed specific limits on U.S. and Soviet strategic offensive nuclear delivery systems, including heavy bombers, but the accord was never ratified by the United States, although it was informally observed some months beyond its expiration date of December 31, 1985. It was designed to be a ten-year treaty.

SAM: Surface-to-air missile

SAM-D: Ground-based air defense system under development in the 1960s by the United States. It would have utilized systems based on "other physical principles", i.e., lasers and particle beams. It was never deployed.

SCC: Standing Consultative Commission. The SCC is the implementing body established by the ABM Treaty.

SCUD: A primitive ballistic missile based on the German V-1 and V-2 rockets

SDI: Strategic Defense Initiative

SDIO: Strategic Defense Initiative Office

SFRC: Senate Foreign Relations Committee

SHAPE: Supreme Headquarters Allies Powers Europe, the headquarters of the NATO military organization

SLBM: Submarine-launched ballistic missile

SLCM: Sea-launched cruise missile

Sprint: Along with the Spartan missile, one of the two U.S. ABM missile systems developed in the 1960s and deployed for six months in 1975

SS-4, SS-5: The U.S. designation for the early Soviet liquid fueled, single warhead, inaccurate medium range nuclear weapon missile delivery systems

ss-7, ss-8: The U.S. designation for early Soviet liquid fueled ICBMs

ss-9: The U.S. designation for the first Soviet heavy ICBM, which had a 25 megaton warhead

ss-11: The U.S. designation for the first Soviet solid fuel ICBM

ss-16: The U.S. designation for the first Soviet mobile ICBM, never deployed

ss-17: The U.S. designation for the more modern Soviet ICBM, which-along with the ss-19-was the first MIRved Soviet light ICBM

ss-18: The U.S. designation for the modern MIRved Soviet (Russian) heavy ICBM. This very large ICBM, with ten warheads, is still deployed.

ss-19: The U.S designation for the modern Soviet (Russian) light ICBM. It is MIRved, accurate, and still deployed.

ss-20: The U.S. designation for the medium range replacement for the Soviet ss-4s and ss-5s. Mobile, MIRved, solid-fueled and highly accurate, it created great alarm in Western Europe and provoked the Dual Track Decision in 1979, which called for a counter deployment in Europe by the United States of the Pershing II and GLCMs unless the problem could be solved in an arms control arrangement in four years. This led to the INF negotiations, which did not meet the deadline, but did result in agreement in 1987.

ss-25: The U.S. designation for the first deployed Soviet (Russian) mobile ICBM. It uses as its first two (of three) stages the engines of the ss-20, which complicated the INF Treaty negotiations.

ss-21, ss-23: The U.S. designation for short-range (300-500km) Soviet (Russian) nuclear missiles

ss-N-5, ss-N-6: The U.S. designation for early Soviet SLBMs

ssbn: Strategic nuclear ballistic missile submarine

START: Strategic Arms Reduction Talks. The first series of negotiations is also referred to as START I, and the second as START II.

START I: The first Strategic Arms Reduction Treaty. Signed in 1991 and entered into force in 1994, it requires Russia and the United States to reduce their strategic nuclear arsenals to 6000 deployed warheads. This objective was officially reached in December 2001.

START II: The second Strategic Arms Reduction Treaty; signed in January 1993, it requires Russia and the United States to reduce their strategic nuclear arsenals to 3000-3500 deployed warheads. It has not entered into force.

State/PM: U.S. State Department Bureau of Political Military Affairs. Other State Department bureaus (before the April 1, 1999, merger with ACDA added three more) included State/ARA (Latin American Affairs), State/EAP (East Asian and Pacific Affairs), State/EUR (European Affairs), State/H (Legislative Affairs), State/L (Legal Affairs), State/NEA (Near Eastern and Asia Affairs), State/OES (Oceanic, Environment and Scientific Affairs), and State/SA (South Asia Bureau).

STRATCOM: The Strategic Command. STRATCOM commands the U.S. nuclear deterrent, now including the missile and bomber force (which formerly comprised the Strategic Air Command) and the SBNN force.

SVC: Standing Verification Commission, the implementing body established by the INF Treaty

Sverdlovsk (Ekaterinburg): Site of an April 1979 release of anthrax spores from an explosion at a suspected Soviet biological weapons facility located in the city, a facility that would constitute a violation of the BWC. Russian President Boris Yeltsin admitted in 1992 that the release was the result of military activities and was evidence of a vast Soviet violation of the BWC.

TEL: Transporter Erector Launcher, the vehicle for a Soviet (Russian) land mobile missile

THAAD: Theater high-altitude area defense, originally part of SDI, subsequently a part of the missile defense system programs of the 1990s

throw-weight: The throw-weight of an ICBM is the weight of its reentry vehicle or vehicles, targeting and navigational devices, and penetration aids, in other words, the weight of what the missile could deliver on a target

Titan II: Older liquid-fueled U.S. ICBM

TMD: Theater missile defense

TNF: Theater nuclear forces

Toxins: Chemical agents produced by biological organisms, covered by the BWC

Treaty of Bangkok: Treaty establishing a nuclear-weapon-free zone in Southeast Asia

Treaty of Pelindaba: Treaty establishing a nuclear-weapon-free zone covering the land area of the African continent

Treaty of Raratonga: Treaty establishing a nuclear-weapon-free zone in the land area of the South Pacific

Treaty of Tlatelolco: Treaty establishing a nuclear-weapon-free zone consisting of the land area of the Western Hemisphere south of the U.S.-Mexican border

Trident: The most modern U.S. ballistic missile submarine, it initially carried the MIRVed, long-range and highly accurate C-4 SLBM and now carries the D-5 SLBM, the highly accurate MIRVed and most modern SLBM.

TTBT: Threshold Test Ban Treaty of 1974. The TTBT banned underground nuclear weapon tests with yields above 150 kilotons.

Typhoon: NATO designation for the most modern Soviet (Russian) ballistic missile submarine

Tyuratam: Soviet ICBM test range, now in Kazakhstan

UNGA: United Nations General Assembly

UNSC: United Nations Security Council

USUN: The United States' permanent mission to the United Nations

Vienna Convention on Law of Treaties: An international agreement on international law affecting treaties. The United States has not ratified the convention, but recognizes the substantive provisions, as opposed to the procedural rules, in the convention as reflective of customary international law and therefore binding on all states.

Votkinsk Machine Building Plant: Construction plant in the Ural Mountains which manufactured the SS-20 and the SS-25

Yankee class submarine: NATO designation for the Soviet ballistic missile submarine of the 1960s and 1970s

Zanger Committee: A committee, named after its chairman (Dr. Zanger of Switzerland), designed to control the export of nuclear technology—as opposed to dual use technology—and thereby implement the NPT

Zero Option: The 1981 Reagan proposal that the Soviet Union dismantle its SS-20s and the United States would not deploy the Pershing II and GLCMs. Regarded as unrealistic and insincere in 1981, it led, however, to the double zero of the INF Treaty in 1987.

INDEX

Grand Forks, North Dakota, 42

Granoff, Jonathan, 307

Graybeal, Sid, 39–40, 57; ABM Treaty and, 152, 156, 158, 161, 164, 166; ACDA and, 219–20

Great Lakes, 34

Greece, 189; Turkish issue and, 191, 195–97

Greenland, 167

Grey, Robert, 103–6, 111

Grinevsky, Oleg, 200

Gromyko, Andrei, 69, 95; INF Treaty and, 115, 120–22, 125; Shultz and, 120–21; START and, 103; Vance and, 85

ground-launched cruise missiles (GLCMs): INF Treaty and, 107, 114; Tomahawk, 107

Guhin, Michael, 149, 170, 172–73, 198

Gzne, 196

Hackett, James, 104

Hadley, Stephen J., 134

Hague Conferences, 20–21, 24, 34, 324

Haig, Alexander, 102–3

Hall, Alexander, 139

Hamilton, Lee, 218

Hancock, William, 17, 39–40

Hanmer, Read, 129

Harlan, Marshall, 10

Harriman, W. Averell, 239

Hartmann, Rudy, 197, 211

Harvard Law School, 7–10

Hatch, Orrin, 103

Hatfield-Mitchell-Exon legislation, 238–40, 246

Havel, Vaclav, 193

heavy bombers, 51, 86; START I and, 132–33; START II and, 140–41; Vladivostok Accord and, 84

Helms, Jesse, 103, 105; ABM Treaty and, 168–69; ACDA absorption and, 306

Helsinki Final Act, 69, 190

herbicides, 22

Heritage Foundation, 147

Hewlett, Daniel, 7

High Level Task Force (HLTF), 194

Hiroshima, ix, 35

Hoinkes, Mary Elizabeth (Mary Lib), 241; ABM Treaty and, 165, 172, 175, 220; ACDA and, 215–20, 306; CTBT and, 242

Holbrooke, Richard, 214

Holgate, Laura, 216, 218

Hollings, Ernest (Fritz), 48

Holum, John, xviii, 32, 210, 217, 226, 228; ACDA absorption and, 305, 307–8, 312; IVI and, 229–31; NPT and, 261–66, 275

House Banking and Currency Committee, 12–13

Housing and Urban Development (HUD), 10

Hryschenko, Konstantin, 212

Humphrey, Hubert, 5, 226–27

Hungary, 22, 187–88

Hussein, Saddam, 332–33

hydrogen bomb, 146

Hyland, William, 67

ICBMS. *See* intercontinental ballistic missiles

Ikle, Fred: chemical/biological weapons and, 25–26, 29; SALT I and II, 48, 56–57; verification and, 88

Inderfurth, Karl (Rick), 244

India, 15, 22, 57, 322, 327–29; CTBT and, 248–49, 253–54; NPT and, 257, 285–86, 289, 295–96; nuclear testing and, 315–17; Pakistan and, 257

Indonesia, 249, 297, 301; CTBT and, 249–50; NPT and, 272–73, 289–90

Inman, Bobby, 102–3

interagency committee, xiv–xv

intercontinental ballistic missiles (STARTS), 36–38; heavy, 51, 71–73; Minuteman, 42, 49, 53–54, 84; MX, 88–89, 105, 120; SALT II and, 51–52, 57–59, 62, 94; Soviet monopoly and, 53; START I and II, 132–33, 140–41; Vladivostok Accord and, 84

Kirkpatrick, Jeanne, 117
Kislyak, Sergei, 183, 272
Kissinger, Henry, 8–9, 40, 53; ACDA
    and, 56, 232; Backfire bomber
    and, 62; Clements and, 66–67;
    Dobrynin agreement and, 60–61;
    Gerard Smith and, 53; SALT I and,
    43–44, 47; SLBMs and, 54; Vladi-
    vostok Accord and, 62–63
Klosson, Boris, 57, 69, 72–73
Kohl, Herbert, 29
Konadu, Nana, 278
Korea: KAL 007, 119–20; North,
    8, 232, 235–36, 296, 330; South,
    8, 330
Korean Institute for Defense Analysis
    (KIDA), 296
Kornblum, John, 210
Korniyenko, 86
Krasnoyarsk, Siberia, xviii
Kravchuk, 135
Kunsman, Eric, 219–20, 223
Kurds, 26
Kuwait, 333
Kvitsinski, Yuli, 113–15, 119
Kyrgyzstan, 181, 232

LaFollette, Robert, 3
Laird, Melvin, 3, 15–16; chemical/
    biological weapons and, 23; SALT I
    and, 45; SDI and, 48
LaJoie, Roland, 129
Lake, Anthony, 216; CTBT and, 241–
    43, 247–48; NPT and, 267
Lampe, Stuart, 5
Lapham, Tony, 198
large phased array radar, 144
Latin America, 17–19; NPT and, 276–
    78; Nuclear-Weapon-Free-Zone
    Treaty, 283
Latvia, 232–33
Laurendieu, Jennifer, 194
LaVera, Damien, xi, 322
Law of Treaties, 102
Lawson, Karin, 126
Lawyers Alliance for World Security
    (LAWS), 308, 313–15, 322
Lebanon, 148

Ledogar, Stephen, 244; ACDA and,
    191, 193, 195
legally correct interpretation (LCI),
    147–48
Lehman, Joe, 117–18
Lehman, John, 56, 71, 103, 112
Lehman, Ronald, 30, 129, 193, 205,
    216, 219
Lembesis, Paul, 138
Leonard, James, 236
Levin, Carl, 157–59
Libya, 30
Limited Test Ban Treaty (LTBT), 50,
    238–39
L'Institut des Sciences Politiques, 7
Lisbon Protocol, 136–37, 141, 181
Lodal, Jan, 65–66, 69
longbows, 34, 323
Lord, Winston, 222
Lott, Trent, 32
Louisville, Kentucky, 6–7
Louisville Courier Journal, 7–8, 12
Louisville Male High School, 6–7
Lucky Dragon, 237
Lugar, Richard, 32–33, 332; ACDA
    and, 207–8

MacArthur, Douglas, xiii
McCaffrey, Barry, 222, 240
McCarthy, Eugene, 14–15
McCloy, John J., xvi
MacEachin, Douglas, 138
MacFarlane, Robert (BUD), 118,
    147–49
McGifford, David, 171
McLarty, Mack, 217
McNamara, Robert, xvi, 318–19, 322
McNamara, Ted, 227, 275
McNeill, Jack, 85, 112, 149
McTate, Patricia, 220
"main battle tank," 198
Malaysia, 249, 300–301; ACDA and,
    302–3; NPT and, 260
Malone, James, 55–56, 63; ACDA and,
    103–4; START and, 103
Mandate talks (ACDA), 191–92; Greek/
    Turkish dispute and, 195–97
Manhattan Project, 34–35

Treaty and, 113–15; Kvitsinski and, 115; "Walk in the Woods" proposal and, 115–16, 124; Warnke and, 78–79

Nixon, Richard M., 3, 15; biological/chemical weapons and, 23, 27–29; Gerard Smith and, 40; resignation of, 61; SALT I and II, 42, 44, 47, 58; SLBMS and, 38

Nolan, Janne, 230

Non-Aligned Movement (NAM), 247, 249; consensus procedures of, 288–89; coordinated opposition of, 260; extension issues and, 262–63; NPT and, 259–66, 280–84, 288–89

nonproliferation, xiii, xv, 228; ACDA and, xvii–xviii; policy structure and, xv–xvi. *See also* disarmament

North Atlantic Treaty Organization (NATO), 106–7, 150, 183; founding of, 329; Greek/Turkish dispute and, 195–97; HLTF and, 194, 211; no-first-use policy and, 331; NPT and, 259, 317–22; revision issues and, 314, 317; tank division and, 187. *See also* Conventional Armed Forces in Europe Treaty

North Korea, 232, 235–36, 296, 330

Norway, 189; ACDA and, 200–203, 212; flank issue and, 209–10

Nosenzo, Lou, 123–24, 171

Nuclear Non-Proliferation Treaty (NPT), xiv, xvii–ix, 18, 28, 327; ACDA and, 259, 262, 264, 281; CTBT and, 242, 245–46, 261, 265; current status of, 317–23, 327, 329, 333; indefinite extension of, 260; provisions of, 257–62, 278–85, 290–93; Review Conferences and, 233, 258–59, 271, 291–94, 320, 327, 334; signing of, 238; Soviet Union and, 238, 259, 280, 288; START I and, 134

Nuclear Non-Proliferation Treaty Review and Extension Conference: aftermath of, 294–306; Canada and, 287; China and, 297–302; Clinton and, 261–62, 265–66,

274–75, 281, 286–87, 303–5; Colombia and, 273–74; Egypt and, 260, 268–72; Ethiopia and, 278; extension policy of, 260, 284; Final Document of, 320; Gore and, 265, 267, 287–88; Graham and, 261–66; Holum and, 305–6; India and, 257, 285–86, 289, 295–96; Indonesia and, 272–73, 289–90; Israel and, 257; Latin America and, 276–78; Mexico and, 260, 274–76, 280–81; Middle East and, 268–72; NAM countries and, 259–66, 280–84, 288–89; negotiations of, 261–66, 290–93; Nigeria and, 282–83, 290; Pakistan and, 257, 295–96; Philippines and, 278; prepcoms of, 261–66, 279–85; Senegal and, 278; South Africa and, 266–68, 287–88, 291; South Pacific Forum and, 259; Statement of Principles and Objectives and, 290–91, 294; strengthening of, 331; Treaty of Pelindaba and, 281, 303–4; United States and, 238, 260–61, 280, 282–83, 286–89, 292–93

Nuclear Suppliers Group (NSG), 258, 267, 328

nuclear test moratorium, xviii, 239–43. *See also* Comprehensive Test Ban Treaty

Nuclear-Weapon-Free-Zone Treaty, 263–64, 281, 283–84, 321

nuclear weapons: ABM Treaty and, 39; ALCMS, 48, 94, 132–33; arms race and, 35–36; core deterrence and, 331; counting rules and, 51–52; CTBT and, 237–56; free zones and, 14, 17–19, 263–64, 281, 283–84, 321; ICBMS, 36, 47; INF Treaty and, 122; missile trajectory and, 44–45; MX deployment and, 88–89, 105; neutron bomb, 106; no-first-use policy and, 331; NTM and, 37, 51–53, 58–59, 82–83; Oppenheimer on, 34; Pershing missiles, 107–8, 111, 114; PNES and, 61; policy structure and, xv; pres-

Protocol on Elimination, 109–10
Protocol on Existing Types (POET), 198
Protocol on Inspection, 110
Provisional Application Protocol, 198, 207–8
Pryor, Elizabeth, 210
Purvis, Hoyt, 94–95

Quai d'Orsay, 196
Quayle, J. Danforth, 127–28

Rada International Security Committee, 142
radar, 143–44, 233
Rand Corporation, 216
Ratterman, George, 12
Reagan, Ronald, xvi–xvii; ABM Treaty and, 146, 151; AWACS and, 104; biological/chemical weapons and, 30; CWC and, 32; INF Treaty and, 106–29; MX deployment and, 105; Reykjavik and, 325–26; SALT II and, 51, 58, 102–3; SDI and, 146, 150–51; START and, 129–42; verification and, SS; warheads and, 102
religion, 323, 325
Reminiscences (MacArthur), xiii
Republicans, 3–4, 16, 77
Resor, Stanley, 64, 77, 229–30
Restatement of Foreign Relations Law of the United States, 180
Reykjavik Summit, 107–8, 124–25, 325–26
Rhinelander, John, 10–11; ABM Treaty and, 154, 158; ACDA and, 199; LAWS and, 313
Rhyne, Charles, 15
Richstein, Richard, 105
Ride, Sally, 229–30
Rindskopf, Elizabeth, 199
Riot Control Agents (RCAS), 22, 24–26, 31
Robinson, Davis, 146
Robinson, Jackie, 7
Roche, Douglas, 318
Roman-Moray, Enrique, 303

Roosevelt, Franklin, 22
Rostow, Eugene, 87, 102–3; ACDA and, 105; AWACS and, 104; firing of, 106, 116; INF Treaty and, 116–17
Roth, William, 271
Rovine, Art, 91–92
Rowny, Ed, xix, 49, 54, 65; ACDA nomination of, 103; Backfire bomber and, 86; "hit list," 117–19; INF Treaty and, 112, 117–19, 122; JCS and, 57; SALT II and, 54–56, 86, 95; START and, 103
Rumsfeld, Donald, 320
Rumsfeld Commission, 180
Rush-Bagot Agreement, 34
Rusk, Dean, xvi
Russell, Richard, 4–5
Russia, 221; ACDA and, 207; CTBT and, 243, 251, 253–55; current status of, 333–34; Memorandum of Understanding on Demarcation and, 234; no-first-use policy and, 331; NPT and, 297, 301; Nunn-Lugar Threat Reduction Program and, 332; START I and II and, 133–37, 138–42, 319; THAAD and, 234–35; TLE allotment and, 206. *See also* Antiballistic Missile Treaty; Soviet Union

St. Germain, Ferdinand, 14
SALT I, ix, 10, 36; ABM Treaty and, 39, 143, 146; common understandings and, 46–47; heavy ICBM launchers and, 47; Jackson and, 40–41, 44; MIRVs and, 38, 41–42; missile trajectory and, 44–45; negotiation strategies of, 42–43; provisions of, 37, 42–43; SAM upgrade and, 39; SDI and, 48; silo dimensions and, 46; Yereskovsky and, 45–46
SALT II, ix, 7, 36–37, 43, 91; amendments and, 97; Annual Arms Control Impact Statement and, 153; Calcutta Cable and, 65–66; Carter and, 76–101; CIA and, 74; common

and, 150; biological/chemical weapons and, 23–24, 27; ACDA and, 188, 190, 194; CSCE and, 191; CTBT and, 239–40, 253, 255; INF Treaty and, 113–14; no-first-use policy and, 331; NPT and, 298; radar and, 167

United Nations: ABM Treaty and, 181; biological/chemical weapons and, 22–23, 30; ACDA and, 198–99; CTBT and, 244–45; Geneva Protocol and, 22; NPT and, 283; UNSCOM, 306

United States: arms spending of, 328; biological/chemical weapons and, 23–24, 27; ACDA and, 188–89; China and, 183; CSCE and, 191; CTBT and, 237–56, 254; CWC and, 32; Geneva Protocol and, 21, 26–27; Great Lakes and, 34; heavy ICBMS and, 71–72; INF Treaty and, 106–29; no-first-use policy and, 331; NPT and, 238, 260–61, 280, 282–83, 286–89, 292–93; NTM and, 37; Nunn-Lugar Threat Reduction Program and, 332; Persian Gulf War and, 332–33; PNET and, 61–62; SALT I and II, 36–49, 50–101; SLBMS and, 38; START I and II, 129–37, 137–42

United States Information Agency (USIA), 214

Vance, Cyrus, 76–77, 85; ACDA and, 96; INF Treaty and, 125; SALT II and, 95

Van Cleave, William, 105

Van Doren, Charles, 17, 19, 63, 148

Velvet Revolution, 193

Venezuela, 279

Verheugen, Gerhard, 313–14

verification, xv, 58–59; ACDA and, 309–10; BWC and, 100–101; CFE and, 186; INF Treaty and, 108–11; IVI and, 229–35; MIRV, 86–87; POET, 198; policy structure and, xvi; SALT II and, 87–88; START I and, 131–33; SVC and, 220

Verification and Compliance Office, 309

Verification Panel, 40

Verification Protocol, 198

Versailles Treaty, 21

Verville, Liz, 135

Vesco, Robert, 67

Vienna Convention, 102; ABM Treaty and, 164–65, 180–81; ACDA and, 193–96

Vietnam War, 3, 8, 13–14, 16; biological/chemical weapons and, 23–25

Vladivostok Accord, 84; SALT II and, 51, 62–63, 65–66

Von Mohr, Hubertus, 197–98

Von Wagner, Adolf, 30

Votkinsk Machine Building Plant, 110–11

Wade, James, 65

Wales, Jane, 243

Walker, Louise, 313

Walker, Edward (Ned), 253

"Walk in the Woods" proposal, 115–16, 124

Warner, John, 15

Warnke, Paul, 16, 44, 76, 219; CTBT and, 239; Nitze and, 78–79; resignation of, 95–96; SALT II and, 86

Warsaw Pact, 329–31; ACDA and, 185, 187–88, 195, 197, 206; NATO and, 197; START treaties and, 108

Washington Naval Disarmament Conference, 21, 34, 324

Waters, Ray, 147

Watson, Sam, 55

Watson, Thomas, 88–89

Webster, David, 209

Weiler, Larry, 39–40

Weinberger, Caspar: ABM Treaty and, 148; SALT II and, 102; "Walk in the Woods" proposal and, 115

West, Robin, 118

Western Group, 260–61, 282, 295

Weston, Michael, 272, 295

Wilson, Heather, 192

Winchester, Lucy, 15